The Paradox
of Passion

AF088655

The Paradox of Passion

How Rewards Covertly Control Motivation

Bobby Hoffman

BLOOMSBURY ACADEMIC
NEW YORK • LONDON • OXFORD • NEW DELHI • SYDNEY

BLOOMSBURY ACADEMIC

Bloomsbury Publishing Inc, 1359 Broadway, New York, NY 10018, USA
Bloomsbury Publishing Plc, 50 Bedford Square, London, WC1B 3DP, UK
Bloomsbury Publishing Ireland, 29 Earlsfort Terrace, Dublin 2, D02 AY28, Ireland

BLOOMSBURY, BLOOMSBURY ACADEMIC and the Diana logo are trademarks of
Bloomsbury Publishing Plc

First published in the United States of America 2025

Copyright © Bloomsbury Publishing Inc, 2025

Cover design: Dustin Watson
Cover image © istock/DrAfter123

All rights reserved. No part of this publication may be: i) reproduced or transmitted in any form, electronic or mechanical, including photocopying, recording or by means of any information storage or retrieval system without prior permission in writing from the publishers; or ii) used or reproduced in any way for the training, development or operation of artificial intelligence (AI) technologies, including generative AI technologies. The rights holders expressly reserve this publication from the text and data mining exception as per Article 4(3) of the Digital Single Market Directive (EU) 2019/790.

Bloomsbury Publishing Inc does not have any control over, or responsibility for, any third-party websites referred to or in this book. All internet addresses given in this book were correct at the time of going to press. The author and publisher regret any inconvenience caused if addresses have changed or sites have ceased to exist, but can accept no responsibility for any such changes.

A catalog record for this book is available from the Library of Congress.

ISBN: HB: 978-1-5381-9719-6
PB: 978-1-5381-9720-2
ePDF: 979-8-8818-5886-5
eBook: 978-1-5381-9721-9

Typeset by Deanta Global Publishing Services, Chennai, India
Printed and bound in the United States of America

For product safety related questions contact productsafety@bloomsbury.com.

To find out more about our authors and books visit www.bloomsbury.com and sign up for our newsletters.

Contents

List of Illustrations viii
Acknowledgements ix
Executive Summary x

1 Introduction 1
The Passion Warriors 1
The Paradox Revealed 4
Three Problems Addressed 8
How This Book Is Different 10
Organization of the Book 11

2 The Shaky Foundation: Popularity ≠ Precision 17
Dead Roosters 18
Determining the Top Fifty 20
Effective Measurement 22
Summary Observations 25
Four Fowl Findings 27
Conclusions 41

3 The Price of Passion: The Reality of Reward 49
The Guts of Motivated Effort 54
The Ties That Bind 57
Leveraging Rewards 61
Getting to the Source 67

Need Satisfaction 80
Moving Forward 94

4 The Rewarded Brain 107
Biology Is Better (Despite Lower Popularity) 111
Neuropsychology Explains How Needs Originate 118
Positive Expectancies + Reward = INMO 138

5 The Modulators 151
Gene Expression and Neuromodulation 151
Dopamine (DA) 154
Other Neuromodulators 171
Team Cohesiveness 186

6 The Impact of Rewards 197
From Brain to Behavior 197
Labels Belong on Cans, Not Motives 198
Rewards and Learning 205
Reward Stipulations 212
Rewards and Persuasion 220
Reward and Social Relationships 228
Reconciling Brain and Behavior Findings 239

7 This Is How We Do It 255
Invert the Curve 255
Embrace Appropriate Evidence 258
Self-Regulation 259
What Do We Want? 266
Enhancing Physiology 266
Maximizing Cognitive Clarity 276
Learning More in Less Time 288
Ten Timeless Tips and One to Avoid 293
Get the Dop(amine) 304
Persuasion 306

8 Epilogue 323
And So, It Goes 323

Glossary 327
Appendix 333
Name Index 355
Subject Index 363

Illustrations

Figure

3.1 The spectrum of internalization 73

Tables

1.1 Popular Passion Perspectives 3
5.1 Neuromodulator Summary 187
7.1 Neuroprotective Realities 257
7.2 Self-regulation in Action 262
7.3 Circadian Rhythm-Supported Strategies 268
7.4 Cognitive Enhancement Strategies 279
7.5 Cultivating a Growth Mindset 288
7.6 Autonomy-Supportive Instructional Behaviors 291
7.7 Maximizing DA Synthesis 305
Appendix Top 50 Most Cited Intrinsic/Extrinsic and/or Reward Empirical Studies 333

Acknowledgements

While solo authorship may suggest that a single person is solely responsible for a creative work, that's far from the truth in the case of *The Paradox of Passion*. This book would not exist without the inspiration, support, and generosity of Grant Hayes, Richard Hartshorne, and Morgan McAfee. Their encouragement—and the time and intellectual freedom they provided—made this work possible.

Like any substantial achievement, writing *The Paradox of Passion* came with its share of conceptual highs and lows, along with practical challenges that often felt like navigating a maze of hurdles and hoops. I'm deeply grateful to Denise Kay, Helen Rose Fives, and Richard Feenstra for their insightful feedback, which helped transform a scattered collection of ideas into a coherent and scientifically grounded work. Chapter 2, in particular, would not exist without the tireless efforts of Kat Hoppe. Her perseverance in managing an overwhelming amount of data was nothing short of heroic. I owe her a special thanks for helping bring that chapter to life.

Motivation doesn't thrive on opportunity alone. It also requires support, recognition, and connection. Without the encouragement and belief of those closest to me, this book may never have been started—let alone completed. As this very book affirms, recognition is a powerful driver of human effort. I'm profoundly thankful to Rebecca, Roy, Rylee, Carter, Neil, Glenn, Patti, Bill C., Kyle D., and Patsy Mae. Their presence has been foundational to my motivation—and to the person I strive to be.

Finally, my thanks to Team Bloomsbury who helped shepherd this project through to completion—despite the chaos of a merger and the quirks of a meticulous author. Their patience and professionalism were indispensable.

Bobby Hoffman

August 13, 2025

Executive Summary

The Paradox of Passion: How Rewards Covertly Control Motivation challenges conventional wisdom about motivation. It reveals why legacy research findings are often misinterpreted and overgeneralized, leading to unrealistic beliefs about the self and others that foster ineffective strategy use impeding optimal learning and performance. The book provides cross-disciplinary evidence emphasizing the essential role of rewards as a biological and behavioral driver of motivation. It challenges the clichéd idea of intrinsic motivation, pointing out the flaws in pursuing passion and purpose without considering how the brain regulates motivation through personalized rewards. Evidence reveals that a singular focus on passion is an unattainable ideal, akin to a mythical "motivation unicorn." Instead of hopes and dreams, the book offers practical insights and research-based strategies for enhancing learning and performance by effectively leveraging how the brain uses innate reward pathways to get what we want and sometimes obtain what we need.

1

Introduction

Chapter Outline

The Passion Warriors	1
The Paradox Revealed	4
Three Problems Addressed	8
How This Book Is Different	10
Organization of the Book	11

The Passion Warriors

Back in 2021, I was watching *Shark Tank*. The popular television show gives aspiring entrepreneurs the opportunity to pitch an idea to celebrity investors, who use their own money to fund or reject the idea being pitched. The producers describe the show as "inspiring a nation to dream bigger" and contend it "gives people from all walks of life the chance to chase the American dream" (ABC.com, 2025, para. 1). One night a woman was hawking vegetable-infused ice cream (Leigh, 2023). These delectable dishes included flavors like Chocolate Cauliflower, Vanilla Beet, and Mint Chip with spinach 🍦. While high on novelty, these treats were missing (excuse the pun) a few key ingredients.

Despite the drawbacks, Shark Laurie Greiner offered the contestant her requested $800,000 for a 5 percent equity stake in the woman's company, but with the caveat that the money was a 6 percent interest loan and contingent upon offering a low-fat ice-cream option. Another Shark, Mr. Wonderful, Kevin O'Leary, also offered the woman a 9 percent interest loan with no other contingencies. The hopeful dairy queen, Jessica Levison, rejected both offers. She claimed that growing her business was a "life-long passion, a dream that she cherished more than anything else." We can only speculate why the offer was rejected based on the limited evidence available, but Levison stated that she wanted a strategic partner, not a loan. However, the goal for a *Shark Tank* appearance is to secure investor funding, not to make friends, feel cajoled, or leave with warm and fuzzy feelings regarding prospective goals. Funding Jessica's passion apparently had a higher psychological or financial price tag. Maybe Jessica was seeking a different type of reward, and the Sharks, despite their investment expertise, didn't realize what Jessica really wanted.

A reasonable interpretation would suggest that the incentive of a loan was insufficient to satisfy her desires. Jessica likely had needs left unfulfilled by the offer. Did she have unconscious, dual, or conflicting motives that were obscured by her relentless pursuit of passion? Perchance. Jessica may have believed that by accepting a financial buyout her "passion" would be tarnished, blemishing her stated aspirations. While we do not know her thinking, based on her deliberations we can conclude that Jessica had some noticeable angst evaluating her options. Minimally, Jessica wrestled with a common decision-making dilemma that many of us face when making choices that have both drawbacks and advantages. In this case, choosing between the pursuit of her alleged passion and selling out to investors created anxiety and uncertainty. In other words, Jessica encountered a paradox, which is what happens when a person is faced with "mutually inconsistent propositions each of which enjoys some plausibility when viewed on its own" (Schiffer, 1994, p. 279).

But why did Jessica have a paradox when she could have landed a deal with two world-renowned investment partners? According to some of the most successful and prominent authors in the history of the world, as well as scholars and researchers of motivation science, the benefits of finding and pursuing passion are numerous and far-reaching. When we turn to popular media to understand what passion is and how it allegedly relates to success, optimal performance, and overall motivation, we are bombarded with a litany of platitudes, imperatives, and exhortations that insist that devoid of passion and purpose, life is nothing more than a mundane routine of unfulfilled dreams and frustrating experiences. Plop

Table 1.1 Popular Passion Perspectives

Person	Paraphrased Proclamation
Daniel Pink, author of the performance improvement book *Drive* that has sold over 2,000,000 copies.	The secret to high performance isn't rewards and punishments, but that unseen intrinsic drive—the drive to do things for their own sake.
Carol Dweck (2006), professor, Stanford University, originator of "mindset" theory	The passion for stretching yourself and sticking to it, even (or especially) when it's not going well, is the hallmark of the growth mindset.
Angela Duckworth (2016), professor, University of Pennsylvania, developer, and proponent of "grit" theory	Passion for your work is a little bit of discovery, followed by a lot of development, and then a lifetime of deepening.
Galileo Galilei, renowned astronomer and inventor (Walters, 2023)	Passion is the genesis of genius.
Malcolm Gladwell (2008), best selling science author with over 23,000,000 books sold	Practice isn't the thing you do once you're good. It's the thing you do that makes you good. And it requires passion to maintain that practice.
Teresa Amabile, professor emerita, Harvard Business School, developer of "creative" theory	People will be most creative when they feel motivated primarily by the interest, enjoyment, satisfaction, and challenge of the work itself.
Dave Ramsey (2013), author and financial advisor, whose book *The Total Money Makeover* has sold over 9,000,000 copies.	Passion is the key in leading and creating excellence that I will hire passion over education and talent every time.

the terminology "quotes about passion" into a search engine and you will see a list of about 425,000,000 passion proclamations including those given in Table 1.1.

The alleged power of passion goes far beyond popular narratives. Media outlets ranging from the esteemed *Handbook of Educational Psychology* (Schutz & Muis, 2024) published by the American Psychological Association to the all-time bestselling books on motivation (Covey, 2020; Peale, 2012; Pink, 2011) wave the passion flag, touting inner "*drive*"[1] as the cure-all for apathy, stagnation, boredom, learning

---

[1] The terms in italicized quotes are defined in the Glossary.

gains, optimal performance, and personal growth. Conversely, the behaviors associated with externally derived "*rewards*," such as financial gain, status, recognition, power, or whatever else an individual values are often deemed unsatisfying, demotivating, or socially inappropriate (Kwon, 2023). Examples of hyperbolic narratives include *The Role of Passion in Education* (Vallerand et al., 2024), where supporters of the treatise advance the inflated claim that "passion *must* be instilled in students to foster life-long learning and the pursuit of knowledge, and students' identity is ultimately tied to understanding what they are passionate about" (Muis & Schultz, 2024, p. 724), or indicating that "the role of passion is imperative in education" (Vallerand et al., 2024, p. 245). Is a successful career or educational achievement unobtainable without passion? Can passion possibly originate from within, when it must be instilled by others and external validation is an apparent necessity? Can individuals lacking passion or something to be passionate about thrive and prosper in a culture where, according to the renowned philosopher Georg Wilhelm Friedrich Hegel (1861), "nothing great in the world has ever been accomplished without passion!" (Volume one). The answer is a resounding "yes" and an examination of the flaws inherent to measuring and generalizing motivation research combined with a deep understanding of how the brain works will illustrate why many contemporary views of motivation are incomplete and unrealistic in today's world. By the way, Jessica Levison's company "Peekaboo Ice-cream" is no longer in business.

The Paradox Revealed

Scholarly research indicates that passion is "a strong inclination toward an activity that one loves, finds important and meaningful, and to which one commits time and energy" (Vallerand, 2012, p. 3). In other words, passion purports to influence the direction and intensity of goal-related behavior, a common definition of motivation (Reeve, 2018). The concepts of passion and motivation are often intimately entwined yet conceptually distinct, but both suggest a quest to engage in an activity for its own sake, characterized by enjoyment and satisfaction derived from the task itself. While clear distinctions between types of passion exist (see Chapter 3), "passion" is generally the term used to represent inner *"drive"* and the type of motivation that supports superior achievement.

The importance of passion is undeniable and includes many aspects of *"intrinsic motivation"* (INMO), the type of motivation demonstrated when an external incentive is not apparent or expected during task engagement, such as what happens when we engage in a task merely for pleasure. Scholars debate the similarities and differences between passion and INMO but what is indisputable is that neither passion nor INMO are sufficient to explain the totality of human behavior. Even the strongest proponents of the passion perspective acknowledge that some forms of passion are maladaptive and detrimental to performance (Curran et al., 2015). Alternatively, *"extrinsic motivation"* (EXMO), the type of motivation that is generated when behavior is focused on gaining money, praise, recognition, and influence can also compel individuals to put forth powerful effort. While Chapter 3 outlines in detail the nuances of INMO and EXMO, the initial goal here is to suggest that based on a wealth of behavioral and biological evidence rewards can supplement and even replace passion to achieve optimal motivation.

As explained later, ultimately, the passion paradox creates a perception that INMO is good while demonizing EXMO. Yes, INMO is desirable, but like sunshine, overexposure results in getting burnt, which can melt your ice cream. Ask Jessica. Whether we reach the conclusion to embrace INMO and its close cousin "passion" because of research recommendations, social influence, idealistic thinking, modeling the behaviors of successful celebrities and athletes, or for any other reason, every breathing individual can also be motivated by accomplishment, reward, recognition, power, or influence. The manifestation of the passion paradox is that people may adopt an ideological stance supporting INMO that paradoxically holds them back because they do not realize the power of rewards and the fundamental biological need to anticipate and receive rewards as a basic part of human functioning (Sapolsky, 2023).

Part of the paradox is the overgeneralization of one of the otherwise most reliable and explanatory theories of motivation, self-determination theory (SDT). The theory, which is based on the satisfaction of fundamental needs of *"autonomy,"* *"competence,"* and *"relatedness,"* is described as one of "the most researched and applied in psychology today" (Ryan et al., 2022, p. 813). SDT suggests that when you feel free to make choices, believe in your abilities, and have social support for your behavior, you will orchestrate a life of "well-being, greater creativity, superior learning, better performance, enhanced well-being, and higher quality relationships" (Ryan & Deci, 2017, p. 17). Who can argue about motherhood and apple pie that self-determination implies? Unfortunately, life rarely mirrors SDT's utopian prognostication, especially for 77 percent of the global workforce who reported being uninvolved or unenthusiastic at work (Gallup, 2023) or the 52 percent who indicated that what is most important to learn for success does not happen in school (Huang, 2018).

According to the champions of passion and intrinsic drive, the best way to achieve psychological satisfaction is to identify an inner spark that allegedly propels them to experience "spontaneous feelings of effectance and enjoyment" (Ryan & Deci, 2017, p. 14). This description suggests that it is highly desirable and psychologically advantageous to discover something that needs no other incentive for engagement besides our own interest and curiosity, otherwise known as INMO. When we discover this elusive motivational formula, we will then have the potential to alter the direction and intensity of our effort to achieve a higher quality of life, or so they say. The idealistic formula is more reminiscent of Alice in Wonderland than the reality of most individuals. You may recall from your childhood readings that during one of her misadventures Alice finds a bottle of potion and the bottle label commands her to "Drink this!" What happened next was not what Alice expected. Similar reactions to the potion of passion may occur after reading the remaining chapters.

We are told that finding meaning in work is a prerequisite for success (Judge & Hurst, 2008; Pink, 2011). The alleged solution is to satisfy our inner voice by seeking passion, purpose, and fulfillment from our jobs or educational endeavors. This advice bombards us constantly, rooted in the belief that INMO is the key to achievement. But what if this belief is founded on flawed assumptions? What if the concept of motivational nirvana is a fanciful myth? Multidisciplinary research on *"engagement,"* productivity, and performance reveals a far murkier picture than the INMO cheerleaders claim. In truth, the factors that drive human behavior often have little to do with passion or calling. Emerging evidence from *"neuropsychology"* and neuroendocrinology is largely ignored by the champions of self-determination (Sapolsky, 2023) and with few exceptions (Hidi, 2016; Reeve & Lee, 2012) eludes the serious attention of motivation researchers. The meaning we claim to extract from achievement often proves illusory upon closer inspection where individuals routinely confuse the roots of behavior and misconstrue what INMO actually means (Hoffman, 2021, 2023).

However, merely complaining about theoretical, conceptual, or methodological incongruence alone does not justify alternative perceptions of motivation. On the contrary, in line with the premiere proponents of INMO and self-determination theory, such as Richard Ryan and Edward Deci, it is often highlighted that many scholars and researchers who challenge their findings contribute little unless they help advance the field. As they emphatically stated, "This leads to reinventing or rebranding of previously explored ideas, as well as a search for hot topics and anomalous findings, rather than the pursuit of incremental science" (Ryan & Deci, 2019, p. 112).

Rebranding is surely a problem, and there have been previous attempts at undermining the power of INMO and the emphasis on passion. Those attempts (Kruglanski et al., 2018; Locke & Schattke, 2019; Reiss, 2012) have been harshly criticized by passion warriors and failed miserably. These efforts faltered because alternative beliefs alone do not justify better theories. These attempts lacked empirical evidence to overturn the notion that a unitary view of INMO is the cure for motivational lapses and subpar accomplishment. Alternative interpretations of what drives human behavior requires objective, confluent, and replicable data like that which is found in 100s of neuroscience studies, many of which support the perspectives advanced in the remaining chapters.

Considering that the world of the typical worker is dull, repetitive, and structured, the vast majority of jobs fail to provide opportunities to attain or even consider INMO. Many organizations emphasize obedience and predictable psychological functioning designed to promote rule following and ideological conformity (Kellogg et al., 2020). Seek your passion, and you wind up finding it after being fired and looking for a new job! Likewise, academic curriculum is mired in government-approved and standardized curriculum, which must be taught in documented ways that conform to timetables and bureaucratic mandates. A substantial number of students do not find passion and purpose until the school day ends (Sandel, 2020). Finally, misconceptions surround INMO/EXMO and what passion means. Clarifying these fallacies is key to harnessing the power of internal drive. Analysis of robust research over the past thirty years, using fresh perspectives is warranted to unveil the truth behind the passion paradox. Flawed, legacy data contains bias: close scrutiny exposes it.

In aggregate, the remainder of this work emphasizes the significance of multicultural and multidisciplinary evidence to unravel the intricate motivations behind optimal performance, while minimizing philosophical and *"essentialist"* debates. I provide a more well-rounded perspective on what fuels motivation, with a strong focus on practical relevance for diverse audiences in pursuit of peak performance. This effort offers valuable insights for leaders, educators, students, and parents who want to maximize their capabilities. It does not shy away from addressing the limitations of INMO while also confronting the potential stigma associated with a desire for reward. The goal is to complement the prevailing views on intrinsic drive and, in doing so, highlight their inherent flaws, biases, and misinterpretations blurring our understanding of motivation.

Three Problems Addressed

There are at least three problems inherent to human motivation addressed in this book. While some may appear more obvious than others, each plagues the accurate interpretation and application of motivation science to improve learning and performance.

Problem #1: Legacy research and media bias overstate the power of passion as the optimal source of motivation while ignoring or discounting other prevailing psychological and physiological factors. The passion perspective is exclusionary and embellished.

What it means: According to many (Falk, 2023; Pink, 2011; Ryan & Deci, 2019), INMO (defined as engaging in a task based on interest and no other anticipated payout), usually described as "passion" in the popular press, is the elixir of champions. The reliance on the one-sided perspective that INMO is superior across tasks, settings, and people is convenient, yet questionable. The premise relies on the results of unreliable self-report information primarily from white, college-educated 18–24-year-old females. This gratuitous group of data providers, who "volunteer" to earn extra school credit by agreeing to research protocols misrepresent the other 90 percent of the population who have limited opportunities to develop INMO. Most jobs are monotonous with a production orientation. Fortunately, those intrinsically starved citizens embrace other sociological values such as external rewards, recognition, and social validation that add to the interpretation of motivated behavior. Some perspectives glorify the merits of passion or emphasize the limits of extrinsic reward (defined as pursuing a task for an expected payout or avoidance of consequences for nonengagement), even implying a social stigma to those that seek reward, recognition, status, or power. In reality, motivation changes according to the situation and varies contingent on a litany of factors, which may or may not reflect the superiority of a motivation preference.

The takeaway: The intricacies of INMO and EXMO are explored in depth. Evidence is presented to verify under which situations each is preferable, with a focus on reward contingencies and the continuum of motivated behavior. Both the limitations and benefits of the intrinsic/extrinsic motivation spectrum are explored as well as which factors change motivated behavior across contexts, individuals, and situations.

Problem #2: The prevailing view of motivated behavior is incomplete because the role of brain functioning is understated. There is more to understanding the source of motives and subsequent performance change than assigning physical and mental properties to hypothetical research constructs.

What it means: The vast majority of motivation research is correlational leading to speculation as to the underlying cause of behavior. Many motivational interventions take place in schools or workplaces involving manipulation of materials, methods, or environmental restructuring to confirm or refute hypotheses. These efforts, while admirable, rarely address the fundamental antecedents of behavior and fail to explain the majority of differences in behavioral outcomes. Biology, not philosophy, should be the initial explanation for motivated behavior (Lanza, 2007) because the influence on behavior is substantial, consistent, and predictable. Biological considerations are often excluded from education and psychology literature because of controversy, complication, and difficulty in understanding. However, in this text how the brain works is simplified and transformed into easily applied performance success strategies.

The takeaway: Analysis of behavior using research from diverse fields provides a more thorough explanation of behavior than using research from motivation science alone. A multidisciplinary approach avoids the singular focus on behavioral strategies as the motivation unicorn.

Problem #3: Some motivation research contributes to overgeneralized conclusions generated from homogeneous populations and lab research, implying that observed results mirror real life. These findings do not account for the key role of context, diversity, or culture. These myopic views can unduly influence strategy choices that may contribute to suboptimal learning and performance.

What it means: Expecting that findings from a self-selected individuals or synthetic laboratory settings will map precisely to authentic practice is speculative and transfer success is often disconfirmed by users (Winne & Jamieson-Noel, 2002). Additionally, the research process can alter the behavior of those being measured (Spradley, 2016). Thus, the collection and interpretation of data should be based primarily on how the data will be used, not on the contrived data collection conditions that are often designed to confirm hypotheses and enhance the likelihood of a scientific study being published. Individuals ascribe psychological meaning to events, experiences, and behavior on an interconnected basis, which demands a situational evaluation of interactive effects. The majority of motivation research is a lagging indicator based on a singular psychological experience captured at one time. Snapshots of past experience discount plasticity and development, which are inherent to everything that we know about brain maturation.

The takeaway: To be effective, research-based strategy recommendations must be both practical and context dependent, not relying on unitary information sources. Application to support optimal performance should account for the totality of human experience, using diverse populations based on the multidisciplinary evidence as described throughout the text.

How This Book Is Different

The foundation of this book is built on the premise that motivation cannot be accurately assessed when excluding the underlying neurobiological mechanisms that provide the linkage between thought and action. Unlike most popular conceptions of motivation, I consider evidence beyond motivation science to explain behavior. Just as a physician would not offer an accurate medical diagnosis based on observing a patient or by merely listening to a list of self-reported symptoms, motivation cannot be determined to a meaningful extent through external validation alone. Accurate identification of motive includes using neuropsychology and the corpus of knowledge amassed from brain science.

By nature, I approach research with a degree of skepticism, meaning that I closely scrutinize prevailing evidence and do not accept it as fact without justification and replication. In particular, I feel obligated to question the veracity of evidence generated by motivational research on methodological, measurement, and philosophical grounds. Through fine-grained analysis, I show that INMO is not the magical solution to enhancing learning and performance outcomes for the vast majority of the population. While I consider the amplified views of motivated behavior perpetuated by well-published theorists and in the popular press as valuable, I provide empirical support for a more encompassing, yet contrarian, view of motivated behavior.

I examine motivation through the lens of situated expectancy-value theory (SEVT) (Eccles & Wigfield, 2020), which is well suited to understanding the spectrum of motives that drive peak performance. SEVT embraces the totality of human experience on a domain specific, case-by-case basis. SEVT advocates that individuals assess goal setting and task engagement based on a series of iterative evaluations founded upon their interests, usefulness of task engagement, and long-term benefits of task completion along with the psychological and logistical costs associated with commitment. In other words, we check the temperature of the water before we jump in the pool! A compelling argument is advanced showing that the SEVT view is far more encompassing and realistic than other typical motivation models used to assess INMO/EXMO and subsequent optimal performance in school and work contexts.

Organization of the Book

The book is divided into three parts based on the premise that exposing the passion paradox is necessary to suggest an alternative solution. Once the problem is clearly identified, we can then objectively describe and deconstruct the evidence to determine gaps, ambiguities, or unknowns concerning motivation while concurrently offering ways to improve the nature of motivation research through scrutiny of materials, methods, and samples. The application of knowledge to solve practical motivation challenges is essential, and the final chapters are devoted to providing multidisciplinary strategy recommendations and describing new perspectives that enhance reward potential and motivated effort across individuals, cultures, and contexts.

In Chapters 1 and 2, I discuss problem identification and analysis. Challenges related to existing views of motivated behavior are described to reveal why a new perspective is needed. The reader learns how scientific evidence is generated, disseminated, and adapted, often morphing into the dubious perception of common sense. Problem identification includes clarity of the basic principles of motivation and examines popular interpretations of what constitutes INMO/EXMO and why consideration of biological perspectives on reward are essential to understanding motivated behavior. The first part includes an expose of the limitations of popular methodologies in motivational research emphasizing the almost exclusive use of WEIRD (Western, educated, industrialized, rich and democratic) research samples in motivation research, the challenge of self-report, replicability of findings, and culturally congruent interpretation of results.

Next, in Chapters 3, 4, and 5, I deconstruct the main premises of human motivation, including which factors enhance and detract from optimal human learning and performance. A deep dive into reward is presented to give the reader a perspective about why views of passion have achieved prominence, while perspectives of reward are demonized. This part describes what constitutes a reward both biologically and psychologically and under which circumstances rewards drive adaptive behavior. Throughout the second part, you will find interspersed neurological findings presented in simplified terms related to the physiological markers associated with motivation and reward. Robust evidence reveals how and why the process of neuromodulation controls motivation and specifically how and why the synthesis of chemicals like dopamine and serotonin can make the difference between optimal performance and failure. Last, this part explores the spectrum of motivated behavior, the role of interest, passion, and curiosity related to motivation, and the caveats associated with unilateral interpretations of reward.

Chapters 6, 7, and 8, address novel evidence-based alternatives to mainstream interpretations of motivated behavior. The part objective is to illustrate how reward influences specific outcomes encountered in everyday life. This part reveals how neuropsychology explains typical learning and performance opportunities where motivation influences success. It is devoted to the practical application of reward and how reward influences attention, thinking, emotion, motivation, learning, persuasion, self-control, and social relationships. Finally, based on the totally of evidence described throughout the text, performance optimization strategies are advanced from diverse disciplines including neuropsychology, education, and behavioral economics that reveal how to use knowledge of reward to maximize productivity and goal attainment of any type. The explicit goal of the last part of the book is on how to use knowledge of rewards to advance personal and professional success.

Now, it is time to embark on a journey of discovery that challenges conventional wisdom about passion and motivation. In a world that often celebrates passion as the ultimate driver of success, this book presents a perspective backed by data and neuropsychology insights. By delving into the complex interplay of rewards and biological mechanisms underlying motivation, you will gain a deeper understanding of the human experience. Whether you are a student seeking academic excellence, a professional aiming for career fulfillment, or simply someone intrigued by the inner workings of the mind, your perspective on what truly motivates us may radically change. Prepare to be informed and enlightened as you uncover the fascinating truths that lie beyond the paradox of passion.

References

ABC.com. (2025, January 10). *Shark Tank/About*. https://abc.com/shows/shark-tank/about-the-show

Covey, S. R. (2020). *The 7 habits of highly effective people*. Simon & Schuster.

Curran, T., Hill, A. P., Appleton, P. R., Vallerand, R. J., & Standage, M. (2015). The psychology of passion: A meta-analytical review of a decade of research on intrapersonal outcomes. *Motivation and Emotion, 39*, 631–655. https://doi.org/10.1007/s11031-015-9503-0

Duckworth, A. L. (2016). *Grit: The power of passion and perseverance*. Simon & Schuster.

Dweck, C. S. (2006). *Mindset: The new psychology of success*. Random House.

Eccles, J. S., & Wigfield, A. (2020). From expectancy-value theory to situated expectancy-value theory: A developmental, social cognitive, and sociocultural perspective on motivation. *Contemporary Educational Psychology, 61*, 101859. https://doi.org/10.1016/j.cedpsych.2020.101859

Falk, S. (2023). *Intrinsic motivation: Learn to love your work and succeed as never before.* St. Martin's Press.

Gallup. (2023). *State of the global workforce: 2023 report.* https://www.gallup.com/workplace/349484/state-of-the-global-workplace-report.aspx?thank-you-report-form=1

Gladwell, M. (2008). *Outliers: The story of success.* Little, Brown.

Hegel, G. W. F. (1861). *Lectures on the philosophy of history.* G. Bell and Sons.

Hidi, S. (2016). Revisiting the role of rewards in motivation and learning: Implications of neuroscientific research. *Educational Psychology Review, 28,* 61–93. https://doi.org/10.1007/s10648-015-9307-5

Hoffman, B. (2021). Teaching for knowledge transfer: Best practices from a graduate-level educational psychology distance learning program. In W. B. James, C. Cobanoglu, & M. Cavusoglu (Eds.), *Advances in global education and research* (Vol. 4, pp. 1–9). USF M3 Publishing. https://www.doi.org/10.5038/9781955833042

Hoffman, B. (2023). *Value and utility: What students learn and transfer from a graduate motivation course.* Paper presented at the bi-annual meeting of the European Association for Research in Learning & Instruction (EARLI), Thessaloniki, Greece, August 22–26.

Huang, H., (2018). How do students feel about their schools. DRA Report No. 18.07. Wake County Public School System Cary, North Carolina. https://files.eric.ed.gov/fulltext/ED606980.pdf

Judge, T. A., & Hurst, C. (2008). How the rich (and happy) get richer (and happier): Relationship of core self-evaluations to trajectories in attaining work success. *Journal of Applied Psychology, 93*(4), 849–863. https://doi.org/10.1037/0021-9010.93.4.849

Kellogg, K. C., Valentine, M. A., & Christin, A. (2020). Algorithms at work: The new contested terrain of control. *Academy of Management Annals, 14*(1), 366–410. https://doi.org/10.5465/annals.2018.0174

Kruglanski, A. W., Fishbach, A., Woolley, K., Bélanger, J. J., Chernikova, M., Molinario, E., & Pierro, A. (2018). A structural model of intrinsic motivation: On the psychology of means-ends fusion. *Psychological Review, 125*(2), 165–182. https://doi.org/10.1037/rev0000095

Kwon, M., Cunningham, J. L., & Jachimowicz, J. M. (2023). Discerning saints: Moralization of intrinsic motivation and selective prosociality at work. *Academy of Management Journal, 66*(6), 1625–1650. https://doi.org/10.5465/amj.2020.1761

Lanza, R. (2007). A new theory of the universe. *The American Scholar.* https://theamericanscholar.org/a-new-theory-of-the-universe/

Leigh, W. (2023). Peekaboo ice cream: Here's what happened after Shark Tank. https://www.foodrepublic.com/1421424/peekaboo-organic-ice-cream-shark-tank-now/

Locke, E. A., & Schattke, K. (2019). Intrinsic and extrinsic motivation: Time for expansion and clarification. *Motivation Science*, 5(4), 277–290. https://doi.org/10.1037/mot0000116

Muis, K. R., & Schutz, P. A. (2024). The prejudiced past and progressive future of educational psychology. In P. A. Schutz & K. R. Muis (Eds.), *Handbook of educational psychology* (4th ed., pp. 721–729). Routledge. https://doi.org/10.4324/9780429433726-37

Peale, N. V. (2012). *The power of positive thinking*. Random House.

Pink, D. H. (2011). *Drive: The surprising truth about what motivates us*. Penguin.

Ramsey, D. (2013). *The total money makeover: A proven plan for financial fitness*. Thomas Nelson.

Reeve, J. (2018). *Understanding motivation and emotion* (7th ed.). John Wiley & Sons.

Reeve, J., & Lee, W. (2012). Neuroscience and human motivation. In R. M. Ryan (Ed.), *The Oxford handbook of human motivation* (pp. 365–380). Oxford University Press. https://doi.org/10.1093/oxfordhb/9780195399820.013.0021

Reiss, S. (2012). Intrinsic and extrinsic motivation. *Teaching of Psychology*, 39(2), 152–156. https://doi.org/10.1177/0098628312437704

Ryan, R. M., & Deci, E. L. (2017). *Self-determination theory: Basic psychological needs in motivation, development, and wellness*. Guilford Publications.

Ryan, R. M., & Deci, E. L. (2019). Brick by brick: The origins, development, and future of self-determination theory. In A. J. Elliot (Ed.), *Advances in motivation science* (Vol. 6, pp. 111–156). Elsevier. https://doi.org/10.1016/bs.adms.2019.01.001

Ryan, R. M., Duineveld, J. J., Di Domenico, S. I., Ryan, W. S., Steward, B. A., & Bradshaw, E. L. (2022). We know this much is (meta-analytically) true: A meta-review of meta-analytic findings evaluating self-determination theory. *Psychological Bulletin*, 148(11–12), 813–842. https://doi.org/10.31234/osf.io/gk5cy

Sandel, M. J. (2020). *The tyranny of merit: What's become of the common good?* Penguin.

Sapolsky, R. M. (2023). *Determined: A science of life without free will*. Penguin.

Schiffer, S. (1994). A paradox of meaning. *Noûs*, 28(3), 279–324. https://doi.org/10.2307/2216061

Schutz, P. A., & Muis, K. R. (2024). In P. A. Schutz & K. R. Muis (Eds.), *Handbook of educational psychology* (4th ed.). Routledge.

Spradley, J. P. (2016). *Participant observation*. Waveland Press.

Vallerand, R. J. (2012). The role of passion in sustainable psychological well-being. *Psychology Well-Being, Theory, Research and Practice, 2*, 1–21. https://doi.org/10.1186/2211-1522-2-1

Vallerand, R. J., Chichekian, T., & Schellenberg, B. (2024). The role of passion in education. In P. A. Schutz & K. R. Muis (Eds.), *Handbook of educational psychology* (4th ed., pp. 245–268). Routledge. https://doi.org/10.4324/9780429433726-14

Walters, S. (2023). Yes, Galileo actually said that. *Discover Magazine.* https://www.discovermagazine.com/the-sciences/yes-galileo-actually-said-that

Winne, P. H., & Jamieson-Noel, D. (2002). Exploring students' calibration of self-reports about study tactics and achievement. *Contemporary Educational Psychology, 27*(4), 551–572. https://doi.org/10.1016/s0361-476x(02)00006-1

2

The Shaky Foundation
Popularity ≠ Precision

Chapter Outline

Dead Roosters	18
Determining the Top Fifty	20
Effective Measurement	22
Summary Observations	25
Four Fowl Findings	27
Conclusions	41

Warning: You may be skeptical about the information you are about to read because it conflicts with your current beliefs. The reaction of some readers may be that the concerns outlined below are legacy and historical issues that formally plagued contemporary motivation research but no longer exist. Some will contend that enhanced methodological rigor, advanced statistical methods, and greater accountability through preregistration of hypotheses and the use of public data depositories have improved the credibility and application of motivation research. While some of these changes indeed have reduced concerns, the data presented below disputes the contention that the issues have been eliminated. In reality, the foundation of motivation research rests on shaky methodological ground, and the problem is getting worse, not better.

Historically, motivational research has had a litany of methodological and experimental criticisms. Scholars lament that the vast majority of motivational research relies on self-reports or correlations among different cognitive, emotional, and behavioral characteristics (Chan, 2010). Validity concerns are rampant due to inaccurately measuring what is purported to being measured (Steel & König, 2006). Much of the research is correlational and does not reveal the cause of motivated behavior but instead suggests that certain situational factors influence behavior under specific and often-simulated conditions (Franco et al., 2014). Heterogeneous samples discount the generalization of results to diverse populations (Henrich et al., 2010). Almost without exception, results from motivation science account for only minimal behavioral variations, with the majority of factors influencing behavior unexplained and usually unaddressed by research (Open Science Collaboration, 2015). Compounding the validity issues is the conspicuous absence of research on the source of motivational beliefs. The prevalence and significance of these problems are so severe and pervasive that this entire chapter is devoted to the exposition and analysis of extremely popular and primarily flawed research related to understanding the continuum of motivation and specifically the impact of rewards on optimal performance.

Dead Roosters

One cultural universal is the presumption that the actions we take are instrumental in achieving specific outcomes. In research, we call this cause and effect; in life, we call it power and influence. We thrive on taking credit for desired outcomes, like the parent who declares, "my children are successful because of my parenting style," or the organization that contends a new corporate initiative like mentoring is the reason for increased staff loyalty. While both of these assertions seem reasonable, are the claims justified? Like most motivation research questions, the answer is, "it depends." While many factors can influence outcomes, no claims of impact or causality are justified in the absence of a reliable way to measure whatever it is we claim to influence.

Whether in daily life or during controlled research, the method and quality of measurement determines the difference between attributing causality between one factor and another compared to merely establishing that two factors are related. In the examples described above, we might challenge the claims with the familiar retort "how do you know?" The typical layperson response is, "I just know," "I saw it," or "I (insert behavior) and then (insert result) happened." A cocksure rooster could refute these explanations in seconds by revealing that said rooster makes the sun rise, because every morning when it crows, the sun immediately shines. The trite example reveals that simple observations and tangential connections are insufficient to assert that whatever occurred would not have happened in the absence of a specific person, behavior, or event. I'm quite sure you will agree that the sun will rise even when the rooster is dead.

In some ways, motivation research and specifically research related to disentangling how rewards contribute to optimal behavior is suffering from the rooster syndrome. In practical terms, this means that some of the most respected, insightful, and frequently cited findings in the field of motivation research that specifically intend to explain differences in intrinsic and extrinsically derived behavior embellish the power of their influence. Both roosters and researchers fail to consider diverse factors that may account for observed results, in addition to or despite their presumed influence. A detailed scrutiny of the top fifty most cited studies focusing on disentangling the differences between intrinsic motivation (INMO) and extrinsic motivation (EXMO), and specifically the etiology and impact of rewards, reveals that over 75 percent of the difference in measured outcomes is *unexplained*. The unexplained difference can be for many reasons including what is (or is not) measured, statistical error, and the qualities of the study participants, among dozens of other factors. Additionally, many of the conclusions advanced by motivation research suffer from the proclivity to attribute cause to correlation results. Sometimes we do not hear the rooster when it crows, and the crow changes under different conditions, like temperature, cloudiness, and which farmer is making the observation. Roosters crow for at least ten distinct reasons (Leonard & Horn, 1995), but to the indiscriminate observer each crow is erroneously assumed to have the same meaning. While we are not interested in roosters, we do want to ensure that any inferences made from motivation research are justified and based on sound measurement practices that include accounting for sample variations and generalizability of results. While hens, capons, and cockerels may all seem the same to nonfarmers, they are indeed different from roosters, just like the enormous differences in motivation found between an undergraduate, white debutant from Harvard University and an Indigenous, food-insecure coffee grower who hails from Batukaru.

Disturbingly, a review of the fifty most cited studies in the history of motivation research intending to decipher distinctions between passion (i.e., INMO) and rewards (i.e., EXMO) are tainted by a variety of methodological challenges. These issues highlight uncertainty as to what is being measured, the conflation of similar terminology for different constructs, embellished or missing statistical inference, and inappropriate generalization from homogeneous samples and contexts to broader and radically diverse cultures. These issues are further exacerbated by research that attempts to decipher the impact of rewards on behavior. Distinct types of rewards are routinely clustered together obfuscating the important distinctions that blur the reality that rewards can be internalized and thus intrinsically motivating for certain individuals, under particular circumstances, and for specific reasons. Considering the litany of concerns, it is imperative to closely examine the foundation of motivation research to decipher the precise impact of reward on motivated behavior, forestalling the perpetuation of popular legacy research that continues to be cited by new research on a much more frequent basis than you would ever imagine.

Determining the Top Fifty

To determine the precise impact of the concerns described above and avoid the sacrifice of more proverbial roosters, a detailed analysis of motivation literature was conducted to determine the soundness of historical research as a foundation of knowledge to improve human performance. A comprehensive search of research citations was conducted first by using Google Scholar, a tool that helps identify the popularity and degree of influence of specific research. A research citation is earned when one author/researcher in their own writing gives credit to another person's work, ideas, or research. Theoretically, the greater the number of citations earned, the more influential the underlying work is to promote and advance the topic or field, with the caveat that the outlet of publication can have broad implications on citation count. Some outlets have higher impact and greater credibility than others, hypothetically leading to a greater number of citations than if the same work had been published in a less-reputable or unpopular journal.

Only empirical research involving human subjects was considered, specifically studies that examined the constructs of *motivation* and *rewards*. The next phase of identification included searching for relevant articles from scientific databases including APA PsycINFO and EBSCOhost. Search terms included *motivation* and various iterations of the terms *rewards, performance, incentives,* and *learning*, along with the filters *human* and *empirical* to refine the search results. Review articles that merely aggregated findings on general topics were excluded from consideration because of the lack of direct experimentation in those article types. The inclusion approach targeted data-driven articles that explored either INMO/EXMO distinctions or studies that sought to determine the motivational impact of rewards on behavior. Articles that focused on topics indirectly related to motivation were excluded. Animal motivation studies were omitted based on the human performance focus. Articles that dealt solely with instrument validation or theoretical discussions without an empirical component were also excluded.

From this process, a total of 1,115 articles were initially identified. To ensure that only the most impactful studies were included, articles with fewer than 200 citations were excluded, resulting in no included study having less than 299 citations. Upon conducting this initial screening, 102 articles warranted individual investigation. A more detailed analysis of the remaining 102 articles assessed eligibility for inclusion in the final top fifty list. The primary inclusion criteria at this stage focused on whether the studies posed clear research questions related to reward and INMO/EXMO distinctions, and if the study sought to determine how various forms of motivation or rewards influenced outcomes such as learning, motivation, or the performance of a specific task. Any study that provided substantial/novel empirical contributions on the relationship between motivation and rewards was retained. Reward-related articles were excluded if they did not involve the practical implementation or removal of rewards. By employing this search strategy, the final fifty articles, as described in the Appendix, were deemed the most relevant and impactful within motivation research on rewards and included in citation count order (as of June 13, 2025). The list served as the foundation for the detailed discussion that follows. This subsequent analysis allowed for a thorough examination of the methodological approaches employed in each study, as well as the suitability of the conclusions drawn concerning the effect of rewards on motivation.

Effective Measurement

For research to be credible and useful, it must meet methodological standards and pass a series of evaluations that determine if inferences from the findings are warranted. Effective measurement begins by ensuring that the methods used to collect data are standardized, with the intent to produce consistent and replicable results across interventions. While intentions are admirable, even the best-planned research can go awry. There are literally dozens of factors that can turn years of research effort into a pile of bile when a scholarly journal reviewer points out critical flaws that should have been addressed in the design phase of the work, which when left unaddressed prohibit publication. While describing every potential methodological morass here is impractical, several keys for rigorous research are discussed.

Two key aspects of effective measurement are reliability and validity. Reliability refers to the consistency of measurement (Kimberlin & Winterstein, 2008). Imagine repeating the same study multiple times—if the results are similar each time, then the measurement is considered reliable. For example, if you were measuring the relationship between self-reported happiness and school attendance over several weeks and students were consistently happy on days when school was attended, we would conclude the happiness measure was reliable. Like using a scale to weigh yourself, assuming stable weight, if the scale measures weight identically each time you step on it, the scale is reliable. Thus, theoretically, for a reward to be considered reliable, it should be consistently motivating after being received.

Validity implies that a measurement is measuring what it claims to measure (Sürücü & Maslakci, 2020). For instance, if a study claims to measure motivation, the questions, or the tools it uses, should reflect the measure of motivation and not something else, like whether someone is just following instructions or imitating others. Valid measures should result in predictable outcomes for whatever is being measured, as well as produce comparable results as other measures purported to measure the same quality. By example, we would expect that a highly productive employee (according to work records) who is subsequently rated by their supervisor on a work performance scale would earn high marks on the rating scale. If the employee was not rated highly, either the scale or the supervisor might be considered invalid. As you might imagine, perceptions of rewards can vary dramatically, and some rewards may not be a valid reinforcer of motivated behavior (even though it affects everyone equally and consistently), but we will cover that in later chapters.

For research findings to be useful and applicable to a larger group of people than those in a particular study, random sampling is preferred (Stratton, 2021). Randomization means that the allocation of participants to experimental conditions is not contingent upon any personal factors. When randomized, if there are forty-nine red straws and one white straw in a cup, the odds are equal that you will pick the white straw whether you are Hindu or Hebrew, hot or cold, vaccinated or not. When randomization works, any observed differences can be attributed to exposure to what is being measured and little else, permitting the researcher to wave the causality flag. Randomization controls bias, ensuring that the people in the study represent a variety of backgrounds, ages, and experiences (Mertens, 2020). For example, if a study only includes white college students, it may not apply to older adults or people with different racial or educational backgrounds. When researchers use convenience samples, such as college students, or when not controlling for preexisting factors like experience or culture, the generalizability of the results becomes limited and the inferences from the study results may not be warranted. In other words, it would be silly to believe that winning two tickets to see Taylor Swift would be equally as motivating for your granddaughter as it would be for your grandmother.

Researchers are typically interested in making comparisons between groups after the researcher clusters study participants into those various groups. By example, a study could examine the influence of reward type on motivation to learn a foreign language. Group one might earn cash for ten minutes of language practice, group two might get digital badges for practicing, and group three may get nothing (the boring control group). Subsequently the researcher could determine which group had better language vocabulary. While the described study is contrived, like any real study, the data creates an outcome called an "*effect size*," which represents the quantitative differences between groups or variables when making comparisons. Effect sizes are usually reported as small (.2), medium (.5), and large (.8) based on the magnitude of differences between groups or association between variables (Sullivan & Feinn, 2012). Larger effect sizes mean a greater impact of whatever is being studied, in this case the type of reward. Effect size does not ensure statistical significance, but typically significant findings imply an outcome substantial enough to have a meaningful performance impact and thus a measurable effect size. Effect sizes help calculate how much variation between the groups can be attributed to whatever is being manipulated or controlled in the study, which is referred to as *"variance explained."* In the current example, we would want to know how much of linguistic ability is associated with providing the reward. If we found that the reward only increased vocabulary marginally, then the reward wasn't that big of a deal and perhaps other factors in addition to the reward explain vocabulary proficiency. Thus, to measure the true worth of an intervention, variance explained should be reported (and be meaningful) to provide context on the merit of the study results (Thalmayer et al., 2020).

Effective research should not only show statistical significance that explains outcomes but also have *"practical significance."* In other words, findings should have real-world implications and not just provide information that is nice to know. Practical significance refers to how important the study's findings are in the real world (Schmidt & Hunter, 1998), such as revealing methods to improve workplace motivation or describing more effective teaching strategies. Even if a study shows statistical significance—meaning the results are not due to chance, measurement, or statistical error—it does not necessarily mean the results matter or can be implemented to improve everyday life. For example, a study might find that a certain teaching method improves test scores by two to three points. Depending on the sample size in the study, results of this type may be statistically significant. While statistically significant, the outcome may lack practical significance if implementation requires spending thousands of dollars for a new software program or if the outcome means teachers devoting hundreds of hours learning a new teaching method. The minor improvement is not enough to justify implementation.

In summary, effective measurement ensures that studies produce results that are accurate, consistent, unbiased, representative of diverse populations and provide inferences that matter beyond advancing a researcher's hypothesis. Considering the numerous ways research can implode, it should be no surprise that the analysis of the fifty most cited studies in motivational research focused on investigating potential methodological and interpretive issues that might undermine the validity and generalizability of findings related to INMO/EXMO and reward, including scrutiny of the general conclusions drawn about the effects of rewards on motivation. The ultimate goal of the analysis was to determine if the explanatory power associated with these studies might be limited by misleading or *"unjustified"* conclusions, thus failing to capture the dynamic nature of human motivation.

Summary Observations

Total Participants and Sample Composition

Over 17,500 individuals participated in the top fifty motivation and reward studies, with samples varying from as few as twenty-four participants in a small experimental study to over 4,400 participants in a large longitudinal design. Most studies included students aged five to seventeen years or college undergraduates from predominantly Western, educated, industrialized, rich, and democratic (WEIRD) populations. The representation of gender and socioeconomic diversity varied but was often limited by the educational and cultural homogeneity of the samples, otherwise known as recruiting, mostly white, middle-class, or rich kids. Many studies relied on volunteers who were offered extra school credit for participation. Regrettably, while volunteerism is socially conscious and altruistic, it promotes self-selection bias and creates a generalization threat because individuals who volunteer have certain motivational qualities that may differ from the general population.

Effect Sizes and Statistical Reporting

While all studies reported statistically significant findings, only 74 percent provided variance explained. When reported, the average variance explained across studies was 24.5 percent. These modest to moderate effect sizes indicated meaningful but not overwhelming influence of the factors measured, emphasizing the complexity and multifaceted nature of motivational outcomes. Furthermore, eight studies (16 percent) reported some p-values > .05, suggesting significance of findings for null results. Many studies focused on reporting statistical significance without considering or discussing how low variance explained limited the validity of practical interpretations and application.

Methodology Type

Out of the fifty studies examined, nineteen (38 percent) used experimental designs, typically involving controlled manipulations of variables including rewards, attitudes toward learning, or the degree of perceived student autonomy. While experimental studies offer strong internal validity due to controlled conditions, they often lack external validity as artificial lab settings rarely reflect real-world dynamics. The paucity of experimental studies was exacerbated by the exclusive use of self-report measures present in all fifty studies (100 percent), limiting the utility of the findings beyond the observed participants. Correlational studies comprised the bulk of studies reviewed (62 percent), but as every rooster knows, correlation studies cannot ensure causality suggesting that participant and researcher bias may account for subsequent inferences, not objective data.

Research Questions and Study Context

Four general types of research questions were classified after an examination of the fifty studies: motivational influences on academic or work performance, thirty-two studies (64 percent); autonomy and control, three studies (6 percent); rewards and motivation, twelve studies (24 percent); and cross-cultural applications, three studies (6 percent). The lack of methodological diversity raised concerns. Twenty-four studies (48 percent) were conducted in laboratory settings or nonexperimental controlled environments, primarily focusing on tasks such as puzzle-solving, headline-writing, or completing surveys. Of the nineteen (38 percent) experimental studies, only six (32 percent) were fully conducted in real-world settings with six conducted in both the lab and the field (32 percent), including classrooms, workplaces, and locations like fire departments or call centers. The usefulness of laboratory-only studies is often scrutinized, as lab tasks may not capture the complexities of motivation in naturalistic, dynamic environments. This reliance on artificial contexts leaves the results vulnerable to application errors concerning behaviors in diverse business, educational, organizational, or cultural settings.

Subsequent to the general results analysis, each study was examined individually to determine citation recency, sample composition, how rewards were defined, categorized, and applied, appropriateness of inferences, and the justification to generalize the results. More specific analysis revealed four factors that consistently influenced the quality and generalizability of the findings related to the interpretation of INMO/EXMO and rewards: ambiguous construct clarity; lack of distinction between reward contingencies; overreliance on WEIRD, biased, and synthetic samples, and unjustified statistical inference. In addition, based on each of these four named concerns, questionable generalization was pervasive. These four factors serve as the framework for a critical analysis concerning how rewards are described in seminal motivation and reward research, and how their effects on behavior may be misunderstood or overstated as a result of methodological flaws. By examining the following four factors, this analysis underscores the need for more complex, intentional, and valid research designs that truly capture the realities of motivation and rewards in educational and organizational settings.

Four Fowl Findings

Construct Clarity

Pretend you own a restaurant and were invited to an industry conference to learn more about trendy foods. Keep in mind that your restaurant might serve only drinks, snacks, appetizers, main courses, desserts, or one or more of these choices. Also consider that some restaurants specialize in particular food cultures such as pasta, ramen, or tacos. As we know, some venues serve only breakfast or lunch, but not dinner. Some have servers, while others require self-service. As you navigate the conference program to determine which session aligns with your business and tastes, you discover that all program descriptions use similar generic language, stating "An overview of food trends," followed by a random restaurant name. Frustration abounds when you, the owner of a hip sushi shop, are trapped in a session about bargain breakfast taco ingredients. Welcome to consequences of questionable construct validity, where you are not sure what various labels or concepts intend to represent.

Construct ambiguity dominated the top fifty studies. This confusion happened in two ways. First, as evidenced in sixteen studies (34 percent), similar constructs were given different names, creating confusion about what was actually being measured. For instance, terms like "INMO," "task engagement," and "interest" were frequently used interchangeably, leading to vague interpretations or, worse, inappropriate inferences. This type of conflation does not involve uncertainty as to what the individual constructs represent but instead suggests that the fundamental behavior that is being described evolves from similar psychological processes. However, as many realize, the same behavior can be exhibited for many varied reasons. For example, deep task engagement at work can signify genuine task interest or fear of getting fired. You can show up at your job or school and act happy when you couldn't care less. Conceptual clarity is essential for accurate interpretation of motivated effort.

The second type of construct ambiguity occurred when different constructs were conflated or misrepresented by using the same term to describe different concepts (Altgassen et al., 2024; Gonzalez et al., 2020). Across the top fifty studies, nineteen (38 percent) showed terminology overlap, leading to potential results misinterpretation. In psychology, INMO is sometimes confused with compliance or task interest, as documented in various meta-analyses of motivational constructs (Reeve, 2022). For example, Aunola et al. (2006), cited 343 times, combined the constructs' "interest value" and "intrinsic motivation" into one entity, "task motivation." This overlap risks conflating interest value (how much the individual likes or is interested in a particular activity) with INMO (being motivated and curious to do an activity for its own sake).

Fisher (1978), cited 655 times, further exemplified this "what do we really mean" conundrum. The research explored "personal control" and "competence" but used the terms "competence" and "internal work motivation" when discussing participants' INMO experience. This conflation of constructs assumes that feelings of competence and internal work motivation are equivalent, ignoring the possibility that one could feel competent without having internal work motivation or vice versa. Such conceptual blending suggests that even widely accepted constructs are not always clearly distinguished, complicating the overall clarity and application of motivation research.

Furthermore, in Corpus et al. (2009), cited 493 times, the researchers used separate scales for intrinsic and extrinsic motivation; however, the EXMO scale included three distinct dimensions: desire for easy work, desire to please authority figures, and dependence on teachers. The inclusion of teacher dependence as an extrinsic factor was problematic, as the study's own findings suggested dependence may actually reflect INMO. The study concluded that both INMO and EXMO were related to academic achievement, yet the small magnitude of these relationships (particularly for INMO) highlighted the failure to clearly distinguish the unique impacts of these motivational orientations on academic outcomes.

Gagné and St. Père (2002), cited 387 times, presented a case of gonzo generalization, based on inadequate construct definitions. Here, the researchers combined three INMO subscales with the identified regulation subscale of intrinsic motivation into a single intrinsic motivation factor, without making clear distinctions among other empirically distinct motivation types. By blending these dimensions, the study concluded that participants' motivation, whether intrinsic or extrinsic, has limited contributions to academic achievement, regardless of the influence of reward. This conclusion is highly misleading as the intrinsic measure included extrinsic components that were not disaggregated. As a result, the findings obscure the true nature of the motivational factors at play, where external incentives may have accounted for their findings (or lack thereof). Compounding the impact of inappropriate generalization, the study participants were exclusively private-school, female students, with above average IQ scores, a group that is not exactly reflective of the typical learner!

Defining constructs with precision allows for more accurate data interpretation and prevents overgeneralization of results (Gonzalez et al., 2020). To accurately measure motivational outcomes, researchers must make clear distinctions between related concepts. Justified inferences are a necessity, not just a cautious recommendation, for the accurate advancement of scientific inquiry. Situations such as those described cloud data interpretation and undermine the specificity of findings regarding what drives perception of reward and the impact on motivation. Failing to capture necessary distinctions propels conclusions that are marginally supported by the data, offering explanations that may mislead individuals to believe that INMO is the sole magical elixir for any effortful endeavor.

Reward Contingencies

Another pervasive issue was the failure of the top fifty to distinguish between different reward types, particularly engagement-contingent (aka task-contingent), completion-contingent, or performance-contingent rewards. Reward types are discussed in great detail in Chapter 3; however, an engagement-contingent reward means that the reward is earned based on engaging in the activity, but not necessarily for finishing the task. A completion-contingent reward refers to those that are given based on task completion. A performance-contingent reward requires specific performance on the task such as earning a particular grade or score. Across the fifty studies analyzed, eighteen (36 percent) examined how reward differences interact with constructs intimately connected to INMO, such as having choices about the type or timing of the reward (i.e., autonomy), and even fewer, nine (18 percent), clearly differentiated these reward types. While these distinctions may seem trivial, let me know how it feels when you order a veggie burger, and the server brings you a beef or turkey burger instead. Minor differences can be monumental!

The clustering of all reward types without acknowledging the distinct effects each reward structure has on motivation (Park et al., 2019) leads to misleading generalizations about reward impact (Hidi & Renninger, 2006). These omissions resulted in oversimplified conclusions, such as the general claim that all rewards undermine INMO, despite the many circumstances when rewards enhance performance. The impact of rewards depends heavily on how they are delivered (Deci et al., 1999). In reality, completion-contingent and performance-based rewards operate in separate ways. Additionally, each reward type enhances or dilutes basic need satisfaction depending on the task and reward type. By examining how each type of reward interacts with INMO/EXMO, a more accurate picture of how rewards can be structured to support or hinder motivation results. Without distinguishing reward type, inferences may mislead researchers, practitioners, and policymakers to vilify rewards, obscuring the specific conditions when rewards support performance (Bell et al., 2018; Schunk, 1984).

For example, in Amabile et al. (1986), cited 1,148 times, the researchers distinguished between contracted-for-rewards and noncontingent rewards, yet narrowly examined or discussed the no reward or noncontingent reward conditions (or their alleged reduction in creativity and INMO). This lack of distinction between reward types led to an inaccurate generalization that task-contingent rewards decreased creativity. This study, among others, missed the critical insight that task-contingent rewards have minimal harmful effects on INMO, particularly in educational settings where task completion is often the only goal (Cameron & Pierce, 1994).

Anderson et al. (1976), cited 647 times, exemplified the muted distinction between noncontingent and task-contingent rewards. Noncontingent rewards, which are administered regardless of performance, are not necessarily detrimental to INMO as they do not generate external pressure on the individual (Manohar et al., 2017). However, by not differentiating between administering rewards regardless of performance versus rewards for quality, the study concluded that money and symbolic rewards decreased subsequent INMO. This oversight obscures the fact that noncontingent rewards, including symbolic rewards, may have a minimal effect on undermining INMO, while task-contingent rewards have a more direct influence on motivated effort as they are tied to task completion (Henderlong & Lapper, 2002)

Tauer and Harackiewicz (2004), cited 663 times, investigated the effects of competitive and cooperative cultures on INMO and performance, yet did not explicitly differentiate between controlling and informational reward contingencies. By focusing on overall competition and cooperation, the study overlooked how specific rewards, such as performance feedback, might be perceived as controlling (undermining autonomy) or informational (enhancing competence). In addition, the researchers used a motor task, not acknowledging the diversity of motivational impact across tasks. The lack of distinctions limited the ability to understand how distinct types of rewards uniquely influenced INMO within competitive and cooperative contexts.

Deci (1971), cited 8,910 times, also failed to adequately distinguish between reward contingencies. In this study, the researchers failed to distinguish between task-contingent and performance-contingent rewards by treating money solely as a broad external reward, rather than differentiating its effects based on the nature of the situation. The experiments primarily focused on rewards given for task engagement, without adequately exploring monetary rewards tied to specific performance levels or accomplishments. Consequently, concluding that monetary rewards undermined INMO was overgeneralized, as monetary rewards are perceived as valued motivation for those in mundane jobs (Medvedev et al., 2024) and the unitary conclusion discounts evidence that motivation and performance actually increase with external "*incentives*" (Cerasoli, 2014). The failure to parse out differences misleads both researchers and practitioners into believing that any form of reward, even those that provide valuable incentives, inherently undermines INMO.

The clustering of reward types across multiple studies leads to generalizations that are not only inappropriate but also highly misleading. By not differentiating between task-contingent, performance-contingent, and noncontingent rewards, many of the listed fifty studies overlooked the possibility that rewards, when intentionally and cautiously structured, can actually enhance INMO. For instance, informational rewards, such as feedback or praise, can reinforce a sense of competence and autonomy, which are critical components of self-determination theory (SDT) (Ryan & Deci, 2000). This lack of precision not only weakens validity but also has real-world consequences in educational and organizational settings where rewards (e.g., grades, prizes, teacher recognition) are believed to enhance performance. By clustering all reward types together, the cited research risks instilling myths about the inherently negative effects of rewards, without recognizing the potential benefits of carefully designed, personally internalized reward programs that often lead to optimal performance.

WEIRD, Biased, and Synthetic Samples

The usefulness of the findings from the top fifty studies was limited by multiple participant selection issues. First, there was an overreliance on WEIRD samples, with 88 percent of reviewed articles drawn primarily from college students who typically volunteered or who sought extra credit for research participation. Homogenous samples introduce significant racial, cultural, and socioeconomic biases, limiting the generalizability of the findings while currently perpetuating issues of exclusion and equity (Arnett, 2008; King et al., 2018). The trajectory of motivation across cultures, genders, ethnicities, socioeconomic backgrounds, and life stages is different. Thus, the use of primarily WEIRD samples excludes important distinctions in how motivation develops and influences behavior. Henrich et al. (2010) highlighted the dangers of overgeneralizing findings from WEIRD samples, noting that these populations represent only a small subset of global cultural diversity and are often already overrepresented in psychological research. The supposition that normative behaviors across cultures are similar, while an artifact of historically myopic and egotistical worldviews, minimally fails to account for the reality that motivated behavior is context dependent (Eccles & Wigfield, 2020). Thus, the analysis below examines how reliance on voluntary WEIRD samples constrains application of findings in addition to skewing results generalization.

The average number of participants across the identified studies was 346, but the composition was often unbalanced and biased. For example, Deci (1972), cited 1,654 times, failed to mention any demographic information whatsoever referring to his sample, as "participants," while concurrently declaring that verbal rewards universally improved work performance. Out classifying Deci, Ross (1975), cited 507 times, revealed participants were both male and female, while also lamenting, "Two additional children (both females) were excused from the study when they expressed an urgent need to go to the washroom" (p. 247). Corpus et al. (2009), cited 493 times, used a larger sample of 1,051 students from Oregon; however, the composition was 78 percent Caucasian participants from middle-class backgrounds. The conclusions drawn from that study, which purported to generalize findings about INMO to all students, overlooked significant differences that may exist in non-Western or lower-income populations (Urdan & Bruchmann, 2018) that are radically different from the Oregon culture, dude.

Among the fifty studies, only twenty (40 percent) indicated racial breakdowns of their participants; within this 40 percent, 75 percent used a majority Caucasian or homogenous Western sample, with only five studies explicitly accounting for or reporting on participants from racially diverse backgrounds. For instance, Lepper et al. (1973), cited 5,055 times, in a study generally considered to be the most influential reward research responsible for the erroneous attribution that rewards universally undermine INMO (i.e., the overjustification hypothesis), indicated "Three black children who would otherwise have been included in the experiment were arbitrarily excluded from the subject pool in order to increase the precision with which the population could be defined" (p. 131). This statement, allegedly under the guise of reducing sampling error, was shrouded in racial bias. However, researcher bias toward WEIRD samples did not stop the authors from stating "subjects were all children who actually manifested some intrinsic interest in the activity," seemingly implying that the impact of rewards inherent to school-based activities did not apply to Black children! Minimally, the exclusion of racial and ethnic minorities created a narrow understanding of rewards and motivation, if not a total mockery of inclusive practice and established research protocols.

Thirty-nine (78 percent) of the fifty studies used children and college-aged young adults as the primary participants, with twenty-seven (54 percent) of these studies involving college students. In Simons et al. (2004), cited 596 times, 100 percent of participants were female nursing students, with the authors concluding that external regulation (a form of EXMO) was related to lower interest, less motivation, and lower exam scores. However, the study did not account for the fact that college-aged females may respond to rewards differently than other populations (Eagly & Wood, 2012; Gilligan, 1993). The gender disparity and demographic homogeneity limit extension of these findings beyond the specific demographic of young, Western women. In Kuvaas (2009), cited 307 times, the sample was 70 percent female and concluded that INMO is a strong predictor of work performance across various tasks, functions, and groups. The study neglected to mention that gender socialization and culture mediate motivation and different age groups, academic, and professional environments produce different motivational outcomes (Korpershoek et al., 2019).

Sample size was another concern, particularly in highly cited studies that attempted to generalize findings from relatively small, homogenous samples. Anderson et al. (1976) used only twenty-eight subjects (Experiment 2), composed primarily of African American children from low socioeconomic status families. In one study aspect, only nine or ten children were assigned to three distinct experimental conditions, a configuration in violation of conventional group size recommendations for statistical accuracy. Despite the limited sample, the study drew broad conclusions about the effects of different control procedures on INMO. With such a small, homogenous sample the conclusions neglected the realities of motivational structures in larger, more diverse populations. In Deci (1971), across two experiments only twenty-four participants were recruited, again from an introductory psychology course from a Western, middle-class university setting. The study suggested that rewards universally undermined INMO; however, homogeneity limited the reliable application of the findings to workplace or school settings outside of Western academic environments (Henrich et al., 2010). Additional sample size data for each study can be found in the Appendix.

Self-selection occurs when individuals volunteer to participate in research studies. Bias develops when particular types of individuals are more likely to be research participants than others. The validity impact is based not on individual willingness to participate but on the unknown reasons for participation. Participants who volunteer may be more academically motivated or familiar with psychological research than those who decline, which means their behavior may not represent the broader population (Eccles & Wigfield, 2002). Nonparticipation motives are inconsequential, except those who are unwilling to participate may have different values and expectations than those who enlist, potentially skewing observed results. Volunteer participants may possess predetermined characteristics, obscuring a researcher's ability to decipher if study protocols or personal characteristics were responsible for the observed outcomes (Henrich et al., 2010).

In addition, self-selection promotes racial biases in sample composition, due to overrepresentation of Caucasian participants, while racial or ethnic minorities are underrepresented or excluded entirely. The lack of diversity raises significant concerns about how well these studies capture motivational dynamics in diverse, global populations (Urdan & Bruchmann, 2018). This issue intensifies the impact of cultural context on how rewards and motivational feedback may be perceived, particularly in collectivist societies (Miller & Goodnow, 1995) where receiving rewards and garnering attention are seen as an undesirable personal quality. In Ryan et al. (1983), cited 1955 times, participants were undergraduate volunteers, participating to complete course credit requirements. This participation incentive impacted generalizability, as the sample overrepresented individuals who were already motivated by external rewards (like extra credit), inaccurately reflecting the motivations of nonacademic populations. In Reeve (1989), cited 336 times, participants were recruited through psychology department announcements and participated to get extra course credit. Contributors were more likely to be students with an interest in psychology, or individuals already engaged in discretionary academic pursuits (Sears, 1986). The conclusion that rewards negatively affected INMO did not take into account the possibility that volunteerism may mean that participants already had heightened sensitivity to reward structures prior to participation (Van den Berg et al., 2010) and might volunteer for numerous reasons beyond perceived passion.

Across the top-cited fifty studies, twenty-four (48 percent) were lab-based designs, where variables like rewards or feedback were manipulated under tightly controlled conditions. These designs involved low-stakes tasks, such as solving puzzles or performing simple, repetitive actions. While simulated designs are valuable for isolating specific variables, some designs fail to capture the complex interactions that modify results. The simplistic tasks and controlled conditions used in the lab do not reflect the many factors influencing motivation in real life. Consequently, the generalizations made from these lab-based findings are often inappropriate and misleading when applied to schools, workplaces, and other diverse environments.

For example, Fisher (1978) investigated the effects of performance-based rewards on perceptions of feeling controlled during work but failed to capture the reality that rewards are often tied to long-term career goals and social dynamics, factors notably absent in lab settings. Similarly, Ryan et al. (1983), cited 1,955 times, involved participants working individually on hidden-figure puzzles in a controlled laboratory setting; and while the results suggested that task-contingent rewards decreased INMO, the study's short-term, task-specific nature did not reflect how people respond to rewards in complex, ongoing work or learning environments (Eccles & Wigfield, 2002). Amabile et al. (1986) employed a collage-making task in a lab environment to study the impact of contracted-for rewards on INMO. However, collage-making does not mirror the complexity of tasks encountered in the workplace or school, where the stakes are higher, and performance is influenced by other social and professional factors (Wigfield & Eccles, 2002) beyond paste and glue. The study's conclusions that contracted-for rewards decreased INMO was misleading, as the context of rewards in daily life is far more delicate and dynamic than created lab artwork.

Laboratories are useful for controlling extraneous variables, but they often reduce multidimensional real-world tasks to simplistic, isolated activities, leading to findings that are difficult to generalize (Baumeister et al., 2007). While the studies described used controlled conditions and manipulation of variables supporting identification of causality, they lacked the complexity and contextual richness of real-world environments, leading to results that may conflict with reality (Mook, 1983; Shadish et al., 2002). Laboratory studies are designed for the convenience of data collection, where tasks are often simplistic and artificial, thus failing to capture the multifaceted dynamics present in schools, workplaces, or other natural environments. In real life, motivation is shaped by social dynamics, long-term goals, and environmental pressures—factors that are often missing from controlled laboratory settings (Pariott et al., 2020). Generalizing from simplified, synthetic tasks to real-world contexts can often result in misleading conclusions about how rewards affect motivation in everyday life.

Statistical Inference

In eight studies (16 percent), inferences of statistical significance were unjustified by the data analyzed (see Appendix). In some cases, reported p-values were as marginal as $p = 0.10$, creating the illusion of explanatory meaning, yet discounting the integrity of valid scientific inquiry. P values describe the probability that reported findings are a result of experimentation, not statistical or methodological error. A p value of .10 suggests there is a 10 percent chance that observed results are *not* a reflection of the researcher's design or experimental control. While contentious, psychologists and educators are willing to accept a 5 percent chance of error; thus, a minimally acceptable p value is < .05. In physical sciences, the value is typically 1 percent, sometimes even lower. Thus, any p values reported at ≥ .05 are not statistically significant. The implication of marginal significance for p ≥ .05 is misleading and often suggests that the hypotheses, research design, or sample configuration was flawed or insufficient to capture a valid or usable result.

In addition, many times at the expense of practical significance, statistical significance was overemphasized, including the omission of crucial details such as effect sizes and variance explained. Practical significance describes whether differences between conditions are substantial enough to warrant changes in practice. Practical significance differs from statistical significance in that results can be statistically significant but have marginal impact whereby implementing changes based on the findings would not be worth the time, cost, or effort. By example, imagine your refrigerator only cooled to 40 degrees. Also, assume that through experimentation it was concluded that the best temperature to store ice cream was 38 degrees. Would it be prudent to spend $2,000 to get a new refrigerator to achieve the ideal ice-cream temperature? For many people, besides those named Ben and Jerry, it would not be practical to buy a new fridge. The same principle applies to many research findings where the recommendations are not justified by the magnitude of the benefits, because mediation may not provide a justifiable return on the investment of cost or effort.

Furthermore, 100 percent of studies relied on results from self-report measures to inform their analyses. These measures are subject to response bias because individuals may respond in socially acceptable ways with subjective interpretations of reality based on feelings and not facts. When self-report is the exclusive means of reporting motivation, it reflects biased evaluation, which severely limits the ability to generalize the results beyond the individuals providing the information. Thus, the subsequent examples show that several of the top fifty studies inflated the importance of their results by focusing on statistical significance while downplaying (or ignoring) practical significance and the magnitude of the effects reported. We also show how self-report measures without corroborating behavioral evidence can lead to misleading conclusions about the effects of rewards on motivation.

Across the fifty studies reviewed, thirteen (26 percent) employed embellished statistical inference, characterized by reporting statistically significant results while failing to provide details such as effect sizes or how much of the variance in outcomes was explained by whatever was manipulated or controlled in the respective study. Thirty-seven (74 percent) reported effect sizes, and of those that did, the average difference between conditions ranged from 0.2 to 0.4 of a standard deviation, indicating moderate real-world effects. Furthermore, in twenty-two when applied to real-world settings where motivational dynamics are far more complex. This tendency to emphasize statistical significance without considering practical significance leaves the conclusions disconnected from their real-world applicability (Hidi & Renninger, 2006). These liberal interpretations and overgeneralizations based on incomplete data or analysis routinely suggested that single variables, such as autonomy, engagement, and persistence, are the primary INMO catalysts. While confluent data does reveal the components and benefits of INMO, the top fifty studies concurrently and with marginal justification vilified the impact of rewards by routinely and falsely suggesting that rewards undermine motivation. In reality, the unexplained variance paints a much more complex picture concerning rewards and motivation. The findings also bring into question the practical significance of any isolated factor as a standalone predictor of motivation, because of the minimal investigation of interactive effects of the numerous factors driving motivation and rewards. The inflated interpretations reported based on ordinary significance levels make the findings appear more meaningful than implied. As we shall soon see, unjustified conclusions can mislead many to blindly idolize INMO, just like the fledgling lamb who sees a roaring lion in the motivational mirror, sometimes even with their eyes closed.

Conclusions

Skeptics interpreting the data presented here and in Appendix may quickly condemn the findings, lamenting that the bulk of the cited research is as stale as the cake your grandmother baked for your fifth birthday. The study dates ranged from 1971 to 2013, with an average publication date of 1998, suggesting that the recency of the findings and the accompanying methodological concerns are anchored in past practices that may no longer exist or do not reflect the current state of motivational research. Indeed, research samples have become more diverse, methodological rigor has improved, and studies with unitary measures of motivation (i.e., self-report) are often rejected by reviewers for inclusion in prominent journals. Research protocols have changed for the better. More rigorous methods are now used that include proposing and preregistering hypotheses before data is collected to avoid "*p-hacking*." More sophisticated statistical methods and software programs are available to analyze results, allowing researchers to better understand how specific contexts and groups influence results. Online public depositories are available to review raw research data to ensure that results are interpreted properly. However, the legacy of what are often described as "seminal findings" still dominates the field of motivational research.

Perhaps the most alarming consequence of the issues identified in this chapter is that the reliance on flawed methodology and questionable findings as support for ongoing research has actually ***increased*** over time! Of the studies listed in the Appendix, the average annual citation count for forty-four out of fifty studies has increased since 2020, with the average increase at the rate of 49 percent compared to average citations before 2020. This increase indicates that the influence of homogenous samples, overgeneralization, or construct misinterpretations continues to be the frame as substantial motivation research applauds these flawed legacy accomplishments. The problem is magnified exponentially as new research accepts the interpretive principles of the past as a sound basis for future inquiries. Even more disturbing is the perpetuation of legacy results as "new to me information" by journalists and social media influencers that amplify these presumed accurate interpretations, thereby increasing the potential for misconceptions among followers who are unfamiliar with the issues described here.

From a practical perspective what results is reliance on views of human motivation that are steeped in tradition and may not completely reflect what drives human behavior.

Across the fifty studies, foundational theories such as SDT (see p. 5) are heavily emphasized, with many articles building upon vague reward contingency research that omits or falsely generalizes the consequences of autonomous incentives. Some of the most cited works, particularly for academic motivation, include studies on autonomy-supportive environments, psychological well-being, and academic performance. However, the lack of novel theoretical perspectives suggests that the field may be entrenched in a cycle of stagnation by validating established theories instead of adequately challenging or evolving them. Moreover, the inordinate focus on INMO excludes examination of critical variables that can close the unexplained variance gap, particularly the vast influence of how the brain processes instrumental and valanced behavior across different situations and circumstances.

The fifty studies examined, while substantial in their contributions to understanding the foundation of motivation, performance, and rewards, are outdated and incomplete. Consideration of the mountains of credible and replicable evidence from innovative domains like neurology, endocrinology, and behavioral economics are not only warranted but also justified by the influence of physiology on motivated effort. As the subsequent chapters reveal, just as humans crave satisfaction of urges like hunger and sex, they have a quest to gain rewards that are not necessarily activated or repressed through the pursuit of passion.

The remaining chapters explain the documented source of motivation, how rewards work across contexts, and which factors influence reward attainment or failure. We investigate the specific influence of rewards on behavior including such topics as the formation and maintenance of beliefs, learning, persuasion, socializing, and ultimately getting whatever makes us get out of bed in the morning (or keeps us there) on a day-to-day basis. Contrary to popular belief, the influence of the brain is not immutable and fixed. Neuronal *"plasticity"* means that within particular boundaries we can change how our reward system functions. As such, specific strategies are advanced that provide the ability to satisfy every desire despite the brutal and unforgiving influence of the brain on behavior.

References

Altgassen, E., Geiger, M., & Wilhelm, O. (2024). Do you mind a closer look? A jingle-jangle fallacy perspective on mindfulness. *European Journal of Personality, 38*(2), 365–387. https://doi.org/10.1177/08902070231174575

Amabile, T. M., Hennessey, B. A., & Grossman, B. S. (1986). Social influences on creativity: The effects of contracted-for reward. *Journal of Personality and Social Psychology, 50*(1), 14–23. https://doi.org/10.1037/0022-3514.50.1.14

Anderson, R., Manoogian, S. T., & Reznick, J. S. (1976). The undermining and enhancing of intrinsic motivation in preschool children. *Journal of Personality and Social Psychology, 34*(5), 915–922. https://doi.org/10.1037/0022-3514.34.5.915

Arnett, J. J. (2008). The neglected 95%: Why American psychology needs to become less American. *American Psychologist, 63*(7), 602–614. https://doi.org/10.1037/14805-008

Aunola, K., Leskinen, E., & Nurmi, J. E. (2006). Developmental dynamics between mathematical performance, task motivation, and teachers' goals during the transition to primary school. *British Journal of Educational Psychology*, 76(1), 21–40. https://doi.org/10.1348/000709905x51608

Baumeister, R. F., Vohs, K. D., & Funder, D. C. (2007). Psychology as the science of self-reports and finger movements: Whatever happened to actual behavior? *Perspectives on Psychological Science*, 2(4), 396–403. https://doi.org/10.1111/j.1745-6916.2007.00051.x

Bell, L., Vogt, J., Willemse, C., Routledge, T., Butler, L. T., & Sakaki, M. (2018). Beyond self-report: A review of physiological and neuroscientific methods to investigate consumer behavior. *Frontiers in Psychology*, 9. https://doi.org/10.3389/fpsyg.2018.01655

Cameron, J., & Pierce, W. D. (1994). Reinforcement, reward, and intrinsic motivation: A meta-analysis. *Review of Educational Research*, 64(3), 363–423. https://doi.org/10.3102/00346543064003363

Cameron, J., Pierce, W. D., Banko, K. M., & Gear, A. (2005). Achievement-based rewards and intrinsic motivation: A test of cognitive mediators. *Journal of Educational Psychology*, 97(4), 641–655. https://doi.org/10.1037/0022-0663.97.4.641

Cerasoli, C. P., Nicklin, J. M., & Ford, M. T. (2014). Intrinsic motivation and extrinsic incentives jointly predict performance: A 40-year meta-analysis. *Psychological Bulletin*, 140(4), 980–1008. https://doi.org/10.1037/a0035661

Chan, D. (2010). So why ask me? Are self-report data really that bad?. In C. E. Lance & R. J. Vandenberg (Eds.), *Statistical and methodological myths and urban legends: received doctrine, verity, and fable in the organizational and social sciences* (pp. 311–338). Routledge.

Corpus, J. H., McClintic-Gilbert, M. S., & Hayenga, A. O. (2009). Within-year changes in children's intrinsic and extrinsic motivational orientations: Contextual predictors and academic outcomes. *Contemporary Educational Psychology*, 34(2), 154–166. https://doi.org/10.1016/j.cedpsych.2009.01.001

Deci, E. L. (1971). Effects of externally mediated rewards on intrinsic motivation. *Journal of Personality and Social Psychology*, 18(1), 105–115. https://doi.org/10.1037/h0030644

Deci, E. L. (1972). The effects of contingent and noncontingent rewards and controls on intrinsic motivation. *Organizational Behavior and Human Performance*, 8(2), 217–229. https://doi.org/10.1016/0030-5073(72)90047-5

Deci, E. L., Koestner, R., & Ryan, R. M. (1999). A meta-analytic review of experiments examining the effects of extrinsic rewards on intrinsic motivation. *Psychological Bulletin, 125*(6), 627–668. https://doi.org/10.1037//0033-2909.125.6.627

Dodd, N. G., & Ganster, D. C. (1996). The interactive effects of variety, autonomy, and feedback on attitudes and performance. *Journal of Organizational Behavior, 17*(4), 329–347. https://doi.org/10.1002/(SICI)1099-1379(199607)17:4<329::AID-JOB754>3.0.CO;2-B

Eagly, A. H., & Wood, W. (2012). Social role theory. In P. A. M. Van Lange, A. W. Kruglanski, & E. T. Higgins (Eds.), *Handbook of theories of social psychology* (pp. 458–476). Sage. https://doi.org/10.4135/9781446249222.n49

Eccles, J. S., & Wigfield, A. (2002). Motivational beliefs, values, and goals. *Annual Review of Psychology, 53*(1), 109–132. https://doi.org/10.1146/annurev.psych.53.100901.135153

Eccles, J. S., & Wigfield, A. (2020). From expectancy-value theory to situated expectancy-value theory: A developmental, social cognitive, and sociocultural perspective on motivation. *Contemporary Educational Psychology, 61*, 101859. https://doi.org/10.1016/j.cedpsych.2020.101859

Elliot, A. J., & McGregor, H. A. (2001). A 2×2 achievement goal framework. *Journal of Personality and Social Psychology, 80*(3), 501–519. https://doi.org/10.1037/0022-3514.80.3.501

Fisher, C. D. (1978). The effects of personal control, competence, and extrinsic reward systems on intrinsic motivation. *Organizational Behavior and Human Performance, 21*, 273–288. https://doi.org/10.1016/0030-5073(78)90054-5

Franco, A., Malhotra, N., & Simonovits, G. (2014). Publication bias in the social sciences: Unlocking the file drawer. *Science, 345*(6203), 1502–1505.

Gagné, F., & St. Père, F. (2002). When IQ is controlled, does motivation still predict achievement? *Intelligence, 30*, 71–100. https://doi.org/10.1016/S0160-2896(01)00068-X

Gilligan, C. (1993). *In a different voice: Psychological theory and women's development.* Harvard University Press.

Graves, L. M., Ruderman, M. N., Ohlott, P. J., & Weber, T. J. (2012). Driven to work and enjoyment of work: Effects on managers' outcomes. *Journal of Management, 38*, 1655–1680. https://doi.org/10.1177/0149206310363612

Gonzalez, O., MacKinnon, D. P., & Muniz, F. B. (2020). Extrinsic convergent validity evidence to prevent jingle and jangle fallacies. *Multivariate Behavioral Research, 56*(1), 3–19. https://doi.org/10.1080/00273171.2019.1707061

Grant, A. M. (2008). The significance of task significance: Job performance effects, relational mechanisms, and boundary conditions. *Journal of*

Applied Psychology, 93(1), 108–124. https://doi.org/10.1037/0021-9010.93.1.108

Harackiewicz, J. M. (1979). The effects of reward contingency and performance feedback on intrinsic motivation. *Journal of Personality and Social Psychology, 37*, 1352–1363. https://doi.org/10.1037/0022-3514.37.8.1352

Henderlong, J., & Lepper, M. R. (2002). The effects of praise on children's intrinsic motivation: A review and synthesis. *Psychological Bulletin, 128*(5), 774–795. https://doi.org/10.1037/0033-2909.128.5.774

Henrich, J., Heine, S. J., & Norenzayan, A. (2010). The weirdest people in the world?. *Behavioral and Brain Sciences, 33*(2–3), 61–83. https://doi.org/10.1017/S0140525X0999152X

Hidi, S., & Renninger, K. A. (2006). The four-phase model of interest development. *Educational Psychologist, 41*(2), 111–127. https://doi.org/10.1207/s15326985ep4102_4

Kimberlin, C. L., & Winterstein, A. G. (2008). Validity and reliability of measurement instruments used in research. *American Journal of Health-System Pharmacy, 65*(23), 2276–2284. https://doi.org/10.2146/ajhp070364

King, R. B., McInerney, D. M., & Pitliya, R. J. (2018). Envisioning a culturally imaginative educational psychology. *Educational Psychology Review, 30*, 1031–1065. https://doi.org/10.1007/s10648-018-9440-z

Korpershoek, H., King, R. B., McInerney, D. M., Nasser, R. N., Ganotice, F. A., & Watkins, D. A. (2019). Gender and cultural differences in school motivation. *Research Papers in Education, 36*(1), 27–51. https://doi.org/10.1080/02671522.2019.1633557

Kuvaas, B. (2009). A test of hypotheses derived from self-determination theory among public sector employees. *Employee Relations, 31*(1), 39–56. https://doi.org/10.1108/01425450910916814

Leonard, M. L., & Horn, A. G. (1995). Crowing in relation to status in roosters. *Animal Behaviour, 49*(5), 1283–1290. https://doi.org/10.1006/anbe.1995.0160

Lepper, M. R., Greene, D., & Nisbett, R. E. (1973). Undermining children's intrinsic interest with extrinsic reward: A test of the "overjustification" hypothesis. *Journal of Personality and Social Psychology, 28*(1), 129–137. https://doi.org/10.1037/h0035519

Manohar, S. G., Finzi, R. D., Drew, D., & Husain, M. (2017). Distinct motivational effects of contingent and noncontingent rewards. *Psychological Science, 28*(7), 1016–1026. https://doi.org/10.1177/0956797617693326

Medvedev, D., Davenport, D., & Talhelm, T. (2024). The motivating effect of monetary over psychological incentives is stronger in WEIRD cultures. *Nature Human Behavior, 8*, 456–470. https://doi.org/10.1038/s41562-023-01769-5

Mertens, D. M. (2020). *Research and evaluation in education and psychology: Integrating diversity with quantitative, qualitative, and mixed methods* (5th ed.). Sage.

Miller, P. J., & Goodnow, J. J. (1995). Cultural practices: Toward an integration of culture and development. In J. J. Goodnow, P. J. Miller, & F. Kessel (Eds.), *Cultural practices as contexts for development* (pp. 5–16). Jossey-Bass/Wiley.

Mook, D. G. (1983). In defense of external invalidity. *American Psychologist, 38*(4), 379–387. https://doi.org/10.1037/0003-066X.38.4.379

Open Science Collaboration. (2015). Estimating the reproducibility of psychological science. *Science, 349*(6251), aac4716. https://doi.org/10.1126/science.aac4716

Pariott, L., Grotrian, S., Griffin, B., Cole, R., Granfors, S., & Becker, A. (2020). Identifying discrepancies between student technology expectations and current resources. *Educational Research: Theory and Practice, 31*(1), 1–6.

Park, J., Kim, S., Kim, A., & Mun, Y. Y. (2019). Learning to be better at the game: Performance vs. completion contingent reward for game-based learning. *Computers & Education, 139*, 1–15. https://doi.org/10.1016/j.compedu.2019.04.016

Reeve, J. (1989). The interest-enjoyment distinction in intrinsic motivation. *Motivation and Emotion, 13*, 83–103. https://doi.org/10.1007/BF00992956

Reeve, J. (2022). A self-determination theory perspective on student engagement. In A. L. Reschly & S. L. Christenson (Eds.), *Handbook of research on student engagement* (pp. 149–172). Springer US. https://doi.org/10.1007/978-1-4614-2018-7_7

Ross, M. (1975). Salience of reward and intrinsic motivation. *Journal of Personality and Social Psychology, 32*(2), 245–254. https://doi.org/10.1037//0022-3514.32.2.245

Ryan, R. M., & Deci, E. L. (2000). Self-determination theory and the facilitation of intrinsic motivation, social development, and well-being. *American Psychologist, 55*(1), 68–78. https://doi.org/10.1037/0003-066X.55.1.68

Ryan, R. M., Mims, V., & Koestner, R. (1983). Relation of reward contingency and interpersonal context to intrinsic motivation: A review and test using cognitive evaluation theory. *Journal of Personality and Social Psychology, 45*(4), 736–750. https://doi.org/10.1037/0022-3514.45.4.736

Schmidt, F. L., & Hunter, J. E. (1998). The validity and utility of selection methods in personnel psychology: Practical and theoretical implications of 85 years of research findings. *Psychological Bulletin, 124*(2), 262–274. http://dx.doi.org/10.1037/0033

Schunk, D. H. (1984). Self-efficacy perspective on achievement behavior. *Educational Psychologist, 19*(1), 48–58. https://doi.org/10.1080/00461528409529281

Sears, D. O. (1986). College sophomores in the laboratory: Influences of a narrow database on social psychology's view of human nature. *Journal of Personality and Social Psychology, 51*(3), 515–530. https://doi.org/10.1037/0022-3514.51.3.515

Shadish, W. R., Cook, T. D., & Campbell, D. T. (2002). *Experimental and quasi-experimental designs for generalized causal inference*. Houghton Mifflin.

Simons, J., Dewitte, S., & Lens, W. (2004). The role of different types of instrumentality in motivation, study strategies, and performance: Know why you learn, so you'll know what you learn!. *British Journal of Educational Psychology, 74*(3), 343–360. https://doi.org/10.1348/0007099041552314

Skinner, E. A., & Belmont, M. J. (1993). Motivation in the classroom: Reciprocal effects of teacher behavior and student engagement across the school year. *Journal of Educational Psychology, 85*(4), 571–581. https://doi.org/10.1037/00220663.85.4.571

Steel, P., & König, C. J. (2006). Integrating theories of motivation. *Academy of Management Review, 31*(4), 889–913. https://doi.org/10.5465/amr.2006.22527462

Stratton, S. J. (2021). Population research: Convenience sampling strategies. *Prehospital and Disaster Medicine, 36*(4), 373–374. https://doi.org/10.1017/s1049023x21000649

Sullivan, G. M., & Feinn, R. (2012). Using effect size—or why the P value is not enough. *Journal of Graduate Medical Education, 4*(3), 279–282. https://doi.org/10.4300/jgme-d-12-00156.1

Sürücü, L., & Maslakci, A. (2020). Validity and reliability in quantitative research. *Business & Management Studies: An International Journal, 8*(3), 2694–2726. https://doi.org/10.15295/bmij.v8i3.1540

Tauer, J. M., & Harackiewicz, J. M. (2004). The effects of cooperation and competition on intrinsic motivation and performance. *Journal of Personality and Social Psychology, 86*(6), 849–861. https://doi.org/10.1037/0022-3514.86.6.849

Thalmayer, A. G., Toscanelli, C., & Arnett, J. J. (2020). The neglected 95% revisited: Is American psychology becoming less American? *American Psychologist, 76*(1), 116–129. https://doi.org/10.1037/amp0000622

Urdan, T., & Bruchmann, K. (2018). Examining the academic motivation of a diverse student population: A consideration of methodology. *Educational Psychologist, 53*(2), 114–130. https://doi.org/10.1080/00461520.2018.1440234

Van den Berg, I., Franken, I. H., & Muris, P. (2010). A new scale for measuring reward responsiveness. *Frontiers in Psychology, 1*, 239. https://doi.org/10.3389/fpsyg.2010.00239

3

The Price of Passion
The Reality of Reward

Chapter Outline

The Guts of Motivated Effort	54
The Ties That Bind	57
Leveraging Rewards	61
Getting to the Source	67
Need Satisfaction	80
Moving Forward	94

A research investigation of passion reveals that passion is a double-edged sword. Researcher Robert Vallerand (2015) has advanced the most empirically supported model of passion, labeled the "dualistic model of passion" (DMP). The model is primarily substantiated through impressions provided by surveys that hope to measure the degree of passion you have about your passion. By rating the extent of agreement with such statements as "This activity is in harmony with the other activities in my life," or "I am completely engaged in this activity, but I am able to live other experiences in my life," and "I spend a lot of time engaging in this activity" or "I cannot live without this activity," we can measure the degree and polarity of purported passion (Vallerand et al., 2003). While self-report data has significant measurement and interpretative liabilities as described in Chapter 2, passion is generally associated with placing high value and enjoyment on what you do. Passion is usually associated with romantic relationships, but love, joy, and fulfillment can be experienced whenever we voluntarily dedicate time and effort toward a task or goal. According to the DMP, there are two types of passion, "harmonious," and "obsessive" (Vallerand et al., 2024, p. 246). Harmonious passion (HP) is related to feeling self-joy, including academic enthusiasm, whereas the obsessive and compulsive version of passion (OP) is linked with greater stress, anxiety, and burnout.

The polarity of passion is determined in part by the extent of how the passion-inducing activities impact other life facets, including behavior. HP suggests that passion-generating activities seamlessly become part of your personal identity due to immense fulfillment, with the caveat that the activities are pursued in absence of any external coercion or incentive such as money, praise, or elevated social status. When describing harmonious passion, Vallerand et al. used words such as "significant" but "not overpowering" (2024, p. 246), implying that HP people control their activity choices and how much effort they dedicate to a task as opposed to the activity controlling them. HP can be realized through leisure activities, but for many the probability of attaining the positive HP feeling can be more easily attained during work or education (Csikszentmihalyi, 1989).

Conversely, OP is just like it sounds, the over the top. I am compelled to engage in this activity or as the jargon junkies described it "outside the integrating self" (Deci & Ryan, 2000; Ryan & Deci, 2017). OP implies that urges to complete a task are "uncontrollable" and task engagement is done for ulterior motives such as ego boosting or to fit in with a group or culture. This maladaptive form of passion is perceived to be much more controlling and of the blend where the individual feels pressured and compelled to persist in the task knowing that other aspects of life (like family) may suffer as a result of the passionate pursuit. As we shall soon learn, the feelings associated with OP are similar to those experienced during addictive behavior, where the individual in pursuit of pleasure is actually engaging in a form of self-punishment that is seemingly beyond their control yet coveted (and intimately related to how reward pathways predictably operate in the brain).

The promoters of passion recognize the paradox. While passion boosts academic engagement (Zhao et al., 2021), contributes to positive self-assessments and elevated perceptions of mental health (Yukhymenko-Lescroart & Sharma, 2022), while fostering task commitment (Scales &

Brown, 2020), in its maladaptive form passion overload contributes to anxiety, stress, and burnout (Vallerand et al., 2010). Educational persistence and career success are linked to adaptive passion with higher self-reported passion associated with more positive evaluations of one's life and satisfaction with vocational outcomes. The benefits of passion go beyond the materialistic, because when passionate, attentional focus increases along with better concentration (Vallerand et al., 2024). But let's not stop there; passion also helps slackers because passion predicts less procrastination, leading to tenacity and task engagement despite perceived challenges.

However, passion is not the idealistic remedy for motivational laggards that is often portrayed by the media (Cozma, 2023). The concern here is not passion denial or debating the merits of passion as a powerful strategy to motivate human learning and performance. The paradox escalates when one universally believes that passion is more beneficial to motivate behavior than other influences, while assuming that effort extended primarily for fame and fortune lacks psychological reward and is potentially *demotivating* (Vallerand et al., 2024). Moeller (2017) and her colleagues investigated the polarity and source of passion to determine the stability of passion over time and if passion was related to specific activities. To find the answers, they beeped 996 high school kids' wristwatches at random times and asked them what they were doing and how passionate they felt about their behavior at the moment (minus the annoying beep intrusion). Results indicated that 20 percent of the variance in passion came from "personal factors" and that 80 percent originated from the specific activity they were doing at the time of the beep. The 80 percent component were described as "situational" factors like the location, time, or perceptions of energy devoted toward the activity. However, "personal factors" measured only demographics like gender, family SES, and race. Conspicuously absent from "personal factors" was anything related to what the person perceived as rewarding or any consideration of how goals, attitudes, task efficacy, and intelligence influenced task selection and the desire to initiate and pursue an activity. In other words, the study revealed *what* generated excitement, but little knowledge was advanced as to *why* enthusiasm was perceived. The source matters and we must recognize that some people perceive some challenges and tasks as having passion potential, while others don't. Minimally, there are individual differences between interesting and worthwhile tasks and those perceived as boring and mundane. Maybe passion is more personal than Moeller and friends might realize (or elected to emphasize) as part of personalization process (see the explanation of framing on p. 282 to read why this exclusion may happen).

Part of the paradox of passion is realizing that neither HP nor OP fully explain where passion originates or why it develops. Yes, researchers conclude passion starts with having strong interests, but the evidence is based almost entirely on observing the correlation among varying factors that can predict passion like task success or positive emotions. As revealed in Chapter 2, correlation research does not explain the root cause of behavior. Having interests may not be the source of passion any more than believing toasters are responsible for larger families, despite the positive correlation between the number of slots in your toaster and reproductive success. Developing interests results from the subjective valuation that occurs when we enjoy something and do it well. Valuation originates in the experience of task pursuit and usually is accompanied by positive emotion generated through social support and approval from others. While Vallerand and colleagues (2024) imply that passion matures through infusion of the passion with one's identity, again, the reason for identity infusion as a prerequisite for the perpetuation of passion remains elusive.

Passion proponents seem to embrace circular logic professing that strong interest, positive emotion, and ascribing value to an activity or task promotes passion and contributes toward "*internalization*," while likewise advocating that internalization reflects multifaceted passion. The internalization logic is based on the presumption that autonomous internalization occurs when individuals feel pressure free, socially supported, and self-determined. Allegedly, the greater degree of internalization the more passionate we become, but passion magnitude does not explain why internalization happens or why the process of internalization is so motivating. Yes, internalization increases task engagement but perhaps it is not because it is identity supportive, but because basic need satisfaction makes us feel good. When we feel good, the associated behavior related to the feeling tends to increase in frequency. But wait, there's more, as even the greatest proponents of INMO (Cerasoli et al., 2014; Ryan & Deci, 2020) consistently acknowledge that some forms of *extrinsic* motivation are not controlling and can be internalized in the self as well, exacerbating the paradox.

Minimally, harmonious passion is a desirable and positive outcome of selective task engagement. However, this reality fails to acknowledge that passion is rarely all intrinsic. It is unlikely that the passionate expression is devoid of any external, materialistic, or psychological benefits beyond task engagement for its own sake. Additionally, assuming that passion is predicated on task love (Vallerand, 2015) and that other forms of motivated effort lack similar emotional enthusiasm is justified by nothing more than self-reported, socially desirable, anthropomorphic ascription of an emotional connection with your teddy bear. I love to internalize a good cheeseburger now and then, but my "love" (the most contentious and ill-defined construct in psychology history (Berscheid, 2010)) quickly fades when I contemplate my next meal.

Understanding motivation is not about the blissful declaration of unwavering devotion cultivating passion, whether it is demonstrated by a 109-year-old man knitting scarves for ailing penguins (ABCnews.go.com, 2015) or by a scientist like Francis Collins, who has dedicated his entire life to finding a cure for rare congenital diseases (Manolio et al., 2009). To understand the basis of optimal performance, we need a better understanding of *why* we insert ourselves into particular situations, adaptive or otherwise. Arguably, passion may be a consequence of the "jingle-jangle fallacy" in which different terms are used to describe the same construct. According to many journalists and soothsayers, passion is conflated with INMO. When you are intrinsically motivated by an activity, it can breed passion. Enjoyment in turn can enhance your intrinsic drive to engage in the activity more frequently. The key difference is that passion is more of an intense emotional state, while INMO is an inner drive or self-regulated reason for acting. Passion often coexists with and amplifies INMO. However, it is also possible to be intrinsically motivated without experiencing the same level of intense passion. We also have the ability to experience passion through extrinsic reward. Those of us who force ourselves to exercise regularly clearly know the difference, by embracing the inherent rewards of better health and sense of personal accomplishment, without necessarily having a burning passion (or even desire) for the activity itself. In many cases, passion and INMO work together, with passion providing the powerful emotional surge that sustains INMO over time, leading to higher levels of engagement, persistence, and potential for excellence. Ah, but alas, passion is not the only way to sustain motivation and thus the paradox perpetuates.

Having illuminated the key passion components, several other points demand clarification to understand how to optimize learning and performance. First, why do we feel good during task pursuit? The emotional benefits typically associated with INMO can emerge even without strong internal passion. Second, what is the role of need satisfaction, if any, achieved through passionate pursuit but left unsatisfied in the absence of passion? While self-determination is fundamental to optimize human performance, perhaps those needs can be satisfied differently. Third, what accounts for the huge motivational differences among people regarding how tasks, goals, and activities are selected and approached? We have yet to discuss how individual variations develop and why there is inconsistency in motivated effort between two individuals on the same task. Also, except for implications from my fickle cheeseburger fascination, no neuropsychological evidence has been presented to explain motivated behavior. While passion is predicated on subjective interests, passion studies revealed minimal consideration of differences relating passion or anything else to reward perceptions and expectations. Perhaps optimal performance is not about passion, but something else more easily and consistently measured. That something else leads us into a deep dive of the structure of motivation, but, more importantly, understanding why none of the theoretical concepts presented thus far explain the source of motivation, how it starts or why it develops in one way and not another.

The Guts of Motivated Effort

Figuring out what influences the source and intensity of motivated effort that contributes to optimal performance means gaining a foundational understanding of motivational theory and some of the basic psychological and physiological principles that instigate behavior. However, summarizing the basic components of motivation theory is likely boring for the reader and tedious for the author especially when other well-supported resources are available elsewhere. Let's also consider that the contemporary history of motivation theory spans about 140 years and thus requires prolonged explanations (see Ryan et al., 2019). For additional historical perspectives on motivation, see Elliot (2005), Hattie et al. (2020), Latham (2012), or Miele et al. (2024). Instead, the focus here is devoted toward what causes motivated behavior and which factors contribute to optimal exertion of motivated effort with a specific focus on the power of rewards. However, to make sense of how rewards covertly control motivation, we must first answer four questions:

- Which principles, constructs, and factors bind diverse theories of motivation?
- What constitutes reward and what are the contingencies for reward effectiveness?
- What are the primary differences (if any) between INMO and EXMO in practice and what are the benefits and limitations of each perspective?
- Which universal needs relate to enhanced understanding of motivation and how are those needs satisfied?

The emphasis here continues to be more practical and less theoretical. Presenting dozens of theoretical orientations with questionable usefulness is like downloading dozens of influencer travel recommendations and never taking a trip. Thus, the philosophical and esoteric musing of some great thinkers are excluded here in favor of strategies and behaviors that illustrate how to maximize the effectiveness of rewards, once we figure out what psychologically *and* physiologically constitutes a reward.

The Evolution of Motivation

The historical definition of motivation is based on the Latin word "movere," which literally means "to move." The intent of the word echoes familiar definitions that describe motivation as the direction and intensity of effort that drives us to think and behave in certain ways (Hoffman, 2015). Motivation also refers to the reasons underlying behavior or the general desire and willingness to do something, with an action contingent on a variety of biological, social, and cultural influences. Motivations compel us to take action (or resist) whether to satisfy a bodily need like hunger, crave attention from others, feel good (or disgusted) about our accomplishments, or act on deeply held values and beliefs. Considering the importance of movement to overall human existence, specific portions of our brain are dedicated to various motivational processes with one or more areas responsible for goal setting, decision-making, reward evaluation, emotional regulation, learning, social adaptation, and responsiveness to feelings such as anger or fear, among others. In essence, motivation is the "why" behind human goals, need satisfaction, personal evaluations, or desires. It drives action and determines when and what we choose to do, including the moments when we decide to give up, sit on the couch, or devour cheese doodles.

Before moving forward, any study of motivation obligates the author to define and distinguish between various constructs as a starting point to understand motivated behavior. Rather than repeat prolonged explanations that can be found in other publications, the Glossary lists key constructs and terminology (as designated throughout by words in quotes and "*italics*") associated with the analysis of motivated effort and terms that are used throughout the book.

Knowing definitions does not pragmatically inform us as to what happens when we choose to exhibit "*agency*" (i.e., act) or describe the factors that guide behavioral decisions. Hattie et al. (2020), in an attempt to consolidate numerous contemporary motivation theories, suggested that all models of motivation address four main components: self-perceptions, task evaluations, goals, and the costs and benefits of engagement. While these four factors are not all-inclusive for understanding what drives behavior, the factors do highlight the basics of how task-related motivated effort is developed and sustained. These factors are extracted from diverse and prominent motivation theories developed and popularized after the 1960s and exclude outdated unitary perspectives of reinforcement learning.[1]

Note that none of these factors/theories recognize the influence of neurological or endocrinological influences on motivation and the physiological regulation of behavior.

---

[1] The popular behavioral perspective on motivation before 1970 was based on stimulus-response models that emphasized external reinforcers and punishments as primary motivators. This view failed to account for the wide range of intrinsic motivations, cognitive and social processes, and personal goals that drive human behavior. The newer models discussed here provide a more nuanced understanding of motivation as a dynamic interaction between cognitive, affective, biological, and environmental influences.

The Ties That Bind

Self-perceptions are self-made evaluations and include expectations of success based on interest, capability, perceived outcomes, and anything related to a person, their beliefs, or circumstances that might support or inhibit setting and reaching goals. Support includes assessments of the role of others in fostering or forestalling personal objectives and places a strong emphasis on one's socialization ability or desire. By example, if deciding whether or not to attend a graduation party for a four-year-old, we might consider how we look and feel, assess social interest and kibbitzing skills, evaluate who is attending, consider the relationship with the person hosting the party, and contemplate whether we believe it is appropriate to be celebrating a preschool graduation.

Other person factors include the awareness and ability to regulate motivated behavior, including attributes described as "self-regulation, or self-generated thoughts, affects, and behaviors that are systematically oriented toward attainment of one's goals" (Hattie et al., 2020, p. 3). In other words, if the goal of party attendance was to instill family harmony, we might consider such things as our ability to maintain composure when Aunt Sally insisted that all the cousins should hold hands during a group picture, or the ability to tolerate drunken Uncle Joe and his bigoted comments about immigration without losing our minds and making a scene. The presumption of self-regulation as a person variable is well justified based on the wide degree of variability between and within individuals on the use and execution of strategies related to planning, monitoring, and evaluating our thoughts, behaviors, and motives. However self-regulation of behavior has far greater biological and emotional influences and implications to be regarded as a cognitive factor alone and thus is discussed in greater detail below as a separate binding attribute of motivated behavior.

The second set of binding factors are **task aspects**. When contemplating a task, individuals reflect upon the skills, knowledge, or strategies needed to complete the task in tandem with outcome expectations related to task achievement, or as Joe Strummer once asked, "should I stay, or should I go?" Although task evaluation is based on the perceived challenges inherent to the task or goal, in many ways task evaluation is the evaluation of one's wants and needs in comparison to anticipated outcomes. A person might contemplate expectations of success or failure as well as search for a compelling reason to engage in the task, but the assessment would not be based on interest alone and would have the potential to change if the circumstances were different. These evaluations are task dependent because in the event the task changes, the assessments will also change.

Task evaluation closely parallels the situated expectancy-value theory (SEVT) perspective described earlier (p. 11) and that will be continually used to interpret how rewards are rated and assessed. The theory dictates that three independent but related evaluations are prerequisites to task engagement, all centering on relative value of a task. High valuations imply avid task engagement, while lower expectancies predict less effortful engagement or task abandonment (Gladstone et al., 2022). First, the individual assesses if a task is aligned with goals (the next binding criterion). Alignment is determined by anticipated interest and enjoyment in the task or in the language of SEVT "*intrinsic value.*" Tasks may not be perceived as enjoyable but still foster engagement because the skills can be applied elsewhere and are posited to have "*utility value.*" By example, university attendance can be painful but the potential outcome of graduation as a result of spending hundreds of hour studying is sufficient motivation for many based on the utility value of the degree. Closely related to utility is "*attainment value,*" which is the relative importance of the task to the individual and an indication of the degree of task internalization. The more important and meaningful the task is, the more it is embraced by the individual in their overall identity. It is important to keep in mind that any singular assessment changes based on the task and subject to broad influences from cultural, social, and personal beliefs. By example, willingness to sing in a church choir would not be the same when auditioning for a leading role in a major theatrical production. Task expectancies can be expected to be reevaluated and modified based on task complexity, progression, timing, and ongoing evaluations as well. The student who initially decides to study premed but changes majors has reevaluated attainment value based on the challenge becoming too formidable or expecting failure, not success, thus lowering the probability of task engagement.

Goals, the next theoretical binder, are highly instrumental in analyzing motivation because goals are the target of motivated effort. Although motivation is studied in nondirective goal-less environments (Elliot & Harackiewicz, 1996), assessing causes of motivation in goal-deficient situations is akin to taking a trip and not knowing where you are going. In practice, those who set goals are more likely to achieve desired long-term outcomes through sustained motivation. Goals are described as both *instrumental* and *ultimate* (Batson, Ahmad, & Stocks, 2011), with the former designed to serve as a means to an end or a steppingstone toward achieving a higher-level or more fundamental, ultimate goal. Instrumental goals are not valued for their own sake but rather for their ability to facilitate the achievement of more important or overarching motives. For example, a person who has social anxiety may ultimately desire to become a successful entrepreneur to amass power and wealth (ultimate motive). To gain experience and confidence, they might join clubs or attend networking events (the instrumental motive) with little interest in the actual event purpose or sponsoring group. Goals have substantial motivational value because goal setting allows the person to assess incremental progress that gives the individual feedback as to the effectiveness of their motivated effort. When progress is perceived as meeting the expectation, the individual will continue to invest effort, while conversely failed assessments of progress can forestall motivation.

Goal orientation is also an important consideration of the goal-setting dynamic. Typically, "orientation" explains why a particular academic goal is set, with orientation irrespective of the goal choice. This means that individuals can have diverse motives for engaging in a particular behavior. By example, the unitary goal of earning a university degree can be motivated by numerous reasons. Some attend higher education to master a topic, some for status, others to find a life partner, and still others who are forced to attend because of "family tradition." The same behavior (university attendance) is thus instigated for many different reasons. When individuals seek to pursue goals for the purposes of intellectual curiosity and knowledge acquisition, they demonstrate a *mastery* goal orientation. When seeking to satisfy other objectives, such as looking good and comparing favorably to others, a *performance* orientation is exhibited. We can also look at the difference in orientation from the perspective of emphasis on the process of reaching a goal (mastery) or a greater focus on the outcome (performance). Although orientation perspectives typically apply to academic endeavors, we can also see goal orientation in action in other domains such as organizationally or in athletics, where some seek to excel for materialistic gain, while others are primarily concerned with gaining recognition or setting records for their own psychological advantage by performing as best as possible considering their skills and abilities.

The fourth motivation theory binder is the assessment of **benefits and costs** associated with a contemplated action. Any potential decision resulting in the exertion of effort must consider the potential advantages as well as the liabilities of the action. You might imagine sitting in a bar deciding if you should slug back one more drink before you leave. Benefit perceptions could be as mundane as watching the end of a sporting event or maybe meeting the person of your dreams that you have been eyeing across the room. Costs would include reduced driving ability from impairment, potential hangovers, explaining your lateness to a roommate, or work that might be delayed because of tardiness. Each factor would have a differential influence but might all loom large in your decision as you evaluated the pros and cons of having another drink. Costs can be allocated to psychological costs (e.g., the anxiety of explaining to your boss why you have to take off work for a DUI court appearance), or physical costs such as missing out on work or paying fines. Effort costs would entail thinking about the decision and the relative worth of the contemplated behavior and how it might reflect on your overall self-appraisals and miserable self-worth if you ruined your life for one more beer.

While most theoretical models of motivation emphasize the importance of self-regulation and self-control as an influence on motivated behavior (Hattie et al., 2020; Werner & Milyavskaya, 2019), the cognitive emphasis alone is insufficient to explain motivated effort. We should fully acknowledge that individuals when contemplating decisive action are guided by other factors in addition to cognitive processes like logic or rationality (Stanovich, 2011). Whether it is deferral of basic biological needs (like waiting to pee in favor of finishing this section), or lack of emotional regulation (getting cranky because the security line at the airport is longer than you expected), a variety of biological and emotional influences will guide the manifestation or repression of motivated behavior.

The four binding elements—self-perceptions, task evaluations, goals, and costs and benefits of engagement—collectively determine the direction and intensity of motivated effort. In tandem, the analysis of the motivational influencers is transformed into action plans that literally catalyze (or stagnate) our movement. Irrespective of what we chose to do or why we elect to pursue or withdraw from a particular objective, we actively (and sometimes subconsciously too) get feedback from the environment in the form of observations, criticism, or praise and from our own meta-monitoring that gives us information on our motivational condition. Described as *self-regulation*, this aspect of motivation involves the perceptual recognition of task progress or futility. During self-regulation, the individual realizes that optimal attainment of goal objectives may require adjustments to evolve from an existing state to a desired state (Winne & Hadwin, 2008). Action is predicated on the degree of change needed, the expectancy that the change matters, and the value ascribed to reaching the goal.

Ironically, individuals may clearly recognize the need to modify behavior but may not know how to make changes, or more likely, may lack the physiological desire or intensity to initiate the change. Sometimes, despite our best intentions, biology and/or emotion highjack our motivational willpower and self-regulatory ability (Baumeister et al., 1994). Spontaneously scarfing (or scoffing) down two slices of creamy chocolate fudge cake after diligently dieting for weeks or succumbing to potentially life-changing road rage despite the insignificance of the transgression, exemplifies self-regulatory lapses. Ultimately, self-regulation of motivated effort involves the ability and willingness to override or alter one's behavior irrespective of the cause of the discrepancy. Regardless of motivational source, styles, or influences, inclusion of self-regulation is a necessary component to understand motivated effort. Overall, while the binding principles of motivation help categorize behavior, a finer-grained analysis is needed to determine why we sometimes strive for progress and yet at other times elect stagnation.

Leveraging Rewards

The next chapter outlines the physiological derivatives of rewards and why we cannot conclude that reward potential is exclusively the reason why effort is or is not exerted when striving toward a goal. Withstanding reward contingencies, there are several circumstances when EXMO and specifically salient rewards can provide vast benefits for learning and performance. One of the most robust findings, often replicated across tasks and contexts, is the power of EXMO to enhance motivation for the things people do not want to do. Extrinsic rewards or incentives can increase motivation and engagement for tasks that are inherently uninteresting or lack intrinsic appeal (Cameron & Pierce, 1994) because the reward shifts focus from the task to the pearly gates of the outcome. For example, offering students a reward for completing an uninteresting assignment can help sustain their motivation and effort and some students will self-reward (e.g., read a chapter first, then take a social media break) to maintain momentum to complete tedious tasks (Wolters & Rosenthal, 2000). Angrist et al. (2009) found that offering merit-based scholarships to high-achieving students in Canada increased their academic performance and persistence in college. Translation, mo money = mo effort, as the saying goes. Perhaps the greatest exploiters of rewards are parents who, hoping to create good habits, often use incentives to motivate their children to complete chores (e.g., "allowance") or otherwise withhold treats as a threat to induce compliant behavior. The philosophic Pink Floyd bassist and composer Roger Waters immortalized this concept with the classic metaphor, "If you don't eat your meat, you can't have any pudding." You might also know this incentive phenomenon as a bribe or pay for performance. Regardless of what we call it, rewards at least temporarily can motivate individuals to exhibit behaviors desired by the reward provider.

Recent neurological findings (Milyavskaya et al., 2019) corroborate behavioral evidence that rewards alleviate the mundane. To test the power of rewards, researchers either had participants stare at four-digit numbers flashed on a screen for twenty minutes and do nothing compared to those in another group who were required to watch the same numbers but were asked to add three to each digit (thus 623 would become 956) and type the response on a keyboard. All it took was the opportunity to earn two M & Ms to get the bored folks to report they were less fatigued and more interested knowing that reward potential existed compared to the participants who had no reward expectations. Feedback evaluation as measured by electroencephalographic (EEG) scalp monitoring (the physiological reaction to the reward) showed greater reward receptivity during boredom than when expending cognitive effort. Apparently, it doesn't take much to change effort investment toward a task (under highly defined and simulated conditions).

EXMO is also helpful to improve skill development in the initial stages of a task when INMO may be low (Deci et al., 1999). For instance, selectively offering a reward for practicing a musical instrument can help establish a consistent routine until INMO potentially develops (Hallam, 2002). Rewards work by generating increased persistence and effort, particularly when the task requires sustained attention or repetitive practice. Continuous engagement during prospective attentional lapses is one reason why many employers offer incentives to employees for meeting productivity targets, especially for easy tasks that lack intellectual challenge. Extrinsic motivators can also be effective in initiating and sustaining positive behavior changes, such as adhering to doctor recommendations (Ng et al., 2012). For instance, providing financial incentives for weight loss or medication adherence can support individuals in making and maintaining desired lifestyle changes, and the approach is often used to foster healthy decisions (Michaelsen & Esch, 2021). In the "let's be green" department, Gneezy et al. (2011) offered monetary incentives to Israeli households increasing their participation in a program for collecting and recycling household waste. Ferraro and Price (2013) showed that providing financial incentives to homeowners in Georgia led to significant reductions in residential water consumption. I often coax my homebody girlfriend into socializing with the promise of lavish food and drink. Summarily, we are willing to be incentivized to do things that we may not do in absence of the reward.

EXMO is most potent under two specific conditions. First, incentives work better when they are directly tied to performance in comparison to when rewards are tangential to performance. This means that incentives deemed "salient" (Cerasoli et al., 2014, p. 983) to the individual, where there is a perception of an unambiguous connection between accomplishment and incentive, tend to maximize reward effectiveness compared to a fuzzy connection between the prospective outcome and the potential incentive. In other words, stronger work-reward connections enhance the value of the reward. While this behavioral evidence is often replicated, the actual basis of the reward effectiveness has deep roots in physiological processes, as we shall soon see. Ultimately, rewards that exceed our expectations are especially powerful for future motivation and can even lead to obsessive behavior to earn the reward.

Second, EXMO works better when quantity counts, such as found in jobs where the volume of output is an important consideration. Low-appeal jobs often include tasks that are usually repetitive, lower in complexity, and generally require less thinking than positions involving creativity, innovation, or complex problem-solving. Considering the repetitive task nature, boredom is alleviated when the person has a separable outcome, such as might occur if you were rewarded based on how many cans you could correctly put in a shipping container every sixty seconds. The reward potential is useful to speed up performance. Individuals can also gamify the production experience through their own specific brand of personalization as a means to sustain motivation, as I might do when writing and mandating myself to write another paragraph before replying to student emails. Ultimately, figuring out the value and impact of a reward as demotivating or beneficial is based on subjective interpretation, and offering materialistic rewards to jack up production should be approached cautiously, unless individual preferences are known and verified.

The Dark Side

Despite these listed advantages, EXMO must contend with a host of reward contingencies that undermine reward effectiveness. While the reason *why* rewards may not meet expected objectives is discussed later, reward effectiveness is generally counterproductive if the reward is perceived as an attempt to control the individual. When people feel controlled, INMO typically suffers and production wanes with the reward blamed as the culprit for reduction in interest or reduced task effort. Rewards can detract from the perception of autonomy (see the "Satisfaction" section that follows) when people feel coerced or manipulated to chase the reward. However, when the reward purpose and methods are clearly communicated, the negative impact of the reward is diminished, provided the individual buys into the reward as something instrumental to their personal objectives. Lacking personal buy-in, an incentive can easily backfire because the individual does not value what is being offered. Thus, do not expect much success when offering discounted African safaris to PETA proponents, free candy to diabetics, or suspending kids who hate school.

Timing and termination of rewards is also a potential instigator for reduced INMO and should be considered as part of the incentive decision.

Rewards that are expected will impact effectiveness because immediately after earning the reward effort expenditures often crash. Thus, intermittent, or unexpected rewards maximize reward effectiveness, productivity, and dumping money in slot machines because the individual never knows when their effort will matter most and be rewarded. The most significant consequence of a reward to INMO is decreased effort and interest when a reward for a task is withdrawn. Typically, the individual will withhold effort under the reasoning that performing a previously rewarded task without the reward is just foolish. When a reward shifts emphasis from the task to the reward, we can reasonably expect reward withholding to negatively impact effort and performance. The most successful gamblers walk away from the machine after hitting the jackpot. However, we should also recognize that anything that diminishes the controlling aspects of a reward will enhance dedicated effort; thus, reward source, salience, and timing are more of a function of the individual preferences than the nature of the reward. Thus, if a reward can effectively satisfy individual needs, EXMO is the preferential choice because nothing is more important than psychological and physiological need satisfaction, which happens when a desired reward is expected and earned.

It is important to note that EXMO is not a panacea, and researchers generally recommend balancing extrinsic and intrinsic motivators to maximize learning and performance outcomes. Distinguishing the specific influences of INMO and EXMO is unlikely because of the reciprocity of effects and disentangling the influence of one on the other. In addition, shifting motives happen regularly. Finally, the effectiveness of extrinsic motivators may depend on factors such as the type of task, the individual's developmental stage, and the way rewards are structured and delivered. Despite all the contingencies described, reward subtly influences behavior because of brain functionality, regardless of being classified as EXMO or INMO!

Highly related, yet often conflated, with motivational disposition and the EXMO/INMO conundrum, is the concept of *"locus of control."* Whereas internalization modifies self-perceptions by incorporating external influences into one's authentic self, locus of control refers to the belief that life is guided either by internal or external forces (Weiner, 2021). Those with an internal locus feel that events in their life are primarily controlled by their own efforts and personal abilities, an expert in your own domain so to speak. Those with an external locus feel that external forces, luck, and powerful others are the primary determinants of their fate, exemplified by the mantra "it's not what you know, but who you know." By example, imagine that you are an ardent supporter of animal rights and exhibit behaviors that back up the beliefs (like volunteering at a pet shelter). The behavior demonstrates that you believe caring for animals is important. Those with an internal locus would likely feel that their efforts could make a difference and perhaps save some of the 920,000 pets euthanized every year (ASPCA, 2024). Likewise, you might dedicate effort to the same animal rights cause but lack the conviction that your efforts would really change anything, displaying an external locus. In other words, the origin of actions and subsequent beliefs can be traced back to internal sources or external ones. In practice, we either act on our internalized beliefs or feel compelled and mandated to act based on controlling external factors.

Internalization and the intrinsic/extrinsic distinction involve the selective internalization of external phenomenon, making them part of one's motivations. By contrast, locus of control refers to one's beliefs about whether the primary causes of life events are internal (within one's control) or external (due to outside forces). Internalization is actively ingraining external values as your own; locus of control is your perspective on whether your life is mainly controlled by internal or external determinants. Higher internalization often contributes to a more internal locus of control. Ultimately, the locus can be explained by the perception of feeling obligated or required to do something because "that's the way it is" or operating under the presumption that what we do is up to us based on the perception of having choice. When embracing an external locus, we feel less self-determined and may resort to externalizing the reasons for our choices by blaming others or the world for our success or failures. Internal locus suggests we are in control and more accountable for what happens in our lives because we believe we have the ability to craft our destiny.

In a practical sense, understanding locus is the first step toward the realization that dominant orientations and whether or not we believe we can effectively control behaviors and subsequent outcomes is one consequence of human need satisfaction. The locus focus shows great variability exists in our need for control and thus we must explore needs as the next step toward fully understanding the roots of motivation. Needs are the antecedents of motivated behavior, and understanding the type of needs we prioritize is a major threshold to cross to get to the root of motivated behavior. In combination, behavior, passion, internalization, EXMO/INMO, and locus do not explain why behavior manifests or the actual sources of the beliefs that mold behaviors. Underlying the manifestation of each type and construct are various needs that humans have that guide their day-to-day choices and corresponding effort investments.

Before we leave passion and the INMO/EXMO superiority debate in the motivational dust, let's remember that the polarity among motivation types is based on the perceived degree of control the individual believes they have over whichever task or activities they choose to engage. When feeling liberated to choose when, where, and how to navigate the task challenges, individuals are perceived as being autonomous, and the conceptual influences on motivation discussed thus far matter less because we are able to express our free will. When feeling controlled, obligated, and a victim of the task requirements, individuals feel manipulated or coerced and motivation suffers regardless of passion, motivation type, or any social influence. Each situation has broad consequences for motivated behavior, and for the ensuing discussion the concept of autonomy and a wide variety of other needs are crucial to understanding motivation behavior.

Getting to the Source

There is little that inspires greater literary contempt than wordsmiths engaging in trivial dialogue over word choice. It reminds me of the old internet debate about the "dress" being black or gold (Gegenfurtner et al., 2015), a clickbait controversy that was resolved by the realization that color perception is not a property of an object but instead determined by the observer. Individual perceptions are subjective and vary based on perspective, personal beliefs, and cultures. Usually, these lexical linguistics foster little more than confusion and semantic debate, but sometimes consensus of word meaning is critical, such as now. The common terminology used to describe "phenomenal sources" (Ryan & Deci, 2017, p. 14) that initiate behavior are often described as *intrinsic* and *extrinsic* motivation. But do these motivational descriptors actually indicate "sources," which implies a point of behavioral origination? I think not, because where something originates and the application of what is generated from the source are mutually exclusive. Describing intrinsic and extrinsic motivation as a "source" is an ontological misrepresentation. The intrinsic and extrinsic labels ascribed to transient motivational states are no more of a "source" than black or gold could be considered sources when it comes to interpreting dress color.

In reality, the terminology (and theories described thus far) do not identify the source of motives but instead categorize the nature of motivation based on "*valence*" and perceptual preference of the individual. This distinction is of the utmost importance because despite the words and morphology, no theory of motivation or the binding commonalities listed earlier actually address motivational sources. While differentiation of motivation types has contributed to the understanding of motivation, the INMO/EXMO labels have morphed into describing people and their dominant intentions. Considering that motives consistently change within and between tasks, the labeling process is no more reliable than describing oneself as permanently happy and content, which, to the dismay of many, changes instantly and frequently.

What has evolved in contemporary motivation literature is the conflation of source and a preferred motivational disposition. Comparatively, describing the dimensions of motivated effort is easy because we can observe the strategies actors use to reach their goals and measure the frequency and utility of exhibited behavior. Finding the source of what drives the behavior is far more elusive and contested. As Deci and Ryan explained, different motivation types are related to different "experiences that accompany them" (2017, p. 14) and to varied behavioral consequences and the "benefits/costs that they yield" (2017, p. 14). Thus, to avoid any source/type conflation, we focus on situational motivation exhibited at a particular time, for a particular task, in a particular context while concurrently describing the distinctions and influences that differentiate the spectrum of motivated effort.

Navigating the INMO/EXMO Rainbow

Scholars have debated and empirically studied the precise description and meaning of intrinsic and extrinsic motivation for at least 120 years (Ryan & Deci, 2017). These inquiries usually focus on determining reasons behind action and under what circumstances individuals are active or passive constituents of their environmental domain. However, we can trace the ambiguity of determining what drives human behavior and what influences a "preferential state" for motivated action back to the philosopher Socrates and his hemlock poisoning disciples, circa 399 BCE (Reshotko, 1992). One of Socrates's primary contentions was that actions were based on the pursuit of self-interest under the pretense of doing what the person thinks is best for them at the time. Socrates recognized that what is "best" today may be unbearable tomorrow and what is preferential for you may seem downright repulsive to me. Socrates' dialogue also recognized that doing what we think is best can conflict with doing what we want. Thus, we have the root of the classic motivational conundrum, the perpetual and contentious human tug of war between want and need, work and play, the pursuit of pleasure, and the avoidance of existential (and/or physical) pain.

Ironically, not much related to conceptualizing motivation has changed in the past 2,400 years. We still struggle deciding between preferential engagement and obligatory compliance, or what Huberman (2022) described as electing to do the "hard things," common lingo representing task persistence in the face of motivational uncertainty. In simplest terms, and exclusive of any specific theoretical interpretation or perspective, INMO means that you autonomously engage in a task based on sheer interest and intellectual curiosity. According to most interpretations of INMO, when you have no incentive to complete a task beyond the pleasure and satisfaction of reaching the goal, you are exhibiting INMO. Intrinsic purism suggests that you get no feedback from others, no anticipated notoriety from your achievement, no consequences for lack of achievement, and do not experience even the tiniest sliver of emotion or ego inflation as a result of your accomplishment (Robinson et al., 2022). Good luck with that.

Contemporary views of EXMO are portrayed radically different. Hypothetically, when one is extrinsically motivated, the emphasis on attainment shifts from the activity to the consequences of reaching the behavioral goal. People often engage in extrinsically motivated behavior to obtain external rewards such as financial gains, social approval, and material possessions. Alternatively, they may do so to avoid negative outcomes, like evading the potential scoff and social stigma of being perceived as lazy or incompetent that might result when failing an exam due to lack of studying. Ultimately, "Extrinsically motivated behaviors are governed by the prospect of instrumental gain and loss (e.g., incentives), whereas intrinsically motivated behaviors are engaged for their very own sake (e.g., task enjoyment), not being instrumental toward some other outcome" (Cerasoli, 2014, p. 980). Nevertheless, in real life the purported motivational dichotomy is not quite as simple as it is described.

So, what is the purpose of distinguishing between INMO and EXMO when hoping to optimize learning and performance? Does it really matter why we do something, or should we focus on learning more about why some individuals are intrinsically motivated while others are not? The answer depends on who you ask. Unfortunately, INMO as described in most motivational research is an unobservable, theoretical representation of a subjective disposition, which in practical terms is about as solid as a brick of Jello. Withstanding the measurement challenges and inconsistencies described in Chapter 2, INMO is a hypothetical, socially derived construct, similar to an attitude and a feeling that can change from moment to moment. Champion INMO and you earn the label of the passion warrior, one whose behaviors are a manifestation of their values. A person who will persist in the face of difficulty and champion idealistic causes without fear of consequence (Kruglanski & Fishman, 2009). If you claim that power and money are your primary motives, you may be labeled as self-absorbed or narcissistic. Worse yet, you could be demonized and face public backlash when compared to notoriously greedy individuals like the avaricious banker J.P. Morgan or the delusional rapper Yeezus.

Also, consider that in the vast majority of performance situations, including school, work, athletics, and many competitive domains, the type of motivation responsible for your effort is secondary. When evaluating optimal learning and performance, success is measured not by what you thought or how you felt before engagement but instead by what you accomplished, what you learned, or how you behaved. In addition, the vast majority of jobs arguably have few opportunities to satisfy the intrinsic desires of curiosity, interest, or pleasure because responsibilities are inherently mundane. Turn screws for eight hours a day or enter 10,000 pieces of data daily in a spreadsheet and you will understand why many people report having no INMO in the vast majority of their lives. For some scholars (Locke & Schattke, 2019; Reiss, 2005, 2012; Silvia, 2019), INMO is an unsustainable myth, a value judgment, and socially constructed based on simulated research situations that are chiefly a means to justify the presumptions of the hypothesizer. Minimally, dichotomizing INMO/EXMO is an oversimplification that does not accurately reflect individual perceptions, especially as espoused by students who are explicitly motivated to study motivation (Hoffman, 2025).

The more viable explanation is that motivational tendencies are perceptual hues, and like the spectrum of the rainbow where light blends into a kaleidoscope of colors, individuals are simultaneously motivated by a sectoral synthesis of dynamic influences. These influences contribute to transient labeling of individuals based on a situational type of motivation, an interim orientation that often erroneously portrays the person as possessing some actionable "*dispositions*" while repressing others. The hypocrisy of labeling someone as intrinsically or extrinsically motivated is exposed when recognizing the transitory nature of motivation and observing changes in engagement when things do not go according to plan. Between the planning and execution stages of a task, a cavalcade of forces can either support or undermine subsequent effort expenditures.

Individuals usually start with a task desirability evaluation in tandem with the degree of perceived challenge or stress they are willing to accept to achieve a goal. If the task assessment passes muster and the person believes they have sufficient skill to master the task, they will approach the objective with vigor and enthusiasm. When the task experience is perceived to be consistent with expectations and skill, the individual continues to strive toward reaching the desired outcome and will persevere in the face of obstacles, provided reaching the desired outcome does not decrease in appeal or potential value. However, if encountering obstacles is deemed too formidable or if task commitment wanes, prior enthusiasm may vanish, resulting in the need to consider other incentives to push forward in an attempt to avoid goal revaluation or eventual task abandonment.

By example, students who register for a course under the pretense of gaining knowledge or professing interest in a topic often shift intentions when struggling to understand content or when earning a grade inconsistent with expectations. Baseline intentions can quickly shift from task mastery to failure avoidance. Similarly, those seeking refuge from a flawed relationship may robustly commit to finding a new partner but quickly abandoning the quest when encountering a litany of mismatches or serial rejections. While every task engagement decision is different, the comparison between expectations and reality broadly impacts ongoing task effort. Perceived differences between expectations and outcomes have significant explanatory power as we explore the upcoming neurological evidence supporting the role of rewards in motivated performance. In the absence of desire, we often shift orientation, needing some other reason or incentive to keep us going. In the absence of reward, we stagnate or even worse become apathetic and unmotivated typically resulting in inferior performance or compromised learning (Salamone & Correa, 2012).

What still remains unexplained is why some objectives are perceived as intrinsically satisfying while others require an incentive and why there is variation in motivational perception among individuals performing the same task. Incentive in this case means a reason or an event that increases the willingness to initiate or continue action toward reaching a goal (Reeve, 2018). The single most important factor predicting ongoing task effort and the alleged reason underlying the type of motivation exhibited is internalization (Ryan & Deci, 2020). When internalizing, individuals incorporate behaviors, rules, or values and infuse those influences as part of one's typical thinking and behavior patterns, exemplifying how they perceive themselves and want to be seen by others. Internalization involves transforming these external demands or values into personally endorsed motivations, kind of like getting your favorite team logo tattooed on your forehead. Internalization matters because it determines whether we do things based solely on external pressures (e.g., to make money or avoid jail time), or whether we are committed to those values and the behavioral choices that follow. When we internalize something, we've gone beyond just conforming to outside demands—we've embraced it as being consistent with who we are and what we believe in. However, like EXMO and INMO, the extent to which we internalize is variable and not an all or nothing proposition but one that evolves in gradients and is not polarized like a light switch.

Perhaps the best explanation of the gradient process of intentional behavior is self-determination theory (SDT; Ryan & Deci, 2000, 2017, 2020) and more specifically organismic integration theory (OIT). Both theories explain the relationship among behavior sheerly categorized as autonomous (meaning fully intrinsic) and engagement predicated on the combination of internalization and external incentives (extrinsic). Integrated regulation represents the fullest form of internalization, where intentions are fully aligned with one's values, needs, and identity. Identified regulation occurs when individuals acknowledge the value or importance of a behavior, but the motivation is at least partially based on a sense of autonomy. Introjected regulation involves partially internalizing external regulations, but the reasons for action are external and involve feelings of guilt, anxiety, or contingent self-worth. External regulation is the least autonomous form of extrinsic motivation, where behavior is solely driven by controlling external rewards or punishments. Finally, a motivation represents the absence of motivation, where individuals lack the intention to act and perceive their behavior as caused by forces beyond their control. Graphically, the spectrum of internalization and the degree of INMO/EXMO looks as shown in Figure 3.1.

AUTONOMOUS			CONTROLLED		
INMO	Integrated	Identified	Introjected	External	EXMO

FIGURE 3.1 The spectrum of internalization.

You might surmise there is a strong correspondence between the degree of internalization of values and the strength of the belief that individuals can control the outcomes to which they aspire. Given the opportunity, the majority of individuals across cultures (Taylor et al., 2014; Walker et al., 2020) prefer to exercise free will over their choice of goals, activities, and behaviors. While the freedom focus is often thwarted by the realities of familial and organizational life, we prefer options that promote individual choice. Behavior driven by an innate curiosity or inherent interest is perceived as discretionary and opportunistic and often described as feeling autonomous. *"Autonomous motivation"* occurs when engaging in an activity because of an inherent interest or personal endorsement of the activity's importance. Not surprisingly, autonomous motivation is associated with greater psychological well-being (Hortop et al., 2013; Tang et al., 2021), persistence (Pelletier et al., 2001), and higher-quality performance across a broad range of learning and performance domains (Cerasoli et al., 2014; Gillet et al., 2015).

Unfortunately, the ability to be behaviorally or physiologically autonomous is more of a pipe dream than a day-to-day reality. The more likely scenario is that we are subjected to statutory, moral, and economic limitations that constrain actions leading to behavior that complies with cultural norms and societal expectations. While some might debate the merits of why you shouldn't be able to go to Walmart in your underwear or why you should have to clean up your pet's poop, behavioral choices are often nonnegotiable if you have empathy for others or any concern about avoiding incarceration. Thus, we may feel constricted resulting in *"controlled motivation"* that describes engaging in activities due to external pressures or internal demands, rather than by personal choice or inherent interest. Pragmatically, controlled motivation means either engaging in activities solely for tangible benefits and avoiding punishments imposed by external authorities, or pursuing a goal to deflect feelings of guilt and anxiety, or enhancing one's ego or self-worth, also known as succumbing to the "have-to's." Thus, controlled motivation is the antithesis of autonomy and is associated with poorer psychological well-being, decreased task persistence, and lower-quality performance.

The more autonomous we feel, the greater the perception of self-determination and the perceived freedom to pursue personal interests and enact meaningful values. Alternatively, controlled motivation is perceived as a product of external pressures or internal demands, promoting malcontent and frustration. The disparity creates another paradox because it is clearly possible, and in some cultures highly probable, to be extrinsically focused while feeling autonomous. Frequently, individuals deliberately elect to pursue tasks largely devoid of INMO and designed specifically to satisfy needs typically described as extrinsic in the chase of fame, fortune, and recognition. According to OIT, when extrinsic motivations are autonomous, they are accompanied by a sense of value, and the pursuit of the outcomes is viewed as worthwhile to substantiate one's identity because the motivated effort is highly *"volitional"*. In the words of SDT theory, "adulthood brings with it more duties, responsibilities, and social obligations that, although not always fun and enjoyable as activities, are nonetheless increasingly salient and ideally capable of being internalized and integrated" (Ryan & Deci, 2017, p. 197). In addition, individuals can simultaneously be intrinsically motivated and autonomous and externally regulated and controlled. By example, a professional athlete may exemplify dual orientations. On the one hand, superstars voluntarily practice beyond the team's requirements, driven by an intrinsic desire for personal excellence. On the other hand, the same athlete recognizes that winning a championship is crucial for achieving historical notoriety and securing a lucrative new contract, which are extrinsic motivators.

Suppose that not all tasks or goals are inherently suited for autonomous motivation. There are many reasons to believe that different types of motivation (i.e., INMO/EXMO) are not entirely discretionary or under our control. Rather, cultivating one type of motivation may come at the expense of the other. Does this mean if you attain an incentive for an intrinsically motivating task, you will be relegated to the ranks of a lowly EXMO because your desire and drive is compromised? No! However, some researchers suggest that when motivational tendencies coexist, one will dominate (Kuvaas et al., 2017). The static view of motivational disposition implies that task challenges are consistent throughout the task and factors affecting motivation such as the perception of autonomy and enthusiasm do not change over time—a highly unlikely scenario as even the sunniest motivational days are vulnerable to occasional clouds. Similarly, the expectation that one motivation type offsets the other is flawed. While some legacy theorists strongly advocate that external incentives undermine INMO and diminish interest (Lepper & Greene, 2015), this antiquated view has numerous contingencies and strong refutational evidence from neuroscience revealing that the two types of motivation do *not* work against each other but instead operate in a reciprocal fashion contingent on a variety of psychological and physiological factors discussed later. However, there are many well-documented and context-dependent distinctions between the goals, methods, and prospective learning and performance outcomes used and achieved by those who exhibit one dominant orientation. While there are many overgeneralizations of motivation type that often lead to erroneous conclusions on the influence of type on performance, each hue of the motivational spectrum (see p. 73) affords documented benefits and prospective liabilities.

Vote for INMO

Fully internalizing tasks and feeling complete autonomy during the process of effort investment is rare. Goal-directed choices in most careers and formal education are seldom made under such idealistic conditions. However, at least hypothetically, unadulterated INMO is the key to many learning and performance advantages. When intrinsically motivated, we enact behaviors based on interest and demonstrate enthusiastic task engagement because there are hardly any rules or consequences limiting behavior. The lack of adverse consequence means that we have no mandates and expect limited, if any, costs (see p. 60) when dedicating effort toward a task. The robust enthusiasm typically associated with intrinsically driven effort is usually accompanied by strong positive emotions such as enjoyment (Ryan & Deci, 2000), emotional and work engagement (Howard et al., 2021; Van den Broeck et al., 2021), along with general feelings of well-being and satisfaction (Ryan & Deci, 2000).

From a learning perspective, INMO is associated with engaging in deeper cognitive processing that contributes to better conceptual understanding and knowledge acquisition (Vansteenkiste et al., 2004, 2006). People with intrinsic motivation are more likely to seek out greater challenges, explore new ideas, and make connections between concepts, which facilitates meaningful learning. Intrinsically motivated students tend to exhibit greater persistence and sustained effort in their learning activities (Ryan & Deci, 2000), leading to increased creativity, cognitive flexibility, and the ability to consider diverse perspectives that enhances problem-solving, critical thinking, and adapting to new learning situations. INMO learning advantages manifest in a variety of examples, such as the aspiring guitar aficionado who practices endlessly, the budding college athlete who carries a basketball wherever they go, and the highest-achieving workers who often claim to have the greatest level of INMO (Cerasoli et al., 2014).

INMO benefits go beyond domains where success reaps material advantages such as work and school. Greater self-reported levels of INMO are linked to numerous life-enhancing characteristics. Individuals with INMO tend to put forth greater effort and persistence in their pursuits compared to those who report lower INMO (Vansteenkiste et al., 2004). Individuals with higher INMO tend to set more challenging goals for themselves compared to those who are primarily extrinsically motivated (Senko & Tropiano, 2016), including investing more time and goal-directed effort in task completion than their extrinsically motivated peers (Dysvik & Kuvaas, 2013). Another steroidal effect of high INMO relates to confidence levels. Elevated INMO is associated with more self-efficacy and confidence compared to those who are primarily extrinsically motivated (Stupnisky et al., 2007). Self-efficacy, which refers to an individual's belief in their ability to perform a specific task or achieve a desired outcome, is critical to performance success but also highly instrumental to overcome resilience and to navigate the inevitable motivation potholes we all encounter when trying to reach goals. INMO and the effect of elevated efficacy are particularly profound for college students who must constantly maintain motivational momentum across a litany of unfamiliar subjects and situations. INMO even takes credit for sustaining New Year's resolutions longer (Greenstein & Koestner, 1996), better adherence to diets (Teixeira et al., 2015), and lowering drinking after completing a substance abuse treatment program (Burton et al., 2010). Thus, assuming these aforementioned outcomes are desirable, elevated INMO is like the frosting on one's motivation cake. Despite the numerous advantages, extreme caution in interpreting results is warranted as discussed in great detail in Chapter 2. The majority of the findings reported cannot reliably imply that INMO *causes* the observed results, and, instead, there is only a positive correlation between reported INMO, and the quality of the outcomes described.

In the "every cherry has pits" department, INMO is not without consequence. As we might imagine, high INMOs are pretty intense characters, who may not be incredibly good at logically evaluating task progress or realizing when it is time to switch gears or call it quits. High INMO individuals may struggle to disengage from goals or activities that have become unattainable or maladaptive, as their motivation is tied to the inherent enjoyment or interest in the activity itself (Ntoumanis et al., 2014) despite the potential for lagging performance. Intense INMO, (i.e., passion) can lead to overconfidence, potentially resulting in excessive risk-taking or disregard for potential negative outcomes (Deci & Ryan, 2000). Kirchler et al. (2018) found that individuals with higher levels of INMO for investing were more likely to make risky financial decisions, exhibiting overconfidence with a tendency to trade stocks more frequently, a practice that often leads to losing money. Pelletier et al. (2001) described that athletes who were highly intrinsically motivated by the enjoyment and excitement of their sport were more likely to engage in risk-taking behaviors during competition, potentially compromising their safety or performance. And of course, there are students who think they know more than they actually do. They show it by exhibiting high levels of INMO, leading to a tendency to underestimate the difficulty of academic tasks or overestimate their preparedness (Harter, 1992), resulting in subpar performance. Finally, you may recall too much passion can lead to early burnout and actually reduce both interest in a task as well as the ability to perform optimally (Vallerand et al., 2003).

Psychologists Jihae Shin and Adam Grant (2019) speculated about the day-to-day lives of people at work and how INMO might promote changes in task performance. The researchers were operating under the presumption that every job has both interesting and tedious aspects and that no job has unbridled INMO joy. By example, the high-powered sales associate has to fill out TPS reports, the teacher needs to grade fifty papers with similar answers to the same boring questions, and even the most polished artist must prep their paints and tools before the opportunity to demonstrate creative brilliance. Shin and Grant wanted to know how different levels of INMO impacted task performance and how those levels might impact subsequent performance on tasks that were less interesting or even boring. The study found that high INMO in one task can lead to lower average and minimum performance on other tasks. Moderate INMO yielded better performance on less-interesting tasks than high INMO, suggesting that high levels of INMO reduce performance in less-interesting tasks by increasing boredom. The study highlighted the potential downsides of high INMO, but, more importantly, brings us to the ongoing realization that INMO is not only elusive (Fay & Freese, 2001) but many times can also be downright undesirable.

Vote for EXMO

Unlike its positively perceived INMO peer, EXMO is often vilified in the popular press. Enacting motives for personal success, monetary gain, or individual recognition has been maligned and suggested as contributory to systematic racism (Kendi, 2023), lower moral standards, and lack of virtuous behavior (Kwon et al., 2023). Those who champion EXMO are presumed to be far less social and riddled with guilt (Gerhart & Fang, 2015.) The negative perception has spawned an entire field of research dedicated to the "moralization of intrinsic motivation" (Kwon, 2022). Paradoxically, EXMOs are stigmatized by their highfalutin INMO rivals who alienate suspected EXMOs through social distancing and reluctance to offer help to those who needed it (Skitka et al., 2005; Wright et al., 2008), suggesting that diversity initiatives might also consider motivation type as part of the inclusion equation!

Ironically, the most expansive research study of its kind reveals that the majority of college students attend university almost exclusively for materialistic benefits. Twenge and Donnelly (2016) analyzed survey data from over 6,000,000 college students concerning their reasons for university attendance. The survey measured "intrinsic values" such as self-acceptance, affiliation, and community as well as extrinsic values contingent on external feedback such as money, fame, and image. The survey responses revealed reasons across generations for going to college. Topping the list were making more money, gaining a general education and appreciation of ideas, and having better job opportunities, all substantial outcomes of extrinsic valuation. None of the reasons for going to college correlated positively with total intrinsic values! According to another survey across twelve countries and over 10,000 individuals (O.C. Tanner Institute, 2023), 89 percent of respondents indicated that a sense of drive and determination is enhanced by the extrinsic motivator of strong recognition. Thus, the paradox of passion escalates as it seems individual philosophy (what we say) and behavioral agency (what we do) are indeed inconsistent. Perhaps EXMO has more explanatory power for behavior than we might think.

While INMO is often touted as preferential motivation, interpretation of EXMO research reveals that in certain learning and performance situations those driven by EXMO actually outperform their INMO peers. Before outlining those circumstances, EXMO is qualified by a few general presumptions. First, EXMO is often described as both a source of motivation and the pursual of outcomes for specific reasons. EXMO is often conflated with the influences that drive motivated behavior such as money, praise, recognition, or any other incentive that is seemingly unrelated to the actual selection of or progress toward completing a task. EXMO is also described as originating from external sources as what might happen if you chose not to go outside because it was raining, or you concluded that you cannot get a job because the global economy stinks. Ascribing EXMO to a source alone obscures understanding of EXMO because source and motive are distinct. In addition, EXMO is often confused with locus of control, a concept that is related but empirically distinct. Ultimately, EXMO is qualified by the point that engagement in a task due to extrinsic motivation occurs when the motivation "arises from some consequence that is separate from the activity itself" (Reeve, 2018, p. 134). Regrettably, every snippet of invested effort has influences beyond the actual activity itself, and that is one reason rewards covertly control behavior, but we will get back to that later.

According to many (Cerasoli et al., 2014; Kuvaas et al., 2017; Reeve, 2018; Ryan & Deci, 2017), to be categorized as EXMO striving toward a "separable outcome" is required and typically described as being caused by "*incentives and reinforcers*," which are known before engaging in the behavior. Incentives are thought to be "instrumental" (Ryan & Deci, 2017, p. 14) toward increasing the likelihood of effort dedicated toward a positive outcome or decreasing the probability of a negative one. In other words, incentives should propel the individual to engage in behavior more robustly or frequently and conversely if trying to avoid a particular outcome the incentive should inhibit behavioral engagement in the particular task or decrease the frequency of effortful behavior. *Rewards* differ from incentives with respect to interpretation and consequence. Unlike incentives, rewards have the potential to change behavior because the reward can satisfy basic physiological or psychological needs. Rewards are subjectively perceived and will vary in salience both between individuals and within individuals. However, a reward per se does not always function as an incentive—it may or may not actually increase the future likelihood of the behavior it follows. If you have ever refused dessert after a big meal or felt little satisfaction after being praised for a menial task, you understand the fickle nature of rewards. That same dessert or reward could be highly motivating at a different time or in another situation. Thus, a reward may or may not increase the frequency of future behavior, and, unlike an incentive, rewards in a practical sense are earned when the person demonstrates a particular behavior or reaches a particular goal. The key distinction is that unlike externally generated incentives something perceived as rewarding is based on both the anticipation of earning the reward and the potential of the reward to satisfy a need.

Need Satisfaction

Thus far, we have transcended down the slippery slope of the motivational iceberg starting with the examination of thoughts, feelings, and dispositions that prompt behaviors. Below the consciousness of many individuals are beliefs that manifest in dominate motivation tendencies, which in a recursive fashion influence the goals we set and the actions we take. Absent from this analysis are the antecedents of motivated behavior or why we acquire certain beliefs and embrace particular motivational perspectives in the first place. We know food is sought to placate the need for hunger, romantic companionship is pursued to satisfy the need for intimacy (and generativity), and politics appeases our need to debate relatives at holidays, but we have many other psychological needs that determine what we do and how we do it.

The source of most human behavior is a quest to satisfy a need, irrespective of the type of need or the reason for the need. A *need* is defined as any discrepant state that an individual chooses to adjust, leading to the elimination of the perceived discrepancy. Need satisfaction encompasses a wide array of requirements for survival, in addition to a host of thoughts, feelings, emotions, and of course motivations that enhance subjective well-being. Getting to the source of motivated behavior requires an overview of some of these most prominent and common needs that motivated humans attempt to satisfy in their quest to enhance learning and performance.

Most of us are familiar with Maslow's Hierarchy of Needs (1943), a motivation theory that hypothesized needs fall into the five distinct and convenient categories of physiological, safety, love, esteem, and self-actualization needs. Lower-level needs like those addressing biological deficits (e.g., hunger) and safety must be satisfied in order to climb the motivational pyramid. Maslow was onto something because he realized that need satisfaction has a pecking order and we are not much concerned about feeling loved when starving to death. He erred by suggesting that the hierarchy was a defined and immutable progression, which we now know is bunk based on lack of evidentiary support for the hierarchy. Personal experience easily falsifies Maslow's theory if you have ever deferred the physical need to urinate when trying to get something done or during a meal. Thus, we will shelve Maslow and focus on those needs that are better supported by replicable evidence avoiding all the interpretive liabilities outlined in Chapter 2. Relegating Maslow to the theory heap does not mean the needs identified are irrelevant but instead suggests that the paradigm lacks explanatory power. For categorization purposes, we will defer discussion of *physiological* needs to the following chapter that primarily focuses on the biopsychology of rewards and the associated brain, hormonal, and neurological mechanisms that dictate reward expectation and impact.

For now, let's get psychological. Depending on who you ask, psychological needs can number from three to dozens. The most prominent and frequently disseminated perspective of needs driving motivated behavior is SDT, which focuses on the importance of autonomy, competence, and relatedness. Collective satisfaction of these organismic needs allows the individual to feel validated and content because they are able to effectively influence their environment, including those with whom they interact. Other theoretical perspectives suggest that needs fall into neat categories like social, psychological, and physiological needs (Reeve, 2018) and include satisfaction of needs such as power and intimacy. According to Brewer (1991), humans have two primary social needs or drives: the need for assimilation and the need for differentiation. The need for assimilation is the desire to feel a sense of inclusion and belonging within larger social groups or collectives. On the other hand, the need for differentiation involves distinguishing oneself from others in a social context and establishing a unique identity separate from the group. While assimilation represents the need for social connection and acceptance, differentiation represents the need for individuality and uniqueness. Every individual has a unique balance of psychological needs. Maintaining equilibrium is crucial, just like keeping a teeter-totter balanced. If one need is overwhelming or summarily neglected, an imbalance ensues, and the disequilibrium may lead to an uncomfortable psychological or physical crash.

Clearerthinking.org (Greenberg, 2023) takes need satisfaction to the next level by identifying over fifty needs that must be satisfied for optimal human functioning. Needs are categorized into survival, mental health, relationships, satisfaction, and intrinsic value needs. There is considerable overlap among these various subjective interpretations; however, the list of intrinsic values includes many of the beliefs that influence INMO such as degrees of virtue, loyalty, justice, fairness, diversity, respect, caring, protection, nature, beauty, purity, spirituality, truth, learning, achievement, and freedom. While we can dispute the differential weighting of one need over another or the variable influence of any particular need driving behavior at a particular time, we can reliably conclude that need satisfaction or frustration at any time influences motivated behavior.

Psychological needs change frequently and vary according to the specific environment in which one chooses to engage. Considering that between the ages of twenty and sixty-five the average full-time worker will work about 90,000 hours, the workplace need satisfaction matters. Consultants at McKinsey (Brassey et al., 2024) identified six primary drivers of workplace health that included social interaction, embracing growth mindsets and beliefs, productive activity, stress elimination, economic security, and sleep. Allegedly, these critical needs must be satisfied for employee longevity and workplace satisfaction. The McKinsey consultants claimed that satisfying workplace needs has substantial psychological implications but also a financial impact. According to McKinsey's hyperbolic claim, need satisfaction was quantifiable with the "total global opportunity for optimizing employee health and well-being at $3.7 trillion to $11.7 trillion, which is equivalent to raising global GDP by 4 to 12 percent" (Brassey et al., 2024, para. 1)

While all the needs described have situational relevance, it is important to recognize that at any one time a need can have far greater priority and impact than another. It is also crucial to realize that in the absence of need satisfaction that need frustration develops resulting in a person devoting substantial cognitive horsepower and emotion grappling with the realization that needs are not met. Need frustration is powerful and can become the overriding force behind motivated behavior. In turn, the frustration or perception of unfulfilled needs can promote the development of aggressive, obsessive, or irrational behavior in an attempt to eliminate the need gap (Vansteenkiste & Ryan, 2013).

Common consequences of frustration center around decreased psychological well-being. Need frustration has been linked to increased anxiety, depression, and negative "affect," and the frustration can lead to reduced life satisfaction, vitality, and self-esteem (Deci & Ryan, 2000). Frustration breeds the use of maladaptive coping strategies and problem behaviors because frustration is associated with compensatory behaviors, such as substance abuse, disordered eating, and aggression (Vansteenkiste & Ryan, 2013). Interpersonal and social problems develop leading to loneliness, social distancing, and interpersonal conflicts. (Deci & Ryan, 2014). Deficits also contribute to reduced empathy, compassion, and helping behavior (Deci & Ryan, 2000; Weinstein & Ryan, 2010). Thus, examination of motivated behavior requires consideration of need satisfaction but also the physical and psychological consequences of need frustration on optimal behavior.

Finally, we should recognize that needs are variable between individuals and will rapidly contract or expand depending on environmental circumstances. The differential emphasis on need satisfaction is broadly influenced by social circumstances, which may either foster need repression or compel the person to devote even more time and effort toward satisfying needs. We can often see the quest for satisfaction accelerate during group behavior, especially in circumstances where emotions trigger spontaneous behavior such as seen during political debates, sports competitions, and posturing while navigating white elephant holiday gatherings. Differences in group versus personal need satisfaction show that while needs might be fundamental to individual functioning, their significance and emphasis could vary among different cultures, societies, and contexts. Let's get specific and focus on those needs directly related to learning and performance and specifically ones that may eventually be mediated by the functionality and availability of rewards.

Autonomy

Basic Psychological Needs Theory (BPNT) is one of the six mini-theories under the umbrella of SDT that specifically addresses how satisfaction or frustration of the fundamental needs of autonomy, competence, and relatedness predict perceptions of well-being. When these basic needs are met, individuals experience optimal functioning, and internalization, whereas the thwarting or frustration of these fundamental needs can undermine motivation and lead to goal revision, effort suspension, or task abandonment. The word "autonomy" originates from the Greek words "autos" meaning "self" and "nomos" meaning "law" or "rule." When we experience autonomy, we engage in self-governance by freely pursuing our own wants, desires, and intentions without external coercion or pressure. We exercise our free will and make choices based on our authentic interests and values, rather than acting due to external mandates or controls.

Autonomy is perceived as rewarding because the person has freedom to act, and, at least hypothetically, people prefer choices because the freedom to choose can potentially increase the likelihood of obtaining better outcomes (Murayama et al., 2016). Having autonomy does not necessarily mean a person *will* act but instead means that they have the unrestricted opportunity to act if they choose to do so. When the need for autonomy is satisfied, a sense of accomplishment accompanied by positive emotion results because the person feels self-endorsed and authentic (Vansteenkiste et al., 2020). When autonomy is frustrated, a person likely feels manipulated and pressured, which can result in both physical and psychological resistance or withdrawal from the source of malcontent. While everyone has personal examples of restricted autonomy, think how you feel when your boss or partner demands that you do something in a certain way or at a specific time that conflicts with your own values or plans and you will easily remember the emotional consequences of autonomy frustration.

Achieving autonomy, like fulfilling any other need, assumes that you want it, know how to attain it, and have the ability to act on your intentions. The psychological conditions necessary for autonomy may exist, but the desire for autonomy can be suppressed by higher-order physical limitations, moral conflicts, or ingrained beliefs inhibiting follow-through. Innate predispositions may also play a role in limiting the extent to which we can exercise autonomous behavior or satisfy certain needs because needs and acting on needs differ neurologically (Kim et al., 2024). Just as biological predispositions limit our ability to run at fifty miles per hour, similar psychological contingencies may interfere with our capacity to say what we think or pursue carnal desires. Just because the metaphorical gun is loaded, we may choose not to pull the trigger. However, when needs are thwarted in one area, an individual will tend to gravitate toward satisfying other needs where the perception of autonomy exists, potentially validating their self-determination in diverse ways.

Competence

Assuming we have the desire and opportunity to exercise autonomy, we want to feel satisfied and accomplished when we elect to pursue an autonomous goal or directive. Competence is defined as the need to feel effective and capable in one's interactions with the environment and to experience opportunities to exercise and express one's skills and abilities (Deci & Ryan, 2000; Ryan & Deci, 2017). Feeling competent means being able to reach goals and master objectives but also feeling authentic in the process of goal progress and attainment. Competence matters because regardless of the specific learning or performance goal, mastery of material or skills leads to a gratifying sense of personal accomplishment when goals are met. The nature of the goal is irrespective of the perception of competence as people can meet the competence objective by being the best parent, the friendliest person in a group, or the best listener in addition to topical expertise. While the objective of competence is mastery of some sort or another, competence does not require attainment of a particular skill level, but the perception of one's abilities to reach desired outcomes. Thus, the sedentary individual with a relatively mediocre accomplishment, such as running a fifteen-minute mile, can feel more competent than the elite athlete who runs the same mile in under five minutes.

The impact of frustration on competence affords similar consequences to most other need frustrations. When competence needs are thwarted, the person feels ineffective and distraught because motivated effort has not achieved the desired outcome. Feelings of shame, guilt, and being overwhelmed can evolve into behavior changes whereby the person withdraws from necessary activities or avoids a situation because engagement might contribute to deeper feelings of inadequacy. Lack of competence perceptions are especially crucial for learning because when doubt influences competence assessments, learners often exert less effort toward important goals, decrease the challenge associated with goal setting, and can even undermine their own performances to keep their self-esteem intact. It is far better for an individual's psychological health to attribute minimal accomplishment to the lack of motivated effort than it is to lack of competence (Covington, 1984).

The need for competence plays a crucial role in motivation and well-being. When individuals feel competent, they are more likely to engage in activities with intrinsic reward, experience enjoyment, and persist in the face of challenges (Deci & Ryan, 2000; Vansteenkiste et al., 2020). Feeling competent enhances an individual's interest, enjoyment, and inherent motivation for engaging in an activity (Deci & Ryan, 2000; Vansteenkiste et al., 2020) while promoting resilience in the face of challenges and obstacles (Ryan & Deci, 2017). The social implications of competence are enormous, as, when feeling accomplished, we are often quite willing and motivated to share our pride as evidenced by avid social media participation portraying idealistic Instagram lives publicizing worthy achievements, a.k.a. "my bass is bigger than yours." Alternatively, self-doubt leads to withdrawal based on inferior comparisons to others and contempt for socialization because of resultant anxiety. Ultimately, competence perceptions can either enhance or inhibit socialization because perceptions of competence are internalized and, consciously or not, determine the probability of engaging in prosocial behaviors.

Relatedness

Also, described as belongness, relatedness is the desire to be connected to others. Satisfying the need for relatedness means that we are at least partially validated by other individuals who recognize and respect us, even if we do not use the words to describe ourselves on resumes or dating profiles. Bonding with others supports satisfaction of the relatedness need because connecting with others implies that we matter to someone beside ourselves. Relatedness is most satisfying and powerful when someone's friendship is unconditional, and limited when someone befriends us because of looks, status, or wealth (Ryan & Deci, 2017). Thus, some relationships may be of insufficient quality to exceed the relatedness threshold, others not. When relatedness needs are frustrated, we feel excluded and often suffer from loneliness (Vansteenkiste et al., 2020), keeping in mind that loneliness is a deficit psychological state that can be realized even in a room full of other people who might enjoy your company.

Relatedness is accomplished in many ways, including through romantic or plutonic relationships, during work associations or affiliation with specific cultural or ethnic groups, and through the alignment of our values with other individuals or collectives that may or may not involve face-to-face interaction. Relatedness is not merely knowing others and having friends. When feeling related, we have strong emotional bonds and shared values and beliefs that are validated through the social connection with the other person(s). The shared experiences and understandings help propel the individual toward more optimal functioning because the individual feels accepted and recognized as a worthy individual who is valued by others.

Relatedness operates under the presumption that we want to have a connection, and that external recognition is valuable for our perceptions of self-worth. However, there are several reasons why a person might suppress the need for relatedness. Individuals who have experienced significant betrayal, rejection, or emotional pain in past relationships may unconsciously repress their need for relatedness as a self-protection mechanism to avoid future discomfort and anxiety. Opening oneself up to forming close connections with others requires a certain level of vulnerability, which some people may find threatening or uncomfortable, leading them to suppress their relatedness needs.

Like perceptions of competence and autonomy, some individuals may hold negative core beliefs about themselves (e.g., "I'm unlovable") or about others (e.g., "People are untrustworthy"), which can cause them to defensively repress their need for human relatedness, sometimes resulting in the accumulation of multiple felines. Individuals with high levels of social anxiety or shyness may find it extremely difficult to form and maintain interpersonal relationships, leading them to defensively repress their need for relatedness. In some cases, individuals may prioritize the pursuit of other needs, such as autonomy or competence, over the need for relatedness, leading to a temporary or situational repression of any particular need. Ultimately, repressing the need for relatedness can have negative consequences for an individual's well-being and development, as this need is considered fundamental for optimal psychological functioning and growth. While social anxiety and the repression of relatedness is suboptimal, the larger consequence is that people who report elevated levels of relatedness are more successful, have better health, and subjectively assess their lives as better than people who lack fulfillment of the belonginess need (King, 2015).

We should operate pragmatically under the premise that satisfaction of the big three SDT needs are highly interconnected and reveal how externally originated influences mediate need satisfaction. Although we strive to achieve all three needs independent of each other, clearly self-perceptions of autonomy and competence cannot be accomplished in isolation. Autonomy perceptions operate within defined social structures that have statutory and moral limitations as we often elect not to exercise autonomy in support of more noble higher-level beliefs. Competence is often assessed, not by mastery of particular skills, knowledge, or ability but by relative comparison to others. Competence perceptions in isolation are a function of consciousness and bias, not meritocracy. Obviously, we must rely on the receptivity of others to meet the need for belongingness. Thus, we should operate on the presumption that other forces, conscious or otherwise, determine not only what needs we hope to satisfy, but the realization that those forces may override our psychological predilection to address what we believe is most important. Regardless, "big three" satisfaction stimulates well-being, while frustration prompts a shift to other more nefarious needs, potentially stagnating adaptive motivation (Chen et al., 2015).

Trust

Trust is a fundamental human need that serves as the foundation for healthy relationships, cooperation, and personal growth. Trust suggests that we believe others are reliable, honest, and have the best of intentions toward us (Rousseau et al., 1998). When the trust need is met, it provides a sense of security, predictability, and confidence, which is essential for forming meaningful connections and engaging in collaborative efforts (Fulmer & Gelfand, 2012), a strong foundation for belongingness. The influence of trust in learning situations is enormous because trust creates a sense of psychological safety that allows learners to take academic risks, like asking questions and making mistakes without fear of negative consequences or judgment. When trust is compromised, learners may become defensive, hindering their ability to engage fully in the learning process. Trust levels also influence the willingness to engage with unfamiliar information or information that conflicts with existing beliefs or individual values. Receptivity to novel ideas without trust is greatly diminished and can forestall the ability to think critically about the meaning of an important message.

Trust plays a crucial role in motivation by influencing our willingness to engage in activities. When trust is present, individuals are more confident in their pursuits because they believe that others will support and act in their best interests. Conversely, a lack of trust can undermine motivation by creating uncertainty, fear, and a reluctance to invest effort or get involved (Kramer, 1999). When the need for trust is satisfied, individuals experience a range of positive outcomes. High levels of trust are associated with increased cooperation, commitment, and organizational citizenship behaviors (Colquitt et al., 2007; Fulmer & Gelfand, 2012). Additionally, trust has been linked to improved psychological well-being, life satisfaction, and overall happiness (Poulin & Haase, 2015). Conversely, when the need for trust is thwarted, individuals may experience negative emotions such as anxiety, fear, and distress, emotions that are especially relevant to both approach and avoidance motivation (Calnan & Rowe, 2008).

Achievement Goals

Goal attainment is sometimes used to represent the psychological manifestation of purpose and refers to setting targets for the pursuit and achievement of desired objectives or outcomes. The need for achievement is rooted in our innate drive to explore, master challenges, and exert influence over our environment (Sheldon & Schüler, 2011), a description closely tied to INMO. Goal setting is an important aspect of achievement because goals show intentionality by providing direction toward desired outcomes. In turn, goal progress is a useful strategy to gain a sense of accomplishment in comparison to premeditated expectations. Goal attainment is closely tied to motivation because when individuals have clear and meaningful goals, they experience heightened enthusiasm, increased effort, and persistence in their pursuits (Schippers et al., 2020). Progress toward goal attainment can foster a sense of competence and self-efficacy, which in turn enhances INMO for future pursuits (Bandura, 2018).

Goal setting and the need for achievement are closely tied. While many interpretations of achievement motivation exist (see Huang, 2011; Wigfield et al., 2021; Senko et al., 2011), the emphasis here is understanding the difference between goals that are set for mastery purposes in comparison to those that are set to demonstrate competence or compare favorably with external standards or other individuals. Depending on the personal emphasis, individuals usually satisfy their need for achievement with the desire to either look good or become experts. While both orientations have specific advantages and disadvantages, reaching the desired outcomes feels rewarding irrespective of the reason for engagement. However, the orientation distinction is important because individuals will use different strategies to satisfy their achievement needs. Approaches that are need satisfying in one situation for one orientation may be inconsequential and need frustrating in another. This diverse reality explains why attempts to change motivation often fail—different needs are addressed by the same strategies! Fast forward to Chapter 7 for more strategy info.

When the need for goal attainment (and achievement) is satisfied, it is associated with increased life satisfaction, positive affect, and overall well-being (Klug & Maier, 2015). Conversely, when the need for goal attainment is thwarted or individuals experience repeated failure in achieving their goals, it can lead to negative consequences such as decreased self-esteem, increased stress, and negative emotions like frustration and hopelessness (Wrosch et al., 2003). Lack of goal attainment will result in reduced challenge or engaging in tasks only when the probability of success is greatly enhanced. Yes, it is also critical to realize that sometimes giving up can be the most rewarding choice for a particular individual.

Esteem

People constantly evaluate how well they fit within their cultural context and the quality of their goal-driven behavior. These self-evaluations shape their perceptions of self-esteem. Self-esteem refers to an individual's subjective overall assessment of their own worth or value. This assessment is based on the specific factors and benchmarks for comparison that each person deems relevant. The subjective evaluation of worth is considered a basic psychological need because it plays a crucial role in shaping our beliefs, behaviors, and overall well-being. Having a healthy sense of self-esteem allows individuals to feel capable, worthy, and deserving of respect. Negative esteem evaluations can lead to a sense of despair, hopelessness, or apathy inhibiting personal growth, the forming of meaningful relationships, and navigating the challenges of life. Self-esteem is closely linked to motivation as it influences an individual's willingness to pursue goals, take on challenges, and persist in the face of obstacles. Individuals with high self-esteem tend to be more motivated and resilient because they believe in their abilities and feel confident in their potential for success (Gebauer et al., 2015). Conversely, low self-esteem can undermine motivation by fostering self-doubt, fear of failure, and a reluctance to take risks or embrace new experiences (Dogan et al., 2013).

Impressions of self-worth originate from internal or external sources. Internal evaluations are based on cumulative assessments of success in comparison to goals and accomplishments, while externally focused assessments originate from social comparisons. Upward comparisons to highly valued others provide useful information for positive self-enhancement (Mussweiler et al., 2000), because the individual strives to improve, such as what happens when our self-esteem evaluation is based on those who are perceived as being successful in a particular group or culture. Downward comparisons can be equally motivating, albeit for different reasons. Downward comparisons enhance positive perceptions and insulate the individual from self-criticism. A downward trajectory is needed when individuals lack the necessary confidence to make upward comparisons. Ultimately, comparisons will influence the degree of challenge a person is willing to tackle. Like perceptions of goal progress, favorable comparisons will accelerate effort, while negative evaluations will often inhibit personal growth.

When the need for self-esteem is satisfied, individuals experience a range of positive outcomes. High self-esteem is associated with increased life satisfaction, happiness, and overall psychological well-being (Moksnes & Espnes, 2013; Zhang et al., 2014). Additionally, individuals with high self-esteem tend to have better interpersonal relationships, cope more effectively with stress, and exhibit greater resilience in the face of adversity (Liu et al., 2016). Conversely, when the need for self-esteem is thwarted or individuals experience chronic low self-esteem, it can lead to negative consequences such as increased risk of depression, anxiety, and other mental health issues (Sowislo & Orth, 2013). Low self-esteem has also been linked to poorer academic and professional performance, as well as a greater vulnerability to peer influence and risky behaviors (Dogan et al., 2015). For some, external perceptions matter more than anything else.

Recognition

High self-esteem, at least in part, is a result of positive recognition from others. Recognition is the need for acknowledgment, appreciation, and respect from others for one's efforts, achievements, and contributions. Recognition is considered a basic psychological need because it fulfills our inherent desire to feel valued, significant, and accepted within our social and professional circles (Deci & Ryan, 2000). Similar to the previous esteem desire, the need for recognition stems from our fundamental human drive to establish a sense of self-worth and gain approval from those we respect. Unlike self-esteem that includes subjective self-perceptions, recognition is 100 percent externally generated.

Recognition is closely tied to motivation as it serves as a powerful incentive for individuals to invest their time, energy, and resources into various pursuits. When individuals feel that their efforts are recognized and appreciated, they experience a heightened sense of motivation and are more likely to maintain or increase their level of engagement and commitment (Bradler et al., 2016). Conversely, a lack of recognition can lead to diminished motivation, disillusionment, and a decreased willingness to exert effort or contribute to collective endeavors, especially in organizational settings (Luthans & Stajkovic, 2000).

Similar to the satisfaction of other needs, when recognition from others is detected and justified, individuals experience a range of positive outcomes. Receiving recognition is associated with increased job satisfaction, organizational commitment, and overall well-being (Özduran & Tanova, 2017). Additionally, recognition can foster a sense of pride, self-confidence, and motivation for further achievement (Deci & Ryan, 2017). Conversely, when the need for recognition is thwarted or individuals feel their contributions are consistently overlooked or undervalued, it can lead to negative consequences including emotional distress and a higher risk of burnout (Haar et al., 2014). A lack of recognition has also been linked to reduced productivity, increased absenteeism, and higher rates of employee turnover (Özduran & Tanova, 2017). Consistent with the other needs described, recognition can be perceived as rewarding and thus is an important consideration when evaluating motivation dispositions.

Pleasure

The last and most rudimentary of needs related to optimal learning and performance is seeking pleasure and avoiding pain. The ubiquitous and fundamental needs for humans and animals are rooted in our evolutionary drive for survival, because when pleasure is experienced the probability of thriving and surviving is increased. Pleasure is associated with subjective perceptions that promote growth, reproduction, and overall flourishing, while pain signals potential threats or harm that should be avoided (Higgins, 1997). Pleasure needs shape our behaviors and decision-making processes, for both physiological and psychological reasons that suggest that we are inherently drawn toward pleasure and averse to pain. To the chagrin of many struggling students, learning gains are often associated with perceptions of pleasure (Berridge & Kringelbach, 2008), and thus an important consideration here.

Pleasure is intricately linked to motivation, as the anticipation or experience of pleasure serves as a powerful reinforcer that energizes and directs our actions (Higgins, 1997; Berridge & Kringelbach, 2015). The pursuit of pleasure is a driving force behind many of our behaviors, from seeking out rewarding activities and relationships to accomplishing goals that bring a sense of satisfaction or enjoyment. Conversely, the avoidance of pain or punishment can also motivate specific actions and decisions aimed at minimizing potential negative consequences or discomfort. When the need for pleasure is satisfied, individuals experience a sense of accomplishment, growth, and eagerness (Schueller & Seligman, 2010). However, people may feel frustrated, disappointed, and less motivated when their need for pleasure is thwarted, or when they do not have positive experiences (Higgins et al., 2001). When the need for pain avoidance is satisfied, people feel safe, secure, and alert, which can encourage them to keep things as they are and avoid possible dangers or losses (Higgins, 1997). On the other hand, people may feel anxious, afraid, and more motivated to stay away from unpleasant situations when pain is inevitable or they are punished, in addition to when they expect negative outcomes (Higgins, 1997).

The pursuit of pleasure and the avoidance of pain as a motivational force is fleeting and fluctuating. Sometimes we are willing to endure temporary pain in satisfaction of longer-term gain. Any student or athlete knows that short-term sacrifice involves deferral of pleasure and tolerance of discomfort, if not outright physical pain. When psychological needs are satisfied in a lasting way, it allows people to function optimally, maintain psychological health, and flourish as human beings. Need satisfaction is much more than just a fleeting pleasure and more focused on gaining essential psychological nutriments for growth and well-being. So, while pleasure can and does result from need satisfaction, oversimplification misses the deeper psychological functions and benefits that need fulfillment provides. Satisfaction of psychological needs is much more than just feeling good in the moment.

Moving Forward

Overall, motivated effort hinges on a deviously simple factor—the fulfillment of our fundamental needs. How we view ourselves, the passion we express, the sense of identity we cultivate, even the beliefs and values that motivate our behavior—all are profoundly shaped by the perception of need satisfaction.

External perceptions from others intertwine with subjective *"self-beliefs,"* weaving an intricate web that defines who we are, what we want, and what we will avoid at all costs. Yet beneath this surface lies a deeper physiological mystery. What exactly transpires within us when a need is satisfied? How does that subjective feeling of gratification chemically manifest and reverberate through our mind and body? The answers may upend our understanding of what truly fuels human contentment and identity. For in the end, despite all its complexities, one primal element governs—motivated action is based on the perception that a personal reward of one kind or another is attainable.

A critical question remains unanswered: What is the source of need satisfaction, and why does it drive our behavior so powerfully? Survival instincts govern our physical actions, but motivational survival—the need to feel fulfilled—is far more elusive to measure and observe. Need satisfaction is, in essence, a form of psychological homeostasis, a delicate equilibrium managed by the intricate balance of reward and punishment that controls the dopaminergic pathways in our brain. As we will explore next, our beliefs, dispositions, and needs are all ultimately servants of our biological imperatives. Our actions, constraints, and abilities to function are directly propelled or limited by when, where, and how we experience rewards. The upcoming discussion will illuminate how this complex neurobiology fundamentally shapes who we are and what drives us to take action or alternatively what fuels brain rot.

References

ABCnews.go.com. (2015). *Check out these tiny penguin sweaters.* https://abcnews.go.com/International/International/tiny-penguins-tiny-sweaters/story?id=28886035

Angrist, J., Lang, D., & Oreopoulos, P. (2009). Incentives and services for college achievement: Evidence from a randomized trial. *American Economic Journal: Applied Economics, 1*(1), 136–163. https://doi.org/10.2139/ssrn.1032118

ASPCA. (2024). Shelter intake and surrender. https://www.aspca.org/helping-people-pets/shelter-intake-and-surrender

Bandura, A. (2018). Toward a psychology of human agency: Pathways and reflections. *Perspectives on Psychological Science, 13*(2), 130–136. https://doi.org/10.1177/1745691617699280

Batson, C., Ahmad, N., & Stocks, E. L. (2011). Four forms of prosocial motivation: Egoism, altruism, collectivism, and principlism. In D. Dunning (Ed.), *Social motivation* (pp. 103–126). Psychology Press.

Baumeister, R. F., Heatherton, T. F., & Tice, D. M. (1994). *Losing control: How and why people fail at self-regulation*. Academic Press.

Berridge, K. C., & Kringelbach, M. L. (2008). Affective neuroscience of pleasure: Reward in humans and animals. *Psychopharmacology, 199*, 457–480. https://doi.org/10.1007/s00213-008-1099-6

Berridge, K. C., & Kringelbach, M. L. (2015). Pleasure systems in the brain. *Neuron, 86*(3), 646–664. https://doi.org/10.1016/j.neuron.2015.02.018

Berscheid, E. (2010). Love in the fourth dimension. *Annual Review of Psychology, 61*, 1–25. https://doi.org/10.1146/annurev.psych.093008.100318

Bradler, C., Dur, R., Neckermann, S., & Non, A. (2016). Employee recognition and performance: A field experiment. *Management Science, 62*(11), 3085–3099. https://doi.org/10.2139/ssrn.2228609

Brassey, J., Hartenstein, L., Jeffrey, B., & Simon, P. (2024). Working nine to thrive. https://www.mckinsey.com/mhi/our-insights/working-nine-to-thrive?

Brewer, M. (1991) The social self: On being the same and different at the same time. *Personality and Social Psychology Bulletin, 17*, 475–482. https://doi.org/10.1177/0146167291175001

Burton, A., Marougka, S., & Priebe, S. (2010). Do financial incentives increase treatment adherence in people with severe mental illness? A systematic review. *Epidemiology and Psychiatric Sciences, 19*(3), 233–242. https://doi.org/10.1017/s1121189x00001160

Calnan, M., & Rowe, R. (2008). *Trust matters in health care*. McGraw-Hill Education.

Cameron, J., & Pierce, W. D. (1994). Reinforcement, reward, and intrinsic motivation: A meta-analysis. *Review of Educational Research, 64*(3), 363–423. https://doi.org/10.2307/1170677

Cerasoli, C. P., Nicklin, J. M., & Ford, M. T. (2014). Intrinsic motivation and extrinsic incentives jointly predict performance: A 40-year meta-analysis. *Psychological Bulletin, 140*(4), 980–1008. https://doi.org/10.1037/a0035661

Chen, B., Vansteenkiste, M., Beyers, W., Boone, L., Deci, E. L., Van der Kaap-Deeder, J., ... & Verstuyf, J. (2015). Basic psychological need satisfaction, need frustration, and need strength across four cultures. *Motivation and Emotion, 39*, 216–236. https://doi.org/10.1007/s11031-014-9450-1

Colquitt, J. A., Scott, B. A., & LePine, J. A. (2007). Trust, trustworthiness, and trust propensity: A meta-analytic test of their unique relationships with risk taking and job performance. *Journal of Applied Psychology, 92*(4), 909–927. https://doi.org/10.1037/0021-9010.92.4.909

Covington, M. V. (1984). The self-worth theory of achievement motivation: Findings and implications. *The Elementary School Journal, 85*(1), 5–20. https://doi.org/10.1086/461388

Cozma, I. (2023). Values, passion, or purpose—which should guide your career? *Harvard Business Review*. https://hbr.org/2023/10/values-passion-or-purpose-which-should-guide-your-career https://hbr.org/2023/10/values-passion-or-purpose-which-should-guide-your-career

Csikszentmihalyi, M., & LeFevre, J. (1989). Optimal experience in work and leisure. *Journal of Personality and Social Psychology, 56*(5), 815–822. https://doi.org/10.1037//0022-3514.56.5.815

Deci, E. L., Koestner, R., & Ryan, R. M. (1999). A meta-analytic review of experiments examining the effects of extrinsic rewards on intrinsic motivation. *Psychological Bulletin, 125*(6), 627–668. https://doi.org/10.1037//0033-2909.125.6.627

Deci, E. L., & Ryan, R. M. (2014). Autonomy and need satisfaction in close relationships: Relationships motivation theory. In N. Weinstein (Ed.), *Human motivation and interpersonal relationships: Theory, research, and applications* (pp. 53–73). Springer. https://doi.org/10.1007/978-94-017-8542-6_3

Dogan, T., Totan, T., & Sapmaz, F. (2013). The role of self-esteem, psychological well-being, emotional self-efficacy, and affect balance on happiness: A path model. *European Scientific Journal, 9*(20), 31–42.

Dysvik, A., & Kuvaas, B. (2013). Intrinsic and extrinsic motivation as predictors of work effort: The moderating role of achievement goals. *British Journal of Social Psychology, 52*(3), 412–430. https://doi.org/10.1111/j.2044-8309.2011.02090.x

Elliot, A. (2005). A conceptual history of the achievement goal construct. In A. Elliot & C. Dweck (Eds.), *Handbook of competence and motivation* (pp. 52–72). Guilford Press.

Elliot, A. J., & Harackiewicz, J. M. (1996). Approach and avoidance achievement goals and intrinsic motivation: A mediational analysis. *Journal of Personality and Social Psychology, 70*(3), 461. https://doi.org/10.1037//0022-3514.70.3.461

Fay, D., & Frese, M. (2001). The concept of personal initiative: An overview of validity studies. *Human Performance, 14*(1), 97–124. https://doi.org/10.1207/s15327043hup1401_06

Ferraro, P. J., & Price, M. K. (2013). Using nonpecuniary strategies to influence behavior: Evidence from a large-scale field experiment. *Review of Economics and Statistics, 95*(1), 64–73. https://doi.org/10.3386/w17189

Fulmer, C. A., & Gelfand, M. J. (2012). At what level (and in whom) we trust: Trust across multiple organizational levels. *Journal of Management, 38*(4), 1167–1230. https://doi.org/10.1177/0149206312439327

Gebauer, J. E., Sedikides, C., Wagner, J., Bleidorn, W., Rentfrow, P. J., Potter, J., & Gosling, S. D. (2015). Cultural norm fulfillment, interpersonal belonging, or getting ahead? A large-scale cross-cultural test of three perspectives on the function of self-esteem. *Journal of Personality and Social Psychology, 109*(3), 526–548. https://doi.org/10.1037/pspp0000052

Gegenfurtner, K. R., Bloj, M., & Toscani, M. (2015). The many colours of "the dress." *Current Biology, 25*(13), R543–R544. https://doi.org/10.1016/j.cub.2015.04.043

Gerhart, B., & Fang, M. (2015). Pay, intrinsic motivation, extrinsic motivation, performance, and creativity in the workplace: Revisiting long-held beliefs. *Annual Review of Organizational Psychology and Organizational Behavior, 2*, 489–521. https://doi.org/10.1146/annurev-orgpsych-032414-111418

Gillet, N., Lafrenière, M.-A., Huyghebaert, T., & Fouquereau, E. (2015). Autonomous and controlled reasons underlying achievement goals: Implications for the 3 × 2 achievement goal model in educational and work settings. *Motivation and Emotion, 39*(6), 858–875. https://doi.org/10.1007/s11031-015-9505-y

Gladstone, J. R., Wigfield, A., & Eccles, J. S. (2022). Situated expectancy-value theory, dimensions of engagement, and academic outcomes. In A. L. Reschly, S. L. Christenson (Eds.), *Handbook of research on student engagement* (2nd ed.) (pp. 57–76). Springer International Publishing. https://doi.org/10.1007/978-3-031-07853-8_3

Gneezy, U., Meier, S., & Rey-Biel, P. (2011). When and why incentives (don't) work to modify behavior. *Journal of Economic Perspectives, 25*(4), 191–210. https://doi.org/10.1257/jep.25.4.191

Greenberg, S. (2023). What are all the things people need. *Clearerthinking.org*. https://www.clearerthinking.org/post/what-are-all-the-things-that-humans-need

Greenstein, A., & Koestner, R. (1996). Success in maintaining new year's resolutions: The value of self-determined reasons. In A. L. Reschly, S. L. Christenson (Eds.), *International Congress of Psychology, Montreal, Quebec, Canada* (2nd ed.) (pp. 57–76).

Haar, J. M., Russo, M., Suñe, A., & Ollier-Malaterre, A. (2014). Outcomes of work–life balance on job satisfaction, life satisfaction and mental health: A study across seven cultures. *Journal of Vocational Behavior, 85*(3), 361–373. https://doi.org/10.1016/j.jvb.2014.08.010

Hallam, S. (2002). Musical motivation: Towards a model synthesising the research. *Music Education Research, 4*(2), 225–244. https://doi.org/10.1080/1461380022000011939

Harter, S. (1992). The relationship between perceived competence, affect, and motivational orientation within the classroom: Processes and patterns of change. In A. K. Boggiano & T. S. Pittman (Eds.), *Achievement and motivation: A social-developmental perspective* (pp. 77–114). Cambridge University Press.

Hattie, J., Hodis, F. A., & Kang, S. H. (2020). Theories of motivation: Integration and ways forward. *Contemporary Educational Psychology, 61*, 101865. https://doi.org/10.1016/j.cedpsych.2020.101865

Higgins, E. T. (1997). Beyond pleasure and pain. *American Psychologist, 52*(12), 1280–1300. https://doi.org/10.1037//0003-066x.52.12.1280

Higgins, E. T., Friedman, R. S., Harlow, R. E., Idson, L. C., Ayduk, O. N., & Taylor, A. (2001). Achievement orientations from subjective histories of success: Promotion pride versus prevention pride. *European Journal of Social Psychology, 31*(1), 3–23. https://doi.org/10.1002/ejsp.27

Hoffman, B. (2015). *Motivation for learning and performance*. Academic Press.

Hoffman, B. (2025). Value and utility: What students learn and transfer from a graduate motivation course. *Scholarship of Teaching and Learning in Psychology*. https://doi.org/10.1037/stl0000448

Hortop, E. G., Wrosch, C., & Gagné, M. (2013). The why and how of goal pursuits: Effects of global autonomous motivation and perceived control on emotional well-being. *Motivation and Emotion, 37*, 675–687. https://doi.org/10.1007/s11031-013-9349-2

Howard, J. L., Bureau, J., Guay, F., Chong, J. X. Y., & Ryan, R. M. (2021). Student motivation and associated outcomes: A meta-analysis from self-determination theory. *Perspectives on Psychological Science, 16*(6), 1300–1323. https://doi.org/10.1177/1745691620966789

Huang, C. (2011). Achievement goals and achievement emotions: A meta-analysis. *Educational Psychology Review, 23*, 359–388. https://doi.org/10.1007/s10648-011-9155-x

Huberman. A. (2022). How to like doing hard things. https://www.youtube.com/watch?v=jNmebDdXXyw

Kendi, I. X. (2023). *How to be an antiracist*. One World.

King, R. B. (2015). Sense of relatedness boosts engagement, achievement, and well-being: A latent growth model study. *Contemporary Educational Psychology, 42*, 26–38. https://doi.org/10.1016/j.cedpsych.2015.04.002

Kim, K. S., Lee, Y. H., Yun, J. W., Kim, Y. B., Song, H. Y., Park, J. S., ... & Choi, H. J. (2024). A normative framework dissociates need and motivation in hypothalamic neurons. *Science Advances, 10*(45), eado1820. https://doi.org/10.1126/sciadv.ado1820

Kirchler, M., Lindner, F., & Weitzel, U. (2018). Rankings and risk-taking in the finance industry. *The Journal of Finance, 73*(5), 2271–2302. https://doi.org/10.1111/jofi.12701

Klug, H. J., & Maier, G. W. (2015). Linking goal progress and subjective well-being: A meta-analysis. *Journal of Happiness Studies, 16*(1), 37–65. https://doi.org/10.1007/s10902-013-9493-0

Kramer, R. M. (1999). Trust and distrust in organizations: Emerging perspectives, enduring questions. *Annual Review of Psychology, 50*(1), 569–598. https://doi.org/10.1146/annurev.psych.50.1.569

Kruglanski, A. W., & Fishman, S. (2009). What makes terrorism tick? Its individual, group and organizational aspects. *International Journal of Social Psychology, 24*(2), 139–162. https://doi.org/10.1174/021347409788041480

Kuvaas, Buch, R., Weib., el, A., Dysvik, A., & Nerstad, C. G. (2017). Do intrinsic and extrinsic motivation relate differently to employee outcomes?. *Journal of Economic Psychology, 61*, 244–258. https://doi.org/10.1016/j.joep.2017.05.004

Kwon, M. (2022). *The moralization of intrinsic motivation* (Doctoral dissertation).

Kwon, M., Cunningham, J. L., & Jachimowicz, J. M. (2023). Discerning saints: Moralization of intrinsic motivation and selective prosociality at work. *Academy of Management Journal, 66*(6), 1625–1650. https://doi.org/10.5465/amj.2020.1761

Latham, G. P. (2012). *Work motivation: History, theory, research, and practice.* Sage.

Lepper, M. R., & Greene, D. (2015). Overjustification research and beyond: Toward a means—ends analysis of intrinsic and extrinsic motivation. In *The hidden costs of reward* (pp. 109–148). Psychology Press. https://doi.org/10.4324/9781315666983-14

Liu, Y., Wang, Z., & Li, Z. (2013). Resilience and affect balance as mediators between trait emotional intelligence and life satisfaction. *Personality and Individual Differences, 54*(7), 850–855. https://doi.org/10.1016/j.paid.2012.12.010

Locke, E. A., & Schattke, K. (2019). Intrinsic and extrinsic motivation: Time for expansion and clarification. *Motivation Science, 5*(4), 277–290. https://doi.org/10.1037/mot0000116

Luthans, F., & Stajkovic, A. D. (2000). Provide recognition for performance improvement. In E.A. Locke (Ed.), *Handbook of principles of organizational behavior: Indispensable knowledge for evidence-*

based management (pp. 166–180). John Wiley & Sons. https://doi.org/10.1002/9781119206422.ch13

Manolio, T. A., Collins, F. S., Cox, N. J., Goldstein, D. B., Hindorff, L. A., Hunter, D. J., . . . & Visscher, P. M. (2009). Finding the missing heritability of complex diseases. *Nature*, 461, 747–753. https://doi.org/10.1038/nature08494

Maslow, A. H. (1943). A theory of human motivation. *Psychological Review*, 50(4), 370–396. https://doi.org/10.1037/h0054346

Michaelsen, M. M., & Esch, T. (2021). Motivation and reward mechanisms in health behavior change processes. *Brain Research, 1757*, 147309. https://doi.org/10.1016/j.brainres.2021.147309

Miele, D. B, Rosenzweig, E. Q., & Browman, A. S. (2024). Motivation. In P. A. Schutz & K. R. Muis (Eds.), *Handbook of educational psychology* (4th ed., pp. 191–218). Routledge.

Milyavskaya, M., Inzlicht, M., Johnson, T., & Larson, M. J. (2019). Reward sensitivity following boredom and cognitive effort: A high-powered neurophysiological investigation. *Neuropsychologia, 123*, 159–168. https://doi.org/10.1016/j.neuropsychologia.2018.03.033

Moeller, J., Dietrich, J., Eccles, J. S., & Schneider, B. (2017). Passionate experiences in adolescence: Situational variability and long-term stability. *Journal of Research on Adolescence, 27*(2), 344–361. https://doi.org/10.1111/jora.12297

Moksnes, U. K., & Espnes, G. A. (2013). Self-esteem and life satisfaction in adolescents—Gender and age as potential moderators. *Quality of Life Research, 22*(10), 2921–2928. https://doi.org/10.1007/s11136-013-0427-4

Murayama, K., Izuma, K., Aoki, R., & Matsumoto, K. (2016). Your choice motivates you in the brain: The emergence of autonomy neuroscience. *Recent developments in neuroscience research on human motivation* (Advances in motivation and achievement, Vol. 19, pp. 95–125). Emerald Group Publishing Limited. https://doi.org/10.1108/S0749-742320160000019004

Mussweiler, T., Gabriel, S., & Bodenhausen, G. V. (2000). Shifting social identities as a strategy for deflecting threatening social comparisons. *Journal of Personality & Social Psychology, 79*(3), 398–409. http://dx.doi.org/10.1037//0022-3514.79.3.398

Ng, J. Y. Y., Ntoumanis, N., Thøgersen-Ntoumani, C., Deci, E. L., Ryan, R. M., Duda, J. L., & Williams, G. C. (2012). Self-determination theory applied to health contexts: A meta-analysis. *Perspectives on Psychological Science, 7*(4), 325–340. https://doi.org/10.1177/1745691612447309

Ntoumanis, N., Healy, L. C., Sedikides, C., Duda, J., Stewart, B., Smith, A., & Bond, J. (2014). When the going gets tough: The "why" of goal striving matters. *Journal of Personality, 82*(3), 225–236. https://doi.org/10.1111/jopy.12047

O. C. Tanner Institute. (2023). The business case for recognition. https://hr.mcmaster.ca/app/uploads/2020/05/Business-Case-for-Recognition.pdf

Özduran, A., & Tanova, C. (2017). Manager mindsets and employee organizational citizenship behaviours. *International Journal of Contemporary Hospitality Management, 29*(1), 589–606. https://doi.org/10.1108/ijchm-03-2016-0141

Pelletier, L. G., Fortier, M. S., Vallerand, R. J., & Brière, N. M. (2001). Associations among perceived autonomy support, forms of self-regulation, and persistence: A prospective study. *Motivation and Emotion, 25*(4), 279–306. https://doi.org/10.1023/a:1014805132406

Poulin, M. J., & Haase, C. M. (2015). Growing to trust: Evidence that trust increases and sustains well-being across the life span. *Social Psychological and Personality Science, 6*(6), 614–621. https://doi.org/10.1177/1948550615574301

Reeve, J. M. (2018). *Motivation and emotion* (7th ed.). Wiley.

Reiss, S. (2005). Extrinsic and intrinsic motivation at 30: Unresolved scientific issues. *The Behavior Analyst, 28*, 1–14. https://doi.org/10.1007/bf03392100

Reiss, S. (2012). Intrinsic and extrinsic motivation. *Teaching of Psychology, 39*(2), 152–156. https://doi.org/10.1177/0098628312437704

Reshotko, N. (1992). The Socratic theory of motivation. *Apeiron, 25*(3), 145–170. https://doi.org/10.1515/apeiron.1992.25.3.145

Robinson, M. D., Persich, M. R., & Irvin, R. L. (2022). An ego effectiveness perspective of successful self-control: An individual difference and its links to social functioning and well-being. *Journal of Research in Personality, 97*, 104207. https://doi.org/10.1016/j.jrp.2022.104207

Rousseau, D. M., Sitkin, S. B., Burt, R. S., & Camerer, C. (1998). Not so different after all: A cross-discipline view of trust. *Academy of Management Review, 23*(3), 393–404. https://doi.org/10.2307/259051

Ryan, R. M., & Deci, E. L. (2000). Self-determination theory and the facilitation of intrinsic motivation, social development, and well-being. *American Psychologist, 55*(1), 68–78. https://doi.org/10.1037/0003-066X.55.1.68

Ryan, R. M., & Deci, E. L. (2017). *Self-determination theory: Basic psychological needs in motivation, development, and wellness.* Guilford Publications.

Ryan, R. M., & Deci, E. L. (2020). Intrinsic and extrinsic motivation from a self-determination theory perspective: Definitions, theory, practices, and future directions. *Contemporary Educational Psychology*, 101860. https://doi.org/10.1016/j.cedpsych.2020.101860

Ryan, R. M., Bradshaw, E., & Deci, E. L. (2019). A history of human motivation theories. In B. Sternberg & W. Pickren (Eds.), *The Cambridge handbook of the intellectual history of psychology* (pp. 391–411). Cambridge University Press. https://doi.org/10.1017/9781108290876.016

Salamone, J. D., & Correa, M. (2012). The mysterious motivational functions of mesolimbic dopamine. *Neuron, 76*(3), 470–485. https://doi.org/10.1016/j.neuron.2012.10.021

Scales, A. N., & Brown, H. Q. (2020). The effects of organizational commitment and harmonious passion on voluntary turnover among social workers: A mixed methods study. *Children and Youth Services Review, 110*, 104782. https://doi.org/10.1016/j.childyouth.2020.104782

Schippers, M. C., Morisano, D., Locke, E. A., Scheepers, A. W., Latham, G. P., & de Jong, E. M. (2020). Writing about personal goals and plans regardless of goal type boosts academic performance. *Contemporary Educational Psychology, 60*, 101823. https://doi.org/10.1016/j.cedpsych.2019.101823

Schueller, S. M., & Seligman, M. E. (2010). Pursuit of pleasure, engagement, and meaning: Relationships to subjective and objective measures of well-being. *The Journal of Positive Psychology, 5*(4), 253–263. https://doi.org/10.1080/17439761003794130

Sheldon, K. M., & Schüler, J. (2011). Wanting, having, and needing: Integrating motive disposition theory and self-determination theory. *Journal of Personality and Social Psychology, 101*(5), 1106–1123. https://doi.org/10.1037/a0024952

Shin, J., & Grant, A. M. (2019). Bored by interest: How intrinsic motivation in one task can reduce performance on other tasks. *Academy of Management Journal, 62*(2), 415–436. https://doi.org/10.5465/amj.2017.0735

Silvia, P. J. (2019). Curiosity and motivation. In R. M. Ryan (Ed.), *The Oxford handbook of human motivation* (2nd ed., pp. 155–167). Oxford University Press. https://doi.org/10.1093/oxfordhb/9780190666453.013.9

Skitka, L. J., Bauman, C. W., & Sargis, E. G. (2005). Moral conviction: Another contributor to attitude strength or something more? *Journal of Personality and Social Psychology, 88*, 895–917. https://doi.org/10.1037/0022-3514.88.6.895

Senko, C., Hulleman, C. S., & Harackiewicz, J. M. (2011). Achievement goal theory at the crossroads: Old controversies, current challenges, and new directions. *Educational Psychologist, 46*(1), 26–47. https://doi.org/10.1080/00461520.2011.538646

Senko, C., & Tropiano, K. L. (2016). Comparing three models of achievement goals: Goal orientations, goal standards, and goal complexes. *Journal of Educational Psychology, 108*(8), 1178. https://doi.org/10.1037/edu0000114

Sowislo, J. F., & Orth, U. (2013). Does low self-esteem predict depression and anxiety? A meta-analysis of longitudinal studies. *Psychological Bulletin, 139*(1), 213–240. https://doi.org/10.1037/a0028931

Stanovich, K. (2011). *Rationality and the reflective mind*. Oxford University Press.

Stupnisky, R. H., Renaud, R. D., Perry, R. P., Ruthig, J. C., Haynes, T. L., & Clifton, R. A. (2007). Comparing self-esteem and perceived control as predictors of first-year college students' academic achievement. *Social Psychology of Education, 10*, 303–330. https://doi.org/10.1007/s11218-007-9020-4

Tang, M., Wang, D., & Guerrien, A. (2021). The contribution of basic psychological need satisfaction to psychological well-being via autonomous motivation among older adults: A cross-cultural study in China and France. *Frontiers in Psychology, 12*, 734461. https://doi.org/10.3389/fpsyg.2021.734461

Taylor, G., Jungert, T., Mageau, G. A., Schattke, K., Dedic, H., Rosenfield, S., & Koestner, R. (2014). A self-determination theory approach to predicting school achievement over time: The unique role of intrinsic motivation. *Contemporary Educational Psychology, 39*(4), 342–358. https://doi.org/10.1016/j.cedpsych.2014.08.002

Teixeira, P. J., Carraça, E. V., Marques, M. M., Rutter, H., Oppert, J. M., De Bourdeaudhuij, I., ... & Brug, J. (2015). Successful behavior change in obesity interventions in adults: A systematic review of self-regulation mediators. *BMC Medicine, 13*(1), 1–16. https://doi.org/10.1186/s12916-015-0323-6

Twenge, J. M., & Donnelly, K. (2016). Generational differences in American students' reasons for going to college, 1971–2014: The rise of extrinsic motives. *The Journal of Social Psychology, 156*(6), 620–629. https://doi.org/10.1080/00224545.2016.1152214

Van den Broeck, A., Howard, J. L., Van Vaerenbergh, Y., Leroy, H., & Gagné, M. (2021). Beyond intrinsic and extrinsic motivation: A meta-analysis on self-determination theory's multidimensional conceptualization of work motivation. *Organizational Psychology Review, 11*(3), 240–273. https://doi.org/10.1177/20413866211006173

Vallerand, R. J. (2015). *The psychology of passion: A dualistic model*. Oxford University Press.

Vallerand, R. J., Blanchard, C., Mageau, G. A., Koestner, R., Ratelle, C., Léonard, M., Gagné, M., & Marsolais, J. (2003). Les passions de l'âme: On obsessive and harmonious passion. *Journal of Personality and Social Psychology, 85*(4), 756–767. https://doi.org/10.1037/0022-3514.85.4.756

Vallerand, R. J., Chichekian, T., & Schellenberg, B. (2024). The role of passion in education. In P. A. Schutz & K. R. Muis (Eds.), *Handbook of educational psychology* (4th ed., pp. 245–268). Routledge. https://doi.org/10.4324/9780429433726-14

Vallerand, R. J., Paquet, Y., Philippe, F. L., & Charest, J. (2010). On the role of passion for work in burnout: A process model. *Journal of Personality, 78*(1), 289–312. https://doi.org/10.1111/j.1467-6494.2009.00616.x

Vansteenkiste, M., Lens, W., & Deci, E. L. (2006). Intrinsic versus extrinsic goal contents in self-determination theory: Another look at the quality of academic motivation. *Educational Psychologist, 41*(1), 19–31. https://doi.org/10.1207/s15326985ep4101_4

Vansteenkiste, M., & Ryan, R. M. (2013). On psychological growth and vulnerability: Basic psychological need satisfaction and need frustration as a unifying principle. *Journal of Psychotherapy Integration, 23*(3), 263–280. https://doi.org/10.1037/a0032359

Vansteenkiste, M., Ryan, R. M., & Soenens, B. (2020). Basic psychological need theory: Advancements, critical themes, and future directions. *Motivation and Emotion, 44*(1), 1–31. https://doi.org/10.1007/s11031-019-09818-1

Vansteenkiste, M., Simons, J., Lens, W., Sheldon, K. M., & Deci, E. L. (2004). Motivating learning, performance, and persistence: The synergistic effects of intrinsic goal contents and autonomy-supportive contexts. *Journal of Personality and Social Psychology, 87*(2), 246–260. https://doi.org/10.1037/0022-3514.87.2.246

Walker, G. J., Yan, N., & Kono, S. (2020). Basic psychological need satisfaction and intrinsic motivation during leisure: A cross-cultural comparison. *Journal of Leisure Research, 51*(4), 489–510. https://doi.org/10.1080/00222216.2020.1735973

Weiner, B. (2021). An attributionally based theory of motivation and emotion: Focus, range, and issues. In N. T. Feather (Ed.), *Expectations and actions* (pp. 163–204). Routledge. https://doi.org/10.4324/9781003150879-8

Weinstein, N., & Ryan, R. M. (2010). When helping helps: Autonomous motivation for prosocial behavior and its influence on well-being for the helper and recipient. *Journal of Personality and Social Psychology, 98*(2), 222–244. https://doi.org/10.1037/a0016984

Werner, K. M., & Milyavskaya, M. (2019). Motivation and self-regulation: The role of want-to motivation in the processes underlying self-regulation and self-control. *Social and Personality Psychology Compass, 13*(1), e12425. https://doi.org/10.31234/osf.io/yq2j7

Wigfield, A., Muenks, K., & Eccles, J. S. (2021). Achievement motivation: What we know and where we are going. *Annual Review of*

Developmental Psychology, *3*, 87–111. https://doi.org/10.1146/annurev-devpsych-050720-103500

Winne, P. H., & Hadwin, A. F. (2008). The weave of motivation and self-regulated learning. In D. H. Schunk & B. J. Zimmerman (Eds.), *Motivation and self-regulated learning: Theory, research, and applications* (pp. 297–314). Lawrence Erlbaum Associates.

Wolters, C. A., & Rosenthal, H. (2000). The relation between students' motivational beliefs and their use of motivational regulation strategies. *International Journal of Educational Research*, *33*(7–8), 801–820. https://doi.org/10.1016/s0883-0355(00)00051-3

Wright, J. C., Cullum, J., & Schwab, N. (2008). The cognitive and affective dimensions of moral conviction: Implications for attitudinal and behavioral measures of interpersonal tolerance. *Personality and Social Psychology Bulletin*, *34*, 1461–1476. https://doi.org/10.1177/0146167208322557

Wrosch, C., Scheier, M. F., Carver, C. S., & Schulz, R. (2003). The importance of goal disengagement in adaptive self-regulation: When giving up is beneficial. *Self and Identity*, *2*(1), 1–20. https://doi.org/10.1080/15298860309021

Yukhymenko-Lescroart, M. A., & Sharma, G. (2022). Passion for work and well-being of working adults. *Journal of Career Development*, *49*(3), 505–518. https://doi.org/10.1177/0894845320946398

Zhang, J., Zhao, S., Lester, D., & Zhou, C. (2014). Life satisfaction and its correlates among college students in China: A test of social reference theory. *Asian Journal of Psychiatry*, *10*, 17–20. https://doi.org/10.1016/j.ajp.2013.06.014

Zhao, H., Liu, X., & Qi, C. (2021). "Want to learn" and "can learn": Influence of academic passion on college students' academic engagement. *Frontiers in Psychology*, *12*, 697822. https://doi.org/10.3389/fpsyg.2021.697822

4

The Rewarded Brain

Chapter Outline

Biology Is Better (Despite Lower Popularity)	111
Neuropsychology Explains How Needs Originate	118
Positive Expectancies + Reward = INMO.	138

We now recognize that the bedrock of motivated behavior involves satisfaction of needs. Indeed, examine just about every theory of mammalian motivation, and you will read descriptions of how and why a variety of nonnegotiable needs must be addressed in order to maximize longevity and psychological health. From a philosophical perspective, few would debate the necessity of food, water, and the avoidance of carnivorous predators as essential for prosperity. When these basic needs are left unattended, the indisputable outcome is death, so there isn't much deliberation concerning the legitimacy or source of the need. Theories that take strictly biological approaches to explain motivated behavior are commonly described as *"drive"* (Hull, 1943) or reinforcement theories, because the reduction of an unpleasant physical state motivates (drives) the individual to act. However, over the course of seventy years of debating the merit of drive theories, psychologists realized there was more to life than biological need satisfaction, and that drive alone was insufficient to explain human agency (Ryan & Deci, 2017).

The demise of drive theory led to a massive surge in perspectives that focused on the inclusion of cerebral needs as integral to becoming "fully functional," and essential for optimal human growth and performance (Vansteenkiste et al., 2020, p. 4). Selectively described as "nutrients," psychological need satisfaction was deemed necessary for well-being because allegedly when needs are thwarted, objective "observable" decrements in "growth, integrity, and wellness" ensue (Ryan & Deci, 2017, p. 10). While it is clear that having a positive self-image and an optimistic outlook are desirable to drive motivated action, the exaggerated emphasis is unwarranted. Minimally, as Chapter 2 described, we should scrutinize the soundness of evidence that leads to the lofty contention that specific strands of human motivation are both necessary and sufficient to drive action. Moreso, for the purposes of this chapter, we can debate the "objective" universality of the needs, as well as the suitability of using frothy words like "nutrients" to describe needs that are necessary "regardless of one's subjective goals and values" (Deci & Ryan, 2017, p. 10). More importantly, neither self-determination theory (SDT), where the italicized terminology originates, nor any other contemporary theory of motivation answers three especially important questions addressed in this chapter.

First, "*why have neuropsychological perspectives been grossly underemphasized by most motivation researchers and psychologists?*" There is a conspicuous gap in psychology and education literature concerning the powerful influence of neurological functioning on motivated behavior. A cursory review of the fourth edition of the multidisciplinary bible *The Handbook of Educational Psychology* finds the word "neuropsychology" appearing four times out of 794 pages, with those four instances relegated to reference citations (Schutz & Muis, 2024). In the handbook chapter summarizing motivation theory (Miele et al., 2024), there is no mention of neuroscience, whatsoever. Despite the repeated call from prominent researchers (see Lee & Reeve; 2017; Reeve; 2019a, 2019b), the neuroscience gap persists. Researchers Andrew Martin and Emma Burns (2023) exclaimed, "until there is greater uptake of biopsychological perspectives and data, there will be persistent gaps in knowledge about the explanatory mechanisms underlying motivation theories" (p. 383). Renowned scholar Suzanne Hidi echoed the sentiment seven years earlier when she stated, "Interestingly, only recently have limited efforts been made to link neuroscience and motivational research. With few exceptions, the importance of neuroscientific data has been underestimated in social, educational, and psychological literature, particularly in the area of motivational research" (2016, p. 3).

The omissions are obvious and ominous, especially in light of neuroimaging measurement advances such as fMRI (functional magnetic resonance imaging), PET (positron emission tomography), and MEG (magnetoencephalography) that can monitor brain activity during behavioral tasks, limiting doubt as to how the brain processes, stores, and retrieves information while concurrently observing brain activity to determine localization of functionality. The ubiquitous trend focusing on how biology and specifically how neuroscience findings explain thinking, learning, and motivation cascades into similar calls from other disciplines besides psychology and education. Benjafield (2020), who investigated vocabulary overlap among the disciplines of mathematics, computing, astronomy, physics, chemistry, biology, psychology, sociology, economics, political science, philosophy, and linguistics, concluded, "Our data suggest that much of what we now call psychology may end up being part of biology" (p. 1979). Rather than try to answer the lingering "why does the omission problem persist?" question, this chapter presents neuropsychological evidence to explain motivated behavior and enhance the myopic disciplinary perspectives that usually consider behavioral evidence as sufficient to explain motivated action.

Second, we must resolve the mystery concerning, "*What is the source of need satisfaction?*" Merely having needs, or correlation evidence of the degrading psychological effects in the absence of need satisfaction are insufficient to imply why the need exists. Based on "Basic Psychology Needs Theory" (BPNT, Deci & Ryan, 2017), "A basic need represents an evolved aspect of our psychological nature due to adaptive advantages associated with need satisfaction" (Vansteenkiste et al., 2020, p. 4). In other words, need satisfaction feels good and we should strive to satisfy needs. While this vernacular does not specifically indicate that a need is "*innate*," the terminology used implies an evolutionary component to need origination and the connotation of "*adaptive*," suggests a genetic basis for psychological need justification. However, neither BPNT, nor the parent theory SDT, provides sufficient evidence to justify that a pattern of resolving psychological shortcomings is what drives all people. Universality aside, from a practical perspective, knowing where and how these needs originate would assist in the development of strategies to maximize the power of their rewarding ability (the point of Chapter 7).

Third, as repeatedly implied here, "*Is there a better explanation than INMO as the most robust version of motivated behavior?*" Hopefully, the previous chapters have shown that there is more to optimal motivation than passion and much of the evidence supporting the superiority of INMO rests on shaky methodological ground. Other researchers have raised similar concerns regarding the power of INMO. Reiss (2012) suggested that the intrinsic-extrinsic dichotomy was an oversimplification of human motivation and contended that appropriate categorization of behavior was based on sixteen "universal reinforcements" (p. 154) that included random desires such as romance, the quest for beauty, saving, companionship, respect, and tranquility, among others. Apparently, Reiss hasn't encountered my grandchildren, who might contest his tranquility agenda. While perhaps more encompassing than SDT's INMO conceptions, his musings were based exclusively on self-reported survey responses, which as we now know are unreliable. However, Reiss provided valuable insight about the nature of rewards as conceived by SDT, indicating that 95 percent of the research used to reach the inference that extrinsic reward has a debilitating effect on INMO was almost entirely based on single-trial studies conducted in laboratories, an approach that is lethal for generalization. He was also a pioneer critic in revealing that INMO in experimental studies can be the result of experimental novelty and that extrinsic rewards can also enhance INMO under certain conditions, challenging the idea that EXMO consistently undermines INMO.

More recently, Locke and Schattke (2019) directly challenged INMO superiority. They contended that INMO can be attained in the absence of achieving competence and that need gratification can be accomplished in multiple ways. They also contested the heavy emphasis of SDT on the undermining influence of reward on INMO. Undermining, in this case, means the alleged universal reduction in INMO when rewards are contingent on task progress or completion. Supposedly subsequent iterations of the same task when rewards are withdrawn inhibit motivation to resume the task. Further, Locke and Schattke expressed disenchantment because they believed that in some situations EXMO was not controlling and thus there was little basis for the universal superiority of INMO. While there is some validity to the noncontrolling aspects of extrinsic reward, Ryan and Deci (2019) easily refuted the claims as conjecture. As you know, the motivation continuum of SDT, described on p. 73, includes acknowledgment that EXMO can be instrumental when it is perceived as noncontrolling or not manipulating to the individual. However, like trying to topple dictatorships with limited resources, INMO refutation efforts have failed, not because of intent but because of lack of disconfirming evidence. Toppling governments requires ammunition, just as overcoming an overgeneralized theory takes reliable and valid evidence, the type consistently provided by neuropsychological findings.

While SDT and the concept of INMO have been widely influential in the field of motivation research, there are vulnerabilities within the theory. The idea that INMO is inherently superior to EXMO is embellished, and recent calls reiterate the need to consider alternative reward perspectives (Bardach & Murayama, 2025). However, the goal here is *not* to discredit the dimensions of SDT or desecrate the influence of INMO. Neurological evidence may suggest that INMO is simply one of a variety of personalized reward types that is person and context dependent. Perhaps INMO is more of a trojan horse, or an imposter disguising the underlying source of motivation and not a unilateral solution to every problem of human agency. As the neurological evidence unfolds, we will soon learn what biology tells us about rewards that behavioral theories cannot. Brace yourself as we finally reveal how your brain's perception of rewards holds the key to not only understanding personal motivations but also predicting the behavior of others. Prepare to unravel the vital connections between biology, needs, and motivation that are glaringly absent from mainstream discourse.

Biology Is Better (Despite Lower Popularity)

First, recall from Chapter 2 that the average variability left unexplained by the top fifty empirical reward/INMO/EXMO studies was 75 percent. This means factors other than what was measured during the experimental interventions accounted for the observed outcomes. Second, the analysis of those same studies revealed that 48 percent were conducted under simulated laboratory conditions. Generalizing from a lab to the complexities of day-to-day experience is speculative at best and often neglects important person-environment interactivity that changes behavior. Third, biology does not discriminate based on demographics, compensating for the WEIRD sample dilemma that plagues motivation research. By example, functional brain localization of a person living in China is identical to someone residing in the United States.[1] Summarily, a biological perspective of motivation offers a more comprehensive understanding of what drives behavior compared to focusing solely on behavioral evidence. Specifically, the focus here is on neuroscience, the strand of psychology research showing the greatest growth trajectory over the past three decades compared with eighty other topics in psychology (Wieczorek, 2021).

While neuroscience is a broad field that investigates relationships between neural functioning, brain structures, and behavior (Yeung et al., 2017), neuropsychology is focused on the relationship among the brain and cognitive, behavioral, and emotional functioning. In particular, motivation research in neuropsychology examines which brain structures, neural circuits, and factors influence attention, goal-directed behavior, beliefs, and decision-making. Specifically, the emphasis here is on how neurodiversity impacts perceptions of INMO, reward processing, learning, conceptual change, socialization, and the regulation of motivation; all factors intimately connected to optimal performance.

Given this backdrop, there are at least four advantages to embracing a neuropsychological perspective of motivated behavior. First, measurement of brain activity is highly valid and reliable, meaning there is consistency in what is measured, and objective measurement avoids much of the subjectivity embedded into the interpretation of behavioral data. Your bathroom scale measures weight (a biometric marker) without bias and does not care about your preferred pronouns, ideology, or whether you think the earth is flat (or how these views influence other aspects of your behavior). Assuming proper scale calibration, you either weigh 250 pounds or you don't. The same reliability applies to neuroimaging systems that measure a variety of chemical, electrical, and hemodynamic responses that reveal brain localization and activation intensity. Neurological measurement is of such precision that through a variety of microbiology techniques we can quantify things like the degree of neural cell excitability,

---

[1] Although localization is similar across the entire human species, variability in brain functionality is widely observed between individuals. Individual variation is a result of the interactive effects of genes and environment and is manifested through gene expression, neurotransmitter activation, hormonal modulation, and peptide synthesis, as discussed on pages 151–154 and elsewhere throughout the subsequent chapters.

which, along with other measures, helps us predict subsequent behavior (Bakermans-Kranenburg & Van Ijzendoorn, 2015). Yes, like all measurements, fluctuations occur in physiological measurement, but variability is a function of individual differences, not a reflection of researcher or experimental bias.

Second, the approach to measuring individual differences in behavioral research is less informative than how similar differences are measured in neuropsychology studies. Behavioral studies typically assemble groups of individuals with certain preexisting conditions with the intent to either manipulate or control a number of factors to see how those factors influence behaviors of interest. Preexisting conditions include demographics, but can also include individual differences in cognitive abilities, beliefs, or emotional states, among many others. Manipulated factors are based on what a researcher believes will influence an outcome such as when trying to determine which circumstances promote optimal motivation when learning a challenging concept. For example, when measuring subject mastery, controls might be put in place to determine the influence of modality of instruction (online vs. face-to-face), instructor temperament (authoritative vs. empathetic), or learner characteristics like degree of interest (high vs. low). Outcome measures would include observable results such as test performance, learning latency, and survey responses. These approaches are designed to elicit specific observable behaviors or capture self-reported experiences.

Behavioral research uses a highly inductive approach to infer general principles or theories based on these observations. This approach is inductive because it moves from specific instances to general conclusions. By example, a researcher might observe that children who are praised for their effort tend to persist longer on completing a jigsaw puzzle. From this observation, they may develop a general theory about the effects of praise on task persistence. Behavioral research often compares an individual's scores on a measure to a normative sample, which represents the typical performance of a population. Individual differences are then interpreted relative to these norms.

Neuropsychology studies, on the other hand, focus on measuring brain-behavior interactions. The same individual differences can be assessed to determine characteristics like reaction time to a request, attentional focus, or the efficiency of learning a new concept to determine how differences relate to underlying neural structures or processes.

Neuropsychological research often begins with existing knowledge about brain-behavior relationships and then seeks to test specific hypotheses based on this knowledge. This approach is more deductive in nature, as it moves from general principles to specific instances. For example, a neuropsychologist might also be interested in the impact of praise on task persistence as described above with the knowledge that the amygdala, the part of the brain that processes fear responses, is crucial for task focus (along with the hippocampus). After all, who cares about task persistence when you're being chased by a rabid dog or more concerned about not appearing dumb in front of your classmates? A study could be designed to test the specific hypothesis that amygdala processing inhibits task persistence because of accelerated anxiety (a fear response). Results could be examined to conclude that focus is maximized when greater brain localization occurs in the prefrontal cortex (PFC), the part of the brain dedicated to *"executive control"* and attention (among others). Neuropsychology studies also use normative comparisons but additionally compare an individual's performance to expectations based on their age, education, and other demographic factors. This approach helps identify deviations from expected performance that may indicate brain impairment, processing optimization, or possible dysfunction. Ultimately, neuropsychological evidence provides a more precise indication of individual differences than the observation type data used in most motivation studies. Comparing the two approaches, we can conclude elevated precision and lower susceptibility to misinterpretation threats when evaluating neuropsychology and behavioral evidence together, than when examining behavioral evidence alone.

Third, biology accounts for factors uncontrollable by behavioral research. A primary criticism of motivation research that relies strictly on behavioral measures is data integrity. Open any book on research methods and you'll see a laundry list of threats to *internal validity*, an explanatory term used to describe the possibility of making false inferences and reaching unjustified conclusions from observed results by erroneously attributing the degree to which a study establishes a trustworthy cause-and-effect relationship between the independent variable (the presumed cause) and the dependent variable (the presumed effect). The potential to reach false conclusions is possible based on dozens of factors far too extensive to discuss here (see Shadish et al., 2002 for a factor list), but plenty can go wrong when dealing with temperamental human beings who are sometimes more concerned about their positive self-image and fragile egos and what impression they might give to others than the actual research study.

As such, indisputable manipulation and control cannot be assured during behavioral interventions. Imagine for a second that you are involved in a research study about work ethics where you couldn't care less about the researcher's success or study outcomes because all you have to do to earn credit for participation is to show up (the standard protocol for college students, upon which much of motivation research is based). It does not matter when responding to questions if you pretend you're George Costanza or if you respond with unwavering honesty because you are conscientious. In other words, behavioral research assumes participant motivation is intact and allegedly equal across individuals. The key word here is "allegedly" because observational data has few controls or standardized ability to determine the intent or integrity of the behavior being measured. Needless to say, integrity of response varies between George Constanza and George Washington. Hypothetically, an individual could feign interest in a measurable outcome while others could robustly invest every ounce of cognitive resources toward task effort, with no way to reliably determine differences between the two differing motivations based on observation of results alone.

Conversely, when using neurological measurement, intent cannot be disguised based on brain localization. If you are afraid of snakes, your insular and amygdala will light up hemodynamically, and your adrenal glands will release neurotransmitters like epinephrine and cortisol, signaling your brain to be alert to the prospective threat. If you are not afraid of snakes and perhaps an aspiring herpetologist, and you encounter a venomous snake (or person), your brain will process the information differently even if you are highly motivated to conceal your bravado. Brain images or electrophysiological recordings do not lie! Neuropsychology data often provides a more direct measure of the underlying neural processes associated with a particular cognitive function or behavior. This can reduce the influence of confounding variables that may affect behavioral measures, such as task difficulty or strategic differences in task performance. Additionally, neurological measures, such as EEG and MEG, have high temporal resolution, allowing researchers to precisely track the timing of neural events. This can help establish temporal precedence between the presumed cause and effect, strengthening causal inferences, an ability impossible to replicate with behavioral research.

Fourth, behavioral and neuropsychological evidence consider the interactivity between context and behavior differently. While neuropsychological research is not without criticism (see below) because of the brief time span of measurement, the basis for interactive influences is cumulative, not situational. When behavioral data is collected (usually in contrived situations) it is the result of the current intervention and nothing more. In fact, most motivation studies will intentionally assess whether prior knowledge or preexisting conditions are not influencing whatever is being measured in the current study. For example, if a researcher is trying to determine if a climate change lesson will change climate change beliefs, an initial measure of climate beliefs is necessary; otherwise there is no way for the researcher to contend that the lesson, not previous knowledge, caused an updated belief change. While this approach is helpful to rule out issues related to sample selection and random distribution of specific traits (like prior knowledge), it discounts the reality that individuals are a sum of collective experiences. The sophistication of measurement to determine cumulative effects of experience are speculative with behavioral measures.

However, neurological research has the ability to measure neurological expression that happened a millisecond, a minute, a day, a month, a year, or 500 years before a specific action is executed by the individual. Robert Sapolsky (2017, 2023), a prominent neuroendocrinologist, explains that understanding the complex interactions between genes, environment, and behavior requires not only examining what happens during a motivation intervention, but also recognizing that true accuracy depends on considering many other past influences. His research reveals there is an intricate interplay between genes and the environment that shapes an individual's behavior and overall functioning, otherwise known as *"gene expression."* More importantly, Sapolsky shows that the influences on gene-environment interactions can be measured by examining neurotransmitters. Sapolsky explains that the levels and functioning of neurotransmitters observed in a "here and now" study, such as how the production of serotonin and dopamine (discussed later), can be influenced by early life stress or trauma, parenting style, and even cultural factors such as whether or not your distant ancestors were farmers or hunters. Gene expression can alter the development of neurological systems as seen in imaging measurements revealing changes in emotional regulation and stress responsivity, among others. In turn, this information can lead to epigenetic changes that alter gene expression and increase or decrease how the brain responds to the cognitive and emotional demands of motivated effort. In summary, neurological approaches reveal the dynamic interplay between genes and the environment in shaping behavior. Knowledge of gene expression ultimately contributes to identifying how individual differences in behavior and psychological functioning develop and persist, information that is unobservable by traditional behavioral inquiries.

Deciphering the neuropsychology of motivated behavior requires clarification of several important points. First, much of the neuropsychology literature examines motivation from an experimental perspective using laboratory rodents. To the casual observer, this type of research is highly reminiscent of behavioral research done by psychologists like B.F. Skinner (Ferster & Skinner, 1957) and Clark Hull (1943), who primarily focused on the mechanics of learning and motivation. Behaviorists believed that motivation for learning was contingent on whether a reward was provided or withheld when an entity demonstrated a desired behavior, otherwise known as *operant conditioning*. Current neuropsychological research is different, relying on evaluations of behavior that consider both external cues and internal brain functioning.

The subsequent discussion here is not advocating a behaviorist or reinforcement perspective of motivation, nor will any research from animal studies be cited to support conclusions. The emphasis here is on the importance of neurological and hormonal functioning as the antecedent of motivated behavior including a strong emphasis on context of application. In this case, context means considering how interactivity among gene expression, neuromodulation, socialization, and culture explains individual differences in motivated behavior. While the behavioral concept of rewards related to approach and avoidance behavior receives particular emphasis throughout the ensuing discussion, rewards are not conceptualized as a result of performing certain actions. Instead, rewards are conceived as the preamble for motivated effort that can either be within the control of the individual or happen spontaneously as a result of the sum of the individual's biological predispositions and environmental tendencies.

Despite the superiority of using biological findings to supplement behavioral interpretations, measures are not flawless. The most contentious concern is the correlational nature of neuropsychological evidence from imaging studies. If presented with a plate of cockroaches and a fork, we do not know if the repulsion sends an avoidance response to your insular cortex or if that brain area produces a motivational reaction prompting your disgust. Likely, there is shared influence, but certainty of origination is questionable (Kim at al., 2016). We must also acknowledge that brain processing is rarely limited to a singular portion of the brain and there can be overlaps, making precise measurement more challenging. Second, the temporality of neurological measurement is limited. Although we can extract information from gene expression and regulation, the practicality of the approach is computationally and pragmatically limited and often invasive; most people don't want electrodes inserted in their brain. Measurement occurs at specific time points and thus only reflects what happens at the precise moment of measurement. Third, neuromonitoring in naturalistic environments is challenging and expensive. While strides have been made to increase the portability of monitoring devices (Tsow et al., 2021), the cost and accuracy of measurement outside of labs leaves plenty of room for improvement. Precise measurement of cell-level neuromodulation is essential going forward (Hu et al., 2024). Fourth, heterogeneity of participants in neuropsychology research can be improved, with recent evidence revealing that social identities have neurological implications (Dhamala et al., 2024). Last, the nomenclature and orientation of most neurological research is highly clinical and, in some cases, lacks both practical significance and application. For example, while it is wonderful to know that orbitofrontal cortex (OFC) neurons in mice dynamically encode different sounds that promote reward discrimination through salience cues (Namboodiri et al., 2019), how can this knowledge be used to promote optimal motivation? Not a whole lot. Thus the following discussion will only include neurological evidence that directly enhances understanding of motivation for human learning and performance.

Neuropsychology Explains How Needs Originate

What gets you out of bed, drives you to tackle challenging tasks, or persevere in the face of obstacles? The answers lie in the intricacies of your brain, where a complex interplay of neural circuits, neurotransmitters, and hormones determine desire, direct attention, and energize actions. The neuropsychology of motivation explores the biological underpinnings of human behavior and how organic changes and differences influence learning and performance. Deciphering neuropsychology means analysis of the brain's reward systems, the bridge between emotion and motivation, and how motivation is regulated and sustained biologically. We will also investigate how individual differences in brain structure and function can influence motivational tendencies, and how external factors like threat perceptions, social context, and cultural or environmental cues can alter motivational states. Now let's see how the sausage is made.

Basic Neurological Functioning

At its core, the nervous system is divided into two main parts, the central nervous system (CNS), comprising the brain and spinal cord, and the peripheral nervous system (PNS), which includes all nerves outside the CNS. The PNS is further subdivided into the somatic nervous system (SNS), controlling voluntary movements, and the autonomic nervous system (ANS), regulating involuntary bodily functions. Neuromodulators influence all systems, with the ANS affecting heart rate, digestion, respiratory rate, pupillary response, urination, and sexual arousal, among others. The ANS plays a crucial role in motivation and is divided into two branches, the sympathetic and parasympathetic systems. These systems work together to maintain homeostasis (the body's brand of internal stability) in response to internal and external environmental demands. Overall, the brain serves as a gatekeeper directing motivational resources to needed areas, while suppressing activity in others. These changes prepare the body for action, a state that can be closely linked to certain types of motivation, particularly those driven by immediate goals or threats.

The sympathetic nervous system, often described as the clichéd "fight or flight" response, mobilizes resources to respond to stress or excitement. When activated, it triggers a cascade of physiological changes including increased heart rate and blood pressure, dilation of airways and pupils, redirection of blood flow to muscles and organs, and the release of glucose for energy. Alternatively, the parasympathetic nervous system, often called the "rest and digest" system, promotes relaxation, conservation of energy, and restoration of bodily functions suppressed by the sympathetic nervous system. Key effects include slowing heart rate, lowering of blood pressure, stimulation of previously repressed digestive function, and trauma recovery via decompression and predisposition for sleep. While seemingly less directly related to motivation, the parasympathetic system plays a vital role in long-term motivational states, particularly those involving sustained effort and goal pursuit, in other words the regulation of motivation. The CNS is the primary focus here because of the crucial role it plays in motivation and learning, and especially because the CNS is responsible for the valuation and processing of reward.

At the lowest level, motivated behavior starts when specialized sensory neurons pick up different environmental cues like sights, sounds, and smells. This sensory information gets passed up to more primitive brain regions like the brainstem and hypothalamus. The sensory inputs are then routed to regions like the amygdala, hippocampus, and frontal cortices where the primary reasoning processes are situated. Motivation emerges from the intricate interplay of various neural circuitry. The PFC is instrumental in goal-directed behavior, playing a key role in planning and executing actions aligned with motivational states (Miller & Cohen, 2001). The PFC's involvement extends to cognitive control, where it regulates motivation and applies learned knowledge to guide behavior during problem-solving. In other words, the PFC assists in the evaluation of "what did I do last time, and did it work?" The PFC integrates the sensory data with our past experiences to guide decision-making based on the current situation and needs. Meanwhile, the orbital PFC (the front part of the brain behind the eyes) makes valuations based on prospective reward, keeping in mind that reward can be anything providing physiological or psychological satisfaction. The cortical outputs target the basil ganglia area and the ventral tegmental area (VTA), which receives converging information about motivationally relevant stimuli. The VTA's dopamine neurons project densely to the nucleus accumbens (NAcc), signaling the motivational value of things and reinforcing actions to obtain rewards or avoid punishments. This dopamine system (described in detail later) is regulated by local GABA neurons in the VTA that activate or inhibit dopamine synthesis conditional on the cost-value calculation (Nieh et al., 2016); high value/low cost and dopamine is optimally synthesized, exceeding baseline levels. By computing mismatches between predicted and actual outcomes, this circuit learns to associate environmental cues with their motivational significance. So, in essence, this hierarchical neural system detects important sensory information, makes predictions about its meaning based on prior experience, evaluates motivational value, and physiologically reinforces behaviors to optimize attainment of goals subjectively determined as vital for survival and well-being.

Emotional considerations are also a critical part of the valuation process. Largely influenced by the limbic system, particularly the amygdala and hippocampus, these areas can either foster or inhibit motivation. The amygdala is crucial for processing emotional salience of stimuli, while the hippocampus contributes to context-dependent emotional responses (Phelps, 2004). Together, they form a circuit important for emotional learning and memory, directly impacting motivational processes. The amygdala and the PFC are cerebral version of the *Hatfields and McCoys*, as the neurological exchange is crucial to assess fear and avoidance learning (don't put you hand on the hot oven or haven't you had enough to drink, Bob?), as well as accounting for the quick emotional response to positive and negative people, places, and things that might easily set us off. The amygdala and the PFC battle it out to determine which behavior is appropriate. By example, after not seeing someone for several years you might want to say "hey, dude you are looking pretty hefty these days" (the amygdala at work). Thankfully, your PFC will intervene preempting the embarrassing snub and keeping a lifetime kinship intact by, instead, saying, "Wow, you look darn healthy!" More information about the unique PFC-amygdala relationship is below, information that is especially valuable when we discuss what it takes to persuade someone to think like you.

Motivation and Neuromodulation

Knowing that motivation to act results from complex interactions between various brain regions, the next step is determining how diverse brain areas communicate with each other, getting us one step closer to the overall goal of optimizing motivation based on neuropsychological evidence. Neuromodulation is the process by which certain neurons alter the properties or activity of other neurons. By analogy, neuromodulation can be conceptualized as functioning like a concert sound board mix where neuromodulators can "turn up" or "turn down" the activity of different neural pathways, just like the sound board technician can accentuate or diminish certain vocals or instruments. Neuromodulators do not necessarily activate or deactivate neural pathways but instead change their sensitivity for response and the degree of connectivity to other inputs. In the context of motivation, neuromodulation plays a crucial role in shaping behavior, including goal-directed decision-making, the valuation of rewards, and the corresponding motivation and emotion that determines when and if we are willing to engage in a task (Sands et al., 2023).

At the most rudimentary level, neuromodulation is like a hormonal delivery system. Some carriers and some products get delivered more efficiently and easier than others. Neuromodulation alters neural excitability, making neurons more or less likely to fire action potentials, which are the shipping points of the neuromodulation process. Through the release of neuromodulators, multiple neurons and synapses can be activated simultaneously (Marder, 2012). *Neurotransmitters* act in similar ways but do not have the broad-based impact of neuromodulators, and the terms, at least in the popular press, are often used interchangeably. However, the timing and duration of neuromodulation does matter for motivation because sometimes we need short bursts of motivated effort, like we do when forcing ourselves out of bed, while other times we need perseverance for longer-term goals, like sustaining motivation to earn a college degree.

For the purposes of understanding motivated behavior, we should recognize that the key deliverable from neuromodulation related to motivation is the synthesis of dopamine (DA), serotonin, norepinephrine (NE), and various endorphins, regardless of delivery by the biological equivalent of Amazon or Federal Express. While the complexity of the reward systems and corresponding pathways justifies its own section, briefly, the major neuromodulatory systems are dopaminergic, serotonergic, noradrenergic, and cholinergic. These systems account for the overall process of neural transmission. DA, the most prominent neuromodulator related to motivation, plays the lead role in reward processing and reinforcement learning. The DA system's activity is closely tied to expectations and valuation, which ultimately determine task-related decision-making and engagement, evaluations that are crucial for updating motivational states based on experience (Schultz, 2007). Serotonin, while less directly linked to reward, plays a significant role in motivational processes by modulating mood, anxiety, and impulsivity. It interacts with the DA system to influence decision-making and behavioral inhibition, key components of motivated behavior (Cools et al., 2011). NE, primarily originating from the locus coeruleus, modulates arousal and attention. Its activity is closely tied to the salience of environmental stimuli, influencing an organism's motivation to engage with its surroundings (Sara & Bouret, 2012). Acetylcholine (ACh), released from basal forebrain nuclei and brainstem regions, influences attention and arousal. It modulates reasoning and can enhance accuracy of sensory perceptions, potentially increasing motivation to attend to specific stimuli (Picciotto et al., 2012). In aggregate, each neurotransmitter has a broad influence on a decision to act. Overall, the nervous system's role in motivation involves various interconnected regions and neuromodulatory systems. Understanding these processes not only advances our knowledge of brain function but also will allow us to determine why sometimes we act and other times in seemingly identical situations we are apathetic, lethargic, and stagnate. Chapter 5 details the impact of neuromodulation on motivation.

Neurologically, when pondering motivated action, the brain roughly recognizes anticipation, execution, and reactivity phases, with each phase reflective of different *types* of neurological processing (Salamone & Correa, 2024). *Anticipation* represents the energizing of prospective action before acting, *execution* is acting upon the expected outcome, while *reactivity* reflects what happens (or doesn't happen) after refractory periods that invigorate future behaviors. If this last sentence triggers a reminder of a male sexual cycle, then you likely understand the temporality of neuromodulation. Although overlap among phases is common, a phase framework is useful to determine what is motivationally relevant at a particular time. Now let's see how all this biological gobbledygook works from a practical perspective.

Anticipation

We all have a waking routine. Pragmatically, getting up might mean letting some light into your room, drinking some water, and heading to the bathroom, or if you are DA deficient, checking your phone before you do anything. Your regime is based in part on the anticipation of your day. While your internal biological clock (i.e., circadian rhythm) matters, your brain does not care if it is Tuesday or Friday. Regardless of day or time, brain function has a significant anticipatory component that activates and energizes the direction and intensity of your subsequent behavior. On face value, it may not seem like much is happening, because most of the neurological calibration takes place automatically, and not in direct consciousness. However neurological functioning will determine everything from the actual movement of your head from your pillow to the speed, vigor, and level of exertion you demonstrate throughout the day. The anticipatory stage is one where there is no doubt concerning the undeniable connection between motivation and motion.

When you transition from sleep to wakefulness, several neurological and physiological changes occur. First, your reticular activating system kicks in to increase overall brain arousal, reducing that groggy, what-day-is-this feeling. Hormone changes such as increased levels of cortisol (a metabolic regulator) promote alertness, while production of melatonin (a sleep neurotransmitter) decreases it. The body temperature, which drops during sleep, begins to rise during the wake-up process. A gradual increase in cognitive functioning occurs as working memory, attention, and decision-making abilities slowly improve through greater production of NE and ACh. Gradual increases in cerebral blood flow follow, particularly in areas involved in arousal and cognitive function. The duration and intensity of this wake-up routine can vary among individuals and can be influenced by factors such as sleep quality, duration, and the stage of sleep from which one awakens. However, neurological circuitry is consistent, continually priming the motivational aspects of your brain, prepping you for whichever environmental conquest you choose to address.

The activation phase is like motivational foreplay. The anticipation of an action involves simultaneous firing of multiple systems related to the impending exertion of effort to reach a goal, whether that goal is three hours of "brain rot" or climbing Mt. Everest. Through the anticipation stage of neurological priming, we can observe the dissociable nature of motivation systems. When unified, urges are a coordinated neural process, such as perceiving a reward not only as having value but also as being helpful to reach an instrumental goal (Salamone et al., 2022). Disassociated means the realization that some aspects of neural circuitry are separated (Berridge, 2007). This distinction becomes increasingly important as we learn how reward manifests neurologically and answer the all-important question concerning whether an intrinsically rewarding activity is associated with similar brain localization and neural pathways as materialistic rewards. While it may not seem obvious, disassociation in motivation-related neural pathways can lead to diminished ability to experience pleasure or satisfaction from typically rewarding activities (Taylor et al., 2022), potentially contributing to conditions such as indecisiveness and poor decision-making, or even worse, anhedonia (Salamone & Corria, 2024).

Neurological disassociation and the differences between the anticipation and execution phases are often examined through a series of tasks where neural activity is tracked. In these situations, an individual is told a task has potentially beneficial outcomes (i.e., do this task correctly and win a prize) or, conversely, the potential action may incur a loss (i.e., do the task wrong and you pay a fine). By no means is this paradigm intended to influence a behavioral action alone but instead is designed to determine which factors make a difference during contemplation of gain or loss and to understand how each situation may project neurologically, based upon quality and satisfaction with achieved outcomes. This paradigm is key because reward anticipation (and prospective loss) engages dopaminergic neurons in the VTA and, as explained below, generates a prediction that may or may not be commensurate with achieved outcomes. Knowing when dopaminergic pathways are optimally activated is the secret sauce to encourage motivation for mastery in a variety of performance outcomes, as described in Chapter 7. If you remember anything from this chapter, remember *you can control DA production*.

DA synthesis from baseline involves numerous comparisons and consistent updating based on historical patterns, emotions, experiences, and interactivity between the individual and their environment (Schultz, 2016). All these factors in combination are highly instrumental in determining what is or is not rewarding and as such have a huge impact on motivated behavior. From the brain's perspective, adaptability builds tenacity and maximizes the power of DA synthesis (Touroutoglou et al., 2020). In other words, how we view outcomes in relation to expectations can foster sustained motivation and impact future performance. English poet Alexander Pope once stated, "Blessed is he who expects nothing, for he shall never be disappointed." Pragmatically, this means some prospective outcomes will be evaluated as satisfying (anticipated value is confirmed), while others will undergo a devaluation process after reflection (anticipated value was questionable). Contingent on the deviation between evaluation and outcomes observed individuals may or may not be satisfied, resulting in some outcomes perceived as rewarding while others are not.

As you might imagine, feeling satisfied about decisions matter, and the brain does not like to be disappointed because dissonance leads to homeostatic imbalance! When considering the possibilities, we can identify four main scenarios: high expectations that are met or exceeded, high expectations that are not met, low expectations that are met or exceeded, and low expectations that are not met. When our expectations are not met, our brain typically responds in one of two ways: first, we may become passive or disengaged, leading to apathy or immobility; alternatively, if the expected outcome was positive and pleasurable, we may develop an intense longing for it and seek more of the same satisfaction. The power of desire can hijack our motivation, determining both our future "likes" and "wants." Perhaps no better illustration of desire is the iconic Lay's potato chip ad campaign engrained in the minds of twentieth-century snackers, "bet you can't eat just one!" As we shall see, we can blame it all on DA, because we almost always want more of whatever we think is a good thing (Lieberman & Long, 2018).

For many of us, even more crucial is what happens when outcomes fall short of expectations, which, according to your neural circuitry, is a form of loss and punishment. Sometimes referred to as a "negative prediction error" (Schultz, 2016) and fully explained below, losses typically result in lower DA. When an outcome is worse than expected (a loss), DA neurons temporarily reduce their firing rate. This causes a transient dip in DA levels below the baseline. In practical terms, dips mean you feel deflated, apathetic, and subject to bouts of procrastination if the task is challenging and important for your success. Imagine the feeling you get when you fail a test, don't get a job offer you want, or your partner leaves you for the postal carrier, and you will know what a DA deficit feels like.

The good news is that DA dips help the brain learn to avoid similar negative outcomes in the future. However, perception of loss triggers a stress response, involving cortisol and other hormones which interact with and modulate DA signaling. While not meeting goals can evoke frustration, disappointment, shame, apathy, indifference, and for some even depression, more importantly DA deficits need to be replaced. When expectations are unfulfilled and we cannot get what we want from goal accomplishment, we resort to less-effective means of DA replacement, like drinking too much coffee, eating carbohydrate dense foods, and engaging in alcohol or substance abuse, all behaviors that evoke DA production. We are also prone to some risky behaviors to fill the DA gap like promiscuity, jumping out of airplanes, or taking imprudent financial risks (Norbury et al., 2013). While some of these strategies *temporarily* improve the situation, other approaches work better (skip to Chapter 7 if you cannot wait to learn how)!

At the most basic level, your brain cares about survival and evolutionary fitness (Stuber, 2023). In this case, survival means optimizing physiological functioning and fitness means interacting with your environment to maximize personal gain. In practice, maximization occurs by securing perceived rewards (i.e., food, sex, and psychological well-being, among others), while concurrently avoiding threats (e.g., illness, aggression, loss of resources, and many more). It does not matter if the reward perception comes from passing by an attractive person who arouses you, the smell of a piece of chocolate cake, or the satisfaction felt when solving a Rubik's cube faster than a robot. While one reward may promote more desire than another at a particular time, from your brain's perspective they each have value. Similarly, you are probably going to flee regardless of being chased by a lion or a bear. In both instances, your neural system will appreciate the flight to safety. What your brain cares about is that familiar concept that you learned about in high school: "homeostasis," or returning your physiological and psychological systems to a state of balance and harmony. The source of the reward, or the method of threat removal is far less consequential than homeostatic restoration (and this is one reason why we can get addicted to bad things; see p. 164). Ultimately, the brain is interested in maximizing resources and minimizing threats. How we satisfy this primal need has consequences, but, as we shall see later, internal stability (i.e., homeostatic balance) matters more than anything else if we want optimal motivation.

The prior few pages have partially explained the concept of reward prediction error (RPE), a foundational neurological principle with substantial explanatory power to explain motivated behavior and described in detail on page 138. Based on whether RPE is achieved or exceeded, a wide variety of neurotransmitters and hormones are activated within the brain and determine how subsequent goals and behaviors will manifest. DA especially plays a crucial role in the neural pathways related to RPE, as it is released when an individual anticipates engaging in an inherently rewarding activity. The release of DA reinforces the behavior that led to the elevated RPE, making it more likely to be repeated in the future. So, it may appear that all we need to do is have low expectations that are exceeded or high expectations that are met and the DA synthesis and subsequent motivational euphoria will be consistent. However, before you get too excited or skip to the chapter on strategies (Chapter 7) to pump up the dope, let's dig deeper into what determines if our reward expectations are met or thwarted.

Execution

First, let's disentangle the meaning of an expectation. After all, what are we seeking and what dictates if we come back for more? Are you looking for a good time? Recognition from your tribe? Feelings of invincibility? Personal development? A second bagel and then a muffin? While a good deal of the neurological research in the past 100 years centers around the pursuit of pleasure and the avoidance of pain (Kringelbach & Berridge, 2010), evaluations of this sort are subjective and based in large part on immutable culture and genetic history (Sapolsky, 2023). In addition, we must account for the reality that sometimes we voluntarily pursue goals that require enduring plenty of pain, like devoting years of your life to earning a college degree or the trauma your body endures when running a marathon. In addition, what you find pleasurable could be repulsive to me. Thus, subjective evaluations of rewards across people are fruitless. Instead, we examine within-person variations as the first step toward understanding what is considered rewarding. Then we can see if any neurological differences exist among different types of rewarding behavior and how we can maximize motivation for goal attainment.

We typically consider something rewarding when it helps us achieve a goal that we find valuable (Simpson & Balsam, 2016), whether the goal is a scoring a plate of french fries or identification of the genetic code to cure a fatal disease. A wide variety of factors will broadly influence value calculations including current physiological states, the environment, personal dispositions, past history, and the degree of success we expect. We will use the value proposition proposed by Simpson and Balsom, who investigated the behavioral neuroscience of motivation from a psychiatric perspective. They indicated that "motivated behaviors represent the actions associated with the highest net value that results from a cost–benefit analysis that encompasses all of the potential influencing factors and processes" (p. 2). Quite simply, our behaviors reflect what is important to us at the moment.

Costs, both psychological and physiological, inhibit perceptions of personal value. Emotional considerations, such as anxiety, fear of failure, and embarrassment associated with attempting a task and failing, can often hold us back. Self-esteem can falter due to damage to one's self-image if the task is not completed successfully. Pragmatically, many humans do not like to exert mental effort when it can be avoided (Toplak et al., 2014); thus, increased *"cognitive load"* is also a consideration. Liabilities aside, even when an outcome is highly desirable, the task complexity and application of skills can be exhausting, such as what we experience when prepping for or taking a high-stakes exam. Alternatively, tasks that are too easy or routine are subject to potential tedium because of repetition and lack of interest. We also have to contend with looking foolish to others; thus, for some, the specter of social comparison is a major psychological cost. Physiological costs are also rampant, including pain, strain, or fatigue associated with the task. Sleep and food deprivation can result if the task requires late night or early morning commitment. Sustained effort might leave less energy for other activities, and too much strain can inhibit motivation for other seemingly less important and easier tasks. Overall, these costs interact with the perceived value and expectancy of success to influence a person's engagement decision.

Thus, to determine value we undertake a complex process of weighing pros and cons. First, your brain assigns values to different outcomes. These values are not fixed—they change based on your past experiences and your current situation. For example, if you're hungry, food becomes more valuable to you. Your brain stores these values from past experiences. When you face a similar situation later, it recalls these stored values. But it does not just use the old information—it updates these values based on your current state and surroundings. Often, there is a gap between when you start an action and when you get the result. During this time, your brain is constantly predicting what the outcome might be. It's like having an inner voice saying, "If I do this, I might get that." Different parts of your brain work together in this process. Some areas focus on predicting rewards, while others help compare different options. Importantly, your brain does not think in terms of absolute values. Instead, it compares options relative to each other and to your current needs. For instance, a small snack might seem great when you're slightly hungry, but not so appealing after a big meal. In other words, reward value shifts depending on the circumstance. This whole process happens automatically, often unconsciously. The cognitive tug-of-war helps you make decisions that are best suited to your current needs and situation. Now that we know cognitively how we determine value and costs, let's look under the hood again and see what's happening neurologically.

Creating Value

To understand how our brain ascribes value to rewards, it is helpful to break down the experience into three main parts. First, we have feelings of pleasure and enjoyment from something rewarding. It's the "yum" factor when you eat your favorite food, let's say tacos. From a neuroscience perspective, this aspect is referred to as "liking." Second, there is motivation or desire to get the reward. It's what makes you crave tacos even when you're not hungry. This aspect of valuation is described as "wanting" and feels like an urge that needs to be satisfied. Neurologically, "wanting" is not about getting to the taco stand, but instead is focused on attention-grabbing cues that increase desire to obtain the taco (more on this later). The third aspect of reward assessment is described as "learning," which happens continuously as the process of evaluation of liking and wanting unfolds. Learning reflects perceptions of satisfaction or frustration when comparing expectations to outcomes and is a key aspect of the reactivity stage of reward valuation. Learning is what happens when connections between the reward and other aspects of reward seeking are forged in your mind, like where you eat your taco or how you felt when you had it. It's how you remember which restaurants have the best taco. Each one of these aspects of reward have different neural mechanisms, each with specific motivational implications (Berridge & Kringelbach, 2015).

On face value, both liking and wanting may appear to be one and the same; however, the neural circuitry of each reveals dramatic differences. "Liking" has hedonic impact due to the sensory benefits derived from a cognitive, social, or cultural experience stimulus or experience (Nyugen et al., 2021), such as doing something that feels good or hanging out with people you enjoy. Hedonic in this case means a conscious, "*affective*" reaction that provides immediate pleasure or enjoyment from an experience. The feeling is typically measured through facial expressions, subjective reports, or behavioral responses. "Wanting," on the other hand, refers to the motivation to obtain a reward and is also referred to as *incentive salience*, or how much something grabs your attention and increases desire toward a goal. Wanting drives goal-directed behavior and can operate both consciously and unconsciously. By example, the smell of coffee has strong incentive salience because it makes you crave a cup, even if you were not thinking about it before. However, even from a definitional and comparison perspective, liking and wanting differ. For example, I like babies, but I definitely do not want one at this point in my life. I try to stay fit and control my weight, but I clearly don't like dieting. Thus, you can want something you don't like and like something you don't want.

While there are important conceptual differences between liking and wanting, the greater impact manifests in where and how the brain reacts to different perceptions of liking and wanting. From a practical perspective, we surely prefer students who possess a strong desire for topic mastery, compared to merely expressing liking of a subject, just as we want unconditional commitment when consummating a long-term relationship in comparison to hearing "I think you are really nice." Fortunately, neuropsychological research reveals the dissociable (separate and different) psychological components of liking and wanting. While there is some overlap, the neural pathways underlying these components are relatively distinct.

You may be curious, now asking yourself "so what do I do with this information?" First, let's remember we strive to determine where and how value is encoded in the brain to potentially enhance value perceptions for the right things. It is challenging to mediate value functioning in absence of localization knowledge. Second, you may have noticed that the preceding three paragraphs under the subheading of "creating value" did not mention DA, and this matters tremendously because when DA synthesis is reduced, so is the insatiable urge to pursue a goal. Third, in the quest to promote optimal learning and performance, most behavioral (and instructional) approaches attempt to generate "interest," a term that implies the need to enjoy (like) the subject that one is studying (Renninger & Hidi, 2022). When learners lack academic motivation or fail to reach their academic goals despite expressing topical interest, we may be puzzled. A closer scrutiny of meta-analysis research exploring the role of interest on achievement indicates a best-case scenario that only 15 percent of the difference in learning outcomes is explained by whether or not a student enjoys/likes a subject, and sometimes interest has little, if any, bearing on knowledge acquisition (Rotgans & Schmidt, 2017). The other 85 percent of the influence on achievement outcomes are a mystery based in part on the reality that liking differs from wanting, and DA synthesis does not necessarily correlate with liking alone. We should not expect optimal motivation in the absence of DA at or below baseline! A similar philosophy applies to performance domains, where tenacity and perseverance are required for success. You could very much want to be an elite athlete, but "When faced with a difficult challenge, such as mastering complex equations or training for a marathon, many individuals will find the effort too costly and withdraw" (Touroutoglou et al., 2020, p. 12). As such, we are left with the ongoing paradox: Why do some of us show grit and resilience and do the harder things, while others bail or resist? Read on and see why DA, not passion, accounts for most of the difference.

Determine Incentive Salience

Wanting comes in several forms, but the form distinction is important based on the relationship with neuromodulation. The type of wanting that we typically encounter is in the form of *cognitive desire*, when we express a deliberate, conscious, and reason-based argument justifying planned behavior. Some examples of this type of wanting might include the longing for a successful career, the desire to learn and understand new concepts, or the yearning for long-term economic security, which could involve saving, investing, and making prudent financial decisions. Wanting can evolve on a more esoteric level too, with desires including the quest to become a more ethical person or fulfilling the moral obligation to reduce one's carbon footprint and live more sustainably, or perhaps the admirable goal of maintaining meaningful personal or professional relationships. While these wants are highly specific, we can also have omnibus desires including the quest for self-improvement in multiple aspects of life, such as being more honest, resilient, or empathetic. The cognitive desires described are characterized by their complexity, the need for planning and sustained effort, and their alignment with personal and cultural values that are highly correlated with long-term goals. Attainment requires balancing multiple factors and may involve overriding more immediate "wants" in pursuit of these broader objectives. We might have to suppress short-term goals like seeing friends or going for a walk to maximize the potential of reaching our long-term objectives. In sum, cognitive desires are often more complex, involving long-term goals, and embrace abstract concepts or values.

When striving toward cognitive desires, it is important to note that brain activation patterns vary depending on the specific cognitive desire and the individual. Cognitive wanting is complex and is primarily mediated by higher-order thinking processes specifically in the PFC, the brain area that is crucial for executive functions, planning, and decision-making. However, several other areas of the brain are typically activated during cognitive desire, particularly those associated with reasoning, and goal-directed behavior. Cognitive wanting implicates the anterior cingulate cortex (ACC), which is primary involved in motivation, error detection, and conflict monitoring, and particularly important for perseverance through challenging tasks (Touroutoglou et al., 2020). In addition, the Orbitofrontal Cortex, which plays a role in decision-making and expectation, encodes the subjective pleasantness of prospective outcomes, which is essential for steering us toward rewarding outcomes and away from aversive ones. However, projections to the striatum (the key part of the reward system) and the part responsible for motivation and goal-directed behavior, while implicated through cognitive desire, has a relatively reduced role especially in comparison to incentive salience wanting and the urges to accomplish a goal.

Incentive salience "wanting" typically refers to a more immediate, visceral, and often-unconscious drive. It is associated with the limbic system in the brain and is tied to emotional and instinctive responses. This type of desire is often related to basic needs or pleasures, like wanting food when you're hungry or wanting to avoid a threatening situation, like putting off a difficult assignment. "Wants" are usually simpler, while cognitive desires can be more nuanced and multifaceted. "Wanting" stems from more primitive brain regions responsible for basic need satisfaction. Yet we may not always be fully aware of our "wants." For example, you might "want" a sugary snack (immediate, visceral desire), but have a cognitive desire to maintain a healthy diet (reasoned, long-term goal). Unfortunately, long-term benefits have discounted reward value, and you can instead easily succumb to these evil impulsive wants under adverse circumstances (such as stress and when you are feeling physically or emotionally overwhelmed). You are especially vulnerable when prompted by a number of incentive salience cues (like advertising or by opening a cabinet and seeing the box of cookies staring back at you)! Long-term reasoning is often subject to failure because we are at the mercy of incentive salience.

Why do we succumb to incentive salience? It's the urge that can lead to great glory or monumental defeat. The thrill of the chase takes priority overachieving the goal. According to hundreds of human reward-based studies (Berridge & Robinson, 2016), only "wanting" is mediated by mesolimbic dopamine systems because wanting promotes desire, and DA is the catalyst, like fuel for the motivational engine. Unlike cognitive wanting, which is consciously experienced and primarily mediated by cortically weighted systems, incentive salience wanting is highly dependent on subcortical mesolimbic DA signals (Berridge, 2023). The challenge is that the DA can either propel us to relentless pursuit of admirable goals or lead us into a downward spiral of uncontrollable addiction.

Deconstructing the liking and wanting distinction has significant practical benefits. When the wanting component becomes dysregulated from DA overload, it can lead to compulsive behavior despite a diminished experience of pleasure (liking) (Berridge & Robinson, 2016). Additionally, the disassociation between incentive salience and liking can inform the development of interventions for disorders involving disruptions in reward processing, such as depression, where anhedonia (a diminished experience of pleasure) is a common symptom. Furthermore, this research has implications for the study of decision-making and reinforcement learning, as it highlights the role of different neural systems in the encoding and retrieval of reward-related information, as well as the attribution of incentive salience to disparate stimuli, which is often exploited by consumer advertising and behavioral economics that are designed to make you want what you didn't know you liked (Bhardwaj et al., 2024).

Reactivity

So, you have engaged in a task. In all likelihood the experience was instrumental, meaning that because of your task engagement there were perceived advantages and/or drawbacks associated with the activity you performed. Keep in mind that the evaluation of outcomes is based on value and mediated by the encoding of positive or negative experiences that are influential on one's future behavior (Schmid et al., 2018). Were you successful (task value increased) or are you now less motivated to engage in the task going forward (task value decreased)? Likely, to determine your ongoing task motivation, you evaluated progress (or lack of) and made a comparison to some sort of standard. That standard might be a prior attempt, a learning standard, or perhaps a comparison of your performance to another person. Contemplating what to do next, you probably considered if task engagement has accomplished anything meaningful. In other words, did the value and utility calculation change, for better or worse?

It is during the reactivity stage, which occurs both during a task and after it is completed, when outcomes are evaluated based on internal and external feedback. Feedback comes in numerous forms and can be as basic as knowing your decisions were correct or incorrect. More substantive feedback might reveal which aspects of your responses, thinking, or strategies were effective and suggesting how you might enhance future outcomes. Self-generated feedback, sometimes called meta-motivational knowledge, would subjectively assess the degree of satisfaction with progress. Regardless of the nature of feedback, the ultimate purpose of the information is to provide useful information for subsequent effort, under the presumption that feedback inspires learning. Feedback valance, either supportive or discouraging, can be instrumental in fostering positive or negative affect based on the evaluation of one's performance. Feedback helps the individual grade their performance and has implications for self-efficacy perceptions or prospective doubt about abilities, subsequent goal setting, and obviously future task motivation. While the type and quality of feedback is important, what matters more is what happens next. From a neuropsychological perspective, regardless of feedback type, feedback perceptions modulate neural activity related to reward processing and almost always reveal that knowledge gains are rewarding (Lee & Kim, 2014).

Learning from experience is motivationally significant because newly acquired knowledge will either increase or decrease future value perceptions. However, not all learning opportunities have a similar or significant impact on learning because some experiences are not considered valuable. We can clearly engage in pointless educational encounters, but even those have consequences on the willingness to engage with particular topics and similar situations going forward. During the reactivity phase, when we assess outcomes that are relevant and meaningful, the experience triggers a complex interplay of several key brain regions and neurotransmitter systems. At the core of ongoing valuation is the ACC and the striatum. The ACC plays a crucial role in tracking uncertainty and facilitating behavioral adaptation, while the striatum is central to reward processing and learning. These regions work in concert with other areas such as the dorsolateral prefrontal cortex, ventromedial prefrontal cortex, and amygdala, forming an interconnected network that enables the brain to adjust behavior based on feedback (Hauser et al., 2014).

Both positive and negative feedback are instrumental in guiding goal-directed behavior, but they operate through somewhat distinct neural pathways. Positive feedback, associated with "Go" learning, increases DA levels in the striatum. This activates D1 dopamine receptors, promoting the repetition of reinforced actions. Conversely, negative feedback, linked to "NoGo" learning, decreases striatal DA, activating D2 dopamine receptors and encouraging the avoidance of unrewarded actions (Frank & Claus, 2006). The role of DA in this process is particularly significant for understanding motivation. When positive outcomes occur, the resulting increase in DA synthesis above baseline in the striatum not only reinforces the associated behavior but also enhances motivation to repeat that action in the future. In other words, when your brain releases dopamine after doing something rewarding, you gradually start to value that action more. On the other hand, negative outcomes lead to a decrease in DA, which reduces the motivation to repeat the unrewarded behavior and incrementally decreases its perceived value.

This dopamine-driven mechanism forms the neurobiological basis for how evaluative feedback shapes motivation and guides goal-directed behavior. Through repeated experiences of positive and negative feedback, the brain continually refines its understanding of which actions are valuable and worth pursuing, and which are better avoided. This process allows for adaptive learning and behavior modification, enabling individuals to optimize their responses to achieve desired outcomes in various situations (Frank et al., 2007). As you might expect, repeated negative evaluations result in apathy toward the responsible task, goal, or experience because in the absence of DA synthesis motivation and movement become stalled or stagnant.

The primary purpose of the reactivity phase is to help predict the viability of similar behavior going forward. In neuroscience terminology, the value/outcome assessment results in a "learned prediction" (Berridge, 2023, p. 933) about future events and the perceived motivation we have to engage in those events. From a neurological perspective, for learning to occur there must be alteration of mental representations or neural pathways. When the individual receives feedback in the form of rewards or punishments for actions, the brain aims to maximize the cumulative reward over time. Considerable research indicates that learning is a type of reward (Galaj & Ranaldi, 2021), and, for the reward to occur, there must be a recognizable difference between the pre- and post-learning state. If the organism finds this beneficial, then learning has occurred and consequently should enhance future predictability of similar behavior (Schultz, 2016). The reward-DA connection is undeniable and ultimately determines what you will or will not do.

Now, we should recognize three broad-based conclusions based on the biology of reward. First, experiences are encoded neurologically. These experiences activate specific brain regions, which results in neuromodulation that either increases or decreases the probability and intensity of the behavior going forward. Second, although not explicitly explained, the brain is in a perpetual mode of making predictions, and these speculations are grounded on what we subjectively perceive to be rewarding. When predictions are better than expected, the person values the behavior more and expects that repeating the behavior is beneficial. If the behavior is unsatisfying, the individual will be less motivated to repeat the behavior. For some, these conclusions may be reminiscent of the basic principles of instrumental learning that suggest individuals acquire behavior and skills based on the consequences of their actions. However, unlike historical behavioral views of learning, the current perspective embraces the influence of cognitive, social, and situational factors as highly influential for value calculations. Withstanding the dynamic influences, as the brain learns what is more or less beneficial than expected, neuromodulation accentuates the consequences of the behavior and ultimately the type and degree of modulation will determine what the person does next.

Positive Expectancies + Reward = INMO

What is explained above is the concept of reward prediction error. RPE links motivation and learning, particularly when instrumental goals are at stake. RPE plays a crucial role in how we respond to task demands (Hamid et al., 2016) and the ensuing decisions we make because RPE serves as a learning signal that drives behavioral adaptation. RPE is the difference between the expected reward and the actual reward received for an action. RPE can be positive (when the reward is better than expected) or negative (when the reward is worse than expected). In essence, RPE is the consequence of the feedback derived from the expectancy-value calculation that ultimately teaches the individual under which circumstances their thoughts and behaviors are personally productive and thus rewarding. In practice, RPE is primarily a learning mechanism. It teaches us whether a behavior is worth repeating by comparing the actual outcome to our expectations. When our actions result in a higher RPE than anticipated, it reinforces that behavior, encouraging us to repeat it in the future. Conversely, when actions lead to a lower RPE than expected, it signals a need for change. This might mean modifying, reducing, or even eliminating specific behaviors to achieve better outcomes. In essence, RPE guides our decision-making process, helping us optimize our actions to maximize positive outcomes and minimize negative ones.

Ironically, RPE is not an error at all, but a way for your brain to realize deviation of outcome from expectation. In the brain, the RPE signals one of two messages, primarily designed to encourage environmental adaptation. If the personal expectation of what is rewarding needs to be adjusted, either the prediction was improperly calibrated with the achieved outcome or the behavior displayed may need to change (Schultz, 2016). As such, RPE serves as a way to update value estimates of actions or states. Positive RPEs strengthen the likelihood of repetition, while negative RPEs decrease the likelihood. Thus, RPE is instrumental in the balance between exploring new options or using known rewards. Large RPEs might encourage exploration of alternatives, while small RPEs might promote exploitation of current knowledge. By continuously updating expectations based on RPEs, we adapt to changing environments and optimize our behavior. In today's world, a negative RPE might be a catalyst for you to buy a different brand of chips the next time you go shopping, or to stop eating junk food altogether. However, historical RPEs have had immense consequences. Just imagine, a naive Christopher Columbus landing on the shores of the Bahamas in 1492 thinking he was in China. While Columbus did not find the expected route to Asia, he did discover new lands with far greater potential for resources resulting in a huge and unexpected RPE. His "error" led to increased investment in exploration and eventually population of the Americas by Europeans. Positive RPE contributed to more "discoveries" and sadly colonization, with the consequences changing the lives of Indigenous peoples for centuries to come.

The anticipation of positive RPEs (i.e., better-than-expected outcomes) not only facilitates learning but also motivates behavior. In the brain, DA neurons encode RPE (Hamid et al., 2016; Rutledge et al., 2010). DA release correlates with positive RPEs, while a dip in DA signaling corresponds to negative RPEs. This DA signaling is believed to modulate synaptic plasticity, facilitating learning at the neural level. DA neurons, primarily located in the VTA and substantia nigra, respond to positive RPEs by increasing their firing rate (Sands et al., 2023). When a positive RPE occurs, it triggers a phasic (short-lived, but intense) release of DA in target areas such as the striatum, NAcc, and PFC. Positive RPEs not only cause immediate DA release but also stimulate increased DA synthesis. The increased DA synthesis resulting from positive RPEs creates a positive feedback loop. More available DA means stronger signaling when future positive RPEs occur, potentially enhancing learning and motivation. In addition, recent evidence suggests a similar but independent network of punishment predictive errors (PPEs), which encode adaptive punishment learning signals (Sands et al., 2023). Like RPEs, PPEs trigger DA fluctuations based on the prospect of loss from engaging in certain behaviors compared to actual losses. This suggests DA release increases for larger-than-expected punishments and decreases for smaller-than-expected punishments. In aggregate, both phasic and tonic release of DA will vastly influence brain receptivity to information with broad impact on future learning, decision-making, and how we engage with others (see Chapter 5 for the dirty details).

The relationship between learning and reward prediction error highlights how our brains are constantly trying to build better models of the world to guide behavior. This process is dynamic, allowing for continuous adaptation to changing circumstances and receptivity for new information. By leveraging RPE knowledge, more effective learning environments can be designed that optimize the brain's natural reward system. For instance, teachers can structure lessons and activities to create positive surprises or exceed students expectations, triggering positive RPEs that strengthen learning and memory formation. This could involve introducing unexpected connections between concepts, presenting information in novel ways, or offering rewards that are slightly better than anticipated. Additionally, understanding RPEs can help educators calibrate the difficulty of tasks to maintain an optimal level of challenge—not too easy to be boring, nor too difficult to be discouraging—keeping students in a state where they frequently experience positive RPEs as they progress. Moreover, knowledge of RPEs can inform feedback practices and assessment strategies. Feedback that highlights unexpected positive outcomes or improvements can be reinforced through positive RPEs. This approach can be particularly effective in gamified learning environments, where the timing and nature of rewards can be carefully controlled to maximize positive RPEs and, consequently, learning outcomes (Luria et al., 2021). By integrating RPE principles into educational practices, teachers can create more engaging, motivating, and effective learning experiences that align with the brain's natural learning mechanisms. It is worth noting that while RPE is a powerful explanatory framework, it does not account for all types of learning. Other learning mechanisms, such as those involved in declarative memory or skill acquisition, generally operate on different principles, as do perceptual and observational learning.

Decisions to engage in and persist with worthwhile endeavors are universally influenced by the balance between achieving desired outcomes and accepting their consequences. This applies to both professional activities in work or school and intrinsically motivated personal development. Motivation cannot develop or persist without perceived benefits. As SDT emphasized, competency perceptions are a fundamental need, and self-determination is unlikely without need satisfaction. Individuals perceive this satisfaction as rewarding, regardless of its form. Consequently, the intensity of expected reward determines how likely an individual will feel and remember the satisfaction experienced, thus influencing behavior repetition (Esch & Stefano, 2010). Michaelsen and

Esch (2021) concluded in their study on how rewards promote healthy behavior, "Reward does not lie in the stimulus or goal itself, but in the composite of active psychological and corresponding neurobiological processes that occur in context of positive anticipation (expectation) and as a subsequent reaction to a stimulus or goal" (p. 4). While biological reactions to reward are relatively predictable, reward perceptions are not. Understanding these contingencies is crucial before we can effectively apply neuropsychological findings to leverage the power of rewards.

Reward Caveats

Chapter 3 outlined a series of contingencies related to the power of rewards, most notably the subjectivity of reward, type of reward, and reward timing. Each one of these factors has a broad influence on reward effectiveness. As we now know, ineffective rewards will lower RPE and cause a negative feedback loop, discounting the power of DA synthesis with the potential for demotivating the individual, if DA remains at or below baseline. Complicating the effectiveness of rewards and the explanatory power of RPE is the reality that many times individuals may not have conscious awareness of what rewards them at a particular time or in a particular context. Implicit learning occurs when the brain learns to associate certain stimuli or behaviors without direct perceptual awareness and when lacking attentional volition. Implicit learning can create unconscious reward associations, such as what happens when young children learn language rules despite minimal corrective feedback, or when individuals succumb to cognitive bias like when unknowingly showing preferences for certain ethnicities or genders. Neurotransmitter release, which is associated with reward, can occur in response to stimuli without realizing the rewarding nature of the stimulus. In other words, we can feel good and motivated yet not know exactly why. Conversely, we can feel apathetic and not be able to understand the reason for seeming unjustified malaise.

Additionally, rewards can backfire, resulting in a "boomerang" effect whereby the behavior intending to be modified changes in an unintended direction. By example, warning labels on high-risk products like vapes are known to increase dangerous behavior because mandated requirements and what some people actually want differ dramatically. History is replete with offering supposed rewards that fail miserably. Some examples include ratings on television programs to curb viewership of violent programs that wound up increasing viewership after the warnings (Bushman & Stack, 1996) and the infamous India snake incident of the early twentieth century. When colonializing India, the British government in Delhi was concerned about the number of venomous cobra snakes in the city. To try and reduce the cobra population, they offered a bounty or reward for every dead cobra brought to the authorities. Initially, this program seemed to work as large numbers of dead cobras were being turned in and people started earning money. However, over time, people began to breed and farm cobras specifically to kill them and claim the reward bounty. When the government became aware of this reverse effect where the bounty was actually increasing the cobra population, they scrapped the reward program. But then the cobra breeders, no longer able to claim bounties, simply released their stockpiled cobras into the city, exacerbating the original snake problem even further. This situation illustrates the "cobra effect" or perverse incentive—when an attempted solution to a problem inadvertently makes the problem worse through people exploiting or responding perversely to the incentive put in place. The parable has become a classic example in economics, game theory, and policy studies of how improperly designed incentive systems can backfire disastrously by failing to account for irrational human motivation and behavior. What it really means is that the business of rewards is highly complex and personalized and subjective to a variety of biases, many of which were discussed in Chapter 3.

Ultimately, the brain is governed by a group of structures and pathways that are activated whenever we experience something rewarding, regardless of motivation or the reward intention. To summarize where we are now, the key parts of the brain involved in reward-based motivated action primarily include the following:

1. Ventral tegmental area: The VTA is the primary source of DA in the reward system, and DA is released when the brain encounters a rewarding stimulus. The VTA primarily projects to the NAcc.
2. Ventral striatum: Processes reward-related information received from the VTA and is primarily activated in response to reward anticipation and reward-based learning translating motivation into action.

3. Nucleus accumbens: The NAcc is part of the ventral striatum. It is often referred to as the brain's "pleasure center" of the brain, where it is responsible for processing and reinforcing the feelings of well-being and satisfaction that encourage us to repeat behaviors that are thought to be beneficial.
4. Substantia nigra: While more associated with motor control, it also plays a role in reward, providing dopaminergic input to the dorsal striatum, influencing motor control and habit formation.
5. Prefrontal cortex: The PFC receives dopaminergic projections from the VTA. It helps in assessing the value of rewards in the context of current goals and long-term consequences. And as such, the PFC acts as the brain's executive control, contributing to decision-making processes related to reward-seeking behaviors.
6. Orbital prefrontal cortex: This part of the PFC is crucial in representing the subjective value of rewards. It helps encode the expected reward or punishment associated with different choices. After an action is taken, the OFC is involved in evaluating RPE. This comparison is essential for learning and updating future expectations.
7. Amygdala: Part of the limbic system that governs the brain's response to fear and threat, the amygdala receives dopaminergic input from the VTA. The amygdala plays a crucial role in attaching emotional significance to stimuli, including rewards. It helps in assessing the emotional valence (positive or negative) of rewards and potential rewards and interfaces with the PFC in the decision-making process.

Ultimately, these areas all interact and contribute to the signaling and transmission of DA, which is the high-octane fuel that keeps the reward engine running. While each area has a specific function, all work together as a team to determine what the organism deems to be important and if the perceived value is worthy of pursuit. The captain of "Team Reward" is DA and thus we delve deeper into how the captain manages the reward process and propels the individual into action or complacency that can often result in stagnation.

References

Bakermans-Kranenburg, M. J., & Van Ijzendoorn, M. H. (2015). The hidden efficacy of interventions: Gene× environment experiments from a differential susceptibility perspective. *Annual Review of Psychology, 66*(1), 381–409. https://doi.org/10.1146/annurev-psych-010814-015407

Bardach, L., & Murayama, K. (2025). The role of rewards in motivation—Beyond dichotomies. *Learning and Instruction, 96*, 102056. https://doi.org/10.31219/osf.io/hgbw4

Benjafield, J. G. (2020). Vocabulary sharing among subjects belonging to the hierarchy of sciences. *Scientometrics, 125*, 1965–1982. https://doi.org/10.1007/s11192-020-03671-7

Berridge, K. C. (2023). Separating desire from prediction of outcome value. *Trends in Cognitive Sciences, 27*(10), 932–946. https://doi.org/10.1016/j.tics.2023.07.007

Berridge, K. C. (2007). The debate over dopamine's role in reward: The case for incentive salience. *Psychopharmacology, 191*(3), 391–431. https://doi.org/10.1007/s00213-006-0578-x

Berridge, K. C., & Kringelbach, M. L. (2015). Pleasure systems in the brain. *Neuron, 86*(3), 646–664. https://doi.org/10.1016/j.neuron.2015.02.018

Berridge, K. C., & Robinson, T. E. (2016). Liking, wanting, and the incentive-sensitization theory of addiction. *American Psychologist, 71*(8), 670–679. https://doi.org/10.1037/amp0000059

Bhardwaj, S., Kaushik, N., & Arora, M. (2024). Does your brain have a buy button?: A neuro marketing approach with sensory branding. In R. Malik, S. Malhan, & M. Arora (Eds.), *Sensible selling through sensory neuromarketing* (pp. 210–229). IGI Global. https://doi.org/10.4018/979-8-3693-4236-7

Bushman, B. J., & Stack, A. D. (1996). Effects of warning labels on attraction to television violence. *Journal of Experimental Psychology: Applied, 2*(3), 207–226. https://doi.org/10.1037/1076-898x.2.3.207

Cools, R., Nakamura, K., & Daw, N. D. (2011). Serotonin and dopamine: unifying affective, activational, and decision functions. *Neuropsychopharmacology, 36*(1), 98–113. https://doi.org/10.1038/npp.2010.121

Dhamala, E., Ricard, J. A., Uddin, L. Q., Galea, L. A., Jacobs, E. G., Yip, S. W., ... & Holmes, A. J. (2024). Considering the interconnected nature of social identities in neuroimaging research. *Nature Neuroscience, 28*(2), 1–12. https://doi.org/10.1038/s41593-024-01832-y

Esch, T., & Stefano, G. B. (2010). Endogenous reward mechanisms and their importance in stress reduction, exercise and the brain. *Archives of Medical Science, 6*(3), 447–455. https://doi.org/10.5114/aoms.2010.14269

Ferster, C. B., & Skinner, B. F. (1957). *Schedules of reinforcement.* Appleton-Century-Crofts. https://doi.org/10.1037/10627-000

Frank, M. J., & Claus, E. D. (2006). Anatomy of a decision: Striato-orbitofrontal interactions in reinforcement learning, decision making, and reversal. *Psychological Review, 113*(2), 300–326. https://doi.org/10.1037/0033-295X.113.2.300

Frank, M. J., Moustafa, A. A., Haughey, H. M., Curran, T., & Hutchison, K. E. (2007). Genetic triple dissociation reveals multiple roles for dopamine in reinforcement learning. *Proceedings of the National Academy of Sciences, 104*(41), 16311–16316. https://doi.org/10.1073/pnas.0706111104

Galaj, E., & Ranaldi, R. (2021). Neurobiology of reward-related learning. *Neuroscience & Biobehavioral Reviews, 124,* 224–234. https://doi.org/10.1016/j.neubiorev.2021.02.007

Hamid, A. A., Pettibone, J. R., Mabrouk, O. S., Hetrick, V. L., Schmidt, R., Vander Weele, C. M., ... & Berke, J. D. (2016). Mesolimbic dopamine signals the value of work. *Nature Neuroscience, 19*(1), 117–126. https://doi.org/10.1038/nn.4173

Hauser, T. U., Iannaccone, R., Stämpfli, P., Drechsler, R., Brandeis, D., Walitza, S., & Brem, S. (2014). The feedback-related negativity (FRN) revisited: New insights into the localization, meaning and network organization. *NeuroImage, 84,* 159–168. http://dx.doi.org/10.1016/j.neuroimage.2013.08.028

Hidi, S. (2016). Revisiting the role of rewards in motivation and learning: Implications of neuroscientific research. *Educational Psychology Review, 28,* 61–93. https://doi.org/10.1007/s10648-015-9307-5

Hu, Z., Yang, Y., Gong, Y., Chukwu, C., Ye, D., & Yue, Y. (2024). Airy-beam holographic sonogenetics for advancing neuromodulation precision and flexibility. *Proceedings of the National Academy of Sciences,* June 17, 2024. https://doi.org/10.1073/pnas.2402200121

Hull, C. (1943). *Principles of behavior: An introduction to behavior theory.* Appelton-Century.

Kim, S. I., Reeve, J., & Bong, M. (2016). Introduction to motivational neuroscience. In S. I. Kim, J. Reeve, & M. Bong (Eds.), *Recent developments in neuroscience research on human motivation* (pp. 1–19). Emerald Group Publishing Limited. https://doi.org/https://doi.org/10.1108/S0749-742320160000019022

Kringelbach, M. L., & Berridge, K. C. (2010). The functional neuroanatomy of pleasure and happiness. *Discovery Medicine, 9*(49), 579–587. https://doi.org/10.1016/j.tics.2009.08.006

Lee, W., & Kim, S. (2014). Effects of achievement goals on challenge seeking and feedback processing: Behavioral and fmri evidence. *PLoS One, 9*(9), e107254. https://doi.org/10.1371/journal.pone.0107254

Lee, W., & Reeve, J. (2017). Identifying the neural substrates of intrinsic motivation during task performance. *Cognitive Affective Behavioral Neuroscience, 17*, 939–953. https://doi.org/10.3758/s13415-017-0524-x

Lieberman, D. Z., & Long, M. E. (2018). *The molecule of more: How a single chemical in your brain drives love, sex, and creativity--and will determine the fate of the human race*. BenBella Books.

Locke, E. A., & Schattke, K. (2019). Intrinsic and extrinsic motivation: Time for expansion and clarification. *Motivation Science, 5*(4), 277–290. https://doi.org/10.1037/mot0000116

Luria, E., Shalom, M., & Levy, D. A. (2021). Cognitive neuroscience perspectives on motivation and learning: Revisiting self-determination theory. *Mind, Brain, and Education, 15*(1), 5–17. https://doi.org/10.1111/mbe.12275

Marder, E. (2012). Neuromodulation of neuronal circuits: Back to the future. *Neuron, 76*(1), 1–11. https://doi.org/10.1016/j.neuron.2012.09.010

Martin, A. J., & Burns, E. C. (2023). Gaps in contemporary motivation research: A biopsychological perspective. In M. Bong, J. Reeve, & Sung-il Kim (Eds.), *Motivation Science: Controversies and insights* (online edition). Oxford Academic. https://doi.org/10.1093/oso/9780197662359.003.0062

Michaelsen, M. M., & Esch, T. (2021). Motivation and reward mechanisms in health behavior change processes. *Brain Research, 1757*, 147309. https://doi.org/10.1016/j.brainres.2021.147309

Miele, D. B., Fujita, K., & Scholer, A. A. (2024). The role of metamotivational knowledge in the regulation of motivation. *Motivation Science*. Advance online publication. https://doi.org/10.1037/mot0000336

Miller, E. K., & Cohen, J. D. (2001). An integrative theory of prefrontal cortex function. *Annual Review of Neuroscience, 24*(1), 167–202. https://doi.org/10.1146/annurev.neuro.24.1.167

Namboodiri, V. M. K., Otis, J. M., van Heeswijk, K., Voets, E. S., Alghorazi, R. A., Rodriguez-Romaguera, J., ... & Stuber, G. D. (2019). Single-cell activity tracking reveals that orbitofrontal neurons acquire and maintain a long-term memory to guide behavioral adaptation. *Nature Neuroscience, 22*(7), 1110–1121. https://doi.org/10.1038/s41593-019-0408-1

Nieh, E. H., Vander Weele, C. M., Matthews, G. A., Presbrey, K. N., Wichmann, R., Leppla, C. A., ... & Tye, K. M. (2016). Inhibitory input from the lateral hypothalamus to the ventral tegmental area disinhibits dopamine neurons and promotes behavioral activation. *Neuron, 90*(6), 1286–1298. https://doi.org/10.1016/j.neuron.2016.04.035

Norbury, A., Manohar, S., Rogers, R. D., & Husain, M. (2013). Dopamine modulates risk-taking as a function of baseline sensation-seeking trait.

Journal of Neuroscience, 33(32), 12982–12986. https://doi.org/10.1523/jneurosci.5587-12.2013

Phelps, E. A. (2004). Human emotion and memory: Interactions of the amygdala and hippocampal complex. *Current Opinion in Neurobiology, 14*(2), 198–202. https://doi.org/10.1016/j.conb.2004.03.015

Picciotto, M. R., Higley, M. J., & Mineur, Y. S. (2012). Acetylcholine as a neuromodulator: Cholinergic signaling shapes nervous system function and behavior. *Neuron, 76*(1), 116–129. https://doi.org/10.1016/j.neuron.2012.08.036

Reeve, J., & Lee, W. (2019a). Motivational neuroscience. In R. M. Ryan (Ed.), *The Oxford handbook of human motivation*. Oxford University Press.

Reeve, J., & Lee, W. (2019b). A neuroscientific perspective on basic psychological needs. *Journal of Personality, 87*(1), 102–114. https://doi.org/10.1111/jopy.12390

Reiss, S. (2012). Intrinsic and extrinsic motivation. *Teaching of Psychology, 39*(2), 152–156. https://doi.org/10.1177/0098628312437704

Renninger, K. A., & Hidi, S. E. (2022). Interest: A unique affective and cognitive motivational variable that develops. In A. J. Elliot (Ed.), *Advances in motivation science* (Vol. 9, pp. 179–239). Elsevier. https://doi.org/10.1016/bs.adms.2021.12.004

Rotgans, J. I., & Schmidt, H. G. (2017). The relation between individual interest and knowledge acquisition. *British Educational Research Journal, 43*(2), 350–371. https://doi.org/10.1002/berj.3268

Rutledge, R. B., Dean, M., Caplin, A., & Glimcher, P. W. (2010). Testing the reward prediction error hypothesis with an axiomatic model. *Journal of Neuroscience, 30*(40), 13525–13536. https://doi.org/10.1523/jneurosci.1747-10.2010

Ryan, R. M., & Deci, E. L. (2017). *Self-determination theory: Basic psychological needs in motivation, development, and wellness*. Guilford Publications.

Ryan, R. M., & Deci, E. L. (2019). Research on intrinsic and extrinsic motivation is alive, well, and reshaping 21st-century management approaches: Brief reply to Locke and Schattke (2019). *Motivation Science, 5*(4), 291–294. https://doi.org/10.1037/mot0000128

Salamone, J. D., & Correa, M. (2024). The neurobiology of activational aspects of motivation: Exertion of effort, effort-based decision making, and the role of dopamine. *Annual Review of Psychology, 75*(1), 1–32. https://doi.org/10.1146/annurev-psych-020223-012208

Salamone, J. D., Ecevitoglu, A., Carratala-Ros, C., Presby, R. E., Edelstein, G. A., Fleeher, R., ... & Correa, M. (2022). Complexities and paradoxes in understanding the role of dopamine in incentive motivation and instrumental action: Exertion of effort vs. anhedonia. *Brain Research Bulletin, 182*, 57–66. https://doi.org/10.1016/j.brainresbull.2022.01.019

Sands, L. P., Jiang, A., Liebenow, B., DiMarco, E., Laxton, A. W., Tatter, S. B., ... & Kishida, K. T. (2023). Subsecond fluctuations in extracellular dopamine encode reward and punishment prediction errors in humans. *Science Advances, 9*(48), eadi4927. https://doi.org/10.1126/sciadv.adi4927

Sapolsky, R. M. (2017). *Behave: The biology of humans at our best and worst*. Penguin.

Sapolsky, R. M. (2023). *Determined: A science of life without free will*. Penguin.

Sara, S. J., & Bouret, S. (2012). Orienting and reorienting: the locus coeruleus mediates cognition through arousal. *Neuron, 76*(1), 130–141. https://doi.org/10.1016/j.neuron.2012.09.011

Schmid, P. C., Hackel, L. M., & Amodio, D. M. (2018). Power effects on instrumental learning: Evidence from the brain and behavior. *Motivation Science, 4*(3), 206–226. https://doi.org/10.1037/mot0000088.supp

Schultz, W. (2007). Multiple dopamine functions at different time courses. *Annual Review Neuroscience, 30*(1), 259–288. https://doi.org/10.1146/annurev.neuro.28.061604.135722

Schultz, W. (2016). Dopamine reward prediction error coding. *Dialogues in Clinical Neuroscience, 18*(1), 23–32. https://doi.org/10.31887/dcns.2016.18.1/wschultz

Schutz, P. A., & Muis, K. R. (Eds.). (2024). *Handbook of educational psychology* (4th ed.). Routledge. https://doi.org/10.4324/9780429433726

Shadish, W. R., Cook, T. D., & Campbell, D. T. (2002). *Experimental and quasi-experimental designs for generalized causal inference*. Houghton Mifflin.

Simpson, E. H., & Balsam, P. D. (2016). *The behavioral neuroscience of motivation: An overview of concepts, measures, and translational applications* (pp. 1–12). Springer International Publishing. https://doi.org/10.1007/7854_2015_402

Stuber, G. D. (2023). Neurocircuits for motivation. *Science, 382*(6669), 394–398. https://doi.org/10.1126/science.adh8287

Taylor, W. D., Zald, D. H., Felger, J. C., Christman, S., Claassen, D. O., Horga, G., ... & Rutherford, B. R. (2022). Influences of dopaminergic system dysfunction on late-life depression. *Molecular Psychiatry, 27*(1), 180–191. https://doi.org/10.1038/s41380-021-01265-0

Toplak, M. E., West, R. F., & Stanovich, K. E. (2014). Assessing miserly information processing: An expansion of the Cognitive Reflection Test. *Thinking & Reasoning, 20*(2), 147–168. https://doi.org/10.1080/13546783.2013.844729

Touroutoglou, A., Andreano, J., Dickerson, B. C., & Barrett, L. F. (2020). The tenacious brain: How the anterior mid-cingulate contributes to achieving goals. *Cortex, 123*, 12–29. https://doi.org/10.1016/j.cortex.2019.09.011

Tsow, F., Kumar, A., Hosseini, S. H., & Bowden, A. (2021). A low-cost, wearable, do-it-yourself functional near-infrared spectroscopy (DIY-fNIRS) headband. *HardwareX, 10*, e00204. https://doi.org/10.1016/j.ohx.2021.e00204

Vansteenkiste, M., Ryan, R. M., & Soenens, B. (2020). Basic psychological need theory: Advancements, critical themes, and future directions. *Motivation and Emotion, 44*(1), 1–31. https://doi.org/10.1007/s11031-019-09818-1

Wieczorek, O., Unger, S., Riebling, J., Erhard, L., Koß, C., & Heiberger, R. (2021). Mapping the field of psychology: Trends in research topics 1995–2015. *Scientometrics, 126*(12), 9699–9731. https://doi.org/10.1007/s11192-021-04069-9

Yeung, A. W., Goto, T. K., & Leung, W. K. (2017). At the leading front of neuroscience: A bibliometric study of the 100 most-cited articles. *Frontiers in Human Neuroscience, 11*, 363. https://doi.org/10.3389/fnhum.2017.00363

5

The Modulators

Chapter Outline

Gene Expression and Neuromodulation	151
Dopamine (DA)	154
Other Neuromodulators	171
Team Cohesiveness	186

Gene Expression and Neuromodulation

Despite the diversity in our goals and motivations, the neurological structure of the human mind remains fundamentally similar across individuals, especially regarding brain localization. While we may seek different things and have unique ways of achieving our goals, motivation and reward processing is essentially identical across individuals. The previous chapter emphasized that we are all driven by internal urges that propel our motivations. However, it is important to understand that these urges stem from *physiological* need satisfaction rather than the specific goals themselves. Whether one aspires to visit Paris or Parsippany, devour pasta or pastry, become a politician or a plumber, the brain's reward system activates in similar ways in the quest to satisfy whatever urge is desired. The uniformity in neural processing is analogous to cultural diversity: while our individual appearance, beliefs, and needs may vary widely, the underlying architecture that governs our thoughts and responses to external stimuli are largely the same across human beings.

The variations we observe are primarily the result of deeply engrained sociocultural differences that have been inherited over time that result in gene expression based on when, where, and how we interact with the environment and others (Sapolsky, 2017). Gene expression is the process by which the information encoded in a gene is used to synthesize a functional gene outcome, like the production of hormones and proteins that eventually manifest in behaviors. The synthesis process has indirect relevance to understanding rewards, so we will skip the gritty synthesis details. However, depending on variations in gene expression, there is a measurable impact on the baseline level of neuromodulators and how the targeted receptor cells respond to neurotransmission. Genes provide the essential instructions for the production and regulation of neuromodulators (e.g., DA, serotonin, epinephrine, and ACh among others) and how those modulators are expressed in specific neurons. Expression levels affect baseline production and thus lead to differences in patterns and variations in neuromodulation between individuals. These variations can impact the amount of neuromodulators produced, the sensitivity of neurons to these neuromodulators, and the rate at which neuromodulators are broken down (Maloney, 2021), eventually influencing our thinking, motivation, and behavior. This process is known as creating neural plasticity, which is a change in the structure and function of the neuronal system.

Gene expression is influenced by environmental factors, potentially leading to long-term changes in neuromodulation systems. For example, early life stress from child abuse or neglect reduces methylation (protein production) in certain genes that result in the compromised ability of the neurotransmitter serotonin (a stress and mood regulator) to fine-tune an appropriate stress response. Basically, the impact of abuse switches off the transporter gene that affects serotonin signaling and reuptake in the brain. The result of under-methylation is an increased risk for depression and other stress-related disorders in adulthood (Beach et al., 2010). In other words, the serotonin example reveals how the gene-environment interaction contributes to the diversity of human behavior and cognition. While the basic processes are similar across individuals, variations in gene expression can lead to differences in how neuromodulatory systems function, potentially influencing traits like personality, cognitive abilities, and susceptibility to certain neurological or psychiatric conditions.

While pharmacological interventions like Prozac can subdue the effects of epigenetic changes like reduced methylation, gene expression patterns also change over our lifespan without using drugs! These changes, particularly those related to neuromodulation, contribute to neural plasticity as well as behavioral differences between individuals. While the fundamental mechanisms of goal-directed behavior are similar across individuals due to shared neurological architecture, there are still individual variations in how these processes play out. Gene expression is key, but not the only factor because the modulators (like DA, serotonin, NE) are also critical in goal-directed behavior and reward attainment. Neuromodulators are the physiological messengers that deliver the psychological rewards that we crave. Just as we need transportation to reach a destination, we need a mechanism to attain our rewards, and neuromodulators serve that role. The modulators influence much of our day-to-day functioning, including how much motivation we have, the effort we put forth, the degree of comfort and satisfaction with our decisions, and what we actually learn from experience. Individuals can broadly differ in the efficiency of these processes, the strength of connections between relevant brain regions, and the balance of different neuromodulatory systems. In essence, while we share common biological mechanisms, the unique combination of gene expression, environmental experiences, and neuromodulation variations all work together contributing to how our wants and desires are expressed and satisfied.

To fully understand how rewards control motivation, we must master the roles of individual neurotransmitters and how they work together to modulate the reward system. The key challenge in describing each influence lies in distinguishing between the types and impacts of neurological messengers, which are confusingly described as both neurotransmitters and neuromodulators. Each is crucial for neural signaling, yet they operate in distinct but interconnected ways. Neurotransmitters directly transmit signals across synapses between neurons, while neuromodulators modify or modulate neurotransmitter effects and overall neuronal excitability. Neurotransmitters are fast-acting, short-lived (phasic) chemical messengers that transmit signals directly across synapses, while neuromodulators have slower-onset, longer-lasting effects and modify the overall excitability of neurons and neural networks (Marder, 2012). In other words, transmitters provide quick hits, while the modulators guide our overall neurological disposition. It is important to note that no neuromodulator or neurotransmitter works in isolation; they often collaborate to achieve neural transmission goals. Like members on a baseball team, optimal functionality only happens when all teammates (systems) work in a coordinated fashion. Understanding this intricate interplay is crucial for grasping the full complexity of neural communication and its effects on behavior and cognition. In the following discussion, each messenger is described in detail, starting with DA, the captain on this complex neurological team. The key objective is to learn how we can influence the neuromodulation process to enhance our motivation, learning, and performance.

Dopamine (DA)

By now, there should be little doubt that neuromodulation broadly influences motivation and specifically behavior that appears to be personally rewarding. The key to the motivational treasure chest is held by DA. However, like many viral internet sensations, DA is overhyped. Popular media often misrepresents the role and effects of DA, leading to misconceptions. First, DA is often described as "the pleasure molecule." This widespread oversimplification is grossly inaccurate because DA is more about reward anticipation rather than about pleasure itself. In addition, DA regulation can be consciously contentious (e.g., fasting, abstinence) and is often reported by research (Wood, 2008) and described by individuals as painful (Lembke, 2021). Second, the alleged addictive properties of DA spikes are often portrayed as some sinister uncontrollable biological conspiracy designed to hijack your desires. While DA dysfunction is implicated in addiction and disease (Beaulieu-Boire & Lang, 2015), the comparison to substance abuse oversimplifies complex neurological processes. Third, the concept of a "DA detox" (Sepah, 2019) and other DA "hacks" (Clear, 2018) are often overgeneralized or not scientifically supported, misrepresenting how DA functions in the brain. However, sensationalism aside, there are specific strategies that can be learned and used to leverage DA modulation and boost motivation.

Withstanding the hyperbolic press, the dopaminergic neuromodulatory system is involved in most aspects of brain function from basic neuronal firing to complex problem-solving (Avery & Krichmar, 2017). As such,

DA has a major influence on many aspects of day-to-day learning and performance, with significant practical benefits for optimal functioning. Primarily, DA helps us feel motivated to pursue goals and rewards, and, as mentioned previously, DA accounts for the "wanting" component that propels action. Once we are in gear and behaviorally engaged, DA supports encoding those experiences and remembering which actions were beneficial to reach goals, with corresponding influence on weighing risks and benefits that contribute to effective decision-making (Schultz, 2016). Proper DA function allows us to adapt our thinking and behavior in response to changing environments and demands by helping to hone attentional resources, especially those that are instrumental for long-term gain. The benefits of DA transcend consciousness and help modulate our circadian cycle, influencing alertness and the transition between sleep and wakefulness (Monti & Monti, 2007). In addition, DA modulates pain perception, potentially helping in pain management (Wood, 2008). While not solely responsible for mood, DA contributes to feelings of pleasure and satisfaction, playing a role in our overall sense of well-being. Yes, DA is the source for much of our agency, but it is important to note that while DA is crucial for many aspects of reward choice and direction, regulation of motivation, and sustained and focused effort, it works in concert with other neurotransmitters and brain systems to produce these effects (Avery & Krichmar, 2017). Now we can figure out *how* DA and other neuromodulators enhance the quest for reward and why coveting rewards dominates a good deal of your behavior.

First, please recall that DA synthesis is about the urge to earn the reward. Urges come in many shapes and sizes, but, pragmatically, the development of an urge is designed to satisfy a need, like those needs described in Chapter 3. Satisfying the need is considered a reward because upon satisfaction the individual returns to a state of homeostasis. Assuming need satisfaction has priority (i.e., value), a series of steps are orchestrated to attain the reward. To enhance your probabilities of goal attainment, you may rearrange your schedule, focus attention, use goal-directed strategies, notice only blue Toyotas (if your goal is buying a new blue Toyota), and restructure your behaviors to align with achieving the goal, because you believe goal attainment is rewarding. While your brain cares about outcomes, for optimal motivation and DA synthesis the thrill of the chase and the anticipation of the goal is the catalyst of your insatiable zest. Yes, getting the reward is satisfying, but once the goal is met the motivation wanes and other neuromodulators take over. Many of us can relate to moments of ecstasy on the precipice of success; walking the commencement stage, designing and decorating the baby's room, romancing that special person, only to feel a lull and that puzzling "now what?" feeling once the reward is earned. DA fuels the anticipation while constantly adjusting our actions as we weigh potential rewards against the effort required to obtain them. It fires us up and propels us into action, while subtly and often unconsciously keeping us in check by controlling impulses, assessing risks, and guiding us to completion. Dysfunctional DA leads to disease (e.g., Parkinson's), addiction, or apathy, but before we understand the anomalies, let's examine what happens consistently across individuals in typical performance situations.

It is beneficial to recognize differences in how DA is synthesized to understand how to maximize the regulatory benefits of DA. The target for optimal motivation is maintaining a steady stream of DA, avoiding troublesome spikes of exhilaration that lead to addiction, or precipitous drops that contribute to malaise or depression. DA signaling in the brain occurs in two modes: "*tonic*" and "*phasic*." *Signaling* is the process of alerting one neuron that a message is on the way from another (kind of like "hey you, pay attention here it comes"), while *transmission* is the actual transfer process. *Tonic* DA release is characterized by a slow, steady discharge maintaining a baseline level of extracellular DA. This continuous, low-level firing of DA neurons results in a consistent background presence of DA, which modulates overall neuronal excitability and influences long-term behavioral states and mood. Tonic signaling contributes to cognitive functions like learning, working memory, and attention while helping to maintain motivational homeostasis.

By contrast, *phasic* DA release involves rapid, transient bursts of neuronal firing, resulting in brief but high potency increases in DA concentration. These phasic bursts are typically triggered by specific stimuli or events, often unexpected rewards, or particularly salient environmental cues (like the ones that increase the urge). The phasic mode of DA signaling is crucial for reinforcement learning, cueing reward prediction errors (RPEs), and driving the "wanting" aspect of motivation discussed earlier. This type of release strengthens synaptic connections associated with rewarding outcomes, guiding goal-directed behavior.

Distinguishing between tonic and phasic DA signaling may seem abstract, but the impact is highly practical, even though we are not consciously aware of DA transmission. We cannot see DA signaling, but we sure can feel it. For instance, tonic DA levels contribute to our overall mood and motivation. When you are having a generally good day, feeling productive and positive, that is partly due to healthy tonic DA signaling. It's what helps you maintain focus during a long workday or stay committed to long-term goals. Phasic DA release, on the other hand, is behind those moments of excitement or surprise that punctuate our daily lives. It is the burst of pleasure you feel when you receive an unexpected text message, win a game, or taste something delicious that you did not think would taste that good. These phasic bursts reinforce future behaviors, helping us learn what things and actions we find satisfying and thus rewarding. And spoiler alert, if you are one of those people, and want to know why you check your phone so frequently, it is because you unconsciously get a phasic DA burst when something on your phone breaks up monotony and routine. Knowing that phasic DA release reinforces behaviors can help us intentionally create positive habits or break negative ones. By consciously creating situations that trigger (or avoid) mega burst phasic DA release (like rewarding ourselves for desired behaviors), we can more effectively shape the habits we want to create and prune the ones we don't.

While the strategies that help us mold our environments and daily routines to support steady-state DA levels are discussed in Chapter 7, summarily DA regulation involves consistent monitoring, regular exercise, a healthy diet, good sleep habits, and engaging in autonomous activities that promote personal meaning. However, throughout life we can see popular strategies and tactics that leverage the physiological power behind DA signaling. By example, breaking down large tasks into smaller, achievable steps can provide more frequent DA "bursts," reinforcing the learning process. Emotional regulation and stress management approaches are specifically designed to disrupt the balance between tonic and phasic DA signaling by cushioning the impact of adverse events, while concurrently tempering the glory of success. Many digital technologies, especially social media and video games, manipulate phasic DA release through crafty gamification design that keeps you playing but rewards you when you level up. Media and advertising exploit the "coming soon" teaser to signal anticipatory DA for the next viral sensation. Child development experts leverage tonic and phasic DA knowledge in numerous recommendations from expediting potty training to assuring that career choices are made for the right reasons. While DA operates behind the scenes, the impact is everywhere!

The complexity of the neuromodulation manifests in four different neural circuits (a.k.a. pathways) that govern DA synthesis and signaling, each with different functionality and a brain "address." These pathways are not mutually exclusive and significant overlap ensues, sometimes confusing both the reader and the author. The focus here is on neuromodulation that has significant motivational influence on optimal performance; thus, this is not an exhaustive overview of DA synthesis and transmission (see Latif et al., 2021; Liu et al., 2021 for more). Also, while most pathway descriptions emphasize the dissociable aspects of DA synthesis, and there are distinct DA pathways with specific functions, pathways work together to regulate various aspects of behavior, motivation, and cognitive processes, and as such the focus here will be less on the origin of the neurological process, but instead on the impact.

First, the Tuberoinfundibular DA Pathway (TIDA) regulates how people respond to unwanted events, potentially influencing behavior under stress. While not directly involved in the brain's reward and motivation circuits like the other DA pathways, the TIDA influences motivational states related to maternal behavior, sexual motivation, appetite, and mood regulation. This pathway highlights how motivation is not solely governed by the more well-known pathways described below but can be influenced by broader physiological states and hormonal balances throughout the body. Considering the lack of influence of the TIDA on learning and performance beyond the nursery and bedroom, we will forge forward. Second, the Nigrostriatal DA Pathway (NSP) is involved in physical movement. The pathway supports smooth execution of voluntary movements; thus, it is crucial for the performance of fine motor tasks, like writing. Beyond motor control and movement, it is involved in procedural learning and working memory, skills that are important to learn any repetitive process like playing a piano or developing muscle memory for athletics. While there is no contesting as to the importance of the influence of the NSP on physical motivation, we will operate under the presumption that NSP is necessary prerequisite for all motivation and move forward.

Considering the specificity of the TIDA and NSP pathways and the lack of direct connection to the expectancy-value nature of motivation that emanates from reward assessment, the ongoing focus will be on the two main DA systems that are implicated in reward and motivation, specifically the "reward" and "control" pathways. These pathways are the center of attention because you will recall that at the most basic level of brain functioning we are concerned with evolutionary fitness and, like all DA producing creatures, the ability to survive and reproduce. In pre-internet days, fitness meant actual gene survival, like the type that required foraging for food and avoiding being consumed by predators. Now, fitness means figuring out how to stay healthy and achieve psychological well-being. The commonality across millenniums and the foundation for both the cave dweller and the Tik-Tok influencer is the same, maximize reward, minimize harm, and DA is what ultimately makes the difference between surviving and thriving.

The *Mesolimbic DA Pathway* is the channel most often referred to as the "DA reward pathway." It plays a crucial role in trial-and-error learning, pleasure perceptions, and reward-seeking behavior. This pathway originates in the ventral tegmental area (VTA) and projects to various limbic system structures, including the nucleus accumbens (NAcc), amygdala, and hippocampus. The *Mesocortical DA Pathway* is frequently referred to as the "DA control pathway." This pathway is involved in cognitive control, risk evaluation, and regulating emotional responses. It also originates in the VTA and projects to the prefrontal cortex (PFC) and other cortical areas. The mesocortical pathway is thought to also play a role in regulating behavior, attention, and working memory. Although the distinctions between the two pathways are significant, they are often described collectively as the *Mesolimbocortical Pathway*. So, in essence, when you experience something rewarding, neurons in the VTA release DA along these mesolimbic and mesocortical pathways, creating the feeling of pleasure and motivating you to repeat the rewarded behavior.

Specifically, the mesolimbic pathway projects to the NAcc in the limbic system. This pathway is the primary route to enhance focus toward rewarding outcomes and create feelings of pleasure/satisfaction during effortful progress. From a DA synthesis perspective, the mesolimbic route generally has a higher baseline DA synthesis and release rate compared to the mesocortical pathway because of the greater responsiveness to the immediacy of rewards (and thus is implicated in instant gratification and addictive behavior). Keep in mind that that limbic system is evolutionary mature, and thus more aligned with basic human instincts like attainment of natural rewards such as food or sex. We can think of the mesolimbic system as the workhorse of motivation. Many mesolimbic studies in animals and humans show the ubiquitous relationship between reward frequency and DA potency and synthesis (Hamid et al., 2016). Irrespective of task, when more reward is gained, more motivational effort is expended going forward. When we work for incentives (however those incentives are conceived and measured), the mesolimbic pathway dominates our goal-directed effort.

The mesocortical pathway acts more like a helicopter parent, supervising the mesolimbic pathway, often in opposition to the reward pathway by inhibiting DA release. The mesocortical pathway also originates in the VTA but is more regulatory because it projects to the PFC, the center for reasoning, logic, and contemplative thinking, not the impulsive "ooh, that looks really cool, I want it now" mesolimbic perspective. The mesocortical pathway modulates cognitive processes related to decision-making, and goal-directed behavior, influencing the choices we make and the commitment we have to those decisions. Generally, the mesocortical pathway has a lower baseline DA synthesis and release rate compared to the mesolimbic pathway, and thus is more instrumental in tonic (sustained) DA release rather than phasic (burst) release. Not surprising, mesocortical dysfunction is implicated in conditions like schizophrenia and ADHD because among other chores the mesocortical pathway influences the ability to delay gratification in order to pursue long-term goals. Excess DA can overwhelm the individual and often creates just as many issues as insufficient DA.

What is really happening below consciousness is a neurological tug-of-war whereby the reward and control pathways either instigate or regulate DA signaling and transmission. The enthusiasm and spontaneity of the mesolimbic system battles it out to see which approach prevails. Rewards that are overly attractive and tap into the limbic system through massive DA signaling are counterbalanced by the relatively more conservative mesocortical pathway. GABA neurons (which inhibit DA neurons) in regions like the ventral pallidum and rostromedial tegmental nucleus in the midbrain project to, and inhibit, the DA neurons in the VTA. This inhibition is thought to dampen the DA signal when an expected reward does not materialize, teaching the brain which cues reliably predict rewarding outcomes and which decrease the enthusiasm toward reaching the goal-directed outcome (i.e., RPE). So, while the reward pathway tells the brain "this is enjoyable, do it again," the control pathway tempers this by signaling "actually, don't expect to get rewarded in this situation." The balance and interplay between these two pathways allow flexible updating of reward expectations and motivations. In summary, while there are distinct DA pathways with specific functions, they work together to regulate various aspects of behavior, motivation, and cognitive processes, rather than being strictly divided into "reward" and "control" pathways.

From a structural perspective, mesolimbic and mesocortical DA synthesis and pathway differences manifest in several ways. The mesocortical pathway is more tightly regulated, with DA synthesis and release more carefully controlled (Salamone & Correa, 2012). Regulation is crucial for maintaining optimal cognitive function. For example, increased DA synthesis in the mesolimbic pathway might enhance reward selectivity, while increased synthesis in the mesocortical pathway might improve cognitive control, working memory, and retention. The mesocortical pathway evaluates what to do when feeling pressured, which can decrease DA synthesis in prefrontal areas under chronic stress conditions (Baik, 2020). Meanwhile the carefree mesolimbic system would generate less DA and more spontaneous and impulsive behavior (London, 2020). Stimulant drugs often have a more pronounced effect on DA synthesis and release in the mesolimbic pathway, contributing to their reinforcing and addictive properties. For example, phasic patterns of DA release within the mesolimbic pathway enhance alcohol seeking, whereas tonic patterns stimulating the mesocortical pathway inhibit consumption (Budygin et al., 2020). While beyond the scope of an overview on rewards but nonetheless important, distinctions in DA signaling have massive implications for the overall maturation of executive functioning and decision-making. DA connections to the PFC continue to increase and mature throughout adolescence, not reaching adult levels until early adulthood. By contrast, DA connections to mesolimbic reward regions like the NAcc seem to reach adultlike density by early adolescence. Some DA axons actually grow from reward regions to the PFC during adolescence, indicating ongoing but delayed development of the mesocortical pathway (Reynolds & Flores, 2021). So yes, you can at least partially blame teenage angst, and the dozens of ways risky teenagers prematurely age their parents on where and how DA is synthesized and transmitted in the brain.

Practical Implications

Besides inducing parental stress, disruptions or enhancements to DA synthesis affect many aspects of day-to-day thinking and behavior, often in absence of conscious awareness. In practice, this means DA synthesis and signaling influences why we gravitate toward learning and performance opportunities with presumed higher payoffs and refrain from those with questionable value and psychological risk that may result in frustration or remorse. By example, imagine the job seeker who decides to apply for a position despite not meeting all of the listed requirements. A mesolimbic DA boost might give that individual the confidence and optimism to apply for the position despite minimal qualifications via enhanced self-efficacy perceptions (Blain & Sharot, 2021). That same individual with DA depletion might instead refrain from applying under the pretense of negative outcome expectations (probable rejection) that would outweigh the potential benefits of earning an interview. In other words, in the short term, DA levels can be the barometer for perception of opportunity versus the anticipation of prospective failure.

DA levels also significantly influence our willingness or reluctance to pursue long-term goals. When DA expression is higher, individuals are more likely to choose options that require more effort but offer greater rewards, rather than settling for easier but less-rewarding alternatives. For instance, high-tonic DA signaling is essential for objectives like completing a university degree, which demands significant deferral of gratification and endurance of short-term inconveniences. In challenging situations, such as a difficult course experience, DA signaling can often be the deciding factor between one student persevering and another dropping out. A key hallmark of DA's impact is its ability to sustain motivation through continuous tonic release, even when immediate rewards are not apparent (Berke, 2018).

Additionally, DA influence extends to our conception of time and the approach toward future rewards. Tonic DA helps individuals overcome "delay discounting," which is a tendency to overvalue immediate rewards and undervalue future rewards when they seem too distant (Pine et al., 2010). Research has shown that people with higher DA levels are more willing and able to voluntarily defer short-term gains in favor of better future outcomes. This delay of gratification description is reminiscent of Walter Mischel's classic marshmallow studies, where children were given the choice between one immediate marshmallow treat or two treats if they could wait fifteen minutes (Mischel, 2014). While Mischel did not use physiological measures, consensus suggests that those with higher baseline DA are more likely to wait (London, 2020) and earn marshmallow "squared." Thus, DA not only affects our willingness to defer rewards but also influences our perception of time and ability to delay gratification, which in turn shapes how we approach and maintain commitment to long-term goals.

The effects of DA on motivation and goal-directed behavior are broad, with confluent findings indicating that DA synthesis matters when completing tasks at work or school (Westbrook & Braver, 2016), sticking to a diet or exercise routine (Ferrario et al., 2016), persistence in pursuing long-term career and personal goals (Schultz, 2016), and balancing excitement and anticipation when working toward a desired outcome (Lembke, 2021). In addition, baseline DA levels often influence how effectively you respond to people and situations (via stress response), as well as the level of success you achieve in those interactions. Elevated DA is highly desirable but regrettably, it is not as simple as "more DA is better." Instead, there is a DA sweet spot; but finding that spot is one of the most elusive aspects of human existence.

Unfortunately, both DA droughts and surpluses lead to a variety of unwanted consequences. By example, London (2020) illustrated the double-edged sword of DA by examining the relation of DA expression with impulsiveness. London concluded that people with lower levels of certain DA receptors, especially in the striatum, tend to be more impulsive and unwilling to delay gratification. Less receptor capability means those individuals may have a harder time stopping themselves from acting on immediate urges or waiting for larger future rewards. In practice, this reality is one reason why individuals who want to control addictions are unsuccessful: DA deficiencies in the control pathway. The same research indicated that higher levels of the same DA receptors may also increase impulsivity, resulting in more risk-seeking behavior and tolerating greater loss aversion during decision-making tasks. In practice, this means the person with an addiction will be more prone to engaging in maladaptive behavior and think their actions are warranted. In other words, too much or too little DA is a problem, especially for those individuals who historically lack self-control. London concluded that an "inverted U-curve" (increases to a point and then steep declines) was the best way to optimize the power and influence of DA, especially for delay discounting, and making longer-term objectives seem superior to living in the moment.

Compounding the DA dilemma, for every DA peak there is a trough. While you may not realize what is happening physiologically, you clearly know when you are in a state of DA depletion because you become disappointed and encounter a motivational lull. Post-DA crashes resemble that sinking feeling in your brain that is often accompanied by a sigh. For most, DA depletion feels like pain, not necessarily physical pain but pain like grief, remorse, apathy, sadness, and in just about every circumstance a sense of loss. Common experiences of DA depletion may be after watching a fantastic movie or finishing a really good book, but deflation also occurs after reaching many of life's most important moments. The classic representation is postpartum depression, or the conclusion of an important relationship, milestone, or reaching the end of a major work project. The "what do I do now?" syndrome, while disturbing, is just the start of what you feel when the dark side of DA reveals its ominous influence.

Tolerance and Addiction

Are you addicted? While addiction is normally defined as "the compulsive nonmedical self-administration of drugs" (Wise & Robble, 2020, p. 80), repetitive behavior manifests in many other forms. That's right, whether you believe it or not, you are addicted to *something*, and DA synthesis is the likely culprit. The addiction could be to something highly coveted and culturally congruent, like working multiple jobs to support your family, or staying in school, earning degree after degree for no apparent reason beyond enjoyment or feeling proud of the accomplishment. You could be the type of person who exercises relentlessly, someone who constantly craves sex, gambles, or isn't satisfied unless they receive compliments during every single social interaction—behaviors that all have an addictive streak. Of course, your urges and personification of reward may be much more mundane but potentially harmful like the inability to refuse a cigarette, excessive coffee drinking, spending endless hours on your phone, or craving your next adult beverage. Your addiction may be even more subtle as might be observed by a person who always needs to be correct, or someone who constantly gnaws at the ear of others to broadcast their complaints, or one who bemoans the totality of their existence on social and economic factors beyond their control. You may deny these addictive suppositions, but some form of psychological dependence is inescapable due to the variations in DA signaling and how those fluctuations govern human neurological systems and the pursuit of whatever it is that *you* find rewarding.

Understanding why certain behaviors are dominant and why others are trivial means a deeper exploration of the relationship between personal reward perceptions and DA synthesis. First, recognize that everyone has a DA baseline. Baseline differences between individuals are primarily determined by genetic variation, which regulates the production, signaling, and reuptake of DA synthesis (Diamond, 2007). Variations occur based on a variety of factors, some of which are within our control, like diet and nutrition, sleep cycles, and physical activity. Other prevailing but largely uncontrollable influences on DA synthesis include hormonal levels, circadian rhythms, and age. Most importantly, it is crucial to realize that DA baseline fluctuates day-to-day and hour-to-hour (just like the more conscious perceptions of hunger and thirst). The variations are consistent within a person at any particular time but vary significantly between individuals. This means that a similar level of DA baseline that motivates you today will be needed to optimize motivation tomorrow. Regardless of a specific baseline, the brain continuously works to maintain a harmonious balance, including regulation of DA synthesis, signaling, and transmission.

Although Issac Newton was not referring to DA synthesis, he was absolutely correct in the supposition that what goes up must come down. Remember, when positive RPE (see Chapter 4) is experienced (regardless of the cause or type of reward), baseline levels of DA increase. Conversely, negative RPE blunts DA signaling and inhibits DA neuron potential. Positive prediction errors reinforce behaviors that led to better-than-expected rewards. Negative prediction errors diminish behaviors that led to worse-than-expected outcomes (Schultz, 2016). When something noteworthy happens (like a reward or a cue predicting a reward), DA neurons rapidly fire. This causes a sharp (phasic), temporary increase in DA above the baseline. These bursts signal the value of an event, helping the brain learn what to pay attention to and what actions to repeat. Concurrently, the DA signaling generates positive affect concerning what transpired and the likelihood of behavioral repetition is enhanced or confirmed (Liu et al., 2008). Hopefully, what instigated the phasic burst is something positive and beneficial like striving toward a work or an academic goal or including an achievement that enhances the lives of others. Regrettably, the brain fails to discriminate reward substance and reaches similar conclusions for other less-favorable and disadvantageous actions as well, meaning that you can get hooked on something like food, drugs, or the girl next door because of the sensations generated from elevated DA.

Soon the euphoria of elevated DA wanes. After attaining the reward, DA levels plummet, as homeostasis governs neural readaptation. Similar to the exertion of muscular effort during and after an endurance event, DA resources dip *below* baseline. In response the brain engages in a refractory period, allowing for DA regeneration, just as rest allows muscles to recover from a strenuous workout. Returning to baseline is important because if DA remains elevated, the brain loses its ability to distinguish between important and unimportant events (Olguín et al., 2016). Additionally, maintaining elevated DA levels is metabolically costly for the brain, usurping a variety of energy-depleting metabolic resources. The timing and longevity of the recovery period varies between individuals and is a function of the degree of elevation and how far below baseline levels drop. Regardless, levels will ultimately recover, and life goes on, except for those with addictions or those who have DA dysregulation.

When baseline dips, we typically want more of whatever it was that brought us above the baseline from the start. This reality is the fundamental DA dilemma, because wanting more is akin to feeling passion, but if left unregulated hedonistic urges turn into addictions. The constant drive to seek out ever-increasing rewards relates to always wanting to trigger DA responses from positive prediction errors. The conundrum escalates when rewards become expected, because only rewards better than before will generate similar positive prediction errors and the coveted DA activation. In other words, the organism becomes habituated to the reward process and as such strives to replicate the circumstances that promoted the initial reward. Perceptually, lack of positive RPE after previous accomplishment results in feelings of boredom and malcontent, which often lead to apathy (Schultz, 2016). Receiving the same reward repeatedly does not work as well because there is lower or no positive RPE. The expectation grows, and the potency or frequency of the reward remains consistent; thus, an important event or a reward cue that previously promoted positive RPE becomes functionally impotent. Greater DA elevation comes at the expense of an ever-greater reward, which in addiction terms means the need for a more frequent or higher dosage. In turn, prolonged exposure to high DA levels can make receptors less sensitive, leading to tolerance. The disturbing DA cycle accounts for the perception and reality that nothing ever feels like the thrill of the first time. Returning to baseline is a letdown tantamount to pain, even for the fully functioning, highly productive individual striving to excel. Luckily, the potential frustration and psychological discomfort from DA deficits are actually what aspires many to their greatest accomplishments.

Under ideal circumstances, during refractory the individual takes a metaphorical DA break, patiently waiting for baseline recovery by pursuing other goals or just waiting out synthesis and preparing for the next reward opportunity. Psychiatrist Anne Lembke (2021) calls the process of returning to DA baseline as an "hedonic set point," meaning that we have a benchmark of contentment and well-being that is closely tied to our DA levels. Think of the set point as how you feel on a typical day when life is going the way you want it to go. According to Lembke, as tolerance develops, our hedonic set point shifts. What once brought pleasure now merely brings us to "normal." The new normal in turn generates feelings of restlessness and unfulfillment because it is not enough. This can lead to a cycle where individuals seek more novel, intense, or frequent stimulation to feel better. What used to work simply fine just does not seem exciting anymore. The adventurous hiker needs a bigger mountain to climb, the content spouse fantasizes about romance from days gone by (or potential infidelity), and the aspiring politician clamors for more votes than the last election. When the shifting hedonic point propels the individual to greater accomplishments, the brain is satisfied, but that result is not always the case. For some, the refractory period is mired in dissatisfaction where anxiety and apathy dominate thought, especially when we are uncertain how to replicate the prior experience and the historical DA crescendo. If you have ever lamented about feeling uninspired and unmotivated after ending a relationship or leaving a job, the complacency is directly attributed to not knowing where or how to replicate the prior feeling. But your brain does not care how, it only wants to replicate the prior experience one way or another, at least that is what Deborah Ann Harry (1978) revealed.

Saddled with low levels of DA, we have choices. The adaptive option is setting long-term goals and using a repertoire of strategies to surmount the motivation lull. Incremental progress stimulates DA production, urging the organism forward and resulting in sustained momentum. While doubt and uncertainty may stall or stagnate progress, the obstacles can also serve as the catalyst to exert extra effort to achieve goals. DA neurons become the benefactor of doing the hard thing, and the more difficult the effort exertion, the better the DA payoff. Nestled in the anterior mid-cingulate cortex (aMCC) and supported by dopaminergic, noradrenergic, and serotonergic synthesis (Bar et al., 2016), tenacity develops, not when the easy option is taken, but from attacking formidable challenges where the individual calculates and realizes the cost/benefit advantages of hard work. The result is integration of neurological signaling by the aMCC that "predicts energy requirements that are needed for attention allocation, encoding of new information, and physical movement, all in the service of goal attainment contributing to better academic achievement, career opportunities and health outcomes" (Touroutoglou et al., 2020, p. 12). In essence, what has transpired is that the discomfort of the DA deficiency (that originated under normative and healthy circumstances) provides sufficient distress to reset the hedonic set point, the overall pleasure system, and subsequent appreciation and striving toward future rewards. Unfortunately, adaptive functioning is not always the norm, because for many people DA originates from dubious sources from the start.

Not everyone synthesizes DA from noble striving and the glory of achievement attained from stellar work or reaching lofty academic goals. There are other more nefarious ways to get your daily DA dosage. Additionally, even the greatest producers are prone to motivational lapses and temporary apathy due to DA deficits, whether weary due to exhaustion, burnout, distraction, or vexing about the uncertainty of what comes next. However, neither temporary lulls nor lower achievement needs reduce the brain's motivational reliance on DA. The wanting need burns bright and must be satisfied somehow, and there are plenty of convenient ways to manufacture DA besides hard work. While elaboration of the measurement of DA synthesis and transmission is beyond the current scope, we can estimate how much DA is generated from a variety of substances and behaviors that result in the same rewarding feeling as climbing a mountain or winning an award. Consensus reveals that eating chocolate increases baseline levels of DA by 55 percent, Sex 100 percent, Nicotine 150 percent, Cocaine 225 percent, and amphetamines (like Adderall) 1,000 percent (Lembke, 2021). Even the caffeine from a cup of coffee will typically increase extracellular DA levels by about 20–30 percent, particularly in the NAcc and PFC, the most crucial areas of the brain that determine reward value (Solinas et al., 2002).

Thus, what matters most is the habitual source of DA. When a person first encounters an addictive substance or engages in a potentially addictive behavior (of any type), it typically causes a large release of DA in the brain's reward system. The phasic DA surge promotes feelings of pleasure and euphoria that increase wanting and motivate the individual to sustain the behavior that prompted the feeling. In situations of dysregulation, such as during addiction, repeated exposure to a pleasurable stimulus (like smoking or social media) results in the initial DA surge becoming less pronounced. The sensitized brain adapts by reducing DA receptor sensitivity or decreasing DA production. This means that over time, more of the stimulus is needed to achieve the same pleasurable effect. The underlying cause is because of how positive RPE has been previously experienced, meaning it takes a higher RPE to feel the same. To replicate the prior sensation, individuals must increase their consumption or engagement in the behavior. Ultimately neuroadaptations result in tolerance, where the same amount of the substance or behavior no longer produces the pleasurable effect that the individual wants.

One easily obtainable and powerful reinforcer prone to addiction (and tolerance) is food. Eating in the minds of many is the easiest (and subjectively the most pleasurable way) to increase baseline DA levels. The problem, again, is habituation to positive RPE. A single serving or simple taste from the past may not illicit the same rewarding response as before, resulting in the potential for overeating far beyond nutritional necessity. For most mammals, the palatability of foods is secondary to nutrition (de Araujo, 2016), yet for the gluttonous human, food taste, texture, and nutrition activate multiple reward pathways with health implications often taking a backseat. Foods with excessive fat and sugar are specifically engineered to promote a dopaminergic surge triggering mesolimbic DA in the ventral striatum (the reward pathway), compared to more nutritious food that activates nigrostriatal DA release in the dorsal striatum (Tellez et al., 2016). The double whammy is additive because fats, carbs, and sugar stimulate multiple DA pathways, and, when combined, the addictive effect increases DA exponentially leading to a more aggressive craving response for dense, high-calorie foods (McDougle et al., 2024). Over time, this cycle can lead to a chronic dysregulation of the DA system, affecting motivation, decision-making, and impulse control, and in many cases, when unregulated, leads to obesity. Luckily, there is a remedy for both addictive behavior and milder forms of substance dependency.

When unregulated, whether it be from one of the insidious DA deviants described, or from equally compelling behaviors like video gaming, social media, exercise, and shopping to name a few, the source is secondary, but the remedy is always abstinence. This means a deliberate and intentional pause that inflicts some degree of psychological discomfort and distress, in order to neutralize the DA dysregulation. Consequently, malaise, boredom and discomfort develop but are integral as part of the "cure." After periods of high stimulation, normal life can feel boring or unfulfilling. This state of despondence is often experienced neurologically just like physical pain (Eisenberger, 2012), both implicating the anterior cingulate cortex (ACC) and insula, suggesting a shared neural basis for the affective component of pain.

We often hear about "getting out of the comfort zone" as the remedy for personal growth and development, and this old cliché actually has a justification from science. Some degree of pain or discomfort is necessary for resetting our DA reward syndrome and appreciating prior rewards. Without experiencing the pain of abstinence, pleasure and the return to optimal satisfaction is impossible. Depending on the substance or behavior, there may be physical withdrawal symptoms. These symptoms can include irritability, anxiety, depression, and cravings. Even without physical dependence, psychological withdrawal can feel painful because whatever addictive behavior or substance is being reduced or eliminated previously served as a primary coping strategy. The suspension leaves a void in how we deal with stress or negative emotions that feel deeply uncomfortable or painful until new coping strategies are developed.

Lembke (2021) argued that to overcome tolerance abstinence is nonnegotiable. This continuous void allows the brain to gradually reset the DA system and return to a more natural hedonic set point, otherwise known as the true genetic baseline. While Lembke advocated a thirty-day period of abstinence for this reset, the time can vary based on the severity of the behavior and individual goals. She contended that "DA fasting" or temporarily abstaining from highly stimulating activities allows the individual to cope with the realities of twenty-first-century life which include constantly being bombarded with DA-triggering stimuli (smartphones, advertising, social media, easy access to high-calorie foods, etc.), which can lead to a general state of tolerance and decreased ability to find pleasure in simpler things. While Lembke's approach does not mean a literal DA fast, it does mean refraining from the trash that causes large DA spikes that play havoc with the ability of otherwise fully functioning individuals to battle their motivational regulation.

While controlling DA synthesis is critical to understanding the power of reward, DA does not act alone but instead has a powerful interactive effect on other neuromodulators. Recall that DA primarily accounts for the motivational urge and the striving toward reaching the reward. Perhaps surprisingly, actual reward attainment is far less important for the dopaminergic brain. When DA is released, it activates a robust network of brain areas that collectively drive an individual to pursue their preferred rewards. This dopaminergic activation is crucial for understanding why many of our behaviors are ultimately linked to maintaining or recreating whatever we find rewarding, regardless of if it is petting a dog or colonizing Mars. Thus, the remaining chapter discusses the roles of other neuromodulators and their impact on motivation for rewards.

Other Neuromodulators

Operating under the assumption that DA is the sole instigator in the pursuit of rewards would be like thinking that only a good pitcher is necessary for a winning baseball team. Just like highly functional teams, an assortment of players impact the ability to satisfy the urges generated by DA. First, we must acknowledge that many aspects of motivated behavior are guided by the dynamic interaction among numerous factors. Any motivational theory developed in the last fifty years acknowledges the role of reciprocal determinism (Bandura, 1986), meaning that demonstrated behaviors are a result of influences that include individual beliefs and perceptual experiences that are molded by environmental experience. These influences can determine which behaviors are demonstrated and to what extent the person is motivated to act. By example, while you might find eating a piece of candy enjoyable, it is unlikely you would steal one from a baby you encounter on the street. However, if you had not eaten for days, you would probably not hesitate to pilfer a baby carriage for a lollypop. The same paradigm applies to analyzing motivated behavior from a neuropsychological perspective. The expectation that one aspect of functioning is operating exclusive of other factors would fail to account for the reciprocal influences of different hormones and neurotransmitters on each other. Thus, the neurotransmitters of norepinephrine (NE)/ epinephrine, serotonin, GABA, acetylcholine (ACh), oxytocin (OT), and cortisol are briefly discussed to illuminate how these molecules and peptides individually and interactively influence the setting, pursual, and attainment of subjective reward.

Norepinephrine/Epinephrine

While DA is clearly the captain of "team modulation," urge satisfaction needs energy for attainment, and epinephrine/norepinephrine is the supplier. While the source and metabolic influences of epinephrine synthesis and that of norepinephrine (NE) differ, the impact on reward processing and specifically the relationship with DA are similar. One relevant distinction is that epinephrine (also called adrenaline) is primarily synthesized in the adrenal medulla, the inner part of the adrenal glands located on top of the kidneys. NE, however, is synthesized in the brain, specifically in the locus coeruleus (LC). Since the emphasis here is on reward pathways, we care more about NE as it participates in alertness and attention, and is intricately connected to the "fight or flight" response described in Chapter 4. Each neuromodulator contributes to the overall arousal and helps determine how rewards are valued and pursued. NE synthesis and activation happens based on calculating the difference between the energy required to perform an action to obtain the reward and the reward value (Bouret & Richmond, 2015). In other words, we may want to satisfy a dopaminergic urge but need to figure out if the potential investment of effort is worthwhile based on the goal. Decisions like how long to study for a test or how many hours to drive on a trip fall into this NE valuation process. We do not always have the energy to secure our desires. The energy needed is modulated by NE, so just like optimizing DA, there are strategies to enhance NE production (see Chapter 7).

In his podcast, Andrew Huberman (2022) described NE as providing the "forward center of mass" that propels individuals toward reaching their desired goals. NE is synthesized from DA by the enzyme DA β-hydroxylase, making NE production dependent on the presence of DA (Gonzalez-Lopez & Vrana, 2019). When the valuation of an urge reaches a sufficient level, DA is converted into NE (Gonzalez-Lopez & Vrana, 2019). This conversion activates specific receptors that mobilize the individual to satisfy the dopaminergic urges. The NE system can modulate DA release, priming the individual for reward-seeking behavior. For instance, Zhang et al. (2023) noted that activation of adrenergic receptors in the VTA can influence DA transmission to the NAcc, the key region in reward processing. NE indirectly influences reward seeking by enhancing attentional focus on the reward and creating a state of physical readiness. By mobilizing energy resources, NE's role is more about preparing the body for action and providing the energy and focus that might be needed in pursuit of rewards, rather than generating the reward sensation itself.

So, what happens when NE kicks in? The physiological effects of epinephrine can improve physical and cognitive performance in pursuit of goals. NE enhances attention, arousal, and vigilance, creating a more focused attention on tasks and goals (Mather et al., 2016), improves working memory and behavioral flexibility, aiding in complex cognitive tasks, and regulates mood and motivation, potentially increasing drive to pursue goals (España et al., 2016). From a practical perspective, The LC-NE system in general calculates the difference between the energy required to perform an action and the reward value. This suggests that epinephrine/norepinephrine helps in evaluating the cost–benefit ratio of pursuing a reward (Zhang et al., 2023). For example, if you are deciding whether to put in extra hours at work for a potential promotion, NE activation would occur when weighing the time and effort that is needed to solidify the potential promotion. As such, as shown in neuroimaging, LC neurons show increased activity during reward-predictive cues and goal-directed actions. This indicates that the NE system is actively engaged when anticipating and pursuing rewards. Imagine you are playing a video game—the LC-NE system might become more active when you see a power-up appear, signaling a potential reward. The LC-NE system helps encode the value of the reward. This means it helps in learning from past experiences to improve future reward-seeking behaviors. For instance, if you have had success using a particular study strategy before an exam (or beating a level), the LC-NE system might reinforce this behavior for future exams.

NE also has an important connection to the regulation of stress (Kreek et al., 2005). It plays a key role in the stress response, mobilizing mental resources to cope with challenges (España et al., 2016). The release of epinephrine during stress can sometimes intensify the pleasure of subsequent rewards, a phenomenon known as stress-induced analgesia, where perceptions of pain are psychologically suppressed, resulting in increased motivation for whichever activity provides you with thrills (Butler & Finn, 2009). And as many of us know, adrenaline is what we need when it comes to jumping off mountains, driving 180 mph in a race car, and even when asking a high-quality prospective partner out for a date. While for some these types of activities are frightening, for others they serve the purpose of the ultimate reward. Elevated NE levels can increase willingness to take on risks, which sets the stage to engage in high-risk, high-reward scenarios. Finally, while it is key to realize that NE contributes to the physiological state that can support reward-seeking behavior, it is not responsible for the feeling of reward itself. The reward sensation (like feelings of contentment and satisfaction) is primarily associated with other neurotransmitters, particularly DA and the next "team modulation" player serotonin.

Serotonin (5-HT)

Heightened perceptions of motivation and energy have obvious benefits for productivity, learning, and elevated self-perceptions about the ability to accomplish goals. Thus, for most individuals when the dopaminergic and noradrenergic circuits are activated, we feel satisfied because we know what we want and feel capable of achieving our goals. However, amplified motivation is not always the brain's objective and instead sometimes we need to chill out and recognize achievements by feeling satisfied and content about what we have accomplished. I was once told that recognition is the greatest motivator, and self-recognition boosted by serotonin is the first step. Thus, serotonin provides the neurological substance for the regulation of our moods and feelings of satiety and is related to our perceptions of happiness and well-being. Serotonin is also responsible for sleep and appetite regulation (Martin et al., 2017), and while these are rewards for some, for the most part these metabolic aspects of 5-HT are of little concern.

Serotonergic projections originate in the raphe nuclei of the brainstem, extending to almost all forebrain areas (Avery & Krichmar, 2017). The raphe is closely connected to the PFC, and thus serotonin gets involved in decision-making and reasoning. When we feel good, serotonin is the mood regulator often associated with positivity. In cases of serotonin deficiency, depression is typically the result leading to the popular press conception that serotonin is the "feel good" neurotransmitter. However, like most media conceptions of reward and brain functioning, this generalization is misleading. Higher serotonin levels can actually decrease motivation in certain contexts. For instance, selective serotonin reuptake inhibitors (like Prozac, Zoloft, and Lexapro) are used to treat depression and can sometimes lead to decreased motivation as a side effect. Ultimately, serotonin works as a control mechanism for the balancing act between active and passive behaviors (Fischer et al., 2015) while generating feelings of contentment.

Serotonin interacts closely with the DA system to influence reward processing. While DA is primarily associated with the wanting and the prediction aspects of reward, serotonin influences how we value rewards. Miyazaki et al. (2014) found that serotonin signaling in the dorsal raphe nucleus encodes reward value and influences decision-making when we decide to defer an available reward. Serotonin, by suppressing impulsive behavior, is crucial for delay of gratification and realizing that waiting can reap excess rewards, provided we have the capacity to wait for the desirable experience. In a similar manner, Meyniel et al. (2016) found that serotonin levels influence the willingness to exert effort for rewards, with higher serotonin levels associated with increased willingness to expend effort in selective contexts. It is not just about the willingness to exert effort, but effort exertion based on the exertion cost. Sometimes we are willing to exert the effort to get what we want and at other times we decline. The chief difference is in the baseline of serotonin. Excess serotonin makes us work harder than when serotonin is lower. Serotonin also helps us control our behavior especially in light of unwelcome information, as it serves to insulate us from responding negatively (Colwell et al., 2024).

In the context of reward pursuit, serotonin can inhibit behavior and keep us in check. According to one study (Macoveanu et al., 2013), artificially blocked serotonin receptors using the drug Ketanserin (used to treat high blood pressure) result in participants becoming more risk-averse and less likely to choose risky options. Serotonin levels were related to suppressing impulsive actions, allowing for more careful evaluation of decision-making during reward-seeking. This finding is particularly important in situations where immediate gratification might be detrimental to long-term goals, as what might happen when a learner drops a course because it appears to be challenging, sacrificing the ability to graduate on a timely basis.

Serotonin does not work in isolation. Its effects on motivation and reward-seeking are often mediated through interactions with other modulators, particularly DA and NE. For example, serotonin can modulate DA release in the NAcc, the key area for reward processing (Browne et al., 2019). While challenging to explicitly control the neurological mix, many behaviors and cognitive functions require a balance between serotonergic and dopaminergic activation rather than dominance of one over the other.

Gamma-aminobutyric Acid (GABA)

In the spirit of homeostasis, sometimes those dopaminergic urges need to be reined in. Imagine that you feel out of control managing desire and need a confirming opinion. The behavior needing regulation may be the result of one of the most likely DA hogs like eating, sex, smoking, drinking, or substance use. Welcome GABA, the neurological counselor to the modulation team. GABA helps modulate DA giving signaling and production a rest. While actually an amino acid, GABA acts like a neuromodulator because it reduces neuronal excitability throughout the nervous system by regulating neural networks, resulting in the inhibition of spontaneous behavior.

GABA's inhibitory function in the brain serves purposes beyond simply preventing overindulgence. A primary function of GABA neurons, particularly in the VTA, is to continuously update our perception of rewards. These GABA neurons modulate DA signaling by adjusting RPEs based on changing circumstances. They play a crucial role in calculating these RPEs by encoding reward expectations and inhibiting DA neurons accordingly. This allows DA neurons to signal the difference between expected and actual rewards more accurately. This inhibitory action of GABA neurons on DA neurons is one reason why repeated experiences often feel less exciting than the first time. By refining and sharpening reward-related signals, GABA neurons enable more precise encoding of reward information, including its timing, magnitude, and context. This process helps regulate our reward expectations and responses, allowing us to adapt to changing environments and learn from our experiences. In essence, GABA neurons function as a sophisticated control system, fine-tuning our reward processing to be more accurate and context-appropriate, rather than simply stopping us from looking like gluttonous fools.

Another essential GABA role is to help direct the energy generated by DA toward appropriate goals. Like serotonin, GABA neurons in the ventral pallidum influence aversive decision-making strategies. This suggests GABA signaling in this region is important for motivational processes underlying risky decision-making (Bouarab et al., 2019). In one study, optogenetic stimulation (brain injection of a light-sensitive protein) of GABA neurons in mice caused a pause in consuming a highly rewarding food, but not the desire to seek out the food (Van Zessen et al., 2012). In other words, subsequent to GABA stimulation, food that formally was perceived as highly rewarding had no greater motivation power than low-grade tasteless lab chow. What it means is that food was consumed for nutritional purposes, not for the perceived quality of the experience. While bad for sales at fancy mice restaurants, the study shows how GABA can inhibit reward seeking. While it would be nice to try this type of stimulation with humans, we would encounter ethical issues injecting students and bombarding them with bright light to see if GABA inhibits DA and stops junk food consumption. Mice are a better choice to show the power of GABA.

GABA has also been implicated in controlling effortful motivation and an individual's capacity to maintain performance over time, otherwise known as "stamina" (Strasser et al., 2020). In a related area, GABA neurons in the ventral pallidum of rats mediate both highly motivated pursuit of salient foods and avoidance of shocks, indicating the role of GABA under high-stakes situations. This finding, like the mouse one, shows that under pressure GABA can help the organism make proper choices maintaining the balance between risk and reward (Farrell et al., 2021). This inhibitory control helps prevent excessive reward-seeking behavior. Without this "brake," the reward system might become overactive, potentially leading to addiction-like behaviors, but we need human data to know for sure.

The GABA-mediated inhibition allows for rapid changes in DA signaling, which is crucial for adapting behavior in changing environments or when learning new information about rewards. Tonic inhibition of DA neurons may help conserve energy by preventing unnecessary DA release when it is not behaviorally relevant. Many neural circuits, including those involving DA neurons, have the potential for spontaneous activity. Tonic inhibition actively suppresses this spontaneous activity, ensuring that energy is not wasted on unnecessary neuronal firing (Benjamin et al., 2010). Since DA catalyzes motivation, we want to be sure to use the power judiciously, just like any other limited resource. The purpose of this inhibition is ultimately to create a balanced, flexible, and precise reward system that can guide adaptive behavior while avoiding maladaptive outcomes like addiction. It's part of the brain's complex system of checks and balances that allows for nuanced responses to environmental stimuli and internal states. Thank GABA for preventing you from running amok!

Acetylcholine (ACh)

In the following chapter, we explore how reward is a catalyst for learning. Now, recognize that ACh is the primary molecule and modulator responsible for enhanced attention, memory, and specifically learning about what is subjectively rewarding to an individual. ACh wields power through its interactions with the DA system and specifically the influence it has on synaptic plasticity. The primary impact of ACh is to hone arousal and attention toward relevant stimuli (like incoming information) focusing on what is important to the individual. Like other neuromodulators, ACh interacts with the mesocorticolimbic DA system, contributing to reward processing because cholinergic neurons in the NAcc respond to rewarding stimuli (Nunes et al., 2022). As the perception of reward is enhanced, DA activates. However, unlike some of the other modulators, ACh is intimately involved in determining and encoding what we believe is most important to know. When ACh is released, it initiates changes in the structure and function of neuronal networks, effectively "bonding" the new information with existing knowledge. This neuroplasticity is the physical basis of learning and memory formation. In essence, ACh does not just facilitate learning; it actively shapes the brain's architecture to encode new knowledge and experiences.

The process of how ACh inspires learning and memory formation is rather intriguing. Instead of just creating neuronal connections to process and absorb new knowledge, ACh releases in the cortex favor the encoding of new sensory information over the retrieval of previously stored memories. In other words, through the synthesis of ACh the brain decides which information is relevant and how existing knowledge can be replaced by information that has more personal utility. Simultaneously, ACh diminishes the influence of previously stored information, allowing for encoding of new information by reducing interference from existing memories and enhancing the impact of incoming sensory data. In essence, ACh acts like an information colander, straining out invaluable excess while solidifying the neuronal pathway by retaining the tasty pasta. Conversely, loss of cholinergic neurons enhances the severity of dementia symptoms (Hasselmo & Sarter, 2011) illustrating the importance of ACh synthesis.

The adaptive ACh filtering process contributes to cognitive reevaluation, permitting behavior modifications based on changing reward contingencies. Similar to the information filtering described, ACh contributes by modulating synaptic plasticity and neural networks. Modulation allows the brain to adapt to new information and change reward contingencies by destabilizing and reconsolidating existing memories (Ray et al., 2015). This flexibility enables individuals to update RPE calculations and hone focus on what continues to be rewarding and meaningful based on evolving environmental influences. ACh is also involved in memory consolidation particularly during sleep, by modulating neural activity that promotes memory strengthening. ACh operates during rapid eye movement (REM) sleep, where wild fluctuations in ACh occur as individuals go from resting to awakening, a phase of sleeping that is associated with the consolidation of memories. ACh promotes theta oscillations in the brain, a type of brain wave activity that is crucial for memory formation. During sleep, particularly REM sleep, the brain replays experiences from the day. ACh facilitates this replay by enhancing the neural circuits involved in these experiences, allowing for the strengthening of reward-related memories (Feld & Born, 2020). ACh helps determine and consolidate memories that are deemed important or relevant, such as those associated with rewards. This selectivity ensures that significant experiences are prioritized for long-term storage. If you have ever wondered why some dreams appear so vivid and bizarre during the period immediately preceding being woken, blame it on elevated levels of ACh during REM sleep that help regulate transitions between sleep stages and wakefulness.

While the role of ACh primarily operates below our level of consciousness, there are practical benefits derived from ACh and thus strategies to promote elevation of ACh are covered in Chapter 7. In aggregate, by facilitating the consolidation of important memories, ACh helps improve learning outcomes and the retention of information. The ability to consolidate reward-related memories allows individuals to adapt their behavior based on past experiences, improving decision-making and goal-directed actions. Maintaining healthy ACh levels can mitigate age-related cognitive decline by ensuring effective memory consolidation during sleep (Haam & Yakel, 2017). These functions of ACh underscore its importance in both cognitive processes and practical applications related to learning and memory. However, like other teammates, no neuromodulator operates independently. The interaction between ACh and DA is complex, with ACh sometimes decreasing when DA increases, creating conditions favorable for learning and memory formation during reward processing (Cragg, 2006). What matters most is that learning can be enhanced biologically when using strategies designed to increase ACh output.

Oxytocin

Socialization and the interaction with others can be highly valued and deeply rewarding, often representing the pinnacle of human experience. While not everyone prioritizes social engagement, activities like sharing experiences, collaborating, expressing emotions, and offering support to others frequently dominates human behavior. From chit-chats to deep emotional bonds, prosocial behavior is a cultural universal that shapes societies, organizations, and families. Fundamentally, socialization satisfies the inherent need for relatedness and fosters a valuable sense of connection to others (Ryan & Deci, 2020). Meeting the relatedness need molds our personal identities and broadly influences individual development, well-being, and, in some cultures, basic survival. To support this important need, our neurological systems have evolved to produce and release oxytocin, a hormone acting as a neuromodulator, reflecting positive social experiences and for many the primary and indisputable influence of day-to-day motivation.

Popular media often glamorizes oxytocin as the "cuddle" or "love" hormone, because it is released during positive social interactions and promotes bonding and trust. Oxytocin is also emitted during physical touching, sexual activity, and childbirth (including nursing), and from prolonged mutual gazing (including when you and your pet stare at each other)! While there is robust evidence to support the belief that oxytocin contributes to romance by enhancing perceptions of partner beauty (Scheele et al., 2013), we will defer that aspect of social reward and explanatory focus to others like Oprah or Gottman and Gottman (2017). Here we consider oxytocin as a neuropeptide synthesized in the hypothalamus that is released both as a hormone in the peripheral nervous system and as a neuromodulator into the brain (Kraus et al., 2023).

Cultivating oxytocin is productive for numerous reasons beyond achieving carnal or affiliative pleasure. Engaging in social interactions boosts mood and reduces stress, alleviating anxiety, and depression, with oxytocin indicated as a potential remedy for conditions characterized by social deficits, such as autism (Yamasue & Domes, 2017). Social connections also improve quality of life by contributing to better self-esteem and overall life satisfaction (Umberson & Karas Montez, 2010), with a newer meta-analysis (Mahalingam et al., 2023) finding that socialization substantially increased longevity. Furthermore, social interactions can slow cognitive decline by stimulating brain activity, which strengthens neural pathways and enhances memory and cognitive skills (Biddle et al., 2019). Another particularly advantageous benefit of oxytocin is stress reduction. Positive social interactions lower cortisol levels, reducing stress and promoting a sense of well-being (Dickman et al., 2020). In absence of oxytocin transmission, these benefits are likely attenuated or eliminated.

Oxytocin neurons are projected to reward relevant regions in the brain including the amygdala, striatum, ventral pallidum, and the PFC (Kraus et al, 2023), which are part of the brain's mesocorticolimbic system. Oxytocin modulates the social reward mechanisms by interacting with DA. The interaction enhances the perception of social stimuli as rewarding, thereby promoting behaviors like attachment and bonding. In humans, oxytocin enhances the attractiveness and subsequent reward value of a romantic partner's face by activating the VTA and NAcc, the focal point of reward processing. In other words, when we think others look better, we find the experience rewarding and both the oxytocin and DA start flowing (Love, 2014). Yes, love is both the researcher and the outcome! A similar reaction occurs (most of the time) when mothers view the face of their children (Strathearn et al., 2008), and the recall of happy faces is more accurate than the memory of frowns, all because of the power of oxytocin synthesis (Guastella et al., 2008).

Social interactions also trigger the release of DA, thereby instilling a reciprocal DA-Oxytocin relationship. Oxytocin influences dopaminergic activity within the mesocorticolimbic system, which processes motivational stimuli and facilitates affiliative behaviors. This suggests that oxytocin can increase the salience of social cues, making them seem more rewarding and motivating. In practice, this means that OT serves as a relationship spotlight, honing the individual's attention and evaluation toward aspects of the individual that are related to socialization such as recognizing a friendly face with a nice smile (Marsh et al., 2010). However, the increased attentional focus works in rather unorthodox ways. Excess OT can instill feelings of trust, love, and empathy, but here's the catch, only for individuals who are considered part of your ingroup (De Dreu et al., 2010). Alternatively, OT can also assign aversive and negative value to individuals who are not considered part of your social clique resulting in unfavorable assessments. Like, the team captain DA, OT is a double-edged sword and acts differently depending on the context of application. Finally, it should be noted that reactions to threat and stress may be accompanied by increases in OT release designed to manage and reduce the anxiety of discomfort (Neumann & Slattery, 2016). However, not everyone is stress adverse. Some individuals perceive moderate stress as rewarding, so again, we have yet another paradox that needs a closer look to fully understand.

Stress Hormones

Stress is defined as any physical, emotional, or mental response to the challenges or demands that exceed an individual's resources, at a particular time and in a particular context (Schneiderman et al., 2005). In other words, stress evaluations and subsequent reactions are subjective based on the circumstances. Stress will broadly impact motivation, and, counterintuitively, stress can be perceived as both rewarding and debilitating. What appears to be a massive challenge to some can alternatively be perceived as an incentive to others. Listen to many successful athletes, performers, or senior executives and you will detect excitement and enthusiasm when they are faced with a formidable challenge, such as what happens during high-stakes competition or when attempting a task where others typically fail. While the circumstances that dictate stress responses are far too numerous to discuss here, we can operate under the presumption that when your brain perceives a threat, specific neurological responses follow. What matters more than the source of stress is the response. Reactions can be negative (distress), or favorable (eustress), with mediation governed by a combination of neural modulation and the use of a vast repertoire of coping strategies.

The neurological response to *distress* is a complex interplay of brain regions and chemical messengers that prepares our body to manage potential threats (Godoy et al., 2018). When we encounter stressful situations, several key brain areas spring into action, including the amygdala, hippocampus, PFC, and hypothalamus. The amygdala, sometimes described as the brain's "alarm system," plays a particularly crucial role. The amygdala acts as a threat detector, constantly scanning the environment for signs of danger. For instance, imagine you are walking alone at night and suddenly hear footsteps behind you. Your amygdala quickly assesses this as a potential threat, setting off a bodily chain reaction.

When the amygdala detects a threat, it activates the hypothalamic-pituitary-adrenal (HPA) axis, triggering the release of stress hormones like cortisol (Godoy et al., 2018). This hormonal cascade prepares your body for a "fight or flight" response. By example, you might notice your heart racing and palms sweating as your body readies itself for quick action. The stress response does not stop there; it also involves other body systems. As Chu et al. (2024) explained, the sympathetic-adreno-medullar (SAM) axis gets activated, releasing adrenaline, and even the immune system is put on high alert. You might find yourself breathing faster and your muscles tensing up, all part of your body's comprehensive danger protocol. The amygdala's role in threat detection has significant implications for our behavior. Because it associates certain stimuli with threats, it can lead to avoidance behaviors (Godoy et al., 2018). If you fear getting mugged, you might find yourself avoiding similar situations in the future or choosing different routes, even if the perceived threat turned out to be harmless. If you fear failure, you might not take a difficult course or you might refrain from starting a social relationship out of fear of rejection.

When encountering stress, the brain increases release of several neurotransmitters, including GABA, NE, and serotonin (Andolina & Borreca, 2017). These modulators help respond to immediate threats and concurrently regulate mood. However, cortisol, released by the adrenal cortex in the kidney is the star player in the stress response and is commonly referred to as the "stress hormone." Cortisol's role is a delicate balancing act. On one hand, it helps us stay alert and responsive to potential risks in our environment. For instance, the surge of cortisol you might feel before an important job interview can help sharpen your focus and boost your energy. On the other hand, we need to be aware of the potential harm that chronic stress can cause (Dedovic et al., 2009). This balance is crucial for maintaining the body's homeostasis and internal stability.

In the short term, cortisol is beneficial. It helps mobilize energy reserves and modulates various bodily functions to help us cope with stress. However, when cortisol levels remain elevated for extended periods, it can become damaging to brain cells and overall health. Imagine a person working in a high-pressure job with constant deadlines and long hours. Initially, the stress might help them stay productive, but, over time, the persistent high cortisol levels could lead to burnout and health issues. Indeed, prolonged exposure to high cortisol levels can result in a range of health problems. These include mental health issues like anxiety and depression, as well as physical conditions such as hypertension, heart disease, and metabolic disorders like diabetes (Knezevic et al., 2023). In extreme cases, it can even lead to Cushing's syndrome, characterized by symptoms such as unexplained weight gain, muscle weakness, and high blood sugar. For example, a person with unmanaged chronic stress might find themselves gaining weight despite no changes in diet, feeling constantly fatigued, and noticing their blood sugar levels creeping up over time.

Ironically, stress is not always detrimental to our well-being. In fact, there is a beneficial form of stress known as *eustress*, which occurs when we perceive a challenge as positive and within our capabilities to manage (Dhabhar, 2018). Unlike harmful stress, eustress is typically short-lived and does not overwhelm our brain's resources. Instead, it enhances performance in several ways. For example, imagine you are preparing to give an important presentation at work. The mix of excitement and nervous energy you feel is eustress in action. This positive stress can improve your cardiovascular functioning, boost endurance, and enhance immunity (Dhabhar, 2018). You might notice a slight increase in heart rate and blood flow, helping you feel more alert and prepared for the momentous occasion.

During eustress, our cognitive functions are also improved. Typical experiences include a sharp focus, sustained attention, and better memory retention, which could enhance performance by easier recall of key presentation points and the ability to respond effectively to questions. Studies using functional near-infrared spectroscopy, which is imaging that detects oxygenated blood flow (Dedovic et al., 2009), show that eustress leads to increased activity in the right frontal hemisphere of the brain, associated with better cognitive processing and emotional regulation. In practical terms, eustress could help you stay calm and think clearly under pressure.

Eustress also triggers the release of several beneficial modulators. DA enhances attention and focus, potentially increasing engagement and responsiveness to your audience. Endorphins, the body's natural painkillers, contribute to a sense of well-being and help you feel more optimistic and confident about your performance. Serotonin, while improving mood, also plays a role in the stress response and could help maintain a positive emotional state during your presentation. NE, involved in arousal and alertness, might help you feel more energized and ready to tackle challenges. In combination, eustress can reframe potentially stressful situations into opportunities for growth and achievement, instead of defaulting to the neurologically inferior flight response.

Eustress activates the brain's reward system with projections from the VTA to the PFC. This activation is associated with feelings of pleasure and motivation, encouraging individuals to engage with and overcome moderate challenges (Bak et al., 2022). This is particularly true in situations where stress is perceived as manageable, and provided the individual possesses adequate coping resources. However, chronic, or excessive stress can negatively affect the reward system, leading to reduced motivation and pleasure in activities that were once rewarding. The balance between stress and reward is crucial, as it determines whether stress will have a motivating effect (remember RPE) or lead to negative health outcomes. Overall, understanding the paradox between stress and reward is essential to effectively use the strategies proposed in Chapter 7.

Team Cohesiveness

Along with the complexity of neuropsychology comes at least two words of caution. The interpretation of the evidence can sometimes be misleading. First, no specific neuromodulator accounts for the unitary function of any specific neuronal, cognitive, or motivational process, and no single modulator controls specific human behavior. Just as no single gene can explain why humans exhibit certain behaviors or contract a specific disease, no single neuromodulator can account for specific brain functionality. Human behavior is the result of complex interactions among multiple genes, environmental factors, and neural processes. For example, as explained earlier cognitive functions like memory involve multiple neural mechanisms and are influenced by various genetic and environmental factors (Sridhar et al., 2023). While neuromodulators play crucial roles in regulating various brain functions and behaviors, their interactions are complex and multifaceted. While generalizing is often speculative, some recurring patterns are indicated in relation to how neuromodulators interact. These interactions create a complex, interconnected system that regulates brain function. The balance and interplay between these neuromodulators influence mood, cognition, motivation, stress responses, and various behaviors. Some examples of the recurring patterns among neuromodulation functionality are summarized below as general guidelines, but variability is substantial:

Second, a criticism of neuropsychology is the reliance on correlational evidence, which can limit the ability to infer causation between brain structures or functions and specific cognitive or behavioral outcomes. Correlational studies measure the association between variables, such as brain activity patterns and reward seeking, without establishing a direct causal link. This limitation occurs because correlation does not account for potential confounding variables or the directionality of the relationship. For example, while a positive correlation exists between increased ACh synthesis and learning, it does not necessarily mean that ACh causes more knowledge retention. Other factors such as instructional methods or degree of interest might be implicated as the reason why certain memories are consolidated and others are not. Despite this general limitation, correlational evidence from neuropsychology is highly beneficial as it provides insights into potential relationships that integrate with behavioral

Table 5.1 Neuromodulator Summary

Primary Neuromodulator	Interactive Partners	Impact
Dopamine	Interacts with serotonin in reward and motivation circuits Modulates GABA transmission	Influences NE release, affecting attention and arousal
Norepinephrine	Interacts with DA in attention and arousal circuits Modulates GABA and glutamate transmission	Influences serotonin release, affecting mood and stress responses
Serotonin	Interacts with DA to regulate mood, reward, and motivation Modulates GABA activity, affecting anxiety and stress responses	Influences ACh release, impacting cognitive functioning
GABA	Primary inhibitory neurotransmitter Interacts with glutamate to balance excitation/inhibition	Modulated by various neuromodulators like serotonin and DA
Acetylcholine	Interacts with DA in reward and learning processes Modulates GABA and glutamate transmission	Influences NE release, affecting attention and arousal
Oxytocin	Interacts with DA in social reward circuits Modulates GABA transmission, influencing anxiety and stress responses	Influences serotonin release, affecting mood and social behavior
Stress hormones	Modulate the release of various neurotransmitters, including GABA, and DA	Interact with the stress response system, influencing cortisol release

findings offering a broader understanding of brain-behavior relationships than behavioral evidence alone. This type of evidence is crucial to understanding complex cognitive and motivational processes because it informs practical strategies to enhance optimal performance, supplementing and improving behavioral approaches.

Finally, you may have noticed that "Team Modulation" only has seven "star" players, and a baseball team needs nine to be complete! The missing pieces are the substantial influence of culture and heredity. The explicit discussion of environmental and genetic influences on behavior is largely omitted from this chapter based on the variable and contextual nature of these prevailing influences. These collaborators are incredibly important to understand human behavior and thus discussed in other chapters throughout the book. The lack of specific focus here does not diminish the powerful role of these behavioral influences. Next, we explore how various neuromodulators influence perceptions of passion, learning, changing minds, and socialization, four of the most critical outcomes influencing optimal motivation.

References

Andolina, D., & Borreca, A. (2017). The key role of the amygdala in stress. In B. Ferry (Ed.), *The amygdala-where emotions shape perception, learning and memories* (Vol. 187). IntechOpen. https://doi.org/10.5772/67826

Avery, M. C., & Krichmar, J. L. (2017). Neuromodulatory systems and their interactions: A review of models, theories, and experiments. *Frontiers in Neural Circuits, 11*, 108. https://doi.org/10.3389/fncir.2017.00108

Baik, J. H. (2020). Stress and the dopaminergic reward system. *Experimental & Molecular Medicine, 52*(12), 1879–1890. https://doi.org/10.1038/s12276-020-00532-4

Bak, S., Shin, J., & Jeong, J. (2022). Subdividing stress groups into eustress and distress groups using laterality index calculated from brain hemodynamic response. *Biosensors, 12*(1), 33. https://doi.org/10.3390/bios12010033

Bandura, A. (1986). *Self-efficacy: The exercise of control.* W. H. Freeman.

Bar, K. J., de la Cruz, F., Schumann, A., Koehler, S., Sauer, H., Critchley, H., & Wagner, G. (2016). Functional connectivity and network analysis of midbrain and brainstem nuclei. *Neuroimage, 134*, 53–63. https://doi.org/10.1016/j.neuroimage.2016.03.071

Beach, S. R., Brody, G. H., Todorov, A. A., Gunter, T. D., & Philibert, R. A. (2010). Methylation at SLC6A4 is linked to family history of child abuse: An examination of the Iowa Adoptee sample. *American Journal of Medical Genetics. Part B, Neuropsychiatric genetics: The official publication of the International Society of Psychiatric Genetics, 153*(2), 710. https://doi.org/10.1002/ajmg.b.31028

Beaulieu-Boire, I., & Lang, A. E. (2015). Behavioral effects of levodopa. *Movement Disorders, 30*(1), 90–102. https://doi.org/10.1002/mds.26121

Benjamin, P. R., Staras, K., & Kemenes, G. (2010). What roles do tonic inhibition and disinhibition play in the control of motor programs? *Frontiers in Behavioral Neuroscience.* https://www.ncbi.nlm.nih.gov/pmc/articles/PMC2893002/

Berke, J. D. (2018). What does dopamine mean?. *Nature Neuroscience, 21*(6), 787–793.

Biddle, K. D., Uquillas, F. D. O., Jacobs, H. I., Zide, B., Kirn, D. R., Rentz, D. M., . . . & Donovan, N. J. (2019). Social engagement and amyloid-β-related cognitive decline in cognitively normal older adults. *The American Journal of Geriatric Psychiatry, 27*(11), 1247–1256. https://doi.org/10.1016/j.jagp.2019.05.005

Blain, B., & Sharot, T. (2021). Intrinsic reward: Potential cognitive and neural mechanisms. *Current Opinion in Behavioral Sciences, 39*, 113–118. https://doi.org/10.1016/j.cobeha.2021.03.008

Bouarab, C., Thompson, B., & Polter, A. M. (2019). VTA GABA neurons at the interface of stress and reward. *Frontiers in Neural Circuits, 13*, 78. https://doi.org/10.3389/fncir.2019.00078

Bouret, S., & Richmond, B. J. (2015). Sensitivity of locus ceruleus neurons to reward value for goal-directed actions. *Journal of Neuroscience, 35*(9), 4005–4014. https://doi.org/10.1523/jneurosci.4553-14.2015

Browne, C. J., Abela, A. R., Chu, D., Li, Z., Ji, X., Lambe, E. K., & Fletcher, P. J. (2019). Dorsal raphe serotonin neurons inhibit operant responding for reward via inputs to the ventral tegmental area but not the nucleus accumbens: Evidence from studies combining optogenetic stimulation and serotonin reuptake inhibition. *Neuropsychopharmacology, 44*(4), 793–804. https://doi.org/10.1038/s41386-018-0271-x

Budygin, E. A., Bass, C. E., Grinevich, V. P., Deal, A. L., Bonin, K. D., & Weiner, J. L. (2020). Opposite consequences of tonic and phasic increases in accumbal DA on alcohol-seeking behavior. *IScience, 23*(3), 100877. https://doi.org/10.1016/j.isci.2020.100877

Butler, R. K., & Finn, D. P. (2009). Stress-induced analgesia. *Progress in Neurobiology, 88*(3), 184–202. https://doi.org/10.1016/j.pneurobio.2009.04.003

Chu, B., Marwaha, K., Sanvictores, T., & Ayers, D. (2024). *Physiology, stress reaction.* StatPearls Publishing. https://www.ncbi.nlm.nih.gov/books/NBK541120/

Clear, J. (2018). *Atomic habits: An easy & proven way to build good habits & break bad ones.* Penguin Random House.

Colwell, M. J., Tagomori, H., Shang, F., Cheng, H. I., Wigg, C. E., Browning, M., ... & Harmer, C. J. (2024). Direct serotonin release in humans shapes aversive learning and inhibition. *Nature Communications, 15*(1), 6617. https://doi.org/10.1038/s41467-024-50394-x

Cragg, S. J. (2006). Meaningful silences: How DA listens to the ACh pause. *Trends in Neurosciences, 29*(3), 125–131. https://doi.org/10.1016/j.tins.2006.01.003

de Araujo, I. E. (2016). Circuit organization of sugar reinforcement. *Physiology & Behavior, 164*, 473–477. https://doi.org/10.1016/j.physbeh.2016.04.041

De Dreu, C. K., Greer, L. L., Handgraaf, M. J., Shalvi, S., Van Kleef, G. A., Baas, M., . . . & Feith, S. W. (2010). The neuropeptide oxytocin regulates parochial altruism in intergroup conflict among humans. *Science, 328*(5984), 1408–1411. https://doi.org/10.1126/science.1189047

Dedovic, K., Duchesne, A., Andrews, J., Engert, V., & Pruessner, J. C. (2009). The brain and the stress axis: the neural correlates of cortisol regulation in response to stress. *Neuroimage, 47*(3), 864–871. https://doi.org/10.1016/j.neuroimage.2009.05.074

Dhabhar, F. S. (2018). The short-term stress response–Mother nature's mechanism for enhancing protection and performance under conditions of threat, challenge, and opportunity. *Frontiers in Neuroendocrinology, 49*, 175–192. https://doi.org/10.1016/j.yfrne.2018.03.004

Diamond, A. (2007). Consequences of variations in genes that affect DA in prefrontal cortex. *Cerebral Cortex, 17*(suppl_1), i161–i170. https://doi.org/10.1093/cercor/bhm082

Dickman, K. D., Thomas, M. C., Anderson, B., Manuck, S. B., & Kamarck, T. W. (2020). Social integration and diurnal cortisol decline: The role of psychosocial and behavioral pathways. *Psychosomatic Medicine, 82*(6), 568–576. https://doi.org/10.1097/psy.0000000000000825

Eisenberger, N. I. (2012). The neural bases of social pain: Evidence for shared representations with physical pain. *Psychosomatic Medicine, 74*(2), 126–135. https://doi.org/10.1097/psy.0b013e3182464dd1

España, R. A., Schmeichel, B. E., & Berridge, C. W. (2016). Norepinephrine at the nexus of arousal, motivation and relapse. *Brain Research, 1641*, 207–216. https://doi.org/10.1016/j.brainres.2016.01.002

Farrell, M. R., Esteban, J. S. D., Faget, L., Floresco, S. B., Hnasko, T. S., & Mahler, S. V. (2021). Ventral pallidum GABA neurons mediate motivation underlying risky choice. *Journal of Neuroscience, 41*(20), 4500–4513. https://doi.org/10.1523/JNEUROSCI.2039-20.2021

Feld, G. B., & Born, J. (2020). Neurochemical mechanisms for memory processing during sleep: Basic findings in humans and neuropsychiatric implications. *Neuropsychopharmacology, 45*(1), 31–44. https://doi.org/10.1038/s41386-019-0490-9

Ferrario, C. R., Labouèbe, G., Liu, S., Nieh, E. H., Routh, V. H., Xu, S., & O'Connor, E. C. (2016). Homeostasis meets motivation in the battle to control food intake. *Journal of Neuroscience, 36*(45), 11469–11481. https://doi.org/10.1523/jneurosci.2338-16.2016

Fischer, A. G., Jocham, G., & Ullsperger, M. (2015). Dual serotonergic signals: A key to understanding paradoxical effects?. *Trends in Cognitive Sciences, 19*(1), 21–26. https://doi.org/10.1016/j.tics.2014.11.004

Godoy, L. D., Rossignoli, M. T., Delfino-Pereira, P., Garcia-Cairasco, N., & de Lima Umeoka, E. H. (2018). A comprehensive overview on stress neurobiology: Basic concepts and clinical implications. *Frontiers in Behavioral Neuroscience, 12,* 127. https://doi.org/10.3389/fnbeh.2018.00127

Gonzalez-Lopez, E., & Vrana, K. E. (2020). Dopamine beta-hydroxylase and its genetic variants in human health and disease. *Journal of Neurochemistry, 152*(2), 157–181. https://doi.org/10.1111/jnc.14893

Gottman, J., & Gottman, J. (2017). The natural principles of love. *Journal of Family Theory & Review, 9*(1), 7–26. https://doi.org/10.1111/jftr.12182

Guastella, A. J., Mitchell, P. B., & Dadds, M. R. (2008). Oxytocin increases gaze to the eye region of human faces. *Biological Psychiatry, 63*(1), 3–5. https://doi.org/10.1016/j.biopsych.2007.06.026

Haam, J., & Yakel, J. L. (2017). Cholinergic modulation of the hippocampal region and memory function. *Journal of Neurochemistry, 142,* 111–121. https://doi.org/10.1111/jnc.14052

Hamid, A. A., Pettibone, J. R., Mabrouk, O. S., Hetrick, V. L., Schmidt, R., Vander Weele, C. M., ... & Berke, J. D. (2016). Mesolimbic dopamine signals the value of work. *Nature Neuroscience, 19*(1), 117–126. https://doi.org/10.1038/nn.4173

Harry, D. A. (1978). One way or another. *Parallel Lines.* Chrysalis records.

Hasselmo, M. E., & Sarter, M. (2011). Modes and models of forebrain cholinergic neuromodulation of cognition. *Neuropsychopharmacology, 36*(1), 52–73. https://doi.org/10.1038/npp.2010.104

Huberman, A. (2022, July 10). *Optimize & control your brain chemistry to improve health & performance.* https://www.hubermanlab.com/episode/optimize-and-control-your-brain-chemistry-to-improve-health-and-performance?timestamp=5170

Knezevic, E., Nenic, K., Milanovic, V., & Knezevic, N. N. (2023). The role of cortisol in chronic stress, neurodegenerative diseases, and psychological disorders. *Cells, 12*(23), 2726. https://doi.org/10.3390/cells12232726

Kraus, J., Výborová, E., & Silani, G. (2023). The effect of intranasal oxytocin on social reward processing in humans: A systematic review. *Frontiers in Psychiatry, 14*, 1244027. https://doi.org/10.3389/fpsyt.2023.1244027

Kreek, M. J., Nielsen, D. A., Butelman, E. R., & LaForge, K. S. (2005). Genetic influences on impulsivity, risk taking, stress responsivity and vulnerability to drug abuse and addiction. *Nature Neuroscience, 8*(11), 1450–1457. https://doi.org/10.1038/nn1583

Latif, S., Jahangeer, M., Razia, D. M., Ashiq, M., Ghaffar, A., Akram, M., . . . & Ansari, M. A. (2021). DA in Parkinson's disease. *Clinica Chimica Acta, 522*, 114–126. https://doi.org/10.1016/j.cca.2021.08.009

Lembke, A. (2021). *DA nation: Finding balance in the age of indulgence.* Penguin.

Liu, C., Goel, P., & Kaeser, P. S. (2021). Spatial and temporal scales of dopamine transmission. *Nature Reviews Neuroscience, 22*(6), 345–358. https://doi.org/10.1038/s41583-021-00455-7

Liu, Z. H., Shin, R., & Ikemoto, S. (2008). Dual role of medial A10 dopamine neurons in affective encoding. *Neuropsychopharmacology, 33*(12), 3010–3020. https://doi.org/10.1038/npp.2008.4

London, E. D. (2020). Human brain imaging links dopaminergic systems to impulsivity. In H. de Wit & J. D. Jentsch (Eds.), *Recent advances in research on impulsivity and impulsive behaviors* (pp. 53–71). Springer International Publishing. https://doi.org/10.1007/7854_2019_125

Love, T. M. (2014). Oxytocin, motivation and the role of dopamine. *Pharmacology Biochemistry and Behavior, 119*, 49–60. https://doi.org/10.1016/j.pbb.2013.06.011

Macoveanu, J., Rowe, J. B., Hornboll, B., Elliott, R., Paulson, O. B., Knudsen, G. M., & Siebner, H. R. (2013). Serotonin 2A receptors contribute to the regulation of risk-averse decisions. *Neuroimage, 83*, 35–44. https://doi.org/10.1016/j.neuroimage.2013.06.063

Mahalingam, G., Samtani, S., Lam, B. C. P., Lipnicki, D. M., Lima-Costa, M. F., Blay, S. L., . . . & shared consortium for the Cohort Studies of Memory in an International Consortium (COSMIC). (2023). Social connections and risk of incident mild cognitive impairment, dementia, and mortality in 13 longitudinal cohort studies of ageing. *Alzheimer's & Dementia, 19*(11), 5114–5128. https://doi.org/10.1002/alz.13072

Maloney, R. T. (2021). Neuromodulation and individuality. *Frontiers in Behavioral Neuroscience, 15*, 777873. https://doi.org/10.3389/fnbeh.2021.777873

Marder, E. (2012). Neuromodulation of neuronal circuits: Back to the future. *Neuron, 76*(1), 1–11. https://doi.org/10.1016/j.neuron.2012.09.010

Marsh, A. A., Yu, H. H., Pine, D. S., & Blair, R. J. R. (2010). Oxytocin improves specific recognition of positive facial expressions. *Psychopharmacology, 209*, 225–232. https://doi.org/10.1007/s00213-010-1780-4

Martin, A. M., Young, R. L., Leong, L., Rogers, G. B., Spencer, N. J., Jessup, C. F., & Keating, D. J. (2017). The diverse metabolic roles of peripheral serotonin. *Endocrinology, 158*(5), 1049–1063. https://doi.org/10.1210/en.2016-1839

Mather, M., Clewett, D., Sakaki, M., & Harley, C. W. (2016). Norepinephrine ignites local hotspots of neuronal excitation: How arousal amplifies selectivity in perception and memory. *Behavioral and Brain Sciences, 39*, e200. https://doi.org/10.1017/s0140525x15000667

McDougle, M., de Araujo, A., Singh, A., Yang, M., Braga, I., Paille, V., ... & de Lartigue, G. (2024). Separate gut-brain circuits for fat and sugar reinforcement combine to promote overeating. *Cell Metabolism, 36*(2), 393–407. https://doi.org/10.1016/j.cmet.2024.05.004

Meyniel, F., Goodwin, G. M., Deakin, J. W., Klinge, C., MacFadyen, C., Milligan, H., ... & Gaillard, R. (2016). A specific role for serotonin in overcoming effort cost. *Elife, 5*, e17282. https://doi.org/10.7554/elife.17282

Mischel, W. (2014). *The marshmallow test: Understanding self-control and how to master it*. Random House.

Miyazaki, K. W., Miyazaki, K., Tanaka, K. F., Yamanaka, A., Takahashi, A., Tabuchi, S., & Doya, K. (2014). Optogenetic activation of dorsal raphe serotonin neurons enhances patience for future rewards. *Current Biology, 24*(17), 2033–2040. https://doi.org/10.1016/j.cub.2014.07.041

Monti, J. M., & Monti, D. (2007). The involvement of dopamine in the modulation of sleep and waking. *Sleep Medicine Reviews, 11*(2), 113–133. https://doi.org/10.1016/j.smrv.2006.08.003

Neumann, I. D., & Slattery, D. A. (2016). Oxytocin in general anxiety and social fear: a translational approach. *Biological Psychiatry, 79*(3), 213–221. https://doi.org/10.1016/j.biopsych.2015.06.004

Nunes, E. J., Kebede, N., Bagdas, D., & Addy, N. A. (2022). Cholinergic and dopaminergic-mediated motivated behavior in healthy states and in substance use and mood disorders. *Journal of the Experimental Analysis of Behavior, 117*(3), 404–419. https://doi.org/10.1002/jeab.747

Olguín, J. H., Guzmán, C. D., García, H. E., & Mejía, B. G. (2016). The role of DA and its dysfunction as a consequence of oxidative stress. *Oxidative Medicine and Cellular Longevity, 2016*(1), 9730467. https://doi.org/10.1155/2016/9730467

Pine, A., Shiner, T., Seymour, B., & Dolan, R. J. (2010). Dopamine, time, and impulsivity in humans. *Journal of Neuroscience, 30*(26), 8888–8896.

Ray, N. J., Metzler-Baddeley, C., Khondoker, M. R., Grothe, M. J., Teipel, S., Wright, P., ... & O'Sullivan, M. J. (2015). Cholinergic basal forebrain structure influences the reconfiguration of white matter connections to support residual memory in mild cognitive impairment. *Journal of Neuroscience, 35*(2), 739–747. https://doi.org/10.1523/jneurosci.6028-09.2010

Reynolds, L. M., & Flores, C. (2021). Mesocorticolimbic dopamine pathways across adolescence: Diversity in development. *Frontiers in Neural Circuits, 15*, 735625. https://doi.org/10.3389/fncir.2021.735625

Ryan, R. M., & Deci, E. L. (2020). Intrinsic and extrinsic motivation from a self-determination theory perspective: Definitions, theory, practices, and future directions. *Contemporary Educational Psychology*, 101860. https://doi.org/10.1016/j.cedpsych.2020.101860

Salamone, J. D., & Correa, M. (2012). The mysterious motivational functions of mesolimbic dopamine. *Neuron, 76*(3), 470–485. https://doi.org/10.1016/j.neuron.2012.10.021

Sapolsky, R. M. (2017). *Behave: The biology of humans at our best and worst*. Penguin.

Scheele, D., Wille, A., Kendrick, K. M., Stoffel-Wagner, B., Becker, B., Güntürkün, O., ... & Hurlemann, R. (2013). Oxytocin enhances brain reward system responses in men viewing the face of their female partner. *Proceedings of the National Academy of Sciences, 110*(50), 20308–20313. https://doi.org/10.1073/pnas.1314190110

Schneiderman, N., Ironson, G., & Siegel, S. D. (2005). Stress and health: Psychological, behavioral, and biological determinants. *Annual Review of Clinical Psychology, 1*(1), 607–628. https://doi.org/10.1146/annurev.clinpsy.1.102803.144141

Schultz, W. (2016). Dopamine reward prediction error coding. *Dialogues in Clinical Neuroscience, 18*(1), 23–32. https://doi.org/10.31887/dcns.2016.18.1/wschultz

Sepah, C. (2019). The definitive guide to DA fasting 2.0: The hot silicon valley trend. *Medium*. https://medium.com/swlh/DA-fasting-2-0-the-hot-silicon-valley-trend-7c4dc3ba2213

Solinas, M., Ferré, S., You, Z. B., Karcz-Kubicha, M., Popoli, P., & Goldberg, S. R. (2002). Caffeine induces DA and glutamate release in the shell of the nucleus accumbens. *Journal of Neuroscience, 22*(15), 6321–6324. https://doi.org/10.1523/jneurosci.22-15-06321.2002

Sridhar, S., Khamaj, A., & Asthana, M. K. (2023). Cognitive neuroscience perspective on memory: Overview and summary. *Frontiers in

Human Neuroscience, *17*, 1217093. https://doi.org/10.3389/fnhum.2023.1217093

Strasser, A., Luksys, G., Xin, L., Pessiglione, M., Gruetter, R., & Sandi, C. (2020). Glutamine-to-glutamate ratio in the nucleus accumbens predicts effort-based motivated performance in humans. *Neuropsychopharmacology*, *45*(12), 2048–2057. https://doi.org/10.1038/s41386-020-0760-6

Strathearn, L., Li, J., Fonagy, P., & Montague, P. R. (2008). What's in a smile? Maternal brain responses to infant facial cues. *Pediatrics*, *122*, 40–51. https://doi.org/10.1542/peds.2007-1566

Tellez, L. A., Han, W., Zhang, X., Ferreira, T. L., Perez, I. O., Shammah-Lagnado, S. J., . . . & De Araujo, I. E. (2016). Separate circuitries encode the hedonic and nutritional values of sugar. *Nature Neuroscience*, *19*(3), 465–470. https://doi.org/10.1038/nn.4224

Touroutoglou, A., Andreano, J., Dickerson, B. C., & Barrett, L. F. (2020). The tenacious brain: How the anterior mid-cingulate contributes to achieving goals. *Cortex*, *123*, 12–29. https://doi.org/10.1016/j.cortex.2019.09.011

Umberson, D., & Karas Montez, J. (2010). Social relationships and health: A flashpoint for health policy. *Journal of Health and Social Behavior*, *51*(1_suppl), S54–S66. https://doi.org/10.1177/0022146510383501

Van Zessen, R., Phillips, J. L., Budygin, E. A., & Stuber, G. D. (2012). Activation of VTA GABA neurons disrupts reward consumption. *Neuron*, *73*(6), 1184–1194. https://doi.org/10.1016/j.neuron.2012.02.016

Westbrook, A., & Braver, T. S. (2016). Dopamine does double duty in motivating cognitive effort. *Neuron*, *89*(4), 695–710. https://doi.org/10.1016/j.neuron.2016.07.020

Wise, R. A., & Robble, M. A. (2020). Dopamine and addiction. *Annual Review of Psychology*, *71*(1), 79–106. https://doi.org/10.1146/annurev-psych-010418-103337

Wood, P. B. (2008). Role of central dopamine in pain and analgesia. *Expert Review of Neurotherapeutics*, *8*(5), 781–797. https://doi.org/10.1586/14737175.8.5.781

Yamasue, H., & Domes, G. (2017). Oxytocin and autism spectrum disorders. In R. Hurlemann & V. Grinevich (Eds.), *Behavioral pharmacology of neuropeptides: Oxytocin* (pp. 449–465). Springer. https://doi.org/10.1007/7854_2017_24

Zhang, Y., Chen, Y., Xin, Y., Peng, B., & Liu, S. (2023). Norepinephrine system at the interface of attention and reward. *Progress in Neuro-Psychopharmacology and Biological Psychiatry*, *125*, 110751. https://doi.org/10.1016/j.pnpbp.2023.110751

6

The Impact of Rewards

Chapter Outline

From Brain to Behavior	197
Labels Belong on Cans, Not Motives	198
Rewards and Learning	205
Reward Stipulations	212
Rewards and Persuasion	220
Reward and Social Relationships	228
Reconciling Brain and Behavior Findings	239

From Brain to Behavior

Surviving the previous two chapters is an accomplishment. The brain barrage shall now subside. Next, we need to generate some positive reward prediction error (RPE) and learn how the biological knowledge of reward can be used to enhance motivation. Knowing the immense influence of the brain on behavior is helpful but applying that information to improve performance and reach personal milestones is the payoff. The objective of this chapter is to illustrate how reward influences specific outcomes. In other words, we need to know how neuropsychology explains some of the everyday learning and performance opportunities where motivation influences success. Remembering that motivation is situational, and that behavior is based in part on context, we will continue using the expectancy-value orientation described in Chapter 1. This chapter is devoted to the practical application of reward and how reward influences overall motivation, learning, belief change, and the desire to socialize.

While it would be advantageous to know how reward perceptions influence every type of achievement opportunity, an exhaustive overview is both impractical and unnecessary, because of the subjective nature of reward. If nothing else was garnered from the previous chapters, the fundamental message advanced is that *whatever the brain perceives as rewarding is what motivates us to act*. The brain does not care *how* the urge for the potential reward is satisfied or achieved. Instead, it craves the associated feelings, thoughts, and physiological sensations. The specific rewards that are achieved by the pursuit and attainment of personal goals do not matter. How the urge is satisfied is neurologically inconsequential, provided desire has been adequately quelled. Satisfying the beast in your brain is not a choice, you can only decide how you will do it. Next, we shall explore some of the most common ways that the pursuit of reward operates on a routine but covert basis.

Labels Belong on Cans, Not Motives

Understanding how rewards explain motivation requires acknowledgment of at least three realities. First, your brain and underlying neurological systems don't give a laboratory rodent's posterior about how psychologists describe hypothetical constructs like INMO and EXMO. External contingencies matter, but the origination of agency and movement starts far more upstream than any behavioral theory of motivation suggests. Many explanations of motivated behavior focus on the reasons and causes of motivation but often neglect the "how did we get there" explanation (Luria et al., 2021). Ultimately, there is no definitive origination source for INMO, and an endless loop exists between internalizing values and experiences that contribute to self-determined actions, which in turn enhance self-perceptions, which promote enhanced INMO. Thus, the presumed source of INMO is achieved by fully internalizing external factors. By this logic, if you bring your lawn chairs into your living room, then the source of your comfort is internalized, but we still don't know where the chairs came from, and IKEA is not a source of INMO.

Second, obviously what is considered rewarding has broad implications for internalization and thus stresses the importance of disentangling EXMO and INMO neurologically. Minimally, we can surmise that the nature of rewards is far more variable than what you might believe. While there is little to debate concerning the debilitating impact of controlling rewards, and we have already described how the perception of autonomy is crucial for motivated behavior, the reality is we live in a highly potent, reward-based culture. Despite claims from the passion proponents, EXMO dominates many individuals. We learned earlier (Twenge & Donnelly, 2016) that the current generation of college students prioritizes incentives. Another recent survey (Clearerthinking.org, 2023) tested which intrinsic values were evaluated as personally valuable, and the results revealed that 50 percent of the listed items had an extrinsic locus of control. For those still skeptical about the value of external reward, good luck finding a book on potty training that promotes intrinsic interest as the preferred method to motivate a diaper-pooping toddler!

Finally, we are still plagued by the ambiguous research that rewards undermine INMO. According to the *"overjustification"* effect (see p. 214–215), when someone is already motivated, providing any incentive will diminish subsequent intrinsic task interest. Despite more recent research indicating that the overjustification effect is null (Peters et al., 2022) and reflects a variety of construct and experimental errors (Cameron & Pierce, 1994; Levy et al., 2017), the EXMO reputation remains tarnished. As we shall soon see, rewards don't necessarily undermine the desire to increase rewarded activities, but some researchers suggest that inhibition of reward from a previously rewarding activity will actually *increase* the drive toward earning the reward (Luria et al., 2021). To finally resolve the INMO/EXMO debate, neuropsychology findings provide evidence to answer two important questions: Do INMO and EXMO have separated or combined neural pathways, and do rewards undermine INMO, or, according to your brain, is INMO just a different type of reward?

Distinct or Shared Neural Pathways?

One consistent conclusion advanced by researchers who attempt to determine if there are neurological distinctions between intrinsic and extrinsic reward is that the research is ambiguous (Lee, 2016; Luria et al.,

2021; Morris et al., 2022). However, upon closer scrutiny, conclusions are far less confusing than you might be led to believe. Several themes emerge indicating under which circumstances common neural pathways are activated during the performance of intrinsically motivating tasks and under what conditions neural disassociation (partitioning) occurs during reward. These studies in aggregate reveal that reward perception is first a function of how your brain processes the reward. Second, the perception of autonomy or control makes an enormous difference in reward perceptions. Third, there are significant correlations among certain types of reward contingencies and corresponding neural circuitry.

What appears ambiguous on the surface can be explained quite succinctly when examining the nuances of reward processing. Luria et al. (2021) speculated that motivation type had little bearing on the effectiveness of reward and instead suggested that learning and motivation were a function of reward and punishment contingencies. Since then, additional evidence has been advanced revealing that the source of the reward is secondary (Blain & Sharot, 2021), and what matters most is how the reward is processed neurologically. As Schultz (2015) projected, "Rewards are not defined by their physical properties but by the behavioral reactions they induce" (p. 853). The next step toward settling the INMO/EXMO debate is determining which reward type activates particular brain regions. Similarities in localization would imply that intrinsic and extrinsic motivation are driven by a common underlying factor, while dissociation would suggest that EXMO and INMO are indeed different.

Both intrinsic and extrinsic rewards target some common brain areas within the neural reward system (Lee, 2016). The mesocorticolimbic pathway, which is the primary reward pathway discussed in Chapter 5, contains key areas that are activated by both extrinsic and intrinsic rewards. These shared areas of activation are specifically housed in the neostriatum and basal ganglia (Kim, 2013; Linke et al., 2010). This pathway originates in the ventral tegmental area (VTA) and projects to the ventral striatum, which includes the nucleus accumbens (NAcc). As the reward pathway ultimately extends to the prefrontal cortex (PFC), both types of rewards also activate common areas in this region, particularly the ventromedial prefrontal cortex (vmPFC). This shared neural activation pattern underscores the similarities in how the brain processes both types of rewards similarly, despite their distinct origins as being classified as either extrinsic or intrinsic. Recall that the vmPFC plays a primary role in evaluating the subjective value of rewards. As such, the transmission is activated regardless of the reward source or valence (Oldham et al., 2018). We can thus conclude that DA synthesis and transmission is activated by anything perceived as rewarding because the brain does not differentiate the source of motivation in terms of DA release (Mohebi & Berke, 2020). Motivational value can be similar regardless of the nature of the reward (Bromberg-Martin et al., 2010).

Neural distinctions are revealed when rewards are intrinsically generated, such as what occurs when someone is motivated to master a new topic for no apparent reason. Intrinsic rewards are genuine and prove instrumental in discretionary learning, as demonstrated by behaviors such as playing a musical instrument or reading a book for merely enjoyment (Schultz, 2015). Unlike extrinsic reward processing, intrinsic rewards are linked to activity in the insula, a brain region associated with sensory perception, emotion and self-awareness, and the sensing of internal feedback (Lee, 2016). The insula's involvement suggests that intrinsic rewards are tied to satisfaction of basic motivational needs such as self-satisfaction and personal fulfillment, needs that are highly related to feeling independent and competent. Effort perceptions change when intrinsically motivated to engage in a task because the inherent satisfaction and enjoyment that accompanies task engagement feels natural. In these cases, effort investment occurs automatically, without conscious consideration of how challenging or demanding the task might be. During INMO, task effort is perceived as lower because the activity is enjoyable and aligns with personal interests and expectations.

Conversely, EXMO typically involves pursuing goals based on external factors. While EXMO activates the striatum and NAcc like INMO, it relies more heavily on learned associations and external validation. In pure EXMO scenarios, the brain's response is shaped by the anticipation of external consequences, which often lead to behavior changes once the reward is obtained. For example, with monetary incentives, the mesolimbic pathway is activated similarly to INMO, but the driving force is the expectation of external rewards. Extrinsic rewards consistently engage a network of brain regions, including the vmPFC and the caudate. These areas are typically associated with processing external incentives such as money and social rewards (e.g., being liked or receiving recognition). They play a role in improving performance and goal achievement through external motivators (Bhanji & Delgado, 2014; Tobler et al., 2005). The key difference between INMO and EXMO processing is that striving toward external rewards feels like outside manipulation or control, while those generated through intrinsic reward are individually determined. Overall, while both intrinsic and extrinsic rewards engage the brain's reward system, intrinsic rewards are more closely associated with personal satisfaction and emotional contentment, while extrinsic rewards have lower emotional value (Chew et al., 2021). These differences highlight the distinct pathways through which each type of reward influences motivation and behavior.

Although both types of rewards involve the release of DA in the brain's reward system, DA pathways respond differently to intrinsic and extrinsic rewards. The key difference in dopaminergic response between intrinsic and extrinsic rewards lies in the endurance and normalization of DA release. Intrinsic rewards tend to sustain DA release over longer periods, as they are self-reinforcing and aligned with personal values and interests. This leads to continued engagement and motivation without the need for external incentives. Extrinsic rewards can lead to a decrease in DA release over time due to habituation. This means a strong dopaminergic response to external rewards happens initially, but, over time, repeated exposure can result in neural tolerance, where the DA synthesis subsides because the previous unknown outcome becomes expected, thus inducing lower RPE (Alcaro et al., 2007). Overall, while both intrinsic and extrinsic rewards activate the same dopaminergic pathways, intrinsic rewards are more likely to sustain motivation and engagement due to their alignment with personal interests and the absence of habituation effects.

However, assuming that intrinsic rewards are always preferred is a mistake. Many individuals set their own rewards and use incentives to motivate and propel performance because the rewards are personally valued. As Ryan and Deci stressed, when extrinsic motivation is "congruent with one's self" (2017, p. 14), rewards are not seen as externally controlling and thus perceptions of choice provide the individual with initiative to act devoid of feeling obligated or coerced. In other words, rewards are highly motivating when the individual feels as if the setting and attainment of the reward is done under their own terms and conditions. Ultimately, control of one's destiny is highly rewarding.

The INMO Mask

Operating under the presumption that all rewards are externally generated and thus controlling (thereby inhibiting INMO) is inaccurate. One main conclusion revealed from the neurological EXMO/INMO distinctions is that the perception of control is one of the most relevant variables to determine subjective value of the reward and corresponding RPE. When reward is perceived as controlling, then individuals feel constrained, and thus EXMO/INMO is conceptually and neurologically disassociated. If reward is subjectively valued and can be set and achieved autonomously, then individuals feel like they are in control and liberated, resulting in a substantial blurring of the hypothetical EXMO/INMO distinctions. Reward source is far less meaningful than individual buy-in.

The blurring of EXMO/INMO is supported by confluent and sound evidence indicating that when we think we have agency, both motivation and performance increase (Patall et al., 2008). This autonomy perspective has been supported through neuropsychology evidence as well, with Blain and Sharot (2021) revealing that the perception of agency is often linked to increased activity in the vmPFC and promotes typical interaction with the mesolimbocortical reward system. Wang and Delgado (2019) found comparable results when determining how the brain encodes the subjective value of perceived control and the consequences of control on decision-making. Individuals given a control or no-control option during a monetary reward game revealed more activity in the reward pathway when individuals had free choice, activating the same brain areas as what were observed when receiving monetary rewards. Participants are even willing to endure a "control premium" (Owens et al., 2014) to retain the ability of control over an outcome. In particular, Owens and his colleagues found that when offered a control option, which refers to individuals' willingness to pay for the autonomy to control their own payoffs, greater activation of the vmPFC was observed and the perceived control option inflated the reward value of choice by 30 percent. The study revealed that perceived control motivates behavior because individuals want to feel responsible for their effort. The Owens meta-analysis neurologically extended the consistent behavioral findings that autonomy enhances motivation, learning, and performance (Reeve & Cheon, 2021) by quantifying the subjective value of control within reward-seeking behaviors, and by demonstrating that control is a desirable quality during decision-making. When having control, individuals feel more autonomous and thus INMO increases.

What can we conclude about the EXMO/INMO debate when neuropsychology findings are considered? What it all means is that the EXMO/INMO distinction is predominately theoretical, and conventional findings are inconsistent with the neurological processing observed during the self-directed striving toward rewards. The perception of having flexibility promotes enhanced activation in the ventral striatum, the core of the DA reward pathway. Autonomy in this case means making discretionary decisions as to the goals of one's actions, with the understanding that neuropsychological evidence consistently reveals that the brain does not care about hypothetical sources of motivation or which type of reward leads to enhanced subjective valuation (Bromberg-Martin & Monosov, 2010; Luria et al., 2021; Mohebi & Berke, 2020; Shultz, 2015). Instead, the neurological objective is to maximize the reward return both psychologically and physiologically. *Valuation does not consider source, and source is not a reliable determinant of human agency.* Consequently, individuals are more open to exploring their domains when they feel they have control over their exploration because personal choice is rewarding, changes the perception of outcomes, and thus facilitates motivation and performance (Murayama et al., 2016).

The neurological evidence suggests that the traditional dichotomy between intrinsic and extrinsic motivation may be oversimplified. Both types of rewards activate similar brain regions and trigger DA release, indicating a common underlying mechanism for motivation. The key difference appears to lie not in the source of the reward, but in the individual's perception of autonomy versus external control. This perspective shift suggests that the labels of "intrinsic" and "extrinsic" motivation may have limited explanatory power when considering the complexities of human behavior and decision-making. Instead, the crucial factor seems to be the individual's sense of agency and autonomy in pursuing a reward, regardless of whether that reward is internally or externally generated. Having addressed the ongoing INMO/EXMO debate, we can now turn to analyzing the critical dynamics of how reward influences some of the typical challenges and activities that optimal performers master in day-to-day life.

Rewards and Learning

Learning is a fundamental aspect of human experience, shaping our careers, social experiences, and culture. At its core, learning involves making connections between events, stimuli, and our interactions with the environment. While definitions of learning vary, they all share a common thread: change resulting from experience. The change can be as simple as associating a clang with a bell or as complex as mastering a new language. Advances in neuroscience reveal an intriguing connection between learning and reward. When we learn something new, our brain does not just store information—it experiences a sense of satisfaction, much like the pleasure felt when receiving a tangible reward (Gruber et al., 2019). This neurological response suggests that despite the lament of many students, learning is inherently rewarding to the brain, regardless of whether the practical benefits of acquiring new knowledge are obvious or not.

During learning, neurons generate a teaching signal in the form of DA release to their downstream targets in the basal ganglia, with the overlap activating the mesocorticolimbic reward pathway (Lee et al., 2021). Learning has many nuances, but, overall, learning occurs when new neural connections are formed in the brain. Constructing new connections primarily occurs when satisfying the motive of intellectual curiosity, meaning that required learning (typically experienced in classrooms) is often counterproductive to knowledge acquisition if interest is lacking (Murayama & Kuhbandner, 2011). DA synthesis via learning is not only perceived as pleasurable, but increased DA synthesis also contributes to better memory of what was learned (Gruber et al., 2014), deeper understanding of information (Grill et al., 2024), and elevated critical thinking about information (Westbrook et al., 2024).

Neuroimaging studies provide confluent evidence that learning activates the same brain regions involved in processing as other types of rewards, suggesting that, neurologically, learning is like earning a monetary incentive. For instance, Daniel and Pollmann (2014) and Ripollés et al. (2014) both found that the ventral striatum, the center of the reward pathway, is activated during successful learning, even in the absence of external feedback confirming knowledge acquisition. Kizilirmak et al. (2016), demonstrated that gaining insight during problem-solving, often associated with conceptual learning, also activates the ventral striatum as well as the anterior cingulate cortex (ACC). Furthermore, Sescousse et al. (2015), in a meta-analysis, revealed that the ventral striatum and the orbitofrontal cortex (OFC) are consistently activated by several types of information rewards. Similarly in another meta-analysis, Oldham et al. (2018) revealed that the anticipation and outcome phases of reward processing involve similar brain regions as those activated during learning tasks. These types of results imply that when we understand something previously unknown or overcome ignorance with an "aha!" moment, the experience delivers the impression of an inherent reward (Kizilirmak et al., 2016). Minimally, these findings show the interconnectedness of learning and reward systems in the brain, suggesting that the brain processes the acquisition of knowledge similarly to other rewarding experiences.

Learning can be accomplished and expressed in various ways, each with unique influences on neurological expression. Most learning research that embraces a neuropsychological perspective focuses on *reinforcement learning* (also described as operant conditioning) and uses nonhuman subjects like mice and rats. In these situations, learning is thought to increase based on positive associations between behavior and reward contingencies for the expression of the learned behavior. Interpretations of results from these types of studies, while important, fail to account for the myriad of variables that influence learning in humans like social context, instructional methods, or the motivation behind knowledge acquisition. Rats do not care about how they look in the mirror, whether their behavior is justified, or worry about earning a college degree, so we will stick with egotistical human learning. Thus, the learning and reward emphasis here is different; we are not interested in reinforcement learning or operant conditioning because those forms of learning do not include conscious decisions related to the value and utility of knowledge, assessments that include evaluation of situational factors such as the social implications, the context, emotions, and the beliefs of the individual involved. Regardless, awareness of the diverse ways learning is accomplished matters because of the implications on reward perceptions.

Associative Learning

Associative learning involves forming connections between stimuli or events, primarily through classical and operant conditioning. In classical conditioning, a neutral stimulus becomes associated with a significant event, while operant conditioning involves learning through consequences, such as rewards or punishments. Rewards significantly enhance associative learning by reinforcing the desired behavior. For example, in operant conditioning, a behavior followed by a reward is more likely to be repeated, as the reinforcement strengthens the association between the behavior and the outcome, making learning more effective. In practice, a classroom teacher may use a sticker chart to encourage students to do homework. Each time a student submits their homework on time, they receive a sticker. Once a student collects a certain number of stickers, they earn a reward, such as extra computer time. This method operates under the assumption that the reward has value and will encourage students to submit their homework on time. However, as we know from Chapter 3, reward perceptions are highly personal and the expectation that a particular reward will be universally effective in changing the learning behavior of everyone is as unlikely as believing everyone likes blue hair and anchovies.

Observational Learning

Observational learning occurs when individuals learn by watching and imitating others (Fryling et al., 2011). This type of learning is influenced by the perceived rewards associated with observed behavior. If an observer sees a respected model excelling, they are more likely to imitate that action, expecting similar rewards. The impact of rewards in observational learning is crucial, as it enhances motivation and the likelihood of behavior replication. Studies reveal that positive outcomes or rewards associated with the behavior heighten motivation, making observational learning more effective (Yoon et al., 2021). By example, many workplace orientation programs have new employees shadow experienced staff members. The inexperienced observe how seasoned employees interact with customers, solve problems, and follow company procedures. When the observed employees receive positive feedback, the new employees are more likely to imitate these behaviors, expecting similar rewards for replicating their performance.

Experiential Learning

Experiential learning involves acquiring knowledge through direct experience and reflecting on those experiences. Rewards can enhance experiential learning by reinforcing the learning process through leveraging the social nature of learning. When learners receive positive feedback or tangible rewards for their efforts, it encourages them to engage more deeply with material and reflect on their experiences, leading to more profound learning outcomes. The anticipation of rewards can also increase engagement and willingness to take on challenging tasks, thereby enriching the experiential learning process (Vassena et al., 2019). In science class, students often participate in hands-on laboratory experiments to learn about chemical reactions. After completing experiments, they reflect on their observations and discuss their findings with peers. The teacher provides positive feedback for insightful reflections and accurate conclusions. This reward system encourages students to engage deeply with the material and enhances their learning through direct interaction and reflection, provided they value the social experience.

Rote Learning and Skill Acquisition

Skill acquisition involves developing new abilities through practice and repetition. Rote learning means recalling information with little or no associated meaning. Rewards can significantly impact the effectiveness of these types of learning through reinforcement of progress through continuous engagement. When learners receive rewards for achieving milestones or mastering specific skills, the reward is suggested to enhance practice motivation and perseverance toward skill mastery. Rewards can also create a positive feedback loop, where the satisfaction of achieving a reward motivates additional practice, leading to skill refinement and mastery. However, this type of learning situation can encourage a focus on reward attainment, with significant deterioration of knowledge once the reward is achieved or when the reward is terminated (Bezzina et al., 2016). By example, when learning to play the piano, an instructor can devise a system where students earn points for mastering specific cords. Once they accumulate enough points, they can participate in a recital. The rewards allegedly motivate the students to practice, thereby improving their skills and promoting recognition opportunities. Unfortunately, removal of the reward typically results in a reduction or elimination of the rewarded behavior.

Conceptual Learning

Conceptual learning focuses on understanding abstract ideas and relationships between concepts. While the intrinsic satisfaction of grasping a concept can be rewarding, external rewards, such as recognition or incentives, can further motivate learners to invest time and effort in conceptual learning. By reinforcing the value of understanding over rote memorization, rewards can encourage deeper cognitive processing and integration of new knowledge (Cowan, 2014). While rewards may enhance critical thinking by increasing motivation and engagement, the relationship may depend on factors such as task complexity, individual differences in cognitive abilities, and the perceived value and relevance of the reward (Hidi, 2016). Despite contingencies, many corporations use incentives to optimize performance. For example, Intuit hosts an annual company-wide award ceremony where they present the "Failure Award" to a team whose unsuccessful idea led to valuable learning. This approach encourages risk-taking and learning from failure, which are crucial for fostering creativity. Google gives employees free time to develop innovative ideas through a practice known as "20% Time." This concept allows employees to spend 20 percent of their work hours, or one day a week, on projects of their choice that are unrelated to their regular job responsibilities. This initiative encourages employees to explore their interests, experiment with new ideas, and collaborate with colleagues, fostering a culture of innovation and creativity within the company. The key here is that promoting conceptual learning is done on an autonomous basis, with little, if any, mandates from the company to meet performance objectives or externally driven measurable goals.

Implicit Learning

Implicit learning occurs without conscious awareness, often through exposure to patterns or regularities in the environment. Implicit learning is especially useful in situations where procedural knowledge matters such as during musical, athletic, or other observable performance domains. While rewards are not directly involved in implicit learning, they can influence the outcomes by shaping behavior through reinforcement and modeling. For example, if an implicitly learned behavior leads to a reward, it is more likely to be repeated, even if the individual is not consciously aware of the learning process. Rewards can thus indirectly enhance implicit learning by reinforcing behaviors that align with learned patterns. For example, in a language immersion program, students are exposed to a foreign language through daily interactions and activities without explicit instruction. Over time, they begin to pick up vocabulary and grammar patterns implicitly. When students successfully use new words or phrases in conversation and receive encouragement it feels rewarding. The feedback reinforces their learning, even if they are not consciously aware of the learning or feedback process (Williams & Rebuschat, 2016).

Social Learning

Social learning involves acquiring knowledge and skills through group collaboration and interaction. Rewards can enhance social learning by fostering a collaborative environment and encouraging participation (Lin et al., 2012). Group rewards or recognition for collective achievements can motivate individuals to contribute to group efforts and share knowledge. By promoting cooperation and communication, rewards can strengthen social bonds and facilitate the exchange of ideas, leading to more effective learning outcomes in collaborative settings. One of the most rewarding aspects of my prior career involved regular participation in a community-based literacy project. Working together with human resources leaders from other companies, collectively we hosted an annual retreat where disadvantaged kids from diverse backgrounds came together to learn about different fields to promote interest in careers underrepresented by minorities. The program encouraged students to collaborate effectively, share knowledge, and support each other's learning to achieve a common goal. The implicit reward fostered a sense of teamwork and enhanced the overall learning experience for both the planners and the participants. Little did we know that through implicit learning everyone involved also developed numerous networking and social skills, showing both the implicit and explicit dimensions of reward-based learning.

Maximizing Learning with Reward

At the heart of understanding how rewards influence learning of any type is understanding the value of satisfying intellectual curiosity, a type of information seeking that motivates learning (Kidd & Hayden, 2015). Seminal research by Berlyne (1954) theorized that curiosity has at least two dimensions. *Perceptual curiosity* occurs because we crave novelty and easily get bored. This driver of knowledge acquisition can often be seen in the behavior of infants, children, and those who are compelled to watch reality TV. For many, acquiring new knowledge is not much different than acquiring any other resources and can be a compelling motivation. Complimenting boredom-reducing exploratory curiosity is *epistemic curiosity*, which Berlyne considered sourcing information with a specific purpose in mind, like you might do when searching for YouTube videos to see how to build a birdhouse or to locate strategies that will stop your dog from perpetually licking their paws. While Berlyne's definitions are helpful to explain the process of acquiring knowledge, the categorizations do not consider what motivates the quest or why some individuals may specifically elect not to seek knowledge or even care about knowledge deficits.

Situated expectancy-value theory (SEVT) (see p. 58) is one approach to consider why people perceive knowledge acquisition as rewarding and under which circumstances knowledge gains could be predicted. According to SEVT, an individual's motivation to engage in a task or behavior is influenced by their expectations for success and the subjective value they place on the contemplated activity (Eccles & Wigfield, 2020). If an individual believes that they are motivated and capable of successfully eliminating knowledge gaps and that doing so will lead to positive outcomes, they are more likely to engage in the learning process. Conversely, if they doubt their ability to master a topic or perceive the process as too cumbersome or challenging, they may be less willing to learn. The value an individual places on learning can significantly influence their willingness to engage in the process. This value assessment is made based on four criteria:

    a. Attainment value: If an individual perceives knowledge as crucial to their self-identity or personal growth, they may be more willing to engage in learning.

b. Intrinsic value: If an individual finds the process of learning is inherently interesting or enjoyable, they may be more motivated to do so.
c. Utility value: If an individual believes that learning new things will be useful or beneficial in achieving their goals or navigating their environment more effectively, they may be more willing to engage in the process.
d. Cost: If an individual perceives the learning process requires too much effort, time, or emotional investment, or if they fear social repercussion for being a jughead, they may be less willing to engage in learning.

Willingness to learn is greater when high expectancy for success and high subjective task value is staked on intellectual growth. Conversely, low expectancy for success and low subjective value may result in a decreased willingness to learn. Furthermore, the situational context of learning will influence an individual's expectancies and values. Context is crucial because specific circumstances, environmental factors, and social/cultural influences that surround the learning experience can alter perceived value (Pugh, 2022). This includes elements such as timing, setting, how learning is delivered, social dynamics, and the recipient's mood when receiving the knowledge reward. For example, a supportive environment that encourages critical thinking and provides peer encouragement for continuing education may increase an individual's willingness to learn compared to an uninspired culture that discourages or stigmatizes personal development, a culture found in many low-performing schools (Brummelman, & Sedikides, 2023).

Reward Stipulations

One of the most contentious aspects related to rewards is the perpetual debate concerning the influence of incentives on learning effectiveness. Scholars, students, and parents contest the wisdom of whether incentives increase or decrease academic performance (Kohn, 1993). Previous chapters have revealed that the definitive answer depends on the reward contingencies, with considerable influence from how the incentives are determined, who initiates and controls the incentive process, and the conditions necessary to earn any incentive. Research in general suggests that extrinsic rewards based on meeting specific task requirements or outcomes decrease interest and thus inhibit INMO (Murayama et al., 2016). In turn, decreased motivation leads to inferior performance, especially regarding academic outcomes (Deci et al., 1999). While intuitively this conclusion makes sense, universally inferring that rewards inhibit achievement without investigating the contingencies is like not considering the climate or weather when deciding on which clothes to wear. Thus, we must take a closer look at the situational variables associated with reward-based learning including reward valuation, reward type, emotion and mood, and neural encoding.

Reward Valuation

Reward valuation means knowing how much a particular incentive motivates an individual. Chapter 4 (p. 64) indicated that individual value is primarily determined by evaluating the incentive salience of a reward. For a reward to have high salience, it must be meaningful and desired by the recipient and not something presumed to be rewarding or something of perceived value to the reward provider. When salience is high, DA neurons in the VTA activate DA synthesis (Nieh et al., 2016) with projection to the NAcc and other regions of the striatum (Berridge & Robinson, 2016) activating perceptions that investing effort and moving forward is beneficial. In turn, the reward valuation influences the attractiveness of the learning goal and incentivizes behavior toward attaining the desired outcome. Review the "Creating Value" section in Chapter 4 for the mechanics of reward valuation.

Reward Type and Context

In practice, salience means careful consideration of the reward contingencies and type of reward but also triggers particular concern as to when rewards do or do not inspire learning. The fundamental incentive decision should be based on whether individual interest is sufficient to promote learning in the absence of a reward. When interest is sufficient, rewards are unnecessary and distract from teaching intentions. Remember, the ultimate purpose of the reward is to increase the probability and intensity of motivated effort toward a learning objective; thus, anything that might distract from the actual objective would defeat the reward intent. The "crowding out effect" (Frey & Jegen, 2001) refers to the phenomenon where external incentives, such as monetary rewards, special privileges, and even external recognition can undermine INMO, leading to a decrease in the desired behavior or intended outcome. This effect is significant in various contexts, especially in organizations and academics.

Inspiring workplace motivation through incentives can inadvertently reduce the natural inclination to excel in absence of rewards, particularly when the baseline compensation systems are considered fair and equitable (Fulmer & Shaw, 2018). Few individuals want to be mandated into bonus programs that require staking potential compensation and reputation on factors beyond their control. However, as expected, when employees can decide when and how to engage with incentive programs, motivation to participate increases. LEGO, the kids building block company, has a program whereby employees can voluntarily earn bonuses for brainstorming new product ideas. When comparing employees who participated in the program to those who did not, findings revealed that only the direct effect of INMO on participation mattered (Baswani et al., 2021). This means that when employees can choose to participate, there is no effect on subsequent INMO. When participants were offered 1 percent of total new product net sales for designs developed and accepted for production during the brainstorming process, 27 percent of employees participated in the program compared to 10 percent when no incentives were offered. The study suggested that LEGO's approach of offering rewards only for excellent performance reduces the negative effect of control associated with extrinsic rewards. These findings support LEGO's innovation strategy, indicating that incentives can effectively boost participation and promote creativity without undermining INMO. The LEGO experiment reveals that it is not the incentive that matters most, but how the incentive program is designed and the degree of choice related to participation.

External rewards for academic performance, like grades or financial incentives, may undermine students' INMO to learn, negatively impacting their long-term engagement and achievement. The well-publicized overjustification effect (Deci, 1971) implies that rewarding learners for engaging in activities where existing interest is already in place is detrimental for ongoing participation when rewards are removed. The conclusion is based on experiments that examined the effects of external rewards on INMO using a puzzle-solving task with students (Lepper et al., 1973). Participants were divided into experimental and control groups, with the experimental group receiving rewards for completing puzzles, while engagement with puzzles during breaks was measured as an indicator of INMO. The authors concluded that INMO decreased when rewards were offered, based on reduced puzzle engagement during breaks for the experimental group compared to the control group. These results are generalized to many learning situations because those learners with the highest levels of INMO are almost always advantageous for learning (Cerasoli et al., 2014). This well-established phenomenon is beyond dispute; however, understanding the limitations of this learning contingency matters more.

The bulk of overjustification studies that reach conclusions that rewards are detrimental to INMO fail to account for the degree of preliminary interest in tasks that are used to determine subsequent interest, suppressing the reality that initial low intrinsic motivation for the task will surely predict future task engagement. In the Deci (1971) study, there were varied patterns of puzzle engagement across subjects in both experimental and control groups, rather than a clear decrease only in the experimental group. Both groups showed average decreases in puzzle engagement over trials, not just the experimental group, and few puzzles were completed within the time limit, suggesting the task may have been too difficult. Subsequent replications of the overjustification effect often fail (Peters et al., 2022), yet learning-related rewards still get bad press!

Allegedly, overjustification occurs due to a shift in the perceived locus of causality from internal to external (see p. 99–100). When we engage in an activity for personal interest or enjoyment, the reward is the actual task engagement. The effort invested in the task is seamless because the individual realizes that task participation is the reward, which organically promotes tenacity toward reaching the desired outcome (Touroutoglou et al., 2020). However, when external rewards are introduced, the perceived locus of causality shifts to external factors, leading individuals to focus their behavior on reward attainment rather than their existing interest. Adding to the reward paradox is the reality that in the absence of choice the reward is perceived as controlling, reducing feelings of autonomy, leading to decreased INMO. What appears to be reduced internal locus is merely less control over reward type and contingencies.

Thus, to avoid overjustification and mitigate the impact of the crowding out effect, the individual must have perceived control over how the reward is designed, attained, and administered. This means tailoring incentives based on individual needs that consider existing interests as well as the overall value individuals place on knowledge acquisition. Effective motivation strategies should focus on the journey, not just the destination. It's crucial to help individuals recognize that the true reward lies in the process of completing a task, rather than solely in its outcome. This shift in perspective can foster greater tenacity, perseverance, and resilience in academic pursuits (Touroutoglou et al., 2020). Optimizing performance means carefully offering appropriate incentives, identifying tasks that naturally spark intrinsic interest, continuously monitoring engagement levels (as they can vary within and between tasks), and experimenting with different reward structures, such as acknowledging effort and progress rather than just results. By emphasizing the value of the learning process itself, INMO accelerates. Remember, the goal is to cultivate a mindset where the act of learning and improving becomes inherently rewarding, leading to sustained motivation and better academic outcomes.

Emotion and Mood

Considering there is little dispute as to how emotion influences motivation (Niedenthal & Ric, 2017; Reeve, 2018), the brief overview here only focuses on the direct impact of rewards on existing motivational processes. Generally, we can operate under the presumption that positive emotions tend to encourage motivation, helping individuals to pursue goals and engage with rewarding stimuli. Positive emotions enhance our perception of rewards, making them seem even more appealing. This is because both DA and oxytocin are generated when mood improves, leading to the activation of "hedonic hotspots," which are specific brain regions that generate intense pleasure or "liking" reactions to certain stimuli (Alexander et al., 2021). Knutson and Greer (2008) found that when people experience positive emotions, there is increased activity in the NAcc due to the anticipation of rewards. This suggests that being in a good mood can make rewards appear more attractive.

In addition, positive mood enhances attention to and memory for stimuli that we suspect is worth noticing. When in a good mood people are more prone to pay attention to stimuli that are potentially rewarding or positive, which in turn increases the likelihood of the experience being encoded into memory (Williams et al., 2022). A positive mood enhances reward-related neural activity, particularly in the corticostriatal regions including the NAcc, caudate, lateral orbitofrontal cortex, and putamen (Young & Nusslock, 2016), areas that are typically involved in reward processing and goal-seeking, which results in triggering DA synthesis. This increased neural activity during positive mood states makes rewarding stimuli more salient and memorable than when feeling apathic or uninterested.

Consider a scenario where you (oh no, not me) are attending a long-awaited Taylor Swift performance. Presumably, this puts you in a good mood; thus, you are more likely to notice and remember the vibrant colors, the upbeat music, and the joyful expressions of Taylor and your fellow Swifties. The upbeat atmosphere enhances attention to sparkly dresses and leather boots, making the experience more vivid and memorable. This effect can lead to a stronger recollection of the event later, as the positive mood has facilitated the encoding of these rewarding aspects into your hippocampus and memory. A positive mood cues individuals to environmental rewards through selective attention. Even when memories are less than favorable, selective recall of the past can enhance positive meaning in past negative experiences. Positively reinterpreting unfavorable experiences adaptively updates them, leading to increased activity in the ventral striatum, where positive reappraisal generates dopaminergic activity (Speer et al., 2021). Call it what you want, chipper mood enhances learning.

Conversely, negative emotions often motivate avoidance behaviors, prompting individuals to avoid undesirable outcomes. Negative emotions can disrupt the function of reward-related brain structures such as the NAcc, PFC, amygdala, and hippocampus. These disruptions lead to abnormalities in how rewards are perceived and interpreted, affecting motivation and decision-making processes (Russo & Nestler, 2013). Prolonged exposure to negative emotions, such as those induced by chronic stress, can cause physical changes in the neurons of reward-related brain regions. This neuroplasticity may fundamentally alter how we process and perceive rewards over time, potentially contributing to long-term changes in emotional experience and behavior (Baik, 2020).

For instance, my friend Lindsay, who once found joy in painting, now feels largely disinterested. Despite knowing that painting might improve her mood, she struggles to muster the energy or desire to pick up a brush. The disruption of her brain's reward system (DA deficits) causes her to perceive painting as unrewarding, leading to motivational malaise and decision-making difficulties regarding her art. This overshadowing of past enjoyment by negative emotions has led Lindsay to abandon her cherished hobby. Stress exacerbates this issue by negatively regulating the dopaminergic reward system, which is crucial for coping with stress. Lindsay is trapped in a downward spiral of negative emotion that clearly impacts her behavior. The debilitating cycle, while amenable to pharmacological interventions, if left unchecked can become a chronic condition resulting in long-term depletion of DA synthesis and a sad Lindsay bear.

Overall, positive emotional states lend themselves to enhancing the impact of positive rewards, while negative emotional states can bias attention away from rewarding or positive stimuli, potentially reducing their perceived value. Emotional states are fluid, changing dynamically over time as emotions and situational factors shift. By carefully considering and understanding these nuances, one can greatly leverage the situational effectiveness of rewards, thereby enhancing the learning process.

Neural Encoding

Neurologically, learning can be measured by the degree of synaptic plasticity in a particular set of neurons which reveal how brain structure evolves as learning takes place. Synaptic plasticity is the brain's mechanism for learning and memory formation at the cellular level. This process involves changes in the strength of connections between neurons (Kandel, 2001; Kennedy, 2016). When we learn something new, certain neural pathways in our brain become more active. As these neurons fire together repeatedly, the synapses connecting them undergo changes that make signal transmission more efficient, a principle often summarized as "neurons that fire together, wire together" based on the seminal research of David Hebb, who in 1949 made the initial discovery that learning occurs through the strengthening of synaptic connections between simultaneously activated neurons (Hebb, 2005).

The strengthening process, known as "long-term potentiation," typically begins when a neuron releases chemical messengers that activate receptors on a neighboring neuron (Lømo, 2003; Magee & Grienberger, 2020; Patihis, 2018). If this activation happens frequently and intensely enough, it triggers a cascade of molecular events inside the receiving neuron. These events lead to lasting changes in the synapses, such as an increase in the number of receptors or alterations in the synapses' structure (Malenka & Bear, 2004). As a result, future signals between these neurons become stronger and more easily transmitted and thus the degree of physiological connectivity determines the extent of what is learned. The more engrained the neuronal connection, the more resilient the knowledge is from decay and the higher the likelihood of accessing the learned information.

Importantly, this process works both ways. While some connections strengthen, others may weaken if they are used less frequently, a process called "long-term depression" (Collingridge et al., 2010). This balance allows the brain to prioritize vital information while pruning less relevant connections. Over time, these changes in synaptic strength can lead to more substantial structural modifications, like the growth of new connection points between neurons or the elimination of unused ones (Matsuzaki et al., 2004). The brain also has mechanisms to prevent excessive strengthening or weakening of connections, maintaining overall stability while still allowing for learning. This process, known as "homeostatic plasticity," enables our brains to continually adapt and learn from new experiences throughout our lives, forming the neurological basis of memory and learning (Turrigiano, 2008). Thus, we can see that homeostasis applies to how we learn, as well as all other functions related to evaluating the perception of reward.

DA and norepinephrine (NE) are both crucial for memory formation, particularly for information we encounter incidentally rather than deliberately trying to remember (Thorp et al., 2020). DA helps us selectively encode prominent features of experiences through a prioritization process that focuses on what is most relevant and meaningful in a situation. In this case, DA works by modulating synaptic plasticity through affecting the synaptic strength of neuronal circuits that induce the long-term potentiation and long-term depression, described earlier (Bazzari & Parri, 2019). During learning, as is typical of overall DA regulation, the potency of expression influences whether a mental task is worthy of attention and effort. For example, if you are trying to read difficult handwriting, DA boosts memory for the unusual font rather than only the word meanings (Hauser et al., 2019), helping determine if deciphering is beneficial. On the other hand, NE boosts overall memory when we are in an aroused or excited state particularly through amygdala activation. NE enhances memory for things that happen around the same time as surprising or rewarding events, such as better remembering a word you saw right before unexpectedly winning a small prize (Hauser, 2019). In essence, DA focuses our memory on what seems most important in the moment, while NE makes us more likely to remember things during the process of emotional arousal. Together, these neurotransmitters help ensure we form strong memories of experiences that are relevant or occur during meaningful moments. This process helps explain why some incidental memories stick, while others just fade away into oblivion (Likhtik & Johansen, 2019).

Rewards and Persuasion

Note: The following section includes interpretations from the published article, "It's time to reconsider: The neuropsychology of belief change," written by the author and his colleagues, Aditi Subramaniam and Kendall Hartley and published in the journal *"Trends in Neuroscience and Education."* https://doi.org/10.1016/j.tine.2025.100261

Sometimes memories and information are more sticky than spilled maple syrup, and it takes some major effort to remove the residue. Manifested in the form of personal beliefs, not all knowledge used to make decisions is justified or verifiable, and the usage of such information can be downright dangerous. The impact of harboring beliefs unsupported by empirical evidence is extensive because it leads to faulty reasoning that impacts decision-making with ramifications for both personal and societal well-being (Sinatra & Hofer, 2021). Yet, unreliable information is routinely used as the basis for the direction and intensity of motivated effort. As such, educators and thought learners often strive to help individuals change their faulty beliefs through persuasive verbal or written efforts.

Most applications of changing minds are engrained in the field of science education, and persuasion efforts are called "conceptual change" (CC) by researchers. Change is devoted toward "the restructuring of existing knowledge" (Nadelson et al., 2018, p. 153), such as what occurs when you realize that mass and weight are two separate concepts and that a pound of feathers weighs the same as a pound of cannabis. However, outside of science classrooms change efforts are widespread and involve shifting one's existing knowledge and beliefs about something to accommodate new information that appears to be personally contradictory to what you already think you know (Posner et al., 1982). CC is different from new learning because CC involves unlearning previously learned information or personal beliefs. While some minor distinctions exist between modifying "concepts" and beliefs, for discussion purposes we will call all persuasion efforts "belief change" (BC), although much of the science literature addresses changing beliefs as CC.

Specific conditions are necessary for BC to occur and last more than a day or two. While many different theoretical models address the cause of false beliefs (Dole & Sinatra, 1998; Gregoire, 2003; Murphy, 2007; Nadelson et al., 2018; Posner et al., 1982), all theorists agree that belief change is more likely when there is dissatisfaction or existential doubt with existing conceptions. The replacement belief must be intelligible, plausible, and fruitful, meaning that the alternative belief has personal value and explanatory power for the individual. In other words, a conceptual shift requires the ascription of value and utility to the added information. From a behavioral perspective, BC requires the person's attention and complete understanding of whatever information that is hoping to persuade impressions. It also helps if the person feels lukewarm about what they are actually thinking. Do we really believe the earth is flat or that Hillary Clinton is running a child sex ring from a Washington, DC, pizza shop or is it just convenient to spread the narrative for other purposes? In combination, the existing belief must be vulnerable and the alternative needs to make sense and provide benefit to the person who is contemplating the change.

Changing beliefs involves revising existing knowledge, but the revision process is similar to what happens when acquiring new knowledge or when examining what motivates people to maintain their existing beliefs. Just as animals instinctively search for food to survive, humans have an innate drive to seek information to understand and navigate their world effectively. Information has real value both conceptually and pragmatically (Murayama, 2022), and when people successfully acquire or retain useful knowledge, it increases their chances of success while reducing the risk of physical or psychological harm caused by lack of information. For example, it is beneficial to know that poison ivy leaves should not be used for exfoliation and that using a hammer to kill a fly is both cartoon content and hazardous. Ultimately, individuals need accurate information to make informative decisions that in the most severe circumstances (i.e., health or economic decisions) may determine their overall well-being or longevity.

When we encounter new information that changes what we previously believed, the brain treats the new information like a reward. Knowledge revision follows the same principles as other types of rewards, specifically RPE, as discussed on page 138. The act of gathering and learning new information has value, both during the process and after we have learned it. When we think there's potentially valuable information to be gained, and it turns out to be better than expected, we become more open to changing our beliefs. In these cases, certain neurons in our brain become more active, reflecting positive RPE. On the flip side, if the information turns out to be less valuable than expected, neurons become less active, showing a negative RPE. These RPE signals activate DA synthesis in the striatum. Here, they're thought to change the strength of connections between neurons and update how much value we associate with certain actions or things we encounter (Pessiglione et al., 2006). Over time, this process helps our brain learn to make decisions that maximize rewards and minimize negative experiences, like encountering (and discounting) information we do not want to hear.

The effectiveness of BC likely depends on how we value and see the usefulness of the added information. Kobayashi and Hsu (2019) refer to the evaluation process as the subjective value of information (SVOI) in the brain. This value is influenced by why we're seeking the information and how useful we think it will be. Interestingly, just the act of seeking information can be rewarding to our brain, similar to expecting money or recognition from others. Neurologically, both these types of rewards activate DA pathways in the striatum and PFC, suggesting that our brain uses a common system to represent the value of information and other basic rewards like food or money.

Typically, when learning or experiencing a reward, we see increased activity between two parts of the brain: the VTA and the NAcc (Bromberg-

Martin & Monosov, 2020). At the same time, if we are open to seeking new information, reduced activity is observed in the emotional center of the brain, the amygdala. One motivation for knowledge receptivity is "instrumental utility" (Shen et al., p. 362). This type of knowledge is pursued with an intended purpose in mind and thus is perceived as rewarding because knowledge anticipation and attainment have intrinsic value that presumably assists the individual in meeting learning goals. When impending knowledge has instrumentality, it also provides materialistic benefits to support progress toward other life goals. By example, knowing that motivational support strategies during teaching propel students toward tackling more challenging academic problems compared to providing instructional feedback only, contributes to the reputation of an educator (while promoting student success). Instrumentality also prevails during avoidance of situations, such as knowing not to consume poisonous fruit or touch hot coals because of the obvious reward and toasted finger repercussions.

However, individuals do not seek information for the value of the information alone. Sometimes, we seek out information without a clear purpose in mind. Simply learning new things can make us feel good about ourselves. This happens because discovering new information can create positive emotions, giving us a warm and pleasant feeling. In other words, the information has "hedonic utility" (Shen et al., p. 362). Individuals are often motivated to acquire, retain, or reject information specifically under the pretenses of enhanced subjective well-being. Imagine having a skeptical reaction to a severe medical diagnosis and searching the internet for information that refutes the physician's recommendation, lending support to intuitive impressions and prior beliefs. While the medical information itself may have functional value, the psychological impact, which was the basis for the inquiry, drives acceptance or rejection of the new information. Sometimes referred to as *"confirmation bias,"* the impact of the knowledge can provide sufficient satisfaction irrespective of the absolute information value. Not surprisingly, individuals are more likely to seek information affirming their beliefs or information that generates positive affect (Charpentier & Dezza, 2022; Sharot & Sunstein, 2020; Westen et al., 2006). Additionally, there is a higher probability of information acceptance when the new information is anticipated to be good and desirable than when the new information has the prospect of being perceived as bad and undesired (Charpentier et al., 2018).

Perhaps most relevant to BC, Sharot and Sunstein (2020) contended that information can refute or support our worldviews and individuals are highly motivated to access information that strengthens their mental representations of the world. They proposed "cognitive utility" (p. 16) as a measurement of how much information might strengthen those internal representations. Theoretically, people are more motivated to seek information related to their perceptual world than to seek out knowledge lacking application. Vegetarians might find new information about plant nutrition far more rewarding than learning about the latest meat-packing methods. This type of individual difference is especially relevant for BC as humans will often ignore information that conflicts with their existing mental models (Chinn & Brewer, 1993), hence the term "blockhead!"

The neural circuitry for each blend of information seeking varies. When information is gathered for no specific purpose, such as when skimming the internet and learning that George Washington preferred cherries more than apples, the brain reacts differently than when information sought has intrinsic value and potentially can help better understand the world around us. The subjective assessment of situational relevance is crucial to the evaluation of incoming change efforts and the distinction is illustrated by the activation of distinct neural circuits that differ from typical learning and associated reward processing (Kaanders et al., 2021). When the brain is just checking out information before committing to future engagement, the pre–supplementary motor area (pre-SMA) and dorsal anterior cingulate cortex (dACC) are activated as indicated by increased BOLD signals (blood oxygenation) during brain imaging. However, when deciding if the new information has anticipatory value and utility (i.e., is the knowledge rewarding?), the more anterior ventromedial prefrontal cortex encodes the information. Recall that the vmPFC is strongly coupled with strong DA input from reward-sensitive parts of the midbrain, so if receptivity to change is the goal, the perception of positive utility is essential.

The Message Is the Medium

For a new message to be considered, the existing conception must be insufficient to explain certain phenomena or solve particular problems facing the person, instilling at least some sort of existential doubt as to the usefulness of existing knowledge. Any replacement idea must make sense to the learner. An individual must be able to comprehend the significance of a novel concept and possess the capability to formulate a logically consistent mental model incorporating the new idea. The new conception must appear initially plausible and consistent with other knowledge they hold with the capacity to solve problems that the old conception could not. To be considered fruitful, new knowledge must reveal unrealized possibilities, solve additional problems, or provide a deeper explanation of subjective experiences. Therefore, the success of a BC effort is heavily influenced by engagement with the message on a personal level, in addition to the potential of incorporating new information into one's values and beliefs.

The characteristics of the message also play a crucial role in determining how knowledge is restructured and the effectiveness of the change effort. Given that most BC attempts are unsolicited, psychologically invasive, and often met with resistance, it is not surprising that some attempts fail. The individual's appraisal of the message as rewarding, ambivalent, or even psychologically offensive depends in part on how the information is presented and the degree of emotional appeal embedded within the persuasion attempt. For a message to garner limited attentional resources, meaning and relevance must be assured; otherwise, the message will likely be ignored.

The perceived worth of a message is partly determined by the brain's assessment of tone (Charpentier et al., 2018). This means that the emotionality infused into a message often dictates the subjective impressions of the message, influencing prospective acceptance or rejection. "Valence" represents the message emphasis and influences whether or not the message is perceived positively or negatively in comparison to one's values and dispositions. A message can be desirable instilling optimism or be evaluated pessimistically based on the content, tone, and overall emotional quality of the communicated information. A message with *positive valence* is pleasant, agreeable, and emphasizes benefits for the receiver, while a message with *negative valence* describes unpleasant, undesirable, disagreeable outcomes that are potentially harmful to the recipient.

Consider a message about a proposed work policy change. The message is intended to inform employees that the company's 100 percent work-from-home (WFH) policy is being rescinded and now WFH is limited to three days a week. A positive valence would use the perspective of an employee who values face-to-face collaboration and misses the social interaction of the office environment. The intended internal reaction generated by the message might be: "This is great news! I have been feeling isolated working from home every day. Going back to the office will help me reconnect with my team and boost my productivity. Plus, I can finally get out of the house and have a change of scenery." Conversely, a message might target an employee who has grown accustomed to the flexibility and autonomy of working from home who may appraise the same message negatively. The internal dialogue developed from the message might be "This sucks! I'm much more productive working from home and enjoy the extra time with my family. Going back to the office will be a major disruption to my routine and will waste my time."

The neural subjective value assessment is irrespective of the exact information but instead is based on a determination of personal relevance and applicability. Information deemed of significant utility will be coded as rewarding, based on the high SVOI (Charpentier & Dezza, 2022), while low SVOI will be held in obeyance or dismissed (Chinn & Brewer, 1993). When the information has personal pizzaz, receptivity is boosted because the person is pleasantly surprised by the information revelation (Cox et al., 2015). Positive valence generates added reward salience (desirability), while negative appraisals result in lower reward salience (undesirability). During positive appraisals, higher reward perceptions trigger greater blood oxygen levels in the brain increasing signal strength to the ventral striatum, the target of DA projections (Bromberg-Martin & Monosov, 2020), while hemodynamic signal variability reveals corresponding DA decrements resulting in the avoidance of learning new material (Shafiei et al., 2019). As subjective value increases, activation in the mesocortical pathway increases coveted DA production (Charpentier & Dezza, 2022).

A message is also deemed rewarding when the message is perceived to be both important and welcomed as good news, compared to less-favorable (but still relevant) bad news. Empirically, "news" has been evaluated by participants as "good" in such situations as when learning they are more attractive than others (Sharot & Garrett, 2016), are less suspect to credit card fraud, or more likely to hit a slot machine jackpot (Sharot & Garrett, 2016). Alternatively, lower attentional resources and reduced belief adaptability are experienced when encountering "bad" news such as when monitoring financial losses compared to gains

(Sicherman et al., 2016). Resistance increases when learning about bad news like being more prone to accidents or when learning we are more vulnerable to illness from a previously unknown disease (Weinstein & Klein, 1995). Thus, the probability of successful knowledge restructuring is enhanced when emphasizing the benefits of future positive outcomes, in comparison to outlining the consequences of risky or apathetic behavior that may foretell future losses.

Receiving good news is associated with increased DA release in the brain's reward system, particularly in the ventral striatum and NAcc. People who are more prone to updating beliefs show greater activity in the PFC and ACC when confronted with information that challenges their existing views. Positive news can also trigger serotonin release, which is involved in regulating mood, anxiety, and happiness. By contrast, individuals who are resistant to changing their beliefs may exhibit increased activity in regions associated with cognitive dissonance and emotional reactivity, such as the amygdala and insula. They may also show reduced activity in the PFC, suggesting a diminished capacity for flexible thinking and belief updating. Bad news can also trigger the norepinephrine (NE) system, much like the fight-or-flight response you feel when facing a sudden fear—such as seeing a cockroach crawling on your kitchen wall. Stress avoidance is likely because the information presented is perceived as threatening, heightening the emotional impact of negative information. In addition, reduced serotonin activity is probable because processing negative information resembles the neural correlates of physical stress. Neurologically, the pattern described earlier for reward-based learning prevails when evaluating information; more optimism, more processing in the areas of the brain associated with reasoning and thinking, and the higher likelihood of the neural pathways associated with DA transmission, not to mention belief change!

Not all new information is perceived as a symbolic reward. Sometimes the reaction to incongruent knowledge feels like being chased by a venomous psychological snake. Just like encountering wild reptiles, the uncomfortable experience can be quelled by a fight (debate it) or flight response (ignore it). Other information exposures can create a perception casting doubt about the quality or veracity of existing knowledge, instilling negative emotion, or implying that one's personal mental models are damaged and need repair. BC literature describes incompatible information as "threatening" when it promotes decreased self-efficacy or feelings of incompetence, gives the perception of loss of control, induces stress, or when the challenged belief promotes negative evaluations from others (Gregoire, 2003). Shen et al. (2024) suggested that threat decreases both instrumental and hedonic utility reducing the motivation to seek information. No doubt in some cases negative evaluation leads to anxiety, which in turn can promote emotional dysregulation, lack of concentration, and negative affect (Aupperle et al., 2023). As such, a cognitive reaction of avoiding the threat may develop with the intention of discounting or escaping the emotional consequences associated with the information doubt, also known as shutting down and clamming up. Thus, if the expectation of reward from new information is not met (negative RPE) additional change efforts may become less fruitful as a result, prompting more avoidance behavior than prior to the initial change effort. BC without consideration of neural circuitry may backfire, causing greater resistance to seemingly convincing arguments supported by strong refutational evidence.

As we can see, the emotional appraisal of reward is tentative and transient resulting in highly variable DA activation. Any prospective belief change must consider the contextual variables associated with change efforts because information utility alone is insufficient to determine the brain's response to a change effort. Prevailing variables including the message valance, intonation, timing, and emphasis of a change message should be considered in tandem with neurological findings for greater assurance of desired change outcomes. Perceptions of constrained autonomy, emotional threat, or any situation implying lack of psychological safety can trigger behavior antithetical to BC. Information sought in safe contexts generates motivationally supportive DA, while anxiety-provoking situations may promote NE, discounting the change effort potential (Shen et al., 2024).

Reward and Social Relationships

Social interaction is a powerful force that ignites the human spirit. For many individuals, the opportunity to form deep, meaningful connections with others represents the highest form of motivated behavior. Relationships create a spark within us that solitude simply cannot replicate (Fareri & Delgado, 2014). These rewards are both tangible and intangible, activating the brain's reward system and increasing our desire to engage in these fulfilling behaviors. Social rewards manifest in various ways, including emotional satisfaction by fulfilling the needs of belonging and relatedness (Deci & Ryan, 2020) that occur during enduring relationships with individuals, groups, or one's community. Rewards from socialization also occur during shared experiences (Wagner et al., 2015), when receiving recognition from others (Izuma et al., 2008), through intimate bonds (Acevedo et al., 2012), and during social learning opportunities (Ruff & Fehr, 2014) such as the types that occur during classroom instruction. These social rewards are crucial for optimal performance, as they motivate us to expend greater effort in pursuing our goals. When we anticipate social rewards, we are more likely to work harder to achieve desired outcomes (Knutson & Wimmer, 2007).

Social rewards are neuroprotective (Fratiglioni et al., 2020) because when avoiding social isolation and when increasing the frequency and degree of meaningful connections such as what happens during cohabitation, when working on community projects, or giving social support, health benefits and wellness perceptions follow (Fareri & Delgado, 2014). Similar advantages are observed when enhancing one's reputation (Izuma et al., 2008) and by merely having a confidante to share intimate secrets (Inagaki et al., 2012). These various forms of social reinforcement trigger the release of DA and serotonin in neural pathways similar to those activated by other types of rewards, like the types discussed throughout the text. Physiological reactions make social interactions inherently pleasurable and accelerate motivation to seek out and maintain social connections (Feng et al., 2021). Consequently, the brain's reward system shapes social behavior and reinforces the importance of social bonds for overall well-being and cognitive health, highlighting the deep neurological roots of our social nature.

Some might suggest that the greatest of all rewards is a long and healthy life. In a massive study of 39,271 individuals across fourteen different countries, Suraj Samtani (2022) and thirty-seven of his colleagues conducted the most extensive study on record to determine which factors contributed to premature mortality and how various behaviors are related to longevity and healthy cognitive functioning across the lifespan. The study highlighted how different aspects of social connections—their structure (e.g., relationship status, living situation), function (e.g., having social support), and quality (e.g., not feeling lonely)—can benefit healthy aging. Specifically, being married or in a relationship, engaging in weekly community activities, having weekly interactions with family and friends, and not feeling lonely were linked to a lower risk of dementia. Having monthly or weekly interactions with family/friends and having a confidante were associated with reduced risk of cognitive impairment and lower mortality risk.

The data collected in the study was used to calculate "hazard ratios" that represent the ratio of the hazard rates between two groups. In this context, the "hazard" refers to the risk of the event occurring (in this case, death) at any given time. Among some of the many noteworthy findings, individuals who engaged in monthly community activities had a 33 percent lower risk of mortality (yearly engagers had a 19 percent lower mortality risk) compared to those who never engaged in such activities. People with a confidante had a 17 percent lower risk of mortality compared to those who did not. Living with others reduced mortality risk by 13 percent compared to those who lived alone. Even regular communication with friends and family makes a huge difference as those who had weekly interactions had a 44 percent lower risk of developing dementia compared to those who never had such interactions. Clearly, the findings emphasize the importance of maintaining diverse social connections. The researchers suggested doctors should "prescribe" social activities, like weekly family visits as part of promoting healthy aging. While more research is needed on precise longevity strategies, it is indisputable that social connectivity benefits cognitive and physical health.

Social Reward and the Brain: Facial Attractiveness

In addition to staying connected, there are many other surprising ways that the brain experiences social reward. One way is through the evaluation of others' faces. The relationship between facial attractiveness and reward has intriguing implications for both behavior and neuroscience with most imaging findings revealing stronger BOLD responses in the PFC and orbital prefrontal cortex when viewing attractive versus unattractive faces (Fareri & Delgado, 2014). In a study conducted at the University of Fukui

(Ogoshi et al., 2016), males were first asked to rate the attractiveness of various female faces. They then completed a word recognition memory task, where correct responses were rewarded with the display of these highly rated facial images. The researchers measured brain activity using EEG, focusing on a specific type of brain response called the contingent negative variation (CNV). The CNV is a slow change in brain activity that occurs when a person is anticipating a stimulus, and it's often associated with attention and expectation. When participants were rewarded with highly attractive facial images, they showed improved accuracy on the memory task compared to when they received moderately attractive images as rewards. This performance boost became more pronounced over time, suggesting a learning effect. Even more intriguing were the neurological findings—the highly attractive facial images elicited larger CNV responses in the participants' brains. This increased CNV activity indicates that the participants were paying more attention and had greater anticipation for the more attractive rewards. Apparently, the "you aren't listening to me" claim resounded by frustrated partners and spouses is real, at least according to neuropsychological research!

Another brilliant study pharmacologically manipulated how men perceived and responded to female faces of varying attractiveness (Chelnokova et al., 2014). They gave participants one of three treatments: morphine (which activates pleasurable opioid receptors), naltrexone (which blocks these receptors), or a placebo. Then, they had the men complete two tasks while viewing female faces. In one task, they rated how attractive they found each face ("liking"). In the other, they could adjust how long they viewed each face ("wanting"). The results were eye-opening, pun intended. When men were given morphine, they rated the most attractive faces as even more appealing and were more motivated to keep looking at them. Conversely, when given naltrexone, they found those same faces less attractive and were less motivated to view them. Interestingly, morphine also made men more eager to avoid looking at the least-attractive faces. These findings suggest that naturally occurring endogenous opioids in the brain (e.g., endorphins) play a significant role in how we perceive facial attractiveness and how motivated we are to look at attractive faces. It's as if the opioid system acts like a spotlight, enhancing our appreciation of the most attractive faces while diminishing our interest in less-attractive ones. This research helps explain why we might feel a rush of pleasure when we see an attractive face and why we are drawn to look at beautiful people. Moreover, it highlights the complex interplay between our brain chemistry and our social perceptions, showing how deeply rooted our responses to facial attractiveness are in our neurological wiring.

Interestingly, biological sex matters when assessing the reward value of a face. Males will wait longer and pay more to see a pretty face compared to one less attractive (Fareri & Delgado, 2014). The male brain reacts to femininity not too differently than it does to a juicy pork chop. Cloutier et al. (2008) had forty-eight participants (twenty-four females, twenty-four males) view and rate ninety faces of different sexes on a four-point attractiveness scale while undergoing fMRI brain scanning. The researchers found that certain brain regions associated with reward processing, particularly the NAcc and orbitofrontal cortex, showed increased activation when participants viewed faces they considered attractive. Interestingly, male participants demonstrated a unique activation pattern in the OFC that distinguished between attractive and unattractive female faces, while female participants did not show this same pattern when viewing male faces. This suggests that for men attractive female faces may be more intrinsically rewarding on a neural level. The study also revealed behavioral differences, with men being less likely to rate faces as "not attractive at all" compared to women. These findings suggest that men place greater importance on physical attractiveness than females and offer additional insight into the neural basis of mate preferences and social reward processing, in addition to explaining the $670.8 billion revenue and 9 percent annual growth of the cosmetics industry (Villena & Hood, 2024).

Social Approach Behavior

We all want to feel as if what we say and do has some value to others in our social group, family, organization, or community. Imagine sharing your feelings or expressing your opinion and no one notices or cares about your concerns. In other words, behavior that elicits a subjectively interpreted positive response from others is socially rewarding (Somerville et al., 2006). Positive recognition doesn't mean adoration and worship from everyone encountered, but it does mean garnering a reaction from others that is generally positive and minimally consistent with your expectations.

While sometimes we exhibit behaviors specifically designed to alienate others, regardless we want to feel accomplished in our endeavors even if it means social acceptance of negativity. Think of characters like Ramsay Bolton, Charlie Sheen, Donald Trump, or Elon Musk if you need some models to illustrate public acceptance of "unorthodox" behavior.

Numerous studies suggest that indirect social rewards come in multiple varieties, including positive evaluation from others (Davey et al., 2010), when demonstrating behaviors that conform to social norms such as returning favors (Izuma et al., 2010) and even when experiencing rewards vicariously, which happens when we observe others experiencing a socially rewarding outcome (Morelli et al., 2015). Simply being told that someone likes you activates key reward-related brain regions, including the NAcc and midbrain areas associated with the VTA (Davey et al., 2010). This suggests that indirect social feedback is processed similarly to other rewarding experiences. Who does the liking also matters. When participants viewed faces of people who supposedly liked them, PFC activation was observed but also brain areas involved in self-related processing and emotional regulation were triggered including the emotionally sensitive amygdala. This indicates that our brains are sensitive to the perceived importance of the person providing social approval, and that the social status of the person who evaluates us has meaningful implications on the potency of the social reward.

Many individuals are concerned about reputations, whether it be online social media presence or just generally how we think others view us. Reputation is a crucial aspect of reward, determining how we act in social situations. To illustrate the extent of influence, we can compare task performance using imaging results when being observed or when alone and then analyze differences. Izuma et al. (2010) had participants rate statements such as "I never drop litter on the streets" and "I never cover up my mistakes" to determine self-evaluation of prosocial or antisocial behaviors, with or without observers. In both conditions, the PFC and striatum (the reward center) showed increased activity, as is typically shown in self-referential processing studies (Finlayson-Short et al., 2020). However, when alone, the striatum activation was significantly less than when being watched. This suggests that simply being watched by others, even devoid of explicit instructions to think about how others view us, can be socially rewarding. It's as if our brains automatically start processing our reputation and the potential social rewards of being seen positively by others. This implies that when we are in social situations, especially ones where we might be judged, our brains are working hard to represent how others view us (in the mPFC) and to process the value of a good reputation (in the striatum). By being able to represent complex social goals (like creating a good impression) and valuing social rewards (like a good reputation), we can engage in the kind of indirect reciprocity that is crucial for human society.

Similar results are observed when we unconsciously compare ourselves to others, such as what happens when someone else is the beneficiary of a social reward. Observing others receive rewards activates many of the same brain regions involved in personal reward processing (Morelli et al., 2015). This phenomenon, known as *vicarious reward processing*, helps explain why we can feel genuinely happy for others and why positive social interactions can be so fulfilling. Primary brain regions activated when observing others include the ventromedial prefrontal cortex, which helps compute the value of experiences, and the amygdala, which processes emotional significance. Interestingly, when we observe others' rewards, we also engage additional brain areas like the dorsomedial prefrontal cortex (DMPFC) and posterior superior temporal sulcus (pSTS), which are associated with understanding others' thoughts and feelings (Morelli et al., 2015). This combination of reward processing and social cognition allows us to not only recognize but also share in others' joy. Interestingly, those who take joy in the *failure* of others (termed Schadenfreude) exhibit similar facial and affective reactions as those who take pleasure in the joy of others (Boecker et al., 2015), but much more research is needed to understand the presumably rewarding aspects of what may be considered a type of convoluted envy.

The implications of this shared neural activity are profound, especially when considering the importance of positive role models in our lives. When we observe admired individuals experiencing success or happiness, our brains may simulate those positive experiences, potentially motivating us to pursue similar achievements. Moreover, by sharing in others' positive experiences, we strengthen social bonds and foster a sense of connection, which is vital for cooperation and community building. However, personal, and vicarious rewards are not processed identically. For instance, the NAcc shows less consistent activation for vicarious rewards. While we can genuinely feel happy for others, the intensity of this vicarious joy is not quite the same as a personal victory. This knowledge not only helps us understand human social behavior better but also provides insights into how to inspire social rewards in those less fortunate.

Social Rejection and Social Isolation

Having outlined the numerous benefits of social reward, it is important to realize that some aspirations are elusive despite our best intentions. Social rewards remain out of reach for many, and this exclusion has far-reaching consequences. The most frequent inhibitor of social reward is social isolation. As of December 2021, 58 percent of US adults are considered lonely (Cigna, 2021), with greater disparate impact on Hispanics (75 percent) and Black/African Americans adults (68 percent), who experience higher rates of loneliness compared to the general population. Additionally, lower-income individuals (63 percent of those earning less than $50,000 per year) reported higher levels of loneliness than their higher-income rivals. Young adults are particularly affected, with 79 percent of 18–24-year-olds reporting that they feel lonely, which is almost double the rate of those over the age of 65 (41 percent). The Cigna study also highlighted that parents and guardians (65 percent), and especially single parents (77 percent), experience greater loneliness than nonparents (55 percent).

If the demographics aren't disturbing enough, social isolation is associated with several negative consequences. Adults with mental health issues are more than twice as likely to feel lonely compared to those with strong mental health, while individuals with physical health issues are about 50 percent more likely to be lonely than those in good health (Cigna, 2021). The impact of loneliness extends into the workplace, where lonely employees report lower productivity and job satisfaction, and are more likely to miss work due to illness or stress (Ozcelik & Barsade., 2018). Individuals who experience social isolation show poorer cognitive performance compared to those with stronger social connections (Maxfield et al., 2023). The loneliness/stress relationship is well documented. Individuals often report that social isolation is a major obstacle and related to faster cognitive decline, poorer executive functioning, increased negativity, and heightened sensitivity to social threats (Cacioppo & Hawkley, 2009: Kelly et al., 2017). Confluent evidence suggests that loneliness perceptions increase production of the stress hormone cortisol. Long-term elevation of cortisol is often associated with higher risk of impaired cognition, cardiovascular disease, lower immune functioning, and sleeplessness among other harmful consequences (Jones & Gwenin, 2021).

Even brief periods of social isolation—just ten hours—can trigger a "craving" response in our brains, like how we crave food when hungry. Tomova et al. (2020) designed an intriguing isolation protocol to simulate loneliness. The researchers locked up volunteers for ten hours alone in a room at a research facility. Individuals were deprived of their personal phones and laptops and were provided with a controlled environment that allowed only nonsocial activities like doing puzzles or playing games, while having laptop access only to complete periodic questionnaires. Post isolation, participants were shown "social cues" such as pictures of smiling faces or their favorite activities while hooked up to fMRI brain imaging equipment. Reward pathways in the now-familiar brain areas of the substantia nigra and VTA became more active, and this activation correlated with how much individuals reported craving social interaction. The brain activity pattern in response to social cues after isolation was remarkably similar to the pattern seen in response to food cues (e.g., pictures of pasta) when participants were deprived of food in the same study. This suggests that our brains may have a common way of signaling "craving," regardless of whether craving food or a prolonging FaceTime with a friend or relative.

Other reward-related brain areas also showed specific responses to social isolation, such as the caudate in the striatum and the orbitofrontal cortex. The researchers also found that people who reported feeling chronically lonely had a reduced brain response to social cues after isolation. This might indicate that prolonged loneliness can lead to a kind of "social withdrawal" at the neural level, potentially making it harder for chronically lonely people to seek out social interaction. These findings support the idea that social interaction is a basic human need, much like food or sleep. Just as our brains motivate us to seek food when we are hungry, they also seem to motivate us to seek social connection when we are isolated.

Isolation induces sensitivity to rewards and is likely to encourage humans to seek social reward. Matthews et al. (2016) explored the neurological impact of social isolation particularly focusing on DA neurons in the dorsal raphe nucleus (DRN) in mice, a brain area that modulates reward-related behaviors, specifically in the context of social isolation and reunion. In just twenty-four hours of social isolation, significant changes in neurons were observed. After isolation, the neurons showed increased excitability and stronger connections, suggesting they became more sensitive, a radical example of almost instant neural plasticity. When isolated mice were reintroduced to social contact, these DRN dopamine neurons showed a marked increase in activity. This activation was much stronger than in mice that had not been isolated or when interacting with an object instead of another mouse. The study suggested that this increased neural activity represents a kind of "craving" for social interaction, similar to how we crave food when hungry. When the researchers artificially activated these neurons, mice showed a stronger preference for social interaction. However, this activation wasn't purely pleasurable—when no social interaction was available, mice avoided places associated with this neural activation. These findings help explain why social interaction feels particularly rewarding after a period of isolation. The brain's reward pathway becomes primed to respond more strongly to social stimuli, motivating us to seek out and engage in social behavior. This mechanism likely evolved to ensure that we maintain necessary social bonds, highlighting the fundamental importance of social connection for well-being, at least in rodents.

The importance of social rewards is also supported by what happens in the "default brain network," a collection of brain areas that is part of the mind's eye and is specifically responsible for internally focused cognition, such as remembering past events, imagining future scenarios, and thinking about social interactions. It overlaps significantly with the "social brain" and is called the "default" network because it is active when we are not focused on the outside world. Lonely people differ from social butterflies in this network (Spreng et al., 2020). Loners have more gray matter (brain cell bodies) in these areas, and the connections between these areas are stronger. Also, a pathway that connects memory areas to this network is more developed in lonely people. Lonely people might spend more time imagining social interactions in their mind to make up for not having enough real-life social experiences. This could explain why the default network, which is involved in imagination and thinking about social situations, is more developed in lonely people. It might be the brain's way of trying to meet social needs through internal thoughts when external social interactions are lacking. Considering that when we dream there are almost always other people involved, those in isolation should take a nap before reading on.

No surprise, loneliness has been associated with reduced reward-related activity in mesolimbic DA circuits when responding to social cues (Vitale & Smith, 2022). Spreng and colleagues speculated that lonely individuals may engage in more internal mental simulation of social experiences to compensate for their lack of actual social interactions. This could lead to greater recruitment of default network regions involved in imagination, memory, and social cognition, potentially as an attempt to fulfill unmet social needs through internally generated thought. Ultimately, we are a species that thrives on reward and opportunities for socialization are crucial for human well-being.

Socioeconomic Differences

Regrettably, the rewarding benefits achieved through the variety of mechanisms described throughout the text and particularly during socialization are influenced by socioeconomic status (SES). SES is a common measure of an individual's or family's economic and social position in relation to others. It typically combines multiple factors to create a social hierarchy composite often reported as a score and includes factors such as income, parental level of formal education, and occupations (i.e., the type of job held by the household earners), in addition to race, ethnicity, and geographic location. Lower SES scores reveal differences in neurological sensitivity to rewards and punishments limiting the many psychological and physiological advantages of rewards outlined throughout the book (Decker et al., 2024).

SES changes reward processing both neurologically and behaviorally. For instance, Palacios-Barrios et al. (2021) found that lower SES was associated with reduced activation in the PFC and specifically the ACC (the area responsible for tenacity) in response to reward cues. The blunted PFC activity when processing reward-related information was particularly prominent for stimuli that was classified as motivating for participants, showing that despite goal-directed intentions reward sensitivity was reduced. While the study did not directly measure DA synthesis, we know that corticostriatal circuits are heavily modulated by DA, suggesting that DA signaling may be reduced in lower SES individuals. Yaple and Yu (2020) in a meta-analytic review of seventeen studies compared high and low SES individuals on patterns of brain activity and structural changes in relation to perceptions of reward. Lower SES was associated with reduced activation in the brain areas typically involved in reasoning and self-control, including the ACC and the PFC. Lower SES was also linked to increased gray matter volume in reward-related areas like the orbital frontal cortex. The authors suggested that the findings supported a "scarcity hypothesis," which proposed that poverty leads individuals to focus more on immediate rewards and neglect long-term planning that is instrumental for overall life success and well-being.

Behaviorally, adolescents with lower SES backgrounds show lower reactivity when receiving a reward, supposedly due to the typical scarcity of the reward in their day-to-day lives (Decker et al., 2024). Instead of being overresponsive to rewards as you might expect when rewards are scarce, lower SES brains exhibit an attenuated reward response, likely because they become habituated to the reality that rewards are few and far between. Neurological findings in the same study revealed that higher-SES adolescents showed greater reward-driven activations than lower-SES adolescents in the putamen, caudate, and marginally in the NAcc, areas all associated with motivation and the *urge* to achieve one's goals. While findings of this nature might suggest that reward deficiencies can motivate adaptive behavior to find opportunities for advancement (i.e., the reward), which prospectively satisfy DA deficits, the results also suggest that less privileged individuals are highly vulnerable to risky behaviors and questionable decision making in the quest to quell the lack of readily available reward potential. In other words, low expectations can lead to not even trying to earn the reward or striving for quick hits that are often dangerous or unhealthy. This growing body of evidence underscores the importance of considering socioeconomic factors in how rewards operate and designing interventions to promote positive outcomes across diverse populations.

Reconciling Brain and Behavior Findings

Having thoroughly discussed the liabilities of measuring motivation using only behavioral techniques and providing volumes of evidence why understanding the nuances of neuromodulation offer explanations above and beyond behavioral findings, we must qualify how behavioral and biological findings can be linked to predict and understand motivated behavior. The obvious focus on the mask of passion and why homeostatic satisfaction of the brain is the most salient factor influencing motivated behavior means taking a holistic approach to understanding what motivates agency. While there is no denial that context and environment have broad influence on determining behavior, we must also acknowledge that masterful recipes cannot be crafted absent of quality ingredients, even with expensive cookware, hungry guests, and the presence of a robust desire to eat (or excel). Thus, while incremental progress through personal development and strategy use is attainable for all, massive change that disregards the evidence explained by neural circuitry and modulation is also undeniable. Neurological systems are regulated by baseline levels of various modulators, and this baseline can be directly linked to genetic expression (Sapolsky, 2017, 2023). Overcoming centuries of genetic predisposition by disregarding the benefit and limitations of under which circumstances certain types of physiological reward occur or are forestalled must be a primary consideration. Rewards, while idiosyncratic, operate within the restrictions of neural architecture. Cravers will always crave but there will be physical limitations, environmentally driven dysfunction, and systemic restrictions that impede how reward systems work.

Additionally, the explanatory power of all scientific findings is limited by the available evidence. Neuroscience findings are primarily correlational and do not reveal precise causes of behavior. Additionally, current imaging and genetic engineering cannot yet identify specific neurons that are solely responsible for behavior. Every finding discussed in these pages is interactive, meaning that multiple brain areas and neuromodulator systems account for observed behavior. What we do know for sure is that passion is nothing more than another form of brain-based reward. INMO-EXMO are socially constructed labels that often conflict with the understanding of neural functioning. Your brain wants reward in the many forms described and will not give up until it dies. While the functioning cannot be negotiated, the supplement and feeding of the mind can be broadly controlled and thus the remaining focus will be on strategies that leverage neuromodulation and help increase progress toward motivation and performance goals.

Considering the strong emphasis on neuropsychology here, the next step is keeping our neural architecture intact and functioning optimally. Neuroprotective refers to mechanisms or factors that protect neurons from damage, degeneration, or death. These processes help preserve the structure and function of the brain against various threats or stressors. Fratiglioni et al. (2020) aggregated strategies that have neuroprotective benefits, with the goal of maintaining cognitive health throughout life to reduce the risk of dementia and cognitive decline. This approach includes pursuing higher education, engaging in occupations with complex mental demands, and maintaining a balance between workload and decision-making autonomy in one's career. Regular physical activity, particularly in midlife, plays a crucial role, as does cultivating large and supportive social networks. Engaging in mentally stimulating leisure activities and adhering to a healthy lifestyle—including a balanced diet, avoiding smoking, and managing conditions like diabetes or depression—further contribute to brain health. The most robust protection against cognitive decline appears to stem from cumulative, lifelong engagement in a combination of mental, social, and physical activities, highlighting the importance of a holistic and sustained approach to cognitive well-being. The next chapter describes specific approaches designed to maximize the adaptive synthesis of reward and apply the neuropsychology evidence described throughout the text to improve our day-to-day lives.

References

Acevedo, B. P., Aron, A., Fisher, H. E., & Brown, L. L. (2012). Neural correlates of long-term intense romantic love. *Social Cognitive and Affective Neuroscience, 7*(2), 145–159. https://doi.org/10.1093/scan/nsq092

Alcaro, A., Huber, R., & Panksepp, J. (2007). Behavioral functions of the mesolimbic dopaminergic system: An affective neuroethological perspective. *Brain Research Reviews, 56*(2), 283–321. https://doi.org/10.1016/j.brainresrev.2007.07.014

Alexander, R., Aragón, O. R., Bookwala, J., Cherbuin, N., Gatt, J. M., Kahrilas, I. J., . . . & Styliadis, C. (2021). The neuroscience of positive emotions and affect: Implications for cultivating happiness and wellbeing. *Neuroscience & Biobehavioral Reviews, 121*, 220–249. https://doi.org/10.1016/j.neubiorev.2020.12.002

Aupperle, R. L., McDermott, T. J., White, E., & Kirlic, N. (2023). The neuropsychology of anxiety: An approach–avoidance decision-making framework. In G. G. Brown, T. Z. King, K. Y. Haaland, & B. Crosson (Eds.), *APA handbook of neuropsychology*, Volume 1: Neurobehavioral disorders and conditions: Accepted science and open questions (pp. 767–787). American Psychological Association. https://doi.org/10.1037/0000307-036

Baik, J. H. (2020). Stress and the dopaminergic reward system. *Experimental & Molecular Medicine*, 52(12), 1879–1890. https://doi.org/10.1038/s12276-020-00532-4

Baswani, S., Townsend, A. M., & Luse, A. (2021). Company-sponsored online co-creation and financial incentives: The impact of intrinsic motivation on participation intention. *International Journal of Electronic Commerce*, 25(4), 394–415. https://doi.org/10.1080/10864415.2021.1967002

Bazzari, A. H., & Parri, H. R. (2019). Neuromodulators and long-term synaptic plasticity in learning and memory: A steered-glutamatergic perspective. *Brain Sciences*, 9(11), 300. https://doi.org/10.3390/brainsci9110300

Berlyne, D. E. (1954). An experimental study of human curiosity. *British Journal of Psychology*, 45(4), 256–265.

Berridge, K. C., & Robinson, T. E. (2016). Liking, wanting, and the incentive-sensitization theory of addiction. *American Psychologist*, 71(8), 670–679. https://doi.org/10.1037/amp0000059

Bezzina, L., Lee, J. C., Lovibond, P. F., & Colagiuri, B. (2016). Extinction and renewal of cue-elicited reward-seeking. *Behaviour Research and Therapy*, 87, 162–169. https://doi.org/10.1016/j.brat.2016.09.009

Bhanji, J. P., & Delgado, M. R. (2014). The social brain and reward: Social information processing in the human striatum. *Wiley Interdisciplinary Reviews: Cognitive Science*, 5(1), 61–73. https://doi.org/10.1002/wcs.1266

Blain, B., & Sharot, T. (2021). Intrinsic reward: Potential cognitive and neural mechanisms. *Current Opinion in Behavioral Sciences*, 39, 113–118. https://doi.org/10.1016/j.cobeha.2021.03.008

Boecker, L., Likowski, K. U., Pauli, P., & Weyers, P. (2015). The face of schadenfreude: Differentiation of joy and schadenfreude by electromyography. *Cognition and Emotion*, 29(6), 111–1125. https://doi.org/10.1080/02699931.2014.966063

Bromberg-Martin, E. S., Matsumoto, M., & Hikosaka, O. (2010). Dopamine in motivational control: Rewarding, aversive, and alerting. *Neuron*, 68(5), 815–834. https://doi.org/10.1016/j.neuron.2010.11.022

Bromberg-Martin, E. S., & Monosov, I. E. (2020). Neural circuitry of information seeking. *Current Opinion in Behavioral Sciences*, 35, 62–70. https://doi.org/10.1016/j.cobeha.2020.07.006

Brummelman, E., & Sedikides, C. (2023). Unequal selves in the classroom: Nature, origins, and consequences of socioeconomic disparities in children's self-views. *Developmental Psychology, 59*(11), 1962–1987. https://doi.org/10.1037/dev0001599

Cacioppo, J. T., & Hawkley, L. C. (2009). Perceived social isolation and cognition. *Trends in Cognitive Sciences, 13*(10), 447–454. https://doi.org/10.1016/j.tics.2009.06.005

Cameron, J., & Pierce, W. D. (1994). Reinforcement, reward, and intrinsic motivation: A meta-analysis. *Review of Educational Research, 64*(3), 363–423. https://doi.org/10.2307/1170677

Cerasoli, C. P., Nicklin, J. M., & Ford, M. T. (2014). Intrinsic motivation and extrinsic incentives jointly predict performance: A 40-year meta-analysis. *Psychological Bulletin, 140*(4), 980. https://doi.org/10.1037/a0035661

Charpentier, C. J., Bromberg-Martin, E. S., & Sharot, T. (2018). Valuation of knowledge and ignorance in mesolimbic reward circuitry. *Proceedings of the National Academy of Sciences, 115*(31), E7255–E7264. https://doi.org/10.1073/pnas.1800547115

Charpentier, C. J., & Dezza, I. C. (2022). Information-seeking in the brain. In I. C. Dezza & E. Schultz (Eds.), *The drive for knowledge: The science of human information seeking* (pp. 195–216). Cambridge University Press. https://doi.org/10.31234/osf.io/qfxgd

Chelnokova, O., Laeng, B., Eikemo, M., Riegels, J., Løseth, G., Maurud, H., ... & Leknes, S. (2014). Rewards of beauty: The opioid system mediates social motivation in humans. *Molecular Psychiatry, 19*(7), 746–747. https://doi.org/10.1038/mp.2014.1

Chew, B., Blain, B., Dolan, R. J., & Rutledge, R. B. (2021). A neurocomputational model for intrinsic reward. *Journal of Neuroscience, 41*(43), 8963–8971. https://doi.org/10.1523/jneurosci.0858-20.2021

Chinn, C. A., & Brewer, W. F. (1993). The role of anomalous data in knowledge acquisition: A theoretical framework and implications for science instruction. *Review of Educational Research, 63*(1), 1–49. https://doi.org/10.2307/1170558

Cigna. (2021). Loneliness in America: A 2021 survey. Retrieved from https://newsroom.thecignagroup.com/loneliness-epidemic-persists-post-pandemic-look

Clearerthinking.org. (2023). https://www.clearerthinking.org/tools/the-intrinsic-values-test

Cloutier, J., Heatherton, T. F., Whalen, P. J., & Kelley, W. M. (2008). Are attractive people rewarding? Sex differences in the neural substrates of facial attractiveness. *Journal of Cognitive Neuroscience, 20*(6), 941–951. https://doi.org/10.1162/jocn.2008.20062

Collingridge, G. L., Peineau, S., Howland, J. G., & Wang, Y. T. (2010). Long-term depression in the CNS. *Nature Reviews Neuroscience, 11*(7), 459–473.

Cowan, N. (2014). Working memory underpins cognitive development, learning, and education. *Educational Psychology Review, 26,* 197–223. https://doi.org/10.1038/nrn2867

Cox, S. M., Frank, M. J., Larcher, K., Fellows, L. K., Clark, C. A., Leyton, M., & Dagher, A. (2015). Striatal D1 and D2 signaling differentially predict learning from positive and negative outcomes. *Neuroimage, 109,* 95–101. https://doi.org/10.1016/j.neuroimage.2014.12.070

Daniel, R., & Pollmann, S. (2014). A universal role of the ventral striatum in reward-based learning: Evidence from human studies. *Neurobiology of Learning and Memory, 114,* 90–100. https://doi.org/10.1016/j.nlm.2014.05.002

Davey, C. G., Allen, N. B., Harrison, B. J., Dwyer, D. B., & Yücel, M. (2010). Being liked activates primary reward and midline self-related brain regions. *Human Brain Mapping, 31*(4), 660–668. https://doi.org/10.1002/hbm.20895

Deci, E. L. (1971). Effects of externally mediated rewards on intrinsic motivation. *Journal of Personality and Social Psychology, 18*(1), 105–115. https://doi.org/10.1037/h0030644

Deci, E. L., Koestner, R., & Ryan, R. M. (1999). A meta-analytic review of experiments examining the effects of extrinsic rewards on intrinsic motivation. *Psychological Bulletin, 125*(6), 627.

Decker, A. L., Meisler, S. L., Hubbard, N. A., Bauer, C. C., Leonard, J., Grotzinger, H., ... & Gabrieli, J. D. (2024). Striatal and behavioral responses to reward vary by socioeconomic status in adolescents. *Journal of Neuroscience, 44*(11), e1633232023. https://doi.org/10.31234/osf.io/xyda8

Dole, J. A., & Sinatra, G. M. (1998). Reconceptualizing change in the cognitive construction of knowledge. *Educational Psychologist, 33,* 109. https://doi.org/10.1207/s15326985ep3302&3_5

Eccles, J. S., & Wigfield, A. (2020). From expectancy-value theory to situated expectancy-value theory: A developmental, social cognitive, and sociocultural perspective on motivation. *Contemporary Educational Psychology, 61,* 101859. https://doi.org/10.1016/j.cedpsych.2020.101859

Fareri, D. S., & Delgado, M. R. (2014). Social rewards and social networks in the human brain. *The Neuroscientist, 20*(4), 387–402. https://doi.org/10.1177/1073858414521869

Feng, C., Eickhoff, S. B., Li, T., Wang, L., Becker, B., Camilleri, J. A., ... & Luo, Y. (2021). Common brain networks underlying human social interactions: Evidence from large-scale neuroimaging meta-analysis. *Neuroscience & Biobehavioral Reviews, 126*, 289–303. https://doi.org/10.1016/j.neubiorev.2021.03.025

Finlayson-Short, L., Davey, C. G., & Harrison, B. J. (2020). Neural correlates of integrated self and social processing. *Social Cognitive and Affective Neuroscience, 15*(9), 941–949. https://doi.org/10.1093/scan/nsaa121

Fratiglioni, L., Marseglia, A., & Dekhtyar, S. (2020). Ageing without dementia: Can stimulating psychosocial and lifestyle experiences make a difference?. *The Lancet Neurology, 19*(6), 533–543. https://doi.org/10.1016/s1474-4422(20)30039-9

Frey, B. S., & Jegen, R. (2001). Motivation crowding theory. *Journal of Economic Surveys, 15*(5), 589–611. https://doi.org/10.2139/ssrn.203330

Fryling, M. J., Johnston, C., & Hayes, L. J. (2011). Understanding observational learning: An interbehavioral approach. *The Analysis of Verbal Behavior, 27*, 191–203. https://doi.org/10.1007/bf03393102

Fulmer, I. S., & Shaw, J. D. (2018). Person-based differences in pay reactions: A compensation-activation theory and integrative conceptual review. *Journal of Applied Psychology, 103*(9), 939–958. https://doi.org/10.1037/apl0000310

Gregoire, M. (2003). Is it a challenge or a threat? A dual-process model of teachers' cognition and appraisal processes during conceptual change. *Educational Psychology Review, 15*, 147–180. https://doi.org/10.1023/A:1023477131081

Grill, F., Guitart-Masip, M., Johansson, J., Stiernman, L., Axelsson, J., Nyberg, L., & Rieckmann, A. (2024). Dopamine release in human associative striatum during reversal learning. *Nature Communications, 15*(1), 59. https://doi.org/10.1038/s41467-023-44358-w

Gruber, M. J., Gelman, B. D., & Ranganath, C. (2014). States of curiosity modulate hippocampus-dependent learning via the dopaminergic circuit. *Neuron, 84*(2), 486–496. https://doi.org/10.1016/j.neuron.2014.08.060

Gruber, M. J., Valji, A., & Ranganath, C. (2019). Curiosity and learning: A neuroscientific perspective. In K. A. Renninger & S. Hidi (Eds.), *The Cambridge handbook of motivation and learning* (pp. 397–417). Cambridge University Press. https://doi.org/10.1017/9781316823279.018

Hauser, T. U., Eldar, E., Purg, N., Moutoussis, M., & Dolan, R. J. (2019). Distinct roles of dopamine and noradrenaline in incidental memory. *Journal of Neuroscience, 39*(39), 7715–7721. https://doi.org/10.1523/jneurosci.0401-19.2019

Hebb, D. O. (2005). *The organization of behavior: A neuropsychological theory*. Psychology Press.

Hidi, S. (2016). Revisiting the role of rewards in motivation and learning: Implications of neuroscientific research. *Educational Psychology Review, 28*, 61–93. https://doi.org/10.1037/h0030644

Hoffman, B., Subramaniam, A., & Hartley, K. (2025). It's time to reconsider: The neuropsychology of belief change. *Trends in Neuroscience and Education, 40*, 100261. https://doi.org/10.1016/j.tine.2025.100261

Inagaki, T. K., & Eisenberger, N. I. (2012). Neural correlates of giving support to a loved one. *Psychosomatic Medicine, 74*(1), 3–7. https://doi.org/10.1097/psy.0b013e3182359335

Izuma, K., Saito, D. N., & Sadato, N. (2008). Processing of social and monetary rewards in the human striatum. *Neuron, 58*(2), 284–294. https://doi.org/10.1016/j.neuron.2008.03.020

Izuma, K., Saito, D. N., & Sadato, N. (2010). The roles of the medial prefrontal cortex and striatum in reputation processing. *Social Neuroscience, 5*(2), 133–147. https://doi.org/10.1080/17470910903202559

Jones, C., & Gwenin, C. (2021). Cortisol level dysregulation and its prevalence—Is it nature's alarm clock?. *Physiological Reports, 8*(24), e14644. https://doi.org/10.14814/phy2.14644

Kaanders, P., Juechems, K., O'Reilly, J., & Hunt, L. (2021). Dissociable mechanisms of information sampling in prefrontal cortex and the dopaminergic system. *Current Opinion in Behavioral Sciences, 41*, 63–70. https://doi.org/10.1016/j.cobeha.2021.04.005

Kandel, E. R. (2001). The molecular biology of memory storage: A dialogue between genes and synapses. *Science, 294*(5544), 1030–1038. https://doi.org/10.1126/science.1067020

Kelly, M. E., Duff, H., Kelly, S., McHugh Power, J. E., Brennan, S., Lawlor, B. A., & Loughrey, D. G. (2017). The impact of social activities, social networks, social support and social relationships on the cognitive functioning of healthy older adults: A systematic review. *Systematic Reviews, 6*, 1–18. https://doi.org/10.1186/s13643-017-0632-2

Kennedy, M. B. (2016). Synaptic signaling in learning and memory. *Cold Spring Harbor Perspectives in Biology, 8*(2), a016824. https://doi.org/10.1101/cshperspect.a016824

Kidd, C., & Hayden, B. Y. (2015). The psychology and neuroscience of curiosity. *Neuron, 88*(3), 449–460. https://doi.org/10.1016/j.neuron.2015.09.010

Kim, S. I. (2013). Neuroscientific model of motivational process. *Frontiers in Psychology, 4*, 98. https://doi.org/10.3389/fpsyg.2013.00098

Kizilirmak, J. M., Galvao Gomes da Silva, J., Imamoglu, F., & Richardson-Klavehn, A. (2016). Generation and the subjective feeling of "aha!" are independently related to learning from insight. *Psychological Research, 80*, 1059–1074. https://doi.org/10.1007/s00426-015-0697-2

Knutson, B., & Greer, S. M. (2008). Anticipatory affect: Neural correlates and consequences for choice. *Philosophical Transactions of the Royal Society B: Biological Sciences, 363*(1511), 3771–3786. https://doi.org/10.1098/rstb.2008.0155

Knutson, B., & Wimmer, G. E. (2007). Reward: Neural circuitry for social valuation. In E. Harmon-Jones & P. Winkielman (Eds.), *Social neuroscience: Integrating biological and psychological explanations of social behavior* (pp. 157–175). Guilford Press.

Kobayashi, K., & Hsu, M. (2019). Common neural code for reward and information value. *Proceedings of the National Academy Sciences, 116*(26), 13061–13066. https://doi.org/10.1073/pnas.1820145116

Kohn, A. (1993). *Punished by rewards: The trouble with gold stars, incentive plans, A's, praise and other bribes.* Houghton Mifflin.

Lee, S. J., Lodder, B., Chen, Y., Patriarchi, T., Tian, L., & Sabatini, B. L. (2021). Cell-type-specific asynchronous modulation of PKA by dopamine in learning. *Nature, 590*(7846), 451–456. doi:10.1038/s41586-020-03050-5

Lee, W. (2016). Insular cortex activity as the neural base of intrinsic motivation. In S. I. Kim, J. Reeve, & M. Bong *Recent developments in Neuroscience research on human motivation* (Vol. 19, pp. 127–148). Emerald Group Publishing Limited.

Lepper, M. R., Greene, D., & Nisbett, R. E. (1973). Undermining children's intrinsic interest with extrinsic reward: A test of the "overjustification" hypothesis. *Journal of Personality and Social Psychology, 28*, 129–137. https://psycnet.apa.org/doi/10.1037/h0035519

Levy, A., DeLeon, I. G., Martinez, C. K., Fernandez, N., Gage, N. A., Sigurdsson, S. Ó., & Frank-Crawford, M. A. (2017). A quantitative review of overjustification effects in persons with intellectual and developmental disabilities. *Journal of Applied Behavior Analysis, 50*(2), 206–221. https://doi.org/10.1037/h0035519

Likhtik, E., & Johansen, J. P. (2019). Neuromodulation in circuits of aversive emotional learning. *Nature Neuroscience, 22*(10), 1586–1597. https://doi.org/10.1038/s41593-019-0503-3

Lin, A., Adolphs, R., & Rangel, A. (2012). Social and monetary reward learning engage overlapping neural substrates. *Social Cognitive and Affective Neuroscience, 7*(3), 274–281. https://doi.org/10.1093/scan/nsr006

Linke, J., Kirsch, P., King, A. V., Gass, A., Hennerici, M. G., Bongers, A., & Wessa, M. (2010). Motivational orientation modulates the neural response to reward. *NeuroImage, 49*, 2618–2625. https://doi.org/10.1016/j.neuroimage.2009.09.013

Lømo, T. (2003). The discovery of long-term potentiation. *Philosophical Transactions of the Royal Society of London. Series B: Biological Sciences, 358*(1432), 617–620. https://doi.org/10.1098/rstb.2002.1226

Luria, E., Shalom, M., & Levy, D. A. (2021). Cognitive neuroscience perspectives on motivation and learning: Revisiting self-determination theory. *Mind, Brain, and Education, 15*(1), 5–17. https://doi.org/10.1111/mbe.12275

Magee, J. C., & Grienberger, C. (2020). Synaptic plasticity forms and functions. *Annual Review of Neuroscience, 43*(1), 95–117. https://doi.org/10.1146/annurev-neuro-090919-022842

Malenka, R. C., & Bear, M. F. (2004). LTP and LTD: An embarrassment of riches. *Neuron, 44*(1), 5–21. https://doi.org/10.1016/j.neuron.2004.09.012

Matsuzaki, M., Honkura, N., Ellis-Davies, G. C., & Kasai, H. (2004). Structural basis of long-term potentiation in single dendritic spines. *Nature, 429*(6993), 761–766. https://doi.org/10.1038/nature02617

Matthews, G. A., Nieh, E. H., Vander Weele, C. M., Halbert, S. A., Pradhan, R. V., Yosafat, A. S., ... & Tye, K. M. (2016). Dorsal raphe dopamine neurons represent the experience of social isolation. *Cell, 164*(4), 617–631. https://doi.org/10.1016/j.cell.2015.12.040

Maxfield, M., Li, X., & Widom, C. S. (2023). Childhood maltreatment and midlife cognitive functioning: A longitudinal study of the roles of social support and social isolation. *Neuropsychology, 37*(8), 943–954. https://psycnet.apa.org/doi/10.1037/neu0000911

Mohebi, A., & Berke, J. D. (2020). Dopamine release drives motivation, independently from dopamine cell firing. *Neuropsychopharmacology, 45*(1), 220. https://doi.org/10.1038/s41386-019-0492-7

Morelli, S. A., Sacchet, M. D., & Zaki, J. (2015). Common and distinct neural correlates of personal and vicarious reward: A quantitative meta-analysis. *NeuroImage, 112*, 244–253. https://doi.org/10.1016/j.neuroimage.2014.12.056

Morris, L. S., Grehl, M. M., Rutter, S. B., Mehta, M., & Westwater, M. L. (2022). On what motivates us: A detailed review of intrinsic v. extrinsic motivation. *Psychological Medicine, 52*(10), 1801–1816. https://doi.org/10.1017/s0033291722001611

Murayama, K. (2022). A reward-learning framework of knowledge acquisition: An integrated account of curiosity, interest, and intrinsic–

extrinsic rewards. *Psychological Review, 129*(1), 175–198. https://doi.org/10.31219/osf.io/zey4k

Murayama, K., Izuma, K., Aoki, R., & Matsumoto, K. (2016). Your choice motivates you in the brain: The emergence of autonomy neuroscience. *Recent Developments in Neuroscience Research on Human Motivation* (Advances in motivation and achievement, Vol. 19, pp. 95–125). Emerald Group Publishing Limited. https://doi.org/10.1108/S0749-742320160000019004

Murayama, K., & Kuhbandner, C. (2011). Money enhances memory consolidation–But only for boring material. *Cognition, 119*(1), 120–124. https://doi.org/10.1016/j.cognition.2011.01.001

Murphy, P. K. (2007). The eye of the beholder: The interplay of social and cognitive components in change. *Educational Psychologist, 42*(1), 41–53. https://doi.org/10.1080/00461520709336917

Nadelson, L. S., Heddy, B. C., Jones, S., Taasoobshirazi, G., & Johnson, M. (2018). Conceptual change in science teaching and learning: Introducing the dynamic model of conceptual change. *International Journal of Educational Psychology, 7*(2), 151–195. https://doi.org/10.17583/ijep.2018.3349

Niedenthal, P. M., & Ric, F. (2017). *Psychology of emotion*. Psychology Press.

Nieh, E. H., Vander Weele, C. M., Matthews, G. A., Presbrey, K. N., Wichmann, R., Leppla, C. A., ... & Tye, K. M. (2016). Inhibitory input from the lateral hypothalamus to the ventral tegmental area disinhibits dopamine neurons and promotes behavioral activation. *Neuron, 90*(6), 1286–1298. https://doi.org/10.1016/j.neuron.2016.04.035

Ogoshi, Y., Ogoshi, S., Takezawa, T., & Mitsuhashi, Y. (2016). Impact of the facial attractiveness of a social reward on event-related potential activities and task performance. *Sensors and Materials, 28*(4), 321–327. https://doi.org/10.18494/sam.2016.1182

Oldham, S., Murawski, C., Fornito, A., Youssef, G., Yücel, M., & Lorenzetti, V. (2018). The anticipation and outcome phases of reward and loss processing: A neuroimaging meta-analysis of the monetary incentive delay task. *Human Brain Mapping, 39*(8), 3398–3418. https://doi.org/10.1002/hbm.24184

Owens, D., Grossman, Z., & Fackler, R. (2014). The control premium: A preference for payoff autonomy. *American Economic Journal: Microeconomics, 6*(4), 138–161. https://doi.org/10.1257/mic.6.4.138

Ozcelik, H., & Barsade, S. G. (2018). No employee an island: Workplace loneliness and job performance. *Academy of Management Journal, 61*(6), 2343–2366. https://doi.org/10.5465/amj.2015.1066

Palacios-Barrios, E. E., Hanson, J. L., Barry, K. R., Albert, W. D., White, S. F., Skinner, A. T., ... & Lansford, J. E. (2021). Lower neural value signaling in the prefrontal cortex is related to childhood family income and depressive symptomatology during adolescence. *Developmental Cognitive Neuroscience, 48*, 100920. https://doi.org/10.1016/j.dcn.2021.100920

Patall, E. A., Cooper, H., & Robinson, J. C. (2008). The effects of choice on intrinsic motivation and related outcomes: A meta-analysis of research findings. *Psychological Bulletin, 134*(2), 270–300. https://doi.org/10.1037/0033-2909.134.2.270

Patihis, L. (2018). The historical significance of the discovery of long-term potentiation: An overview and evaluation for nonexperts. *The American Journal of Psychology, 131*(3), 369–380. https://doi.org/10.5406/amerjpsyc.131.3.0369

Pessiglione, M., Seymour, B., Flandin, G., Dolan, R. J., & Frith, C. D. (2006). Dopamine-dependent prediction errors underpin reward-seeking behaviour in humans. *Nature, 442*(7106), 1042–1045. https://doi.org/10.1038/nature05051

Peters, K. P., Grauerholz-Fisher, E., Vollmer, T. R., & Van Arsdale, A. (2022). An evaluation of the overjustification hypothesis: A replication of Deci (1971). *Behavior Analysis: Research and Practice, 22*(3), 258–264. https://doi.org/10.1037/bar0000245

Posner, G. J., Strike, K. A., Hewson, P. W., & Gertzog, W. A. (1982). Accommodation of a scientific conception: Toward a theory of conceptual change. *Science Education, 66*(2), 211–227. https://doi.org/10.1002/sce.3730660207

Pugh, Z. H., Choo, S., Leshin, J. C., Lindquist, K. A., & Nam, C. S. (2022). Emotion depends on context, culture and their interaction: Evidence from effective connectivity. *Social Cognitive and Affective Neuroscience, 17*(2), 206–217. https://doi.org/10.1093/scan/nsab092

Reeve, J. (2018). *Understanding motivation and emotion*. John Wiley & Sons.

Reeve, J., & Cheon, S. H. (2021). Autonomy-supportive teaching: Its malleability, benefits, and potential to improve educational practice. *Educational Psychologist, 56*(1), 54–77. https://doi.org/10.1080/00461520.2020.1862657

Ripollés, P., Marco-Pallarés, J., Hielscher, U., Mestres-Missé, A., Tempelmann, C., Heinze, H. J., ... & Noesselt, T. (2014). The role of reward in word learning and its implications for language acquisition. *Current Biology, 24*(21), 2606–2611. https://doi.org/10.1016/j.cub.2014.09.044

Ruff, C. C., & Fehr, E. (2014). The neurobiology of rewards and values in social decision making. *Nature Reviews Neuroscience, 15*(8), 549–562. https://doi.org/10.1038/nrn3776

Russo, S. J., & Nestler, E. J. (2013). The brain reward circuitry in mood disorders. *Nature Reviews Neuroscience, 14*(9), 609–625. https://doi.org/10.1038/nrn3381

Ryan, R. M., & Deci, E. L. (2017). *Self-determination theory: Basic psychological needs in motivation, development, and wellness.* Guilford Publications

Ryan, R. M., & Deci, E. L. (2020). Intrinsic and extrinsic motivation from a self-determination theory perspective: Definitions, theory, practices, and future directions. *Contemporary Educational Psychology,* 101860. https://doi.org/10.1016/j.cedpsych.2020.101860

Samtani, S., Mahalingam, G., Lam, B. C. P., Lipnicki, D. M., Lima-Costa, M. F., Blay, S. L., ... & Brodaty, H. (2022). Associations between social connections and cognition: A global collaborative individual participant data meta-analysis. *The Lancet Healthy Longevity, 3*(11), e740–e753. https://doi.org/10.1016/s2666-7568(22)00199-4

Sapolsky, R. M. (2017). *Behave: The biology of humans at our best and worst.* Penguin.

Sapolsky, R. M. (2023). *Determined: A science of life without free will.* Penguin.

Schultz, W. (2015). Neuronal reward and decision signals: From theories to data. *Physiological Reviews, 95*(3), 853–951. https://doi.org/10.1152/physrev.00023.2014

Sescousse, G., Li, Y., & Dreher, J. C. (2015). A common currency for the computation of motivational values in the human striatum. *Social Cognitive and Affective Neuroscience, 10*(4), 467–473. https://doi.org/10.1093/scan/nsu074

Shafiei, G., Zeighami, Y., Clark, C. A., Coull, J. T., Nagano-Saito, A., Leyton, M., ... & Mišić, B. (2019). Dopamine signaling modulates the stability and integration of intrinsic brain networks. *Cerebral Cortex, 29*(1), 397–409. https://doi.org/10.1093/cercor/bhy264

Sharot, T., & Garrett, N. (2016). Forming beliefs: Why valence matters. *Trends in Cognitive Sciences, 20*(1), 25–33. https://doi.org/10.1016/j.tics.2015.11.002

Sharot, T., & Sunstein, C. R. (2020). How people decide what they want to know. *Nature Human Behaviour, 4*(1), 14–19. https://doi.org/10.1038/s41562-019-0793-1

Shen, X., Helion, C., Smith, D. V., & Murty, V. P. (2024). Motivation as a lens for understanding information-seeking behaviors. *Journal of Cognitive Neuroscience, 36*(2), 362–376. https://doi.org/10.1162/jocn_a_02083

Sicherman, N., Loewenstein, G., Seppi, D. J., & Utkus, S. P. (2016). Financial attention. *The Review of Financial Studies, 29*(4), 863–897. https://doi.org/10.1093/rfs/hhv073

Sinatra, G. M., & Hofer, B. K. (2021). *Science denial: Why it happens and what to do about it.* Oxford University Press.

Somerville, L. H., Heatherton, T. F., & Kelley, W. M. (2006). Anterior cingulate cortex responds differentially to expectancy violation and social rejection. *Nature Neuroscience, 9*(8), 1007–1008. https://doi.org/10.1038/nn1728

Speer, M. E., Ibrahim, S., Schiller, D., & Delgado, M. R. (2021). Finding positive meaning in memories of negative events adaptively updates memory. *Nature Communications, 12*(1), 6601. https://doi.org/10.1038/s41467-021-26906-4

Spreng, R. N., Dimas, E., Mwilambwe-Tshilobo, L., Dagher, A., Koellinger, P., Nave, G., ... & Bzdok, D. (2020). The default network of the human brain is associated with perceived social isolation. *Nature Communications, 11*(1), 6393. https://doi.org/10.1038/s41467-020-20039-w

Thorp, J., Clewett, D., & Riegel, M. (2020). Two routes to incidental memory under arousal: Dopamine and norepinephrine. *Journal of Neuroscience, 40*(9), 1790–1792. https://doi.org/10.1523/jneurosci.2698-19.2020

Tobler, P. N., Fiorillo, C. D., & Schultz, W. (2005). Adaptive coding of reward value by dopamine neurons. *Science, 307*(5715), 1642–1645. https://doi.org/10.1126/science.1105370

Tomova, L., Wang, K. L., Thompson, T., Matthews, G. A., Takahashi, A., Tye, K. M., & Saxe, R. (2020). Acute social isolation evokes midbrain craving responses similar to hunger. *Nature Neuroscience, 23*(12), 1597–1605. https://doi.org/10.1038/s41593-020-00742-z

Touroutoglou, A., Andreano, J., Dickerson, B. C., & Barrett, L. F. (2020). The tenacious brain: How the anterior mid-cingulate contributes to achieving goals. *Cortex, 123,* 12–29. https://doi.org/10.1016/j.cortex.2019.09.011

Turrigiano, G. G. (2008). The self-tuning neuron: Synaptic scaling of excitatory synapses. *Cell, 135*(3), 422–435. https://doi.org/10.1016/j.cell.2008.10.008

Twenge, J. M., & Donnelly, K. (2016). Generational differences in American students' reasons for going to college, 1971–2014: The rise of extrinsic motives. *The Journal of Social Psychology, 156*(6), 620–629. https://doi.org/10.1080/00224545.2016.1152214

Vassena, E., Deraeve, J., & Alexander, W. H. (2019). Task-specific prioritization of reward and effort information: Novel insights from behavior and computational modeling. *Cognitive, Affective, & Behavioral Neuroscience, 19,* 619–636. https://doi.org/10.3758/s13415-018-00685-w

Villena, K., & Hood, E. (2024). Top trends shaping the beauty and personal care industry in 2024. https://tks-hpc.h5mag.com/hpc_today_6_2024/market_trends_-_top_four_trends_shaping_the_beauty_and_personal_care_industry_in_2024

Vitale, E. M., & Smith, A. S. (2022). Neurobiology of loneliness, isolation, and loss: Integrating human and animal perspectives. *Frontiers in Behavioral Neuroscience, 16*, 846315. https://doi.org/10.3389/fnbeh.2022.846315

Wagner, U., Galli, L., Schott, B. H., Wold, A., van der Schalk, J., Manstead, A. S., ... & Walter, H. (2015). Beautiful friendship: Social sharing of emotions improves subjective feelings and activates the neural reward circuitry. *Social Cognitive and Affective Neuroscience, 10*(6), 801–808. https://doi.org/10.1093/scan/nsu121

Wang, K. S., & Delgado, M. R. (2019). Corticostriatal circuits encode the subjective value of perceived control. *Cerebral Cortex, 29*(12), 5049–5060. https://doi.org/10.1093/cercor/bhz045

Weinstein, N. D., & Klein, W. M. (1995). Resistance of personal risk perceptions to debiasing interventions. *Health Psychology, 14*(2), 132–140. https://doi.org/10.1037//0278-6133.14.2.132

Westbrook, A., van den Bosch, R., Hofmans, L., Papadopetraki, D., Maatta, J. I., Collins, A. G. E., ... & Cools, R. (2024). Striatal dopamine can enhance learning, both fast and slow, and also make it cheaper. *BioRxiv*, 2024-02. https://doi.org/10.1101/2024.02.14.580392

Westen, D., Blagov, P. S., Harenski, K., Kilts, C., & Hamann, S. (2006). Neural bases of motivated reasoning: An fMRI study of emotional constraints on partisan political judgment in the 2004 US presidential election. *Journal of Cognitive Neuroscience, 18*(11), 1947–1958. https://doi.org/10.1162/jocn.2006.18.11.1947

Williams, J., & Rebuschat, P. (2016). *Implicit learning and second language acquisition*. Routledge.

Williams, S. E., Ford, J. H., & Kensinger, E. A. (2022). The power of negative and positive episodic memories. *Cognitive Affective Behavioral Neuroscience, 22*, 869–903. https://doi.org/10.3758/s13415-022-01013-z

Yaple, Z. A., & Yu, R. (2020). Functional and structural brain correlates of socioeconomic status. *Cerebral Cortex, 30*(1), 181–196. https://doi.org/10.1093/cercor/bhz080

Yoon, H., Scopelliti, I., & Morewedge, C. K. (2021). Decision making can be improved through observational learning. *Organizational Behavior and Human Decision Processes, 162*, 155–188. https://doi.org/10.1016/j.obhdp.2020.10.011

Young, C. B., & Nusslock, R. (2016). Positive mood enhances reward-related neural activity. *Social Cognitive and Affective Neuroscience, 11*(6), 934–944. https://doi.org/10.1093/scan/nsw012

7

This Is How We Do It

Chapter Outline

Invert the Curve	255
Embrace Appropriate Evidence	258
Self-Regulation	259
What Do We Want?	266
Enhancing Physiology	266
Maximizing Cognitive Clarity	276
Learning More in Less Time	288
Ten Timeless Tips and One to Avoid	293
Get the Dop(amine)	304
Persuasion	306

Invert the Curve

One important goal of psychological research is the ability to develop practical recommendations that foster well-being. While some researchers might disagree, theory devoid of relevant application and usefulness is little more than junk food for the mind. The theories may sound or taste good, but are they useful and nutritious? While theoretical frameworks in neuropsychology provide the foundation for understanding brain and neural functioning, their true value emerges when the findings are translated into tangible solutions that solve real-world problems, probably like the challenges most humans encounter every day in the quest to become valuable, fully functioning, contributing members of society.

This chapter is designed to apply the complicated inferences from all the other chapters. The remaining content is specifically designed to improve lives. It is time to put the knowledge to work to make a stronger, better, faster, more efficient, and productive version of you. While *not* a self-help troupe based on expert recommendations, this chapter advances neurologically consistent approaches designed to maximize overall functioning and productivity. Unlike many strategies and techniques typically amplified in the media, the recommendations here embrace both neuropsychological findings and behavioral realities and have little or nothing to do with individual success stories, or "proven" formulas. However, all recommendations here are geared toward the firsthand experiences you will likely encounter regardless of your age, gender, ethnicity, culture, or location.

Humans are in a perpetual state of trying to delay cognitive decline and physiological aging. "*Entropy*" is the general term to describe how over time the universe evolves toward death and disorder, a process that mathematician James R. Newman, described as "degradation." Whether we believe it, or like it, our cognitive and motivation capabilities will diminish as we age. The only way to delay entropy is by taking demonstrative steps to invert the entropy curve, which means intentionally doing hard things. Hard in this case means exerting extra effort beyond the minimum requirements when setting, striving for, and attaining goals (Raman et al., 2019; Touroutoglou et al., 2020). For instance, when you exercise more than planned, eat a smaller portion despite being hungry, or act pleasant when you are really aggravated, your brain is in a mode of perseverance and resilience. Hard means delay of gratification, deliberately feeling uncomfortable, enduring short-term pain for long-term gain, and potentially sacrificing pleasure when it is within your immediate grasp. Ultimately, any hard strategy meets the objective of being "neuroprotective" by fortifying neurons and insulating brain cells from damage, degeneration, or death (Fratiglioni et al., 2020), with the focused intent of preserving the structure and function of the brain against various threats or stressors.

Fratiglioni et al. (2020) when reviewing how to reduce early onset of dementia described many supportive behaviors that were hypothesized to have neuroprotective benefits. Notice how every conclusion on the list below involves the exertion of effort, short-term inconvenience for long-term gain, or taking a deliberate and intentional focus to improve lifestyle and overall well-being:

While the prosocial and lifestyle approaches advanced here are all documented through replicable and confluent empirical evidence, the results are primarily based on observation data and do not completely explain the precise mechanisms of neuroprotection. Some variables might function via pathways that are both neuroprotective (avoiding harm and risk) and compensatory (dealing with damage). Nevertheless, the desired outcomes partially serve as the foundation for the subsequent recommendations. In addition, strategies from educational, organizational, and consulting psychology that enhance productivity, contribute to positive self-perceptions, and support general well-being are advanced. Based on the specific neuromodulator functionality described throughout the text, behaviors that cultivate desirable neurotransmission are also described.

Table 7.1 Neuroprotective Realities

Education	There is a continuous correlation between a higher education level and a decreased incidence of dementia.
Occupational complexity	High-stress jobs, particularly those demanding intricate data analysis or interpersonal activities, may be protective against cognitive deterioration.
Physical activity	Engaging in regular exercise, especially in middle age, is linked to a lower incidence of dementia.
Social interaction	Broadening and encouraging social networks may function as a buffer against dementia and cognitive deterioration.
Leisure activities that stimulate the mind	Throughout life, partaking in mentally taxing hobbies may assist and preserve brain function.
Balanced job demands	Jobs with low job strain and a healthy workload/decision-making autonomy may be protective.
Healthy lifestyle factors	Maintaining a healthy diet, abstaining from smoking, and not having diabetes or depression may all be protective.
Cumulative engagement	The best defense against dementia evolves from a lifetime of participation in mentally, socially, and physically engaging activities.

Embrace Appropriate Evidence

When considering which strategies will be effective for a diverse group of individuals, we should always question the recommendation source. It is speculative to assume that a successful approach based on the experience of one individual will be equally effective for others. This reality is true because unless the heritability, contextual circumstances, background knowledge, and experiences of different individuals are similar, the strategy approach cannot be assumed to have the same degree of effectiveness. Yet, we often hear of "proven" techniques and expert claims that are supposedly failproof and life changing. These difficult-to-verify assertions often perpetuate, becoming engrained in cultures and resulting in conventional wisdom, common sense, and a variety of misconceptions. Some of these dubious claims were exposed in Chapter 2, but we must remember that many well-accepted practices are often grounded in tradition, yet unsupported by research, resulting in the use of strategies that may not work or in some cases inhibit effective learning and performance. Approaches like teaching to a preferred learning style, assuming mastery of a topic takes 10,000 hours, or believing that more homework promotes higher grades are all beliefs unsupported by reliable evidence! Add in the faulty presumption that multitasking increases productivity, punishment decreases undesirable behavior, and cramming is a fantastic way to excel on exams and you will cultivate failure.

So how can we counter the proliferation of misconceptions? First, emphasize your own critical thinking and scrutinize why personal experience and pop psychology claims may not accurately reflect reality. Second, seek counterexamples and use debunking strategies that refute conventional wisdom and misconceptions lodged in memory. In other words, avoid confirmation bias by not gravitating toward evidence that supports beliefs while ignoring or rationalizing away disconfirming perspectives. Third, consider that approaches that work in one context and culture may not work in another. In practice, recall the "backfire effect," where individuals become more stubborn in holding true to false beliefs when challenged to consider alternative perspectives. Finally, recall that whether conscious or not, practices advocated by the media and journalists are often mutated pseudoscience beliefs that may be misjudged or politicized interpretations of the actual scientific evidence.

Instead, ask yourself the question, "How do I know?" If the answer is "just because" or "I have always done it this way," or if the response is based only on personal experience (or the experience of limited others), then think again! Do not focus on wishful thinking and try to take an objective perspective. Consider alternative explanations. Rather than focusing only on why your approach is correct, ideate other possible outcomes. Brainstorm with others or critically reflect on the proposed direction to see under which conditions and circumstances you are wrong or why the intended plan might cause more harm than good. Analyze the logic. Distinguish between what you want to happen and what may happen. Finally, do not reach spontaneous conclusions or those made in the heat of emotion. That new car might look really nice in your driveway, but not when you have to make the first payment and don't have enough money left to pay for food. Never forget that we have limited cognitive resources, and when those resources are consumed by emotion (positive or negative), we make errors in judgment. In addition, dopamine (DA) overloads caused by intoxication, hedonism, or overindulgence reduce sound reasoning ability and capacity, and almost always result in long-term regret.

Self-Regulation

After the prior diatribe, you may be thinking that maximizing the value of rewards is based on exhibiting self-control or at least being closely supervised by a mommy figure, significant other, or an annoying self-help app. Well, you are partially correct, but the significant other is you! To effectively maximize the stimulating power of rewarding neuromodulators such as dopamine (DA), serotonin, and norepinephrine (NE), we need to exert some conscious control over actions, even if that only means taking your supplements at the right time. Typically, perceptions of self-control imply the need for restraint, but, in reality, conventional definitions of self-regulation encompass much more than merely avoiding overindulgence or risk. One definition suggests that self-control is "the process of advancing one goal over a second goal when the two come into conflict" (Inzlicht et al., 2021, p. 321). However, in practice self-regulation is more holistic, whereby the individual consciously and perpetually examines the planning, monitoring, and regulation of their behavior, motivation, and emotion with the intent of maximizing learning or performance.

The key element underlying all self-regulatory activities is intent, meaning there is a conscious emphasis associated with all phases of self-regulation and the individual uses specific, measurable targets to guide goal navigation. Awareness also means reflecting on what has been accomplished in comparison to desired outcomes. The crux of self-regulation starts with having predetermined plans and goals. While spontaneous activities can be perceived as rewarding based on being unexpected (thereby increasing reward prediction error (RPE)), almost always those who have a plan outperform those who do not. Regulatory efforts typically unfold in a cyclical process, starting with setting task goals, continuing with monitoring performance progress and conditions, and ending with qualitative evaluation of results (Winne & Hadwin, 2008).

The mechanics of the regulatory process start with a planning phase that decides on the target and proactively projects what obstacles might inhibit goal attainment. Via planning, the individual can prepare in advance for inevitable skill or motivational lapses or lulls and have a remedy before starting the task. Next, the individual conducts ongoing assessments of task performance, keeping in mind the need to switch strategies if the current approach does not meet expectations. Like planning, during the monitoring phase the individual anticipates what might go awry and has an alternative plan in place before task engagement. The third phase, reflection, allows retrospective evaluation to determine what could have been done differently to achieve more favorable results, such as asking oneself "how could have I done this quicker" or "was there a more efficient process than the one I used?" Regardless of the potential areas for improvement, the key metric is not indiscriminately moving on but consciously and seriously considering that one's performance always has opportunities for improvement, even when reaching for stretch goals or when demonstrating superior achievement.

To understand how self-regulation works in practice, let's examine the portrait of an aspiring athlete, 56-year-old Caucasian male, Jonny Wheeler, an avid bicycler living in the swamps of Florida. Most days he sits in his humid garage waiting for the daily deluge of thunderstorms to dwindle so he can go outside and sweat. Considering the weather, he is always in search of the perfect jacket for his daily rides. Once, he bought a windbreaker thinking that would protect him from getting drenched. Jonny is a firm believer that rain hinders exercise performance, so he needs to grab every edge to be his best. He wanted to find something that would make him look fit but also glow in traffic. He was once hit by a car when cycling, breaking nine of his brittle bones. He also wanted to stay dry. After evaluating his options, he decided upon a skintight, vinyl(ish), neon green jacket. The choice was based in part on the material's label, which stated, "*outer shell waterproof.*" To his chagrin, the first time he wore the jacket, he felt gross, all hot and clammy. His immediate thought was to blame the manufacturer. He felt like he was duped because what he wanted and what he experienced from the clothing conundrum were radically different.

Jonny reflected on his sweat dilemma and thought maybe he was the problem. After all, he's a prolific perspirer, who, based on his NYC roots, usually moves like someone being chased by the cops. That walking style can burn. Then it occurred to him that perhaps something was lost in the translation. Maybe the Chinese jacket manufacturer didn't really understand the semantic difference between water resistant, water repellant, and waterproof. He also questioned his motives and beliefs. Did he even need a jacket considering exercising makes you sweat? He wondered how varied materials reacted to increased body temperature. Had he unconsciously succumbed to the litany of "just do it" advertisements that bombard him every time he watched football? Ultimately, it didn't matter what he thought because it was clear based on the evidence (wet skin) that the jacket did not serve the intended purpose of keeping him dry. Ultimately, he decided to hang up the jacket in his closet next to the ten or so others that he had purchased but rarely wears.

Despite his feeble attempts at looking glamorous while cycling, egotistical Jonny was savvy enough to embark on a self-regulatory evaluation when contemplating his jacketed journey. Table 7.2 analyzes his noble self-regulatory attempts, skills which are decisively advanced, far exceeding his athletic prowess and ambiguous motivation.

Despite getting drenched and feeling dissatisfied with his choices, Jonny's thought process was valuable because he contemplated his decisions in advance. This deliberate approach demonstrates how self-regulation can improve performance even when outcomes aren't ideal. From a reward perspective, he was likely jacking up his DA and NE in anticipation of an exhilarating cycling experience, motivated in part by prominently displaying his fashion faux pas. Jonny gets kudos for self-regulation, although his cycling likely would have prospered much more with better knowledge about heat and humidity.

In practical terms, self-regulation is optimized when the goal setter is perpetually monitoring goal progress. As the task unfolds, objective self-feedback (e.g., I am crushing this!) or constructive external feedback (e.g., scores or grades) are used to enhance performance and improve the probability of having a rewarding experience. For example, instead of sitting in traffic on the same route you always take to work, you might consider alternatives such as leaving at an earlier time or taking a different route. When successful, self-regulation can be the difference between mediocre performance and excellence, leading Eccles and Wigfield (2002) to conclude that self-regulation is the bridge between motivation and achievement. When using objective evaluation, the individual adapts their mindset not only by expecting obstacles but also by realizing that steps can be taken to influence and hopefully improve the goal-directed journey.

Benefitting from the power of self-regulatory activities minimally requires several prerequisites. First, one must be aware that improvement is always possible and be open and inspired to make changes when necessary. Second, the individual must be receptive to feedback and consciously repress the spontaneous emotional reaction that subpar performance is a

Table 7.2 Self-Regulation in Action

Statements	Type of Regulation	Strategy
"Once, he bought a windbreaker thinking that would protect him from getting drenched."	Planning	Anticipating potential performance obstacles
"After evaluating his options, he decided upon a skintight, vinyl(ish), neon green jacket."	Planning and monitoring	Reflecting on the suitability and sustainability of goals
"To his chagrin, the first time he wore the jacket he felt gross, all hot and clammy."	Monitoring	Realizing that the intended goal (staying dry) was not reached
"Jonny reflected on his sweat dilemma and thought maybe he was the problem. He also questioned his motives and beliefs."	Reflection	Post-purchase evaluation after task completion by reflecting on goal credibility and buying motivation

negative self-reflection. Conscious effort must be dedicated toward realizing that receptivity to change is the hallmark of seasoned learners and performers (Hoffman, 2015a), which ultimately results in higher levels of achievement. Third, merely knowing that change is required is only part of the process. The person must also possess sufficient strategy knowledge and know when and how to use strategies to effectively revise behavior. Fourth, harkening back to the situational nature of motivation and rewards (Eccles & Wigfield, 2020), the person must see appropriate value in the modification process as many regulatory activities are abandoned as a result of low RPE and the expectation that the modification is not worth the effort to achieve the results. In addition, elevated self-efficacy beliefs are essential for the effective use of any strategies. We might know what it takes to achieve a desired outcome but are often reluctant to invest the effort if there is any inkling that the approach might not work based on doubting personal ability or questioning if we have the personal resources to reach the goal (Bandura, 1986).

Thus, apathy and questionable confidence, not lack of strategy knowledge, can be the greatest culprit for lack of effective self-regulation. As such, emotional and motivational self-regulation is necessary. This means being aware of potential motivational lulls and what factors might trigger performance-inhibiting emotions such as anger, frustration, and boredom (among others). While many regulatory approaches are preplanned, some motivational strategies may be spontaneous, based upon swift deferral to entrenched beliefs, habits, or learned experiences (Wolters et al., 2011). For instance, if you live by the maxim "if at first you don't succeed, try again," you would be prone to using a variety of approaches in the event of initial failure. If you were a believer in the clichéd notion that "When one door closes, another opens," you might not even consider alternative means to reach a thwarted goal.

Specifically related to regulation of motivation, Wolters (2003) suggested four reward-based approaches designed to maximize the urge to complete required tasks. These strategies directly engage the brain's reward system, primarily the mesolimbic DA pathway. Start by using *self-consequating strategies* that are designed to maintain focus and forestall task abandonment. Self-consequating behaviors involve rewarding oneself with whatever is deemed valuable after a task milestone is completed. The reward can be anything pleasurable with the result potentially activating DA in anticipation of the reward and serotonin via attainment. The key is to choose rewards that are personally meaningful as well as realistically attainable. Settle for a few M & Ms instead of wishing for world peace. Set goals within your control.

A second approach is using positive *self-talk*, which happens when thoughts are articulated vocally, and the individual is auditorily reinforced that their effort is contributing toward a desired outcome. This strategy engages multiple brain regions, including the prefrontal cortex (PFC; involved in decision-making) and the limbic system (involved in emotion regulation). Self-talk is especially useful to overcoming effort fluctuations when the going gets tough. Statements such as "just get past this next section, or just go for another five minutes and you can relax," are effective because closer proximity to a goal enhances the probability of reaching the goal (e.g., the goal gradient effect; Kivetz et al., 2006). Engaging in positive self-talk essentially serves the purpose of providing your brain with verbal rewards, similar to the feeling cultivated when receiving external praise.

A third useful strategy to instill motivational momentum is finding ways to maintain interest in boring tasks. As everyone has experienced, even though some goals are highly desired and task effort can be invigorating, sustained intensity is often challenging. We are motivated in part by the quest to stimulate the brain's novelty-seeking behavior and natural curiosity (p. 211). Finding ways to transform boring into stimulating can get us past the predictable lulls. Task interest can be generated by incorporating novel routines or rituals into task completion, such as using gamification, or by seeing how quickly a mundane task can be completed (Baumeister & Heatherton,1996; Sailer et al., 2017). For example, gamification is associated with a greater frequency in stock investment (Chapkovski et al., 2024), greater persistence in learning a language (Wulantari et al., 2023), and higher completion rates in corporate training (Noyes et al., 2020), among many other domains where user tedium is probable.

Fourth, changing the physical environment associated with a motivational challenge can broadly influence performance outcomes. *Environmental restructuring* increases attention on task requirements, neutralizing external distractions, thereby reducing overall cognitive load. Elimination or control of external distractors like noise, intrusive thoughts, dirty dishes, swollen dog bladders, or any other factor that can impede task focus supports application of limited cognitive resources to focus on task demands. Restructuring means creating external cues that support goal attainment, resulting in the elimination of excuses for not focusing attention on task-related requirements. This means structuring the environment in a way that is best suited to conditions that promote your optimal performance. How the environment is restructured is subjective but usually focuses on either the physical modification of the workspace or the restructuring of task requirements. One approach may be to find the most productive location such as a library. Another might consider time of day, room temperature, degree of background noise, removal of distractions like social media, or intrusive roommates. Restructuring might also mean more realistic task goals, reducing stress and controlling potential negative appraisals from slower progress than expected. However, like most rewards, the precise method is a personal choice, and one size does not fit all.

Each of these self-regulatory strategies interacts with your brain's reward system in unique ways. Decisions related to restructuring goals and the renegotiation of which circumstances are most conducive to productivity are a function of the PFC, specifically the lateral PFC, which is often implicated in self-control (Knoch & Nash, 2015). However, activation patterns are clearly idiosyncratic, with individual differences akin to a neural fingerprint, again suggesting that everyone has a unique perspective on what is or is not rewarding (Boettiger et al., 2007). As described earlier, overcoming potential spontaneous motivational and emotional pitfalls means avoiding a reactive situation and instead relying on PFC reasoning and logic to avoid deferring to the emotionally laden amygdala activation. From a neuromodulator perspective, DA helps regulate goal-directed behavior and the ability to maintain focus on long-term rewards, while serotonin helps manage emotional responses and impulsivity. NE exerts influence on focus and managing the physiological aspects of stress, which are important when making strategy adjustments. GABA contributes to the ability to stay calm and make reasoned decisions, while acetylcholine (ACh) influences the ability to focus and maintain attention, which are crucial for effective self-regulation.

Last, despite strategy suggestions advanced by confluent research findings, self-regulation is a highly personalized process. It can take many years of trial-and-error experimentation to find which strategy blend is most effective for a particular individual or situation. The reward system is highly personalized, so what works for one person may not work as well for another. It literally took me years to learn that the best approach for writing was to take breaks when encountering the dreaded writer's block, instead of wasting hours hoping to grind out a few extra paragraphs.

However, despite the individualism of reward, we have broad commonality that suggests there are universally rewarding factors and strategies for attaining those rewards, which is the remaining chapter focus.

What Do We Want?

So, what does everyone want? Besides the right to party (Horowitz et al., 1986), according to a McKinsey survey of more than 30,000 employees across thirty countries (Brassey et al., 2023), there is a commonality as to what we consider rewarding. What everyone wants, regardless of race, gender, ethnicity, age, or geography, is *holistic health*, which encompasses physical, mental, social, and spiritual well-being. McKinsey estimated that attainment of objectives such as the ability to confidently complete physical tasks absent of discomfort, form strong social bonds, experience joy, limit harmful impulsive behavior, and avoid serious depressive episodes will add six years of life to the average person or contribute forty-five billion extra years to global longevity (Coe et al., 2022)! A closer examination of these desires reveals there are modifiable drivers of individual satisfaction that can be categorized. Staying healthy, avoiding stress, getting rest, and feeling energetic falls under the umbrella of enhancing physiology. Thinking effectively means maintaining cognitive clarity, enhancing focus, and being mindful. Finding ways to enhance productivity, learn more in less time, and retain information is an indisputable desire across cultures, as is the ability to maintain motivational momentum to achieve goals. Finally, interpersonal savvy and the ability to effectively persuade others to align with your point of view can mean the difference between success and failure, and in some cultures life or death. Let's take a closer look.

Enhancing Physiology

Staying healthy, in both mind and body, means having sufficient resources to ensure a safe, secure, and nurturing environment. Under ideal conditions, there are few obstacles to acquiring nutritious food, housing, education, and health care. However, even under the most prosperous conditions, individuals are vulnerable to environmental threats such as those experienced during the Covid-19 pandemic, where seemingly healthy individuals succumbed to illness. Thus, a universally rewarding attribute that many of us rarely consciously consider is cultivating a robust immune system, which is accomplished through proper nutrition, sufficient sleep, and exercise. While some may roll their eyes at these simplistic suggestions, only one in ten adults meet the US government's fruit and vegetable recommendations (Lee-Kwan, 2017), about 35 percent of adults in the United States report sleeping less than seven hours per night (Centers for Disease Control, 2016), and one in four adults globally do not meet the recommended levels for physical activity (Strain et al., 2024).

The immune system is regulated in part by circadian rhythm (CR), which is the body's internal clock that regulates the sleep-wake cycle. CR and the immune system are closely intwined especially at the cellular level, with many immune responses working on a cyclical basis with greater activity at specific times in the day. This rhythm often explains why we feel sicker at night, and there is evidence to suggest that we are more prone to disease at certain times of day than others (Scheiermann et al., 2013). CR controls many aspects of overall health and well-being, including hormone regulation, body temperature, and how efficiently we digest food. CR also has psychological implications because when the natural CR cycle is disrupted, the efficiency of concentration and memory suffers, contributing to mood disorders and depression.

The CR implications for thinking clearly are especially revealing. Lack of sleep affects the functioning of working memory and lowers activation in related brain areas such as the PFC. Younger adults tend to have higher alertness and better working memory efficiency in the evening, while older adults are more efficient in the morning (West et al., 2002). It is more likely that you will get into an argument when sleep deprived and take greater risks than when your CR is in check (Xu et al., 2021). Because of CR, individuals are more flexible and open to negotiation during the early hours of the day. Evidence also supports the benefits of being a "morning person" compared to a "night owl." Individuals who prefer morning work have improved tendency for strategic planning and self-regulation, which could explain why morning types often have better academic and health outcomes even independent of sleep (Heimola et al., 2021). It is interesting to note that impulsive thinking that weakens late at night and is lowest between 4 and 7 a.m. is highly conducive to creative problem-solving. This shows that sleep and thinking have a complex interaction and may explain why we have the most ridiculous thoughts when trying to get back to sleep (Xu et al., 2021)!

Table 7.3 Circadian Rhythm-Supported Strategies

Maintain a consistent sleep schedule.	Go to bed and wake up at the same time every day, even on weekends. The body needs standardization to perform best.
Control light exposure.	Follow the routine advocated by Huberman (2021, 2024). Starting four hours before sleep, lower artificial lighting to a point of safe navigation only. Reduce blue light from screens in the evening (use night mode or blue light blocking glasses). Do NOT use your phone within two hours of sleep. Keep your bedroom as dark as possible.
Exercise (see next section).	Aim for earlier in the day, as late-night exercise can be stimulating.
Manage mealtimes.	Eat at consistent times and avoid large meals close to bedtime.
Create a presleep routine.	Relaxing activities like reading or gentle stretching tell your body it is time to sleep. Do not consume caffeine within eight hours of sleep. Limit alcohol consumption if you want good sleep. Contrary to beliefs, drinking is NOT biologically relaxing.
Control bedroom environment.	Keep it cool, quiet, and comfortable. Your body prefers a cold sleeping environment. Use multiple blankets, if necessary. Avoid sleeping with pets who have different CRs than humans.
Get outside.	Natural light exposure during the day helps regulate your internal clock. Start your day by going outside for 20 minutes (without sunglasses). Productivity will increase immensely.
Avoid long naps.	Late day naps can disrupt nighttime sleep. Follow Huberman's (2021) recommendation of limiting naps to no more than 45 minutes to avoid nighttime sleep issues.

Boosting an immune response and leveraging CR for optimal performance means adhering to a specific schedule that is designed to regulate your circadian rhythm. The Table 7.3 approaches work best.

Finally, consider the poignant words of Maria Popova (2023), who, when reflecting on the indignity of sleep deprivation, stated, "We tend to wear our ability to get by on little sleep as some sort of badge of honor that validates our work ethic. But what it really is, is a profound failure of self-respect and of priorities. What could possibly be more important than your health and your sanity, from which all else springs?"

Stress Management

A detailed etiology of stress was described in Chapter 5 (pp. 182–185). Now we need to decide how to respond to perceived stress. Keeping in mind that the classic definition of stress suggests that reactions may be physical, emotional, or mental when we subjectively believe that situational challenges exceed available resources (Schneiderman et al., 2005). The key emphasis here is on two factors: *subjective beliefs* and *situational emphasis*. Both aspects of the definition suggest that stress perceptions will change moment to moment and differ based on the perceived formidability of an individual challenge. This definition implies that to resolve stress perceptions we have three options: modify our beliefs, influence the perceived challenge, or increase the quantity and potency of resources that will navigate the stress. The definition also implies that a stress response is accomplished through some sort of behavior, thought process, or emotional regulation, and the realization that at times *increasing* stress may be beneficial.

Changing stress perceptions means embarking on a regime of self-evaluation and personal renegotiation. The individual must minimally believe they can adjust reactions to environmental stressors, which is not always the perception. Individuals with elevated control beliefs and an internal locus of control (see p. 65) presume they can influence the metaphorical hand they are dealt. Alternatively, those with an external locus operate under the premise that they have minimal influence over the circumstances and challenges they encounter in life (Weiner, 2021). Thus, if you think "everything happens for a reason," and embrace an external locus of control, the prospect of changing your subjective stress perceptions is slim. Alternatively, if you feel empowered and believe the world is your oyster, then you are primed to alter stress perceptions because you realize that stress is situational and thus surmountable.

Even when believing stress is controllable, some perceived challenges are impervious to change. Effective stress management is predicated in part on exerting control over task requirements and desired outcomes, within reasonable boundaries. By example, if you are preparing for a final exam in a course needed to earn a degree, your options are limited.

Suggesting to the instructor that the exam should be eliminated or petitioning the university to remove courses from the required curriculum, while potentially stress reducing, would be frivolous. However, the anxious test taker might adjust exam preparation strategies, such as studying more, forming a study group with friends, and planning to take more challenging courses during a less-demanding semester. Additionally, the individual could recalibrate goals and course expectations accepting that some subjects are more difficult than others and that mastery levels change based on course complexity and personal interest. Revision of the learning goal would clearly reduce the stress perception, allowing the individual to move on to more valued and long-term priorities.

Although we can take the initiative to consciously avoid negative stress, there is little doubt that stress reactions are entwined with the body's automatic immune and protective responses (Seiler et al., 2020). When a threat is perceived, the brain releases important stress response hormones, such as cortisol, adrenaline, and NE, which are essential for biological defense against the stressor. These messengers communicate with various organs and bodily systems to mobilize energy reserves that activate antibodies to protect the body from the threat. It is because of this automatic response that low levels of stress are desired because immunity fighting resources are mobilized because of the stress response. These resistance responses provide tolerance and protection against more aggressive stressors such as allergies and autoimmune diseases (Theodoratou, 2023). As a result, catecholamines (hormones that act as neurotransmitters) like NE jumpstart changes like a faster heartbeat, higher blood pressure, and heightened alertness. Increases in adrenaline and DA in the brain lead to heightened alertness, increased energy, and elevated focus, biologically moderating the stressor.

While the aforementioned reactions mostly occur automatically, there are also ways to consciously manipulate a biological stress response. The most effective and simplistic method to either calm the body down to avoid the consequences of stress or alert the body to fend off pathogens is breathing. No, not just any type of breathing, but cyclic breathwork (Balban et al., 2023). This type of breathing routine improves energy, mood, and cardio vascular functioning through manipulation of the diaphragm. The routine differs from typical automatic breathing by using deliberate modifications in the duration and intensity of inhales versus exhales, which will either decrease heart rate leading to relaxation or create greater arousal when the heart beats faster.

During inhalation, the diaphragm moves down, allowing the lungs to expand. The deeper the inhale, the greater the volume of oxygen that is taken into the lungs. As a result of respiratory changes, neuronal signaling provides messages from the cardiovascular system to the brain, resulting in the heart beating faster during longer inhalations. Thus, longer inhalation leads to a faster heart rate, increased attentional focus, and overall arousal. Slowing down the heart, which is necessary during stress, works in the opposite way. Exhaling moves the diaphragm up, and through neuronal signaling to the brain, tells the heart to slow down. Calming down quickly requires longer and more vigorous exhales. Anyone who has gone through natural childbirth training will know how important breathing is in the calming process as well as for partner harmony. The true benefit of this approach is that it works immediately, and unlike many popular meditation or mindfulness techniques, no preparation or expensive yoga pants are required!

Another variation of the cyclic sighing described above and useful for longer-term stress management is the "physiological sigh," which activates the parasympathetic nervous system. This strategy uses two consecutive inhales through the nose, one substantial inhale, followed by a short second inhale, with no exhalation in between. After the lungs are maximally inflated, a long and complete mouth exhale is done until the lungs are completely empty. According to Huberman (2023), the technique can quickly shift an individual from a state of elevated arousal and agitation toward a state of feeling calmer. The ancillary benefits are substantial. Evidence reveals that if done regularly for only five minutes a day, cyclic sighing reduces stress, promotes relaxation, improves sleep, lowers resting heart rate, enhances mood (Balban et al., 2023). Plus, blowing out all that hot air probably increases breath mint sales, which is helpful to reduce stress for those in the confectionary business.

In many ways stress is a conscious evaluation of environmental circumstances that occur through cognitive appraisal. In other words, you choose your reality. You may see someone hurl a rock in your direction and think to yourself "If this hits me it will sting," and you respond by ducking. Alternatively, you might pull a "carpe diem" (seize the day) and fire back a larger rock at the perpetrator thinking "ha-ha, this muggle doesn't know I won the 8th grade shot-putt contest!" Either way, the behavioral response is guided by personal experience and a jolt of logic and reason supplied by the PFC. In turn, cognitive stress evaluation leads to the generation of varied emotions. Negative appraisals may lead to anxiety, fear, frustration, and anger, among others. Alternatively, confidence and experience may trigger a "fight" response motivated by the reward of earning recognition for your catching superpowers. Catching that rock with your bare hand might convince the aggressor that rock hurlers never win, leading to a discussion about why verbal dispute resolution is far superior to a geological joust.

Revising stress reactions happens through the use of emotional regulation strategies. These approaches start by appraising stress as a challenge instead of a threat. When an event is perceived as challenging, the individual acknowledges the potential impact and risks of the stressor, but instead of succumbing to negative emotions the person takes decisive action to fend off the potential negative connotations associated with the stress. This approach is reminiscent of finding the silver lining in an otherwise dark cloud. This process intentionally transforms negative emotions into more positive ones, altering core affects. Restructuring promotes emotional homeostasis, whereby the person is not overwhelmed by the reality of potential negative consequences but instead reallocates cognitive resources toward coping with the stressor. Make lemonade from lemons.

This reallocation is crucial as it allows the individual to maximize their cognitive focus and engage in more rational, goal-oriented thinking. Restructuring serves as a mental triage, prioritizing resources toward productive behaviors rather than on emotionally draining ruminations. While the shift in thinking softens the impact of negative events, it does *not* eliminate their consequences altogether. However, the shift channels thought toward performance goals, by creating cognitive clarity and instilling a future orientation with a focus on life after the stress. Ultimately emotional regulation is a coping mechanism designed to achieve positive outcomes despite negative perceptions. Obstacles become motivating factors, rather than debilitating consequences that can result from the unavoidable reality of the human condition.

Perhaps the most salient example of restructuring is what happened to me when my son unexpectedly passed away at the age of thirty-one a few days before Thanksgiving in 2016. This tragic event provided the morbid opportunity to deal with the pain of grief while taking intentional value-based actions, a core tenet of Acceptance and Commitment Therapy (Jones et al., 2022). While devastated by the loss, during bereavement I channeled my gloomy feelings toward appreciating my son's demeanor and temperament to a far greater extent than I did when he was alive. As a young man, Robert was always in an upbeat mood, constantly entertaining his friends or helping others, with kinship and loyalty dominating his personality and behavior. Focusing on his positive traits provided me with the inspiration to tackle a new yet formidable writing project, leading to the authorship of the self-development book *Hack Your Motivation*, which was dedicated to Robert's influence on me. The positivity that he radiated guided me to take a more altruistic approach to life and led me to create something that might not have happened if he were alive. While the approach did not suspend the grief typical to mourning the death of a loved one, his influence was channeled into a commemorative effort that has helped almost 10,000 readers enhance their own lives. As is often the case with "calm stress" like that just described, the transformation can serve as the catalyst for accomplishment. Through confrontation of stressors, resilience may develop leading to the acquisition of new and unexpected abilities. As Huberman (2024) so bluntly described, "Even though stress will not always feel good in the moment, adjust your mindset to remind yourself that stress puts you in an action-oriented state to enhance performance." Stress ultimately provides you with the opportunity to choose your reality.

Exercise, Nutrition, and Mindfulness

The health benefits of regular exercise and proper nutrition are well known and highly publicized. Regular exercise is linked to lower mortality. In particular, one massive study accounting for 2,286,806 person-years of physical activity and 317,908 person-years of cardiorespiratory fitness indicated a significantly lower likelihood of developing chronic heart disease and stroke for those who exercise regularly compared to those who do not (Williams, 2001). Similarly, improper nutrition has substantial mortality implications. Insufficient food supply increases cancer probability (Zhou et al., 2023), and lack of proper nutrition leads to a higher incidence of Type 2 diabetes (Aune et al., 2013). Additionally, diets with a greater intake of vegetables, legumes, fruits, nuts, cereals, and olive oil combined with lower intake of saturated fats and meat (e.g., the Mediterranean Diet) not only increases longevity but also improves cognitive functioning, including recall, working memory, processing speed, and reasoning (Loughrey et al., 2017). Considering these indisputable health benefits, as superhero creator Stan Lee often proclaimed, "Nuff said!"

Less attention has been devoted to the *psychological* rewards of healthy living. Exercise has been shown to help reduce psychological distress through numerous neurological mechanisms. Exercise stimulates endorphin production, which is the body's organic equivalent of ibuprofen (Advil) and acetaminophen (Tylenol), resulting in anti-inflammatory effects, which may help reduce inflammation-related mood disturbances. In addition, exercise promotes both DA and serotonin production, contributing to an overall sense of well-being. Perhaps the most remarkable benefit from exercise is that consistent physical activity promotes neuroplasticity, particularly in the hippocampus, a brain area involved in mood regulation and stress response (Gourgouvelis et al., 2017). These epigenetic changes are also related to improved emotional resilience, meaning exercise promotes more tolerance and higher thresholds for noxious environmental stimuli (Saner & Burell, 2012), like dealing with road rage or tolerating airport delays. Regular exercise can also enhance sleep quality, which provides many mental health benefits as described in the previous section.

Exercise is so powerful that it can significantly reduce mental distress, even in people with severe physical limitations. Studies show that the psychological benefits of exercise occur regardless of a person's physical condition, helping even those who are most vulnerable to stress and anxiety, such as being confined at home due to illness. When comparing patients who embark on exercise routines to those who do not, benefits are found for cancer survivors (Kamen et al., 2016), cardiac patients (Saner & Burell, 2012), and individuals with urological disease (Galvão et al., 2021). Across cultures, ethnicities, and genders, exercise substantially reduces symptoms of depression, anxiety, hostility, and overall psychological distress and its effectiveness is on par with antidepressant medications (Milani & Lavie, 2009). However, one of the most striking findings is the potential impact of exercise on mortality rates, where a regular fitness routine is associated with a 31 percent higher probability of survival, despite chronic conditions like coronary heart disease (Saner & Burell, 2012).

Like many of the strategy recommendations advanced, context should be considered. While the benefits of increased physical activity are substantial, exercising with others works even better (Maher et al., 2015). Loneliness is one of the greatest concerns impacting the health of older adults, with social isolation neurologically comparable to food deprivation (Tomova et al., 2020)! Group participation obviously increases the opportunity for socialization but participation with others also promotes greater adherence and accountability for exercise routines (Carron et al., 1996). In addition, collective physical activity primes individuals to assess the actual experience of exercise to be more interesting, enjoyable, and challenging (Maher et al., 2015). In one study, which included a group of highly anxious medical school students, group fitness classes led to a significant decrease in perceived stress and an increase in perceptions of physical, mental, and emotional well-being compared to those who exercised alone (Yorks et al., 2017). While most evidence suggests that working out with others provides more overall benefits, adherence, and enjoyment than working out alone, slow down. Before you join a health club or plan a group Everest expedition, it is crucial to remember that personal preferences should take precedence, as overall self-regulation is a highly idiosyncratic process and for some solo exercise works just as well (Hoffman, 2015a).

Finally, a brief word about *mindfulness*, defined as the nonjudgmental awareness of the present moment. Whenever we can devote conscious attention to the here and now, there are both physiological and psychological advantages. Being in the present leverages the satiating power of serotonin to alter mood and disposition, in addition to accentuating an internal locus of control (Esch, 2013). Mindfulness interventions develop nonjudgmental attention and present-moment awareness by utilizing breathing and focusing techniques that emphasize body awareness, acceptance of feelings, promotion of acute sensory awareness, and an approach to daily tasks with intention (Creswell, 2017). These types of interventions are essential as research concludes that our minds can wander up to 47 percent of the time and that lack of focus is predictive of unhappiness (Killingsworth & Gilbert, 2010). Mindfulness interventions can help reduce symptoms of stress, anxiety, and depression as well as change attitudes and motivation related to maintaining one's health (Remskar et al, 2024). By concentrating attention on the present rather than dwelling on the past or worrying about the future, mindfulness practitioners learn to observe their thoughts and emotions without getting consumed by them. Daily short mindfulness practices can significantly enhance mental health, increase immunity, and encourage healthier lifestyles, with sustained benefits over time (Creswell et al., 2017). Thus, anyone who perceives self-care as rewarding should consider a mindfulness component as part of their daily activities.

Maximizing Cognitive Clarity

Clarity of thought is a prerequisite to taming many of our motivational desires and attaining the rewards we want. Devoid of clear reasoning skills, problem-solving ability, and effective decision making, we can wind up haphazardly chasing our personal holy grail and never reaching the proverbial promised land. The ability to suspend personal bias and use rational thought is especially important for navigating a world of information overload, where the average person is estimated to make 35,000 decisions daily (Pignatiello et al., 2020). We want to be certain that in the pursuit of rewards we take actions grounded in reality, with our thought process both consistent with how the world works and sufficient to help us reach our goals. Maximizing cognitive clarity is not about intelligence but instead means having the energy and know-how to determine what is true and what to do about it (Stanovich et al., 2016). With the average attention span at forty-seven seconds (Mark, 2023), intentionality of thought is essential to achieving goals. Two aspects are crucial for success. First, we need to develop strategies that enhance our focus and attention, enabling us to concentrate on what matters. Second, we must cultivate humility and rationality, recognizing that everyone, even those considered expert thinkers, have room to improve their thinking and reasoning skills.

Attention

Achieving cognitive clarity starts with the ability to maintain attention. When attentional focus is optimized, we discriminate between what is important and relevant while weeding out trivial information (Valdez, 2019). Although much of our attentional resources operate on an unconscious basis, we can override automatic responses with intentional monitoring and cognitive control (Esterman & Rothlein, 2019). With effort, we have the ability to exercise voluntary control over attention while concurrently repressing involuntary distractors. While it is feeble to believe we can eliminate the attention-grabbing power of barking dogs or piercing jet noise, we can take demonstrative steps to limit the disrupting power of cognitive intrusions. What commands attention depends on the objectives of the individual. An object or idea will attract attention if the key features match the goals on our perceptual radar (Büsel et al., 2020). If the prominent characteristics are irrelevant to objectives, the same object would lack attentional power. This "contingent capture" perspective was best illustrated by one of the pioneers of educational psychology, William James (1890), who observed, "A faint tap in and of itself is not an interesting sound; it may well escape being discriminated from the general rumor of the world. However, if it's a signal—like a lover's kiss on a windowpane—it won't go unnoticed" (p. 418). Attention is thus individually determined, and with careful training we can block out cognitive invaders.

A variety of neuromodulators assist in this information pruning process. NE helps hone alertness and perceptual vigilance and is released by the locus coeruleus (LC) in the brainstem. DA released in the ventral tegmental area (VTA) is important based on the reward value of what we seek. More anticipatory DA is released as we get closer to achieving the targeted rewarding goal. The greater the need for enhanced cognitive control and the more sustained effort, the greater the DA transmission, particularly in the PFC. Acetylcholine (ACh) is crucial for attention, learning, and memory and is released by the basal forebrain and brainstem nuclei. The encoding process of learning and the formation of memories is highly dependent on the efficiency of ACh and dysfunction in the cholinergic system is often associated with cognitive impairments, like Alzheimer's disease (Ferreira-Vieira et al., 2016). Overall, neuromodulation helps explain individual differences between attentive states (see Chapter 5 for a detailed overview of each neuromodulator).

Sustained attention is the ability to focus attention over extended periods of time. This type of resource allocation is the kind used during studying or intense periods of mental focus, like those tasks that have little leeway for error such as driving on a rainy mountainous road or trying to thread a needle with a tiny opening. Sustained attention is regulated by both capacity and allocation (Esterman & Rothlein, 2019). Allocation is the individual difference in the ability to exert top-down control over attention, resisting the tendency to mind-wander. Capacity is genetically influenced, but also contingent on the ongoing motivation to overcome the fatigue of sustained effort. Focused attention, like many aspects of motivation, is depletable. We are indeed limited by how long we are willing and able to sustain attention and regardless of capacity or intent, performance will diminish over time. However, in addition to monitoring and strategy knowledge, such factors as task challenge and arousal levels (i.e., boredom, sleep, stress) broadly mediate attentional control (Seli et al., 2016; Unsworth & Robinson, 2018).

A variety of mechanisms can support focused attention. All components of attention tend to be worse in the early morning hours and best in the evening. Daily patterns of behavior and discretionary scheduling should be considered to blunt the reality that we perform best at certain times of the day and under specific circumstances (Nelson et al., 2021). If someone suggests meeting during a less-than-optimal time for you, then negotiate! Individual differences in cognitive clarity can include age, sleep habits, exercise, and whether you are a "morning person" or "night owl." Understanding these rhythms can help in planning daily activities for optimal cognitive performance. However, despite limitations brought about by these individual differences, some general approaches will improve cognitive focus and sustainability, as shown in Table 7.4.

Some of us might believe that the strategies suggested are in fact time consumers, not time savers, and that using these approaches may be more distractive than beneficial. There is some substance to this perception, because we subject ourselves to "self-interruptions" throughout the day. We are conditioned and expect to have our concentration disrupted by rude coworkers, environmental noise, and phone notifications among many other annoyances (Mark, 2023). Breaking this anticipatory habit of disruption is challenging, but scheduling specific times for valued activities is one key remedy. Do not disturb (DND) signs and technology help tremendously to eliminate intrusions. Unfortunately, many people dismiss strategies because of an inflated perception concerning the ominous and patently false supposition of multitasking. While shifting cognitive attention quickly between tasks is possible, multitasking is one of the most prevalent myths based on misleading interpretations of cognitive psychology (Kirschner & Hendrick, 2020). While we can do some tasks without thinking (like brushing your teeth and deciding which outfit to wear), tasks that require simultaneous information processing cannot be

Table 7.4 Cognitive Enhancement Strategies

Goal	Strategies	Specifics
Reduce mind wandering.	Mindfulness meditation Digital detox Environment restructuring	• Practice actively knowing when attention wanes by recording what influences fluctuations. • Remove electronics from immediate access. • Aim for 7–9 hours of quality sleep per night. • Schedule socializing activities immediately following goal attainment, contingent on successful task completion.
Avoid being easily fatigued.	Manage arousal Nature breaks Optimize environment	• Actively control excitability or disinterest, by making incremental progress daily. • Take breaks at least every 45 minutes, preferably outside. • Consider the Pomodoro method and work in 25-minute intervals, followed by short recovery periods. • Reduce environmental distractions like music, TV, and social media. • Control sugar intake to avoid sudden energy crashes.
Focus on the right things.	Prioritization Eisenhower method SMART goals	• Use journals and online scheduling to prioritize tasks. • Create specific, daily, weekly, and monthly measurable goals. • Evaluate task complexity completing the most challenging projects early in the day. • Monitor progress by recording specific interim milestones.
Increase motivation.	Rewards Gamification Exercise	• Use self-consequating strategies to reward specific measurable achievements. • Motivate progress on boring tasks by setting and achieving productivity and efficiency targets. Do more in less time as a game. • Engage in both aerobic exercise and strength.
Promote greater awareness.	Metacognitive strategies	• Analyze under which circumstances optimal focus is achieved. • Monitor thought process to anticipate motivational lulls. • Reevaluate strategy use based on achieved results. • Reconsider goal feasibility.

done without a loss of speed or accuracy. If you don't believe it, try reciting the alphabet while you memorize a phone number and let me know how that works for you. As such, it is crucial to critically evaluate any information that we consider as part of our strategy repertoire and be sure there is a scientific basis for adapting the approach.

Judgment

To leverage the rewarding power of a decision, it is imperative to use sound reasoning skills during the thinking process. Unfortunately, sometimes we know and are motivated to use appropriate approaches, but make biased decisions based on flawed interpretations of information. Stanovich et al. (2016) referred to the process of using the incorrect information as succumbing to "irrationality." When thinking rationally, we seek to accomplish specific goals and solve our personal challenges in the most expeditious and efficient way possible. Rationality also means executing actions based on sound interpretation of evidence, not intuition, wishful thinking, or what we like to believe is possible. Not a day goes by when people who appear gifted and intelligent make irrational decisions that have disastrous outcomes. These errors frequently lead to tragedy, financial ruin, embarrassment, or shame. Hoffman (2019) published several headlines revealing alarming stories based on irrational thoughts, such as the fact that twenty-eight million Americans smoke cigarettes despite the known health risks (Centers for Disease Control, 2021) and that fifty people witnessed a boy bleeding to death and did nothing (Haworth, 2019). Two tourists were also arrested for "thermal trespassing" when they stuck their faces in the infamous Yellowstone Park geyser, "Old Faithful," which spouts 200-degree water every 35 to 120 minutes. Successful people like the late, financial whiz Bernie Madoff, the movie mogul and sexual offender Harvey Weinstein, and the actor Lori Loughlin, who masterminded a fraudulent college admissions scandal, are household names because of their questionable judgment.

Many poor decisions are made for clear and specific reasons (Erwin, 2019). Among the causes are physical illness, fatigue, laziness, being uninformed, overloaded, or distracted. We will not focus on these causes because they are easily fixable by the strategies already described, and the reasons for the mistakes are typically obvious. Nonetheless, many intellectual errors are made without the offender's conscious knowledge. The cognitive culprits are frequently the product of erroneous reasoning that is driven by personal bias. Many individuals are unable to objectively evaluate evidence and do not understand the concept of base rates, probability, or logical reasoning (Kahneman, 2011). By example, irrespective of formal education level, many individuals cannot correctly answer the question, "If a bat and a ball together cost $1.10, and the bat sells for $1.00 more than the ball, how much does the ball cost?" Individuals often quickly assert the answer is .10, because they rely on snap judgment and not thoughtful reasoning. Too bad .10 is wrong.

The remedy to overcome the liabilities of flawed information evaluation falls into two broad categories. First, evaluation of the thinking process. As evidenced by the previous ball and bat riddle, intuitive and spontaneous thinking is often incorrect. In case you were wondering, the ball cost .05 and the bat cost $1.05. Often individuals will not have the motivation or perceive arriving at an unequivocally correct solution as the primary reward. Frequently, we are satisfied by just being in the decision-making ballpark and tolerate arriving at the most likely solution. This principle is exemplified by both individuals and organizations and often is a product of having incomplete knowledge when deciding or when operating under stressful and high-stakes circumstances like a test or a looming deadline. Even absent of pressure, the phenomenon occurs because humans are generally "*cognitive misers*," unwilling to expend cognitive effort when there appears to be a less mentally taxing option to arrive at a solution. Instead, we use "*heuristics*," which are convenient strategies to approximate understanding of worldly phenomena, sometimes called rules of thumb. By example, we often think librarians are conservative and bookish, until we see them outside of a library setting. Unfortunately, while heuristics often work, mental shortcuts are the first and only reasoning option for some individuals, leading to a consistent pattern of wrong conclusions.

Encouraging slower, more deliberate reasoning can help counteract quick, subjective, and spontaneous thinking. First, we need to recognize when intuitive thinking is being used. Stanovich (2016) called this recognizing process a "detection error," which in practical terms means the willingness to admit that shortcuts may have led to mistakes. Next, patience is needed to carefully consider how decisions were made by reviewing which evidence was or was not thoroughly analyzed before making the decision. Two of the most common decision-making omissions are only considering confirming evidence supporting a predetermined intended direction, or reaching conclusions before all information is collected and analyzed. In practice, many initiatives are blundered when leaders prematurely generalize conclusions based on limited information, eventually regretting the hasty approach (Peters et al., 2024).

Next, initial assumptions should be questioned to determine if they are based on sufficient evidence or gut reactions. One particularly effective approach for individuals who jump to snap conclusions is asking them to argue whichever position is in opposition to the one they believe is true. The process continues by requiring them to critique their own argument and reflecting on how the reasoning approach might be flawed. The purpose of the strategy is to apply a similar cognitive process and the same degree of scrutiny to other perspectives. This method, sometimes called "debiasing" (Warner, 2023), helps combat confirmation bias by forcing individuals to consider alternative viewpoints and critically evaluate their own beliefs.

Awareness of at least three biases is necessary to overcome other aspects of rationality and poor judgment. The *"availability bias"* occurs when relying on more recent memories and when contemplating a decision rather than considering a full corpus of experience or evidence. By example, avoidance of salad for months after learning of a reported breakout of listeria in one processing plant would not be an objective evaluation of potential harmful impact of the bacteria. Instead, the focus should be on the future probability of infection with an objective analysis of all data to determine the likelihood of a problem. *"Framing"* involves selecting certain aspects of a desired reality and making those attributes more prominent when communicating text, speech, or visuals relating to a message. Framing uses a particular interpretation or evaluation emphasizing some facts, values, and philosophies over others. To battle the unitary perspectives of framing, it is essential to see a problem state from multiple viewpoints, not merely the one being described. Imagine bantering with an animal rights supporter who advocates protecting animal rights under all circumstances. While conservation efforts are critical for many species, it would also be relevant to understand the frequency of human fatalities from animal injuries, costs, and environmental impacts before making a decision on animal control.

Third, many individuals base decisions on tradition. The "we have always done it this way" mentality results in preserving the status quo in favor of excluding potential solutions that are perceived to be riskier than existing solutions. While known consequences are valuable, the presumption that the status quo is a less risky alternative is a logical fallacy. Doing nothing may be far riskier than converting a legacy belief. By example, individuals declining vaccinations often think they have a higher incidence of staying healthy when avoiding a vaccine then when being vaccinated. However, objective evidence would not support this conclusion (Agrawal et al., 2023).

Nikolić (2018) advocated several approaches to address the challenge of bias control. The process begins with the baseline understanding that preserving the status quo is not the least hazardous course of action. Second, personal risk aversion should be suspended under the pretense that individual expectations and beliefs may underestimate or overestimate true probabilities of an event occurrence. Generally, individuals overestimate the probabilities of catastrophic events occurring yet underestimate the impact on themselves. As Moore and Healy (2008) pointed out, women overestimate the frequency of contracting breast cancer but think they are less likely than others to contract the disease. A similar pattern applies to predictions involving a terrorist attack. We believe the incidence of attack is higher than statistical reality, but the chances of it happening to us are estimated to be much lower than the general public. Individuals overestimate their risk of dying but believe they are at less risk of untimely demise than their friends or family.

To offset the biases described, multiple solutions must be considered. Verification of using the same evaluation criteria is critical to objectively evaluate each possibility. Any approach should be examined with critical skepticism to determine the optimal course of action. Instead of convincing yourself that your idea is the best choice, brainstorm reasons why choices might be wrong and under which circumstances intended outcomes may not result. The objective evaluation of the information source and the integrity of a message matters. The neuroscience of message content and valuation was discussed in the previous chapter (p. 224), but we should always consider RPE. Any information we encounter that is perceived as rewarding must have inherent value and usefulness. We often accept information as true when it comes from people we respect and trust, despite the information content. Alternatively, even the most convincing and articulate message will be conceptually trashed when it comes from sources we do not like or value.

This person/information preference implies that when news comes from people whose opinions diverge from our own, we may disregard the information because we believe them to be prejudiced, uneducated, or misinformed. Regretfully, the reverse is also true, as we are more likely to accept misleading or incorrect information when it originates from reputable organizations and people. As Kim and Dennis (2019) explained, "When we talk with people, we consider who they are before we think about what they say. We use our prior knowledge of the source when we consider a story, and our knowledge of the source shapes how we evaluate the content that follows" (p. 1027). Ultimately, even when information is difficult to accept, it is immensely satisfying to feel like we have a direct line of communication with a source that we personally evaluate as dependable and authoritative. Everybody loves having privy information!

When assessing the veracity of information, the source is extremely important, but this is especially true when we are the ones creating the knowledge we plan to share. There is no greater degree of information inflation than when the source is you! In practice, this implies that we are more willing to share knowledge, whether it is true or not, the more confident we are. Overconfidence occurs when we believe there is a higher probability of achieving favorable outcomes from our proclamations than the outcomes that might be achieved when relying on other sources. Overconfidence originates from unjustified optimism and usually occurs when information analysis is incomplete (Nikolić, 2018). Ironically, those who are most confident in the veracity of their knowledge are least likely to be knowledgeable. As Dunning (2019) indicated, "Importantly, this over belief in one's answers is the most pronounced among those most likely to make the most mistakes. Namely, people largely fail to anticipate those topics and areas in life where they are likely to be incompetent and provide answers that are wrong" (p. 219). People who consider themselves to be "experts" on a subject also have a tendency to believe fake news to be accurate (Pennycook & Rand, 2019), which leads to more people spreading incorrect information. Luckily, there are opportunities to narrow knowledge gaps and forestall communicating bullshit, but only when individuals have one incredibly special inclination.

Display a Growth Mindset

Hidden beneath the conceptual surface of our waking experience resides a series of powerful influences that cultivate and direct our aspirations and capabilities—self-beliefs (see p. 95). Many of these demonstrative beliefs like esteem and perceptions of control have been described throughout the discussion of rewards. One belief remains undisclosed, yet its pervasive power has likely guided you to this point in the book. Persevering through unfamiliar terminology, grappling with complex ideas, and using knowledge to enhance your personal and professional life means that you are optimistic about the future and the prospect of achieving your goals. You are not discouraged by adversity and do not shy away from opportunities to improve. You embrace a growth mindset (GM).

When individuals champion a GM, they operate under some very narrow but highly desirable presumptions. Little holds them back and they think large. Let's call those people "GMs," who have the unwavering belief that skills and intelligence are developed via commitment, hard work, and self-development, and not by chance or manifest destiny. Embracing a growth mentality means welcoming challenges, persevering despite setbacks, and seeing failures as chances for growth, not a blemish on the portfolio of life. Instead of only concentrating on results, GMs emphasize learning from all experiences and every individual, a worldview that promotes flexibility, compassion, inclusion, and resilience. By encouraging a positive attitude toward difficulties and self-development, GMs are competence builders, progressing through life with a love of discovery and learning, which ultimately leads to greater success in personal and professional undertakings.

Adopting a GM is positively associated with many desirable attributes and behaviors. GMs often outperform their peers in academic and professional settings, as they are more likely to take on challenges and innovate (Yeager & Dweck, 2020). Moreover, those with a GM feel like they are earning intrinsic rewards, because they find pleasure in both mundane chores and effortful achievements rather than dwelling on the need for external validation or proving their abilities. Their stress responses are adaptive, with challenges seen as opportunities for growth leading to improved performance on difficult cognitive tasks (Crum et al., 2013). During social relationships and when demonstrating leadership skills, GMs promote empathy, understanding, and the creation of psychologically safe environments that foster innovation and learning. Individuals with a GM are reported to be better leaders than their pessimistic peers (Kouzes et al., 2019).

The adoption of a GM can also have positive effects on mental health, potentially reducing stress and anxiety while increasing self-esteem (Tao et al., 2022). Perhaps most importantly, the benefits of a GM compound over time, promoting continuous improvement and adaptability even in the face of changing circumstances or when encountering personal obstacles (Sheffler et al., 2023).

The challenge of developing a GM can be formidable. Unlike strategies that promote physical well-being or those that monitor the self-regulation of performance, creating or enhancing self-beliefs is far more abstract. Transitioning from a fixed to a GM requires both openness and a strong motivation to change. The first step is realizing that continuous development is a fundamental life goal and that progress, not perfection, is the barometer of success. However, a willingness to grow is only the first step; behaviors must mirror the developmental philosophy. Demonstrating a GM means recognizing and overcoming the vulnerability to use the availability heuristic and the avoidance of confirmation bias, by acknowledging that past experiences and solutions are not necessarily predictive of future success. What matters more is the use of critical thinking, by questioning goals and methods through the eyes of an objective observer and not as someone who only cares about the desire to improve. A growth mentality is essentially accepting the ongoing struggle of personal advancement as a challenging puzzle and not a thumbs-only video game where everyone eventually wins.

There are specific GM techniques that can be seamlessly infused into behaviors. When confronted with obstacles, begin by using self-talk to highlight opportunities for growth, not obstacles for failure. Take the attitude that lack of understanding or experience is only temporary by using "yet" words. For example, consider expressing "I will master this after a few more tries" instead of "I can't do this." Instead of only targeting performance outcomes, set learning objectives that emphasize skill development and personal growth as part of the goal achievement process. Habitually, reflect on the quality of achievements, targeting areas of weakness but celebrating accomplishments. Instead of being afraid of making a mistake or being judged, cultivate curiosity by viewing challenges as an opportunity to learn new skills or recharge intellectual skills that might have become dormant from lack of use. Lastly, praise yourself by giving credit not only for what you have accomplished but also for the effort invested. Focus on the repertoire of strategies used rather than just the acquired outcome. By using these methods on a regular basis, the personal transition to a GM is not only possible but also predictable.

Facilitating a GM in others is far more mechanized. Burnette et al. (2023), in a meta-analytic review of fifty-two mindset intervention studies using 30,403 participants, revealed that mindset interventions generally work, albeit to a nominal extent. The variability among potential intervention types is diverse, with the use of group training sessions as the most frequently cited approach to cultivate a GM. Some of the more effective interventions included:

- Teaching students about neural plasticity and how the brain changes as learning occurs, while asking students to write a letter to a younger student explaining how abilities can be developed through practice and effort
- Sharing stories of famous people who succeeded through hard work and learning from failures, rather than from natural talent
- Playing games or doing activities that reward effort and improvement, not just attainment of high scores
- Teaching students to say things like "I can't do it yet" instead of "I can't do it," emphasizing that abilities are developed over time

More importantly, modeling a growth mindset is essential. When a teacher models a GM through behaviors, the student directly experiences the positive benefits of the GM. Students have the best experiences, put in the most effort, and earn the highest grades when the instructor communicates a GM combined with a warm demeanor (White et al., 2024). Rather than only being personable, communicative, and empathetic, the GM teacher exemplifies someone who can confidently exclaim "I don't know" to a learner and then subsequently model how to narrow the knowledge deficit. Table 7.5 summarizes approaches to cultivate a GM in the self and others.

Ultimately, the benefit and foundation of a GM is the acknowledgment that even those with the most experience can learn more. The realization that expertise is a moving target, and that perpetual development is essential for professional growth, can be demonstrated by following the prescriptive formulas recommended above.

Table 7.5 Cultivating a Growth Mindset

Strategy	Self-Development	Development in Others
Clear expectations	Set stretch goals, but ones that are attainable with effort.	Create measurable objectives designed to promote results *and* enhance self-esteem.
Incremental goals	Build interim milestones into long-term projects.	Develop performance thresholds that measure incremental successes.
Nonjudgmental feedback	Seek constructive feedback.	Provide developmental feedback focusing on effort and resilience.
Positive error climate	Analyze the source of mistakes and revise strategies and behavior.	Cultivate a climate that supports taking risks to foster long-term gain.
Experience failure	Build humility and realize that failure is part of eventual success, and embrace obstacles as a challenge.	Do not stress expertise but instead focus on tackling difficult goals and making progress.
Future visualization	Mentally forecast the results of achievement.	Provide regular focus and feedback on effort and the satisfaction of reaching long-term goals.
Model expertise	Replicate behaviors of valued GM models.	Exemplify a GM, in voice and actions.
Consequation for results	Self-reward for achievement of goal milestones.	Give recognition for risk tolerance, resilience, and effort.

Learning More in Less Time

Memorializing the knowledge we encounter involves more than feeling healthy, being optimistic, and thinking clearly. The learning process is a complex interplay among multiple players including neurotransmitters, teaching methods, instructional design, and enthusiastic effort from the learner. The most effective learning occurs when individuals are active participants in knowledge acquisition. Instead of soaking up water like a sponge, optimal learning requires exhibiting a variety of demonstrative behaviors that foster knowledge gains. Behind these adaptive behaviors are specific strategies designed to accelerate and enhance attainment of learning objectives. Considering the emphasis on knowledge as reward, the focus here is on factors within control of the learner with less emphasis on teaching methods, instructor, or the influence of instructional modality (online vs. face-to-face) on cultivating achievement.

We have already discussed that some knowledge gain prerequisites such as attention, focus, and clarity of thought. These factors are crucial because to be an active learner you need to have some degree of engagement with what you hope to learn. Contrary to urban myths, you cannot master new material while asleep or when lacking conscious awareness (De Bruyckere et al., 2015). Engagement requires harnessing cognitive resources, combined with an emotional and behavioral commitment to whatever is being learned. However, the basic encoding of prospective information minimally requires focused attention (as described earlier), which usually originates when the material to be learned is perceived as interesting. No surprise, higher interest learners almost always outperform academically, retain more information, and remember what they learn compared to their aloof and apathetic peers (Renninger & Hidi, 2011).

One aspect of effective learning cannot be overemphasized. For knowledge to appear rewarding, it must be perceived as both valuable and relevant with usefulness beyond the instructional situation. Ideally, knowledge gains contribute toward personal growth, with the learning material seen as a bridge toward a longer-term goal. When we anticipate prospective gains, either through elevated status, material benefits, or merely the satisfaction of satisfying intellectual curiosity, our self-perceptions of competence increase. The prospect of feeling capable and knowledgeable feels gratifying, thus motivating us to learn even more. However, efficient learning takes more than feeling good about oneself. Open-mindedness flourishes when it is not forced and when learners believe they have some influence on what is learned and how mastery is determined. By example, giving students the ability to choose term-paper topics, or providing the option to demonstrate expertise in writing, verbally, or through a portfolio contributes to receptivity and situational interest (Flowerday & Shell, 2015). Conversely, when learning is demanded, the perception of choice is reduced and a natural disdain toward the material and (the teacher) may follow (Reeve & Jang, 2006).

Thus, the perception of autonomy in the learning situation is crucial to foster engagement and subsequently enhance interest. Meta-analytic results show that autonomy-supportive instructors promote high-quality learning outcomes (Bureau et al., 2022). Regardless of age, grade level, type of school, nationality, or gender, students who see knowledge gains as rewarding want discretion during instruction because it contributes toward internalizing what they learn. Considering the importance of internalization (as described throughout the text), knowing how to inspire autonomy is essential. While not all of these approaches are within the control of the educator, teachers, parents, or anyone in a leadership role may prosper by considering the recommendations of Reeve and Cheon (2021), who described numerous *"autonomy-supportive instructional behaviors"* to leverage what we know about choice and learning. Table 7.6 recommendations have applications across learning contexts and specifically focus on how a supportive message can enhance engagement, curiosity, and interest while encouraging perceptions of relevance concerning whatever is being communicated.

Promoting Plasticity

The preliminary behavioral strategies described set the stage for what happens next. Learning does not occur in the absence of some sort of measurable brain transformation, which, as described on pages 178–180, is assisted by the activation of numerous neuromodulators. As previously discussed, DA has a crucial role in learning by reinforcing, rewarding, and motivating desired behavior. Serotonin modulates the mood for learning with potential to impact learning efficiency, because, when distracted by negative emotion, focus suffers. NE is needed to increase alertness and attention span. However, the champion neurotransmitter for learning is ACh. Choline, the primary nutrient supporting the synthesis of ACh, plays a vital role in memory, attention, and muscle control, and is also needed for proper functioning of the liver and brain (Kansakar et al., 2023). Higher concentrations of choline improve cognitive functioning, enhance memory, and potentially slow cognitive decline in conditions like Alzheimer's disease and dementia (Poly et al., 2011). Higher choline consumption is associated with better memory performance, particularly verbal and visual memory. These findings suggest that intake from sources rich in choline, which include egg yolks, liver, fish (especially salmon and cod), soybeans, and nuts (as well as dietary supplements), may help maintain cognitive function as the brain ages.

Table 7.6 Autonomy-Supportive Instructional Behaviors

Strategy	Objective	Say
Take the others' perspective.	Show support.	What are *your* objectives?
	Avoid "me" vs. "them."	Tell me more. . . .
	Show curiosity.	What are you thinking?
	Clarify.	If I understand you correctly, then . . .
	Promote interest.	How can we make this work?
Present in need-satisfying ways.	Foster autonomy.	I have some options for us . . .
	Build competency.	This will help you develop. . . .
	Emphasize internalization.	What are *your* personal goals?
	Promote interest.	How can we make this more compelling?
	Create social bonds.	Who do you want to collaborate with?
Provide explanatory rationales.	Show hidden value in assignments.	This is what's in it for you . . .
	Prime utility.	You can use this experience to . . .
	Generate transparency.	This is the first step toward . . .
	Vision the outcome.	When we accomplish this goal . . .
Acknowledge negative feelings.	Exhibit emotional intelligence.	I know this is boring, but . . .
	Demonstrate empathy.	Sometimes work is frustrating.
	Reinforce validity of feelings.	Feeling this way is expected.
Use invitational language.	Avoid mandates.	Do not use the words "must" or "have to."
	De-emphasize deadlines.	What matters most is showing your skills . . .
	Encourage initiative.	You may want to . . . You might consider. . . . . What do you think about . . .

Neuroplasticity is not just an unconscious process unraveling in your body—it makes a difference in behavior. Practical examples of neuroplasticity in action abound. London taxi drivers, who must pass a rigorous road map test to be licensed, have better recall than their underemployed Uber peers. Their enhanced memory is a result of neuroplasticity and the repeated firing of neurons in the hippocampus resulting in structural changes in the region of the brain associated with spatial memory (Griesbauer et al., 2022). Similar findings are found with musicians who have more neuronally dense gray matter in the corpus callosum, the brain area that is responsible for auditory processing and motor control, obvious skills needed to play an instrument (Chatterjee, 2021). Language learning follows a similar pattern, as individuals who speak multiple languages have a higher density of gray matter in the left inferior parietal cortex after language fluency than before language training (Li et al., 2014). Many more examples of training-induced brain transformation include golfers (Jäncke et al., 2009), expert spellers (Tan et al., 2000), and even voracious readers (Goldman & Manis, 2013), where neuroimaging results show higher concentration of gray matter or cortical thickness in the corresponding brain area associated with the advanced lexical skill.

So, besides eating bundles of liver and cod omelets, what should be done to enhance learning efficiency? In addition to a balanced diet, regular exercise, and getting sufficient sleep as previously described, specific actions can be taken. First, remember that DA transmission is increased when unexpected learning occurs. Thus, getting away from habitual patterns of existence can be sufficiently rewarding to stimulate motivation for learning. While not everyone has the desire or resources to travel, clearly experiencing new cultures and geographies contributes to novelty learning. Embracing a diverse social group and engaging with others may potentially increase both serotonin and oxytocin synthesis when casual bonds typical to acquaintances morph into meaningful friendships. In the absence of a desire to find Carmen Santiago, novelty can occur vicariously. Read books on unknown topics, meet people who are unlike you, and try new things. Even reading about new food choices promotes neural plasticity (González et al., 2006)!

Another approach is "mindful meditation," a process that helps to reduce stress but also has the power to clear your mind of obtrusive thoughts that interfere with learning. Those who meditate have better memory recall and consolidation than those who do not (Immink, 2016). Even a ten-second break during learning enhances content memory (Buch et al., 2021). Do not discount the power of a short nap. Taking brief respites from a hectic world can have an exponential return. It is no crime to allow depletable motivation to rebound and many studies indicate that naps of fifteen to twenty minutes are highly beneficial for learning and knowledge retention (Wilson & McNaughton, 1994).

Ten Timeless Tips and One to Avoid

Learning science offers a variety of seamless suggestions designed to spark the learning urge and elevate achievement. The philosophy supporting these findings is based on comparing different approaches to achieve a predetermined outcome. For instance, if you wanted to know the best way to motivate students to prepare for a biology exam, what would you tell them? Should they study in a certain way? Should they rewrite their class notes or is that a waste of time? Do flash cards work better than rereading material? To answer questions like these, after measuring students pre-studying knowledge, we could divide the students into three groups. Group one students are told to test themselves using flash cards and practice quizzes without referring to their notes. Group two students are told to create concept maps and write note summaries. Group three students are asked to reread their notes and textbook chapters, highlighting and underlining key information. Assuming all students were skilled in the approach they were told to use and explicitly followed the provided instructions, we could then determine which approach resulted in the most study time (i.e., motivation) and which group performed best on the exam (i.e., achievement). If the results were consistently replicated with different students, then we would be more confident about which method was most motivational and/or conducive to higher test scores. However, even when studies consistently replicate results, we should remain cautious about broad generalization. While replication gives us confidence, it is important to remember that no method is infallible and there is always the possibility that better techniques have not been discovered yet.

While the example above was contrived, the results closely mirror many of the consolidated findings from learning science that reveal behavioral (and thus neural) repetition is a foundation of learning. In other words, "practice makes progress," but more realistically, "proper practice generates peak performance." As such, several of the recommendations below emphasize repetition, while others describe the ubiquitous findings from educational psychology research that are directly related to achieving better teaching, learning, and motivational outcomes. By no means is this list exhaustive but the findings reported here are supported by both the confluence of behavioral and neuropsychological evidence. Of course, we should always keep in mind the situational nature of learning and realize that some approaches will work better with particular individuals, in specific contexts, and not assume that a recommended strategy will be optimal in every circumstance.

Before proceeding there is one point that cannot be made any clearer. Many educators and writers advocate that learning styles, a preference to be taught or learn in a particular way, makes a difference in both learner motivation and subsequent academic performance. Believing in learning styles means among other things that if you enjoy sight, information should be presented visually. Similarly, if you adore sound, information should be presented verbally, and if you like to touch things, information should have a tactile component. Unfortunately, little, if any, evidence supports the superiority of preference, and learning styles is the most popular and enduring myth in the history of education (De Bruyckere et al., 2015). If you are like most people, when you learn, you use all sensory modalities in unison. In reality, reliance on a learning style is detrimental to achievement. Hoffman (2015b) outlined five consequences of teaching to or using a learning style. First, learning styles can foster confirmation bias and create false impressions of content mastery, potentially impeding future motivation and learning. Second, focusing on a preferred learning style may draw attention to irrelevant aspects of the material, hindering rather than helping the learning process. Third, overreliance on learning styles can limit students from developing a broad repertoire of learning strategies, which is crucial for effective self-regulation. Fourth, emphasizing learning styles can shift accountability for learning outcomes from students to teachers, potentially blaming the education process for poor learning outcomes and rationalizing away personal accountability. Finally, the learning styles approach may lead to an ill-advised dependence on technology in the classroom, despite research showing that competent instruction is more influential than the method of content delivery. So, forget learning styles and instead focus on the ten tips below to promote enhanced motivation, learning, and performance during the instructional and studying process.

Active Recall

Consider what happens when you meet a new person and want to remember their name. If you are like most people, you will mentally repeat the name over and over or perhaps try to associate that person with something in your long-term memory like a familiar object, place, or another person. What is happening cognitively is called "rehearsal," where you are attempting to form memories via stronger connections between those previously discussed neurons in the hippocampus. You may have noticed if you write the person's name down, or verbally say the name aloud while trying to remember the name that you are more likely to recall the name. Considering that memory has an auditory and a visual "channel" and two channels are better than one, "dual coding" supports better retention of information than a unitary memory approach.

Thus, rehearsal helps recall because it instills neural repetition. One of the most effective but often underutilized tools to promote memory is via self-testing (Kornell & Son, 2009). The strategy can incorporate flash cards, practice tests, and content interactions with others, but any approach that attempts to verify the depth of knowledge would be useful for retention. The technique is especially valuable when combined with constructive feedback about answer quality in addition to only knowing if you are right or wrong. Other approaches include concept mapping such as what happens when making flow charts, computer-based animations illustrating concepts, and watching online lectures with both audio and video components (Xu et al., 2024).

Learning from Mistakes

Capitalizing on errors involves receptivity to mistakes and suspension of negative self-evaluation, allowing oneself to tolerate and even seek out errors during learning, rather than believing mistakes should be avoided

(Metcalfe, 2017). During the use of "errorful learning" (Metcalf, 2017, p. 465), individuals must generate answers before a correct response is revealed. If correct, the learner moves on. If inaccurate, reassessment is required. Mistakes must not only be recognized but the learner should be able to articulate why the answer was wrong and how and why an alternative response was preferred. Unsurprisingly, error recognition is a huge part of the growth mindset described on p. 284, because psychologically the approach aligns with an incremental belief that knowledge is cumulative and grows according to a developmental trajectory. Contrary to YouTube video and ad sponsors, there are no baby Einstein's! Summarily, error recognition and subsequent correction promotes active learning. The exploration of solutions, even those that are wrong, is highly preferred to relying on passive study methods like only reviewing grades and comparing mistakes to teacher or textbook answers (Käfer et al., 2019).

Distributed Practice

If you have ever crammed for a test or pulled the almighty all-nighter, then you know the benefits of distributed practice. Research as far back as before your great-grandparents were born (Ebbinghaus, 1885) reveals that if the learning goal is content recall in the near or distant future, then studying over time is far superior to mass information overload in quick succession or during compressed time (Gerbier et al., 2015). In other words, cramming does not work! Like the support for most other results described here, brain imagining studies reveal less efficiency and depth of processing during the second *rapid* exposure to information compared to the second presentation of a spaced item. Several interpretations for the reasoning behind this "spacing effect" (Benjamin & Tullis, 2010) are proposed but consensus reveals, and imaging results confirm, that individuals feel too familiar when the same information is presented in rapid succession. Rapid exposure gives a false sense of security that the information is already known and thus can be virtually ignored. Distributed practice works because later presentation of information primes (reminds) the learner of a previous learning episode. The second presentation requires more processing, leading to improved memory for the prior exposure (Roediger & Butler, 2011).

There is no perfect spacing interval and when information should be repeated depends on the background knowledge of the learner, type of content, and how the information will be used. The ability to apply knowledge enhances recall better than merely knowing useless trivia (Hoffman, 2025). Extensive prior experience and depth of knowledge also matter. Some general guidelines suggest that for retention over days or weeks, repetition one to seven days later is sufficient, such as studying material twenty-four hours after initial exposure and then, again, a week later (Cepeda et al., 2008). For retention over months or years, gradually longer intervals are recommended. A general rule of thumb suggests to space study sessions apart by about 10–20 percent of the desired retention time; for instance, if recall is needed in one-year, initial review intervals might be around one to two months later (Carpenter et al., 2012). Shorter practice sessions are often more effective for skill-based learning (like driving or learning how to knit) than longer, massed practice, with daily or every other day practice usually preferred (Rohrer & Pashler, 2007).

Appropriate Challenge

One of the greatest challenges facing an educator is calibrating the complexity of learning material commensurate with the background knowledge and capability of the learner. Instructional material perceived as either too difficult or appraised as overly simplistic may foster learner disengagement (Kalyuga, 2007). Reduced engagement has motivational implications because lack of positive perceptions about learning will reduce the reward value of learning (i.e., RPE). Thus, one goal for teachers and learners alike is to be sure any instructional material aligns precisely with the learner's developmental level. As such, material should be within the individual's zone of proximal development (ZPD), reducing the gap between what a learner can achieve independently and what they can accomplish with support from an educator.

Aligning instruction with the learner's ZPD requires judicious scaffolding of the learner. Scaffolding means providing support to the extent necessary for the learner to avoid frustration from lack of progress toward a learning goal. In other words, educators should intermittently fade help when the learner demonstrates mastery of a particular concept or skill (Taber, 2018). Like training wheels on a bike, support should be removed when no longer useful to the learner. The primary mechanism to support the ZPD is the mouth. Balanced communication between instructors and learners, and learners and peers, provides the foundation for determining existing levels and making strides toward meeting the individuals' learning trajectory. Questioning knowledge, providing feedback, and answering questions all accomplish the scaffolding goal. Keep in mind that self-scaffolding is also possible by creating an instructional plan that includes the anticipation of challenge areas and acquiring appropriate resources and materials to support learning progression.

Rest Stops

One of the most underappreciated approaches to incentivizing learning is the realization that cognitive resources, like motivational effort, are limited. Similar to feeling physically drained from engaging in prolonged exercise or sports, our brain needs time to assimilate information and recover from extended periods of intense activity. Perhaps more important is overcoming the psychological stigma associated with intentionally pausing work to relax. Tell the typical boss you plan to take a nap in the middle of the day and observe the reaction. Despite the evidence that resting promotes productivity (Sio & Ormerod, 2009; Steffey et al., 2023), expect a scowl and a reminder about the company break policy. A litany of "experts" from Alibaba cofounder Jack Ma to motivational speaker Tony Robbins erroneously spout clichéd epitaphs advocating persistence, resilience, and overcoming goal obstacles at all costs. But they are wrong about the relentless pursuit of goals. While individual productivity patterns vary, and some individuals are productive despite compromised mental resources, powering through fatigue is counterproductive (Hoffman, 2017).

Knowing when your productivity wanes and what to do about it is personal. When writing my first book, it took me about six months to realize that after three hours of continuous writing my ongoing effort was useless. Powering through for extra hours to write a few sentences was completely unproductive. Through trial and error, I realized my writing limitation. I learned to rest when plateaued, resulting in greater productivity after a forty-five-minute nap. In other words, I would mathematically write more with a little sleep than spending the same amount of time getting frustrated and trying to write. The power of short breaks is especially relevant for learning. During a motor sequence task, Buch et al. (2021) noticed significantly improved accuracy when participants were afforded short ten-second rest intervals during performance. They speculated that during these brief rest periods "neural replay" occurred, whereby neural patterns were rapidly reactivated solidifying learning. The replay happened about twenty times faster than the actual physical practice and occurred primarily in areas like the hippocampus, the brain area for memory consolidation. Interestingly, most of the skill improvement happened during these brief rest periods rather than during the active practice itself. Do not listen to the "experts"; instead, listen to yourself and take a break, and your motivation and focus will likely improve.

Advanced Organizers and Worked Examples

There are many ubiquitous learning science findings that reveal simple techniques to enhance learning efficiency and achievement. These techniques primarily emphasize preparing learners to learn before instruction begins. *Learning objectives*, such as "by the time you finish this lesson you will be able to describe 10 strategies that boost learning efficiency and accuracy," signal to the learner what material should be mastered as a result of instruction. Another technique, "advanced organizers," presented before the main content, categorizes prospective knowledge for learners in a way that helps them connect new knowledge to existing knowledge. Similar to a table of contents, the goal of the organizer is to focus attention on key points. For example, an abridged advanced organizer for this book might look like this:

Key concepts to be covered:
1. The differences between passion and reward
2. Why motivation research is incomplete
3. The influence of neuromodulation on optimal performance
4. Reward and INMO, same or different?

5. Strategies to increase motivation, learning, and productivity

Advanced organizers can also be posed as questions to consider, prompting learners to seek responses to questions like "under which circumstances are rewards preferential to passion?" The overall intention is to focus learners on the primary objectives of instruction; so, as the lesson unfolds, attention is appropriately targeted. Once immersed in content, many learners struggle unless concrete examples are provided. Particularly for math and science learning, where procedural knowledge and order of operations are crucial, "worked examples" are especially powerful. Examples show how to complete a specific problem step-by-step with the intention of helping learners understand the process of problem-solving before attempting to solve a particular problem on their own. A worked example for the addition problem (28 + 35) is below:

Question: Find the solution to the problem (28 + 35) =

Step 1	Line up the numbers 28 and 35 vertically	28 35
Step 2	Add the ones column 8 + 5 = 13. Write down 3 in the ones column, carry 1 to the tens column	Ones column = 3 Tens column = 1 + 2 + 3
Step 3	Add the tens column, including the carried 1	2 + 3 + 1 (carried) = 6
Step 4	Record each column answer	6 (column one) and 3 (column two)
Step 5	Final Answer	28 + 35 = 63

Finally, leveraging the principles of active recall, neural repetition, and distributed practice, writing summaries of a learned experience creates connections to existing knowledge while also imbedding key points and relationships among concepts. When learners write summaries, they have no choice but to reflect on knowledge gains or describe any potential knowledge gaps. Restating information in one's own words, which is a form of rehearsal, helps encode information in memory (Chi et al., 1994). Summaries are especially effective for transfer of knowledge, where learners apply what they know to real-life situations (Leopold et al., 2013), thereby enhancing utility.

Gamification

The purpose of gamification, typically accomplished via a technology interface, is to encourage content engagement and leverage the power of active learning. By connecting elements of gaming to learning through such incentives as competition with other learners/players and recognition of mastery levels, gamification enhances motivation to learn (Kawachi, 2017). However, the effectiveness of gamification is debated, favoring increased focus and attention (Sailer & Homner, 2020), yet research indicates that gamified learning sporadically transfers knowledge gained to real-world problem-solving and application. Bai et al. (2020) concluded that gamifying learning accomplished four goals: creating enthusiasm, providing feedback, recognition of learners, and promotion of goal setting. Attainment of Bai's four outcomes are consistent with generating both DA and serotonin, as the strategy theoretically cultivates a desired reward and also instills novelty that may be absent from traditional learning. Gamification can also be customized beyond merely using a standard computer interface to view animated learning or earn virtual badges. Some individuals use personal gamification as a form of self-regulation to complete mundane tasks and to exceed productivity targets (see p. 264).

At least three considerations should guide the implementation of gaming as a prospective learning strategy. Remember the overjustification effect discussed on p. 214 and how a focus on externally controlled rewards can inhibit internalization and future performance. Gamification may unintentionally blunt topic interest. Similar learning outcomes may be attained without the liability of inhibiting INMO. Second, gamification can backfire. Heavy emphasis on reward or frustration from lack of game progress may develop, thereby impeding the purpose of gamified learning. In addition, some learners are uninterested in gamification and may perceive the gamified elements as an annoyance unnecessarily increasing cognitive load associated with learning (Turan et al., 2016; Zhan, 2022). Third, learning is a serious endeavor for many and incorporating "fun" elements into learning can sometimes distract learners from the primary purpose of instruction. Thus, any gamified approach should directly support learning and performance goals and not be included for amusement purposes only (Mayer, 2019).

Personalize Reward

In the drama *Hamlet*, written by playwright William Shakespeare, Polonius tells his son Laertes, "to thine own self be true." While Willy wasn't thinking about optimizing motivation and the power of reward, he was on to something. Shakespeare recognized the importance of creating circumstances conducive to one's own success. The message behind the quote is similar to the intention of rewards, which is to create a catalyst for one's desired achievements, recognizing that no one other than the individual can determine their path of optimal success. All too often individual's surrender to external persuasion, indulge in compliant behavior based on social desirability, and even succumb to *"pluralistic ignorance"* supporting minority perspectives under the guise of believing everyone thinks or acts in a certain way. When it comes to deciding on appropriate rewards, individual choice and diligence is essential for effectiveness. No one can reliably know what reward is best for you, except you.

A reward that works for one person may be ineffective for another. Thus, reward composition, timing, and eventual removal are all determined by personal valuation. Intermittent timing of reward works best, but the nature and contingencies of reward are totally within the discretion of the individual who determines the reward. Once rewards become controlled by others, they lose motivational power. Predictable rewards discount the key principles of RPE, which emphasize a reward must exceed individual expectations. By example, do you really get excited earning the same paycheck every week? While appreciated, the routine payment is no longer a DA catalyst and does not enhance motivation to attain the reward. Key considerations should be the degree of autonomy in structuring the reward, with little or no reliance on others as to how the reward is structured, administered, or earned. For maximum impact, the reward should be based on the learning process and not only attaining the outcome. In addition, consider timing as what may be rewarding today can be functionally useless tomorrow (Cerasoli et al., 2014).

Environmental Restructuring

Whenever steps are actively taken to create a working or learning environment that promotes greater productivity, environmental restructuring occurs. While research evidence reveals under which general conditions performance is optimized, the process of restructuring should be viewed similarly to making choices from a menu. Just as food preferences are personalized based on experience and culture, so are the idiosyncratic choices related to productivity. The reasoning behind the benefits and neuropsychology of environmental restructuring were discussed under the umbrella of self-regulation (p. 259), but what form it takes is up to you. The primary goal of the restructuring process is to reduce or remove anything that may be intrusive to optimal performance (Johnson et al., 2013), and only the individual can determine the nature of distractions. One person's distraction is another person's inspiration.

The most important aspect of restructuring is to actively evaluate under which conditions you work best. First, imagine your greatest accomplishment and think of the process used to attain that outcome that was *unrelated* to the task and to the necessary ability, or was influenced by motivational fluctuations. Once those optimal conditions are identified, replicate the conditions. Restructuring can include simplistic workplace evaluations and cosmetic changes, such as reducing ambient noise, finding a comfortable chair, wearing your favorite green shirt, or creating personalized conditions that optimize learning or performance (Hoffman, 2015a). Other times restructuring is a compartmentalization of invasive emotions, moods, and attitudes. Many individuals are incapable of focusing on important projects when fixated on personal challenges such as health, financial, and family well-being concerns. No doubt avoiding mental and emotional distractions are just as critical as controlling elements of the physical environment. While it is fruitless to suggest that these concerns can be eliminated, they can be relegated to defined periods of breaks after sustained task effort. Whether it is avoidance of checking social media for thirty minutes or not lamenting on how you are going to pay the rent, regulate your thought process. After you cross an item off your "to-do list," then go back to ruminating about the realities of life. A deliberate focus on creating conditions for productivity is nonnegotiable, and absent of contextual control, the context controls you.

Get the Dop(amine)

Chapters 5 and 6 thoroughly described DA synthesis related to motivated behavior and the pursuit of rewards. Absent of sufficient excitatory resources, movement is compromised and the degree of intensity toward reward attainment suffers. Whether intentions are productive or hedonistic, there is no magical DA formula that will thrust you into decisive action and relentless goal pursuit. However, multiple steps can be taken to enhance DA from baseline assisting in progress toward meeting or surpassing objectives. Unfortunately, like the subjectivity of rewards, there is no standardized method, object, or process to boost DA synthesis. Reward is a hypothetical objective that changes frequently, and although DA provides the energy to sustain pursuit of the reward, the specific reward is inconsequential. You may crave a date with a buffalo or fantasize about a week in Hawaii. Either way, determined targets are subjective and personal, and thus DA synthesis will also be individualized based on the integration of genetics, experience, context, and the host of beliefs discussed throughout the text.

Despite the unique nature of DA synthesis, there are some universal strategies that apply to any attempt to shift DA above baseline. To achieve any goal, it must first be clearly defined. The goal should be specific, measurable, and achievable through actions you can control. Without well-defined goals, it is virtually impossible to create conditions that increase DA synthesis enough to make you feel motivated. Unfortunately for some, goal setting is in service of physiological homeostasis, meaning that for many goals have little to do with optimal performance, such as when your primary objectives are sleeping, eating, or having sex. While satisfaction of these basic needs may not appear to be goal oriented, they can be the sole motivation for many individuals and the primary way of generating DA above baseline. As previously discussed, however, the fixation on these hedonistic goals often leads to overindulgence and addiction, resulting in a variety of nondesirable behaviors and negative perceptions from the self and others.

Assuming that your motivational urges are more substantial than bread and brassieres, there are a number of DA protocols that are designed to moderate DA synthesis, inducing greater cognitive clarity and motivational

Table 7.7 Maximizing DA Synthesis

Production Strategy	Method/Analysis	Source
Maximize early morning light.	Arousal neuromodulators are triggered by natural light. Minimally, get 20 minutes of early morning natural sunlight. Do not wear sunglasses (or look directly into the sun). Avoid caffeine until after exposure.	Tsai et al., 2011
Eat DA supportive foods.	DA synthesis is boosted by the amino acid tyrosine found in eggs, chicken, yogurt, soybeans, avocadoes, and bananas.	Kühn et al., 2019
Avoid DA stacking.	Too many simultaneous DA boosts cause overload, diminishing the effectiveness of any one source. Do not regularly mix caffeine, exercise, music, or other personalized DA sources.	Huberman, 2021, 2024
Exercise regularly.	Consistent exercise is a primary DA source. Exercise type doesn't matter. Any exercise increases the number and sensitivity of DA receptors in the brain and tyrosine activity.	See p. 273
Exceed goal plans.	Set a daily target and then do a bit more than expected to maximize RPE. Harder things promote synthesis and shift emphasis to the process of goal attainment.	(Touroutoglou et al., 2020).
Minimize evening light.	Avoid digital screens and bright light at least two hours before scheduled sleep to reduce arousal hormones and excitatory neuromodulators.	Tosini et al., 2016
Sleep.	Circadian rhythm influences DA production. Imbalance inhibits the receptivity of DA receptors in the brain.	Sardi et al., 2018

effort. Each one of these approaches is designed to moderate levels of DA, keeping in mind that too much DA sets an individual up for a tolerance plateau (p. 164) and an eventual DA crash. Thus, avoidance of strategy overload is essential to maximize the power of DA and sustain long-term goal striving. The following protocols, many of which are advocated by Huberman (2021, 2023), should be used in moderation. Think of DA strategies like taking vitamins or supplements; taking too many can make you sick. Finally, remember that the greatest value of DA is providing the oomph toward reaching one's goals. Everyone reaches a point where the same outcomes will no longer feel as exhilarating as the prior experience. Thus, planned pauses and periods of abstinence are essential to avoid tolerance and ward off the accompanying apathy associated with low DA levels.

Persuasion

Persuasion attempts occur when we try to convince someone to think differently. Typically, those who are prone to persuasion embrace beliefs that conflict with scientific evidence or exhibit behavior that closely aligns with the expectations of their cultural or social group. By example, thinking that you are more powerful than a locomotive minimally shows flawed knowledge of speed, velocity, inertia and also unfamiliarity with Superman. Beliefs that mismatch reality can result in misconceptions, like what happens when individuals ignore the health impact of such behaviors as driving while intoxicated, smoking, or sticking their hand in a lion's mouth (Beltrao, 2002). Persuasion does *not* involve learning new information but instead requires unlearning previously flawed knowledge and replacing it with evidence-based information gained in ways beyond personal experience. Chapter 6 discussed how the brain processes information differently based on reward perceptions, how it handles incongruous information, and how utility is assessed. Now we turn to the development of targeted strategies to change someone's mind, which has been described throughout as belief change (BC).

Four key considerations are important when using neuropsychological evidence to change beliefs. First, new information must be perceived as more desirable than anticipated, surpassing the learner's initial expectations, and capturing their interest. Remember, more novelty, greater RPE. Second, the revisionist knowledge should have reward value and salience for the learner, suggesting that the new information is meaningful and applicable to their life or goals. Third, the new knowledge should generate uncertainty regarding the learner's existing conceptions, thus creating cognitive dissonance and motivation to consider the alternative information. Last, the timing and manner in which the reward (i.e., the benefits of adopting the new conception) occurs should be uncertain, as this uncertainty can enhance the learner's engagement and anticipation of the rewarding outcome.

Generating uncertainty implies that BC is more likely when learners realize that all knowledge is subject to change. What we consider to be "known" at any given time is based on the best available evidence and the prevailing scientific consensus. However, as new discoveries emerge and new ideas are proposed, existing knowledge can be challenged, refined, or even overturned (Kühn, 1997). Emphasizing the uncertainty of existing beliefs facilitates change by making the cost of holding false beliefs perceptually worse than making a change, motivating learners to adopt new concepts (Tobler et al., 2005). Timing matters because changing attitudes and beliefs happens gradually. First, introduce the idea that new knowledge may be more beneficial to the individual. Following the introduction and followed by a time lag, provide additional information, keeping in mind that DA is about striving toward goal-directed behavior. When the individual anticipates the value of changing impressions for their future long-term benefit, the anticipation will set a spark, creating an urge toward reaching the goal.

Persuasion initiatives should be personalized, as the variable nature of reward makes a one-size-fits-all approach ineffective. To promote change, it is essential to understand what learners already know and what they find rewarding (Vosniadou, 2013). Information that may be rewarding initially can be perceived as downright boring or useless with repeated exposure and has famously been relegated to the "expertise reversal" effect in psychology literature (Kalyuga, 2007), suggesting that "experts" reject basic information and "novices" are easily confused when information is inconsistent with their background knowledge. Nagging someone with the same information over and over will backfire as the large majority of reform efforts fail to show sustained change over time (Ecker et al., 2022). The repeated presentation of similar knowledge loses rewarding value over time and eventually will be ignored (Rankin et al., 2009). Similarly, the more frequent presentation of refutational evidence, the stronger the resistance. As you might imagine, hearing the same perceptually useless information repeatedly can lead to frustration and anger, not consideration. Thus, avoid repeating the same approach and instead consider creating novel ways to communicate the knowledge that avoids the habituation trap.

Encourage cognitive and not affective processing of the change message. Information that is perceived as controversial or inconsistent with existing belief structures can stimulate a reactive, opinionated, angry, fearful, or anxiety-provoking response from the individual, activating information processing in the amygdala and not the PFC. In those circumstances, emotion takes over, and emotionally processed information is contemplated far differently than information, which is evaluated objectively using principles of logic and reason. Gut responses and intuitive rejection of alternative conceptions are the enemy of persuasion, and demonstrative steps should be taken to ensure that incoming information is processed in neurologically supported ways.

Thus, a crucial persuasion step is determining whether information is being processed cognitively or emotionally. If processed cognitively, revert to the previously described strategies. If processed emotionally, focus on reducing threat perceptions and associated negative emotion by reassurance that belief revision is a strength of moral character, not a sign of weakness or lack of intellectual capability. Consider that when evaluating affectively charged information, individuals attach emotional significance based on group or cultural identification because group affiliation is part of social identity (Spears, 2021). Information that conflicts with group identification can be a powerful instigator of information opposition.

One particular promising approach is to emphasize positivity, novelty, and benefits in change messages. Ironically, many refutational messages attempt to instill doubt about prior conceptions emphasizing the negative consequences of embracing existing beliefs, an emphasis that is neurologically inconsistent with BC. Instead, reform messages should focus on prospective gains from knowledge reconstruction, not prospective losses from continuing to embrace false beliefs (Sharot & Garrett, 2016). By example, you can try and convince someone to give up smoking by telling them they will get cancer, smell horrible, or be perceived as stupid by the nonsmoking public, or you can tell others that people who don't smoke are admired, have higher-paying jobs, and appear more frequently on the cover of *Vogue*. Susceptibility to belief revision is more probable when we believe that our knowledge representations have positive payoffs with specific utility that can potentially lead to elevated self-perceptions and more positive life outcomes (Loewenstein & Molnar, 2018).

Finally, leverage the power of socialization and autonomy. Although beliefs are personalized and idiosyncratic, there is a robust corpus of research indicating that social context is a meaningful mediator of what we think and believe. In circumstances where doubt and uncertainty are rampant, we often turn to others to guide our decisions and actions (Shen et al., 2024). Gregoire (2003) argued that individuals who feel supported by their social network may be more open to considering new ideas and changing their beliefs because discussions and debates with others expose individuals to diverse perspectives and facilitate the exchange of ideas, potentially promoting BC.

Similarly, the change climate matters. One key is promoting autonomy in information choices. Autonomy in this case means encouraging exploration of alternative conceptions but not through suggestions from others like teachers or bosses who can inhibit independent exploration (Chen et al., 2025). Instead, induce receptivity through natural exploration that is typical during group problem-solving and the exchange of ideas. When learners believe they have agency and choice, the inhibitory response for knowledge exploration, which often occurs during change initiatives, is repressed (Chakroun et al., 2020). Thus, given the opportunity to persuade, it is imperative to provide meaningful choices, while using noncontrolling language. Authoritative refutational efforts that demand thinking in a particular way for a specific purpose are often rejected based on mandate alone.

In practice, the strategies described here mean creating opportunities for learners to pursue their own interests and curiosities within the limitations of the change effort. The success of changing minds depends on effectively modifying false beliefs by focusing on the prospective gains from belief revision rather than emphasizing the risks associated with maintaining existing beliefs. All recommendations align with neurological findings that suggest positive and rewarding information enhance the probability of acceptance and adaptive neuromodulation.

References

Agrawal, V., Sood, N., & Whaley, C. M. (2023). *The impact of the global COVID-19 vaccination campaign on all-cause mortality* (No. w31812). National Bureau of Economic Research. https://doi.org/10.3386/w31812

Aune, D., Norat, T., Romundstad, P., & Vatten, L. J. (2013). Whole grain and refined grain consumption and the risk of type 2 diabetes: A systematic review and dose–response meta-analysis of cohort studies. *European Journal of Epidemiology, 28*, 845–858. https://doi.org/10.1007/s10654-013-9852-5

Bai, S., Hew, K. F., & Huang, B. (2020). Does gamification improve student learning outcome? Evidence from a meta-analysis and synthesis of qualitative data in educational contexts. *Educational Research Review, 30*, 100322. https://doi.org/10.1016/j.edurev.2020.100322

Balban, M. Y., Neri, E., Kogon, M. M., Weed, L., Nouriani, B., Jo, B., ... & Huberman, A. D. (2023). Brief structured respiration practices enhance mood and reduce physiological arousal. *Cell Reports Medicine, 4*(1), 1–10. https://doi.org/10.1016/j.xcrm.2022.100895

Bandura, A. (1986). *Self-efficacy: The exercise of control.* W.H. Freeman.

Baumeister, R. F., & Heatherton, T. F. (1996). Self-regulation failure: An overview. *Psychological Inquiry, 7*(1), 1–15. https://doi.org/10.1207/s15327965pli0701_1

Beltrao, A. (2002). Chewed off. *The Sun.* https://www.the-sun.com/news/5404141/horrifying-lion-attack-zoo-keeper-senegal/

Benjamin, A. S., & Tullis, J. (2010). What makes distributed practice effective? *Cognitive Psychology, 61*(3), 228–247. https://doi.org/10.1016/j.cogpsych.2010.05.004

Boettiger, C. A., Mitchell, J. M., Tavares, V. C., Robertson, M., Joslyn, G., D'esposito, M., & Fields, H. L. (2007). Immediate reward bias in humans: Fronto-parietal networks and a role for the catechol-O-methyltransferase 158(Val/Val) genotype. *Journal of Neuroscience, 27*, 14383–14391. https://doi.org/10.1523/jneurosci.2551-07.2007

Brassey, J., Herbig, B., Jeffery, B., & Ungerman, D. (2023). Reframing employee health: Moving beyond burnout to holistic health. https://www.mckinsey.com/mhi/our-insights/reframing-employee-health-moving-beyond-burnout-to-holistic-health

Buch, E. R., Claudino, L., Quentin, R., Bönstrup, M., & Cohen, L. G. (2021). Consolidation of human skill linked to waking hippocampo-neocortical replay. *Cell Reports, 35*(10), 109193. https://doi.org/10.1016/j.celrep.2021.109193

Bureau, J. S., Howard, J. L., Chong, J. X., & Guay, F. (2022). Pathways to student motivation: A meta-analysis of antecedents of autonomous and controlled motivations. *Review of Educational Research, 92*(1), 46–72. https://doi.org/10.3102/00346543211042426

Burnette, J. L., Billingsley, J., Banks, G. C., Knouse, L. E., Hoyt, C. L., Pollack, J. M., & Simon, S. (2023). A systematic review and meta-analysis of growth mindset interventions: For whom, how, and why might such interventions work?. *Psychological Bulletin, 149*(3–4), 174. https://doi.org/10.1037/bul0000368

Büsel, C., Voracek, M., & Ansorge, U. (2020). A meta-analysis of contingent-capture effects. *Psychological Research, 84*(3), 784–809. https://doi.org/10.1007/s00426-018-1087-3

Carpenter, S. K., Cepeda, N. J., Rohrer, D., Kang, S. H., & Pashler, H. (2012). Using spacing to enhance diverse forms of learning: Review of recent research and implications for instruction. *Educational Psychology Review, 24*, 369–378. https://doi.org/10.1007/s10648-012-9205-z

Carron, A. V., Hausenblas, H. A., & Mack, D. (1996). Social influence and exercise: A meta-analysis. *Journal of Sport and Exercise Psychology, 18*(1), 1–16. https://doi.org/10.1123/jsep.18.1.1

Centers for Disease Control. (2016). *1 in 3 adults don't get enough sleep.* https://archive.cdc.gov/www_cdc_gov/media/releases/2016/p0215-enough-sleep.html

Centers for Disease Control. (2021). Current cigarette smoking among adults in the U.S. https://www.cdc.gov/tobacco/php/data-statistics/adult-data-cigarettes/index.html

Cepeda, N. J., Vul, E., Rohrer, D., Wixted, J. T., & Pashler, H. (2008). Spacing effects in learning: A temporal ridgeline of optimal retention. *Psychological Science, 19*(11), 1095–1102. https://doi.org/10.1111/j.1467-9280.2008.02209.x

Cerasoli, C. P., Nicklin, J. M., & Ford, M. T. (2014). Intrinsic motivation and extrinsic incentives jointly predict performance: A 40-year meta-analysis. *Psychological Bulletin, 140*(4), 980–1008. https://doi.org/10.1037/a0035661

Chakroun, K., Mathar, D., Wiehler, A., Ganzer, F., & Peters, J. (2020). Dopaminergic modulation of the exploration/exploitation trade-off in human decision-making. *Elife, 9*, e51260. https://doi.org/10.7554/elife.51260

Chapkovski, P., Khapko, M., & Zoican, M. (2024). Trading gamification and investor behavior. *Management Science.* https://doi.org/10.1287/mnsc.2022.02650

Chatterjee, D., Hegde, S., & Thaut, M. (2021). Neural plasticity: The substratum of music-based interventions in neurorehabilitation. *NeuroRehabilitation, 48*(2), 155–166. https://doi.org/10.3233/nre-208011

Chen L. X., Li H. X. The impact mechanism of teaching strategies on student reading achievement in PISA 2018, *Asia Pacific Journal Education* (2025) 1–18, https:// doi.org/10.1080/02188791.2024.2441699

Chi, M. T., De Leeuw, N., Chiu, M. H., & LaVancher, C. (1994). Eliciting self-explanations improves understanding. *Cognitive Science, 18*(3), 439–477. https://doi.org/10.1207/s15516709cog1803_3

Coe, E., Dewhurst, M., Hartenstein, L., Hextall, A., & Latkovic, T. (2022). *Adding years to life and life to years.* https://www.mckinsey.com/mhi/our-insights/adding-years-to-life-and-life-to-years

Creswell, J. D. (2017). Mindfulness interventions. *Annual Review of Psychology, 68*(1), 491–516. https://doi.org/10.1146/annurev-psych-042716-051139

Crum, A. J., Salovey, P., & Achor, S. (2013). Rethinking stress: The role of mindsets in determining the stress response. *Journal of Personality and Social Psychology, 104*(4), 716–733. https://doi.org/10.1037/a0031201

De Bruyckere, P., Kirschner, P. A., & Hulshof, C. D. (2015). *Urban myths about learning and education.* Academic Press.

Dunning, D. (2019). *Gullible to ourselves.* In J. P. Forgas & R. Baumeister (Eds.), *The social psychology of gullibility: Fake news, conspiracy theories and irrational beliefs* (pp. 217–233). Routledge. https://doi.org/10.4324/9780429203787-12

Ebbinghaus, H. (1964; 1885). *Memory: A contribution to experimental psychology.* Original work published 1885.

Eccles, J. S., & Wigfield, A. (2002). Motivational beliefs, values, and goals. *Annual Review of Psychology, 53*(1), 109–132. https://doi.org/10.1146/annurev.psych.53.100901.135153

Eccles, J. S., & Wigfield, A. (2020). From expectancy-value theory to situated expectancy-value theory: A developmental, social cognitive, and sociocultural perspective on motivation. *Contemporary Educational Psychology, 61,* 101859. https://doi.org/10.1016/j.cedpsych.2020.101859

Ecker, U. K., Lewandowsky, S., Cook, J., Schmid, P., Fazio, L. K., Brashier, N., ... & Amazeen, M. A. (2022). The psychological drivers of misinformation belief and its resistance to correction. *Nature Reviews Psychology, 1*(1), 13–29. https://doi.org/10.1038/s44159-021-00006-y

Erwin. M. (2019). 6 reasons we make bad decisions, and what to do about them. *Harvard Business Review.* https://hbr.org/2019/08/6-reasons-we-make-bad-decisions-and-what-to-do-about-them

Esch, T. (2013). The neurobiology of meditation and mindfulness. In S. Schmidt & H. Walach (Eds.), *Meditation–neuroscientific approaches and philosophical implications* (pp. 153–173). Springer International Publishing.

Esterman, M., & Rothlein, D. (2019). Models of sustained attention. *Current Opinion in Psychology, 29,* 174–180. https://doi.org/10.1016/j.copsyc.2019.03.005

Ferreira-Vieira, T., M Guimaraes, I., R Silva, F., & M Ribeiro, F. (2016). Alzheimer's disease: Targeting the cholinergic system. *Current Neuropharmacology, 14*(1), 101–115. https://doi.org/10.2174/1570159x13666150716165726

Flowerday, T., & Shell, D. F. (2015). Disentangling the effects of interest and choice on learning, engagement, and attitude. *Learning and Individual Differences, 40*, 134–140. https://doi.org/10.1016/j.lindif.2015.05.003

Fratiglioni, L., Marseglia, A., & Dekhtyar, S. (2020). Ageing without dementia: Can stimulating psychosocial and lifestyle experiences make a difference?. *The Lancet Neurology, 19*(6), 533–543. https://doi.org/10.1016/s1474-4422(20)30039-9

Galvão, D. A., Newton, R. U., Chambers, S. K., Spry, N., Joseph, D., Gardiner, R. A., ... & Taaffe, D. R. (2021). Psychological distress in men with prostate cancer undertaking androgen deprivation therapy: Modifying effects of exercise from a year-long randomized controlled trial. *Prostate Cancer and Prostatic Diseases, 24*(3), 758–766. https://doi.org/10.1038/s41391-021-00327-2

Gerbier, E., & Toppino, T. C. (2015). The effect of distributed practice: Neuroscience, cognition, and education. *Trends in Neuroscience and Education, 4*(3), 49–59. https://doi.org/10.1016/j.tine.2015.01.001

Goldman, J. G., & Manis, F. R. (2013). Relationships among cortical thickness, reading skill, and print exposure in adults. *Scientific Studies of Reading, 17*(3), 163–176. https://doi.org/10.1080/10888438.2011.620673

González, J., Barros-Loscertales, A., Pulvermüller, F., Meseguer, V., Sanjuán, A., Belloch, V., & Ávila, C. (2006). Reading cinnamon activates olfactory brain regions. *Neuroimage, 32*(2), 906–912. https://doi.org/10.1016/j.neuroimage.2006.03.037

Gourgouvelis, J., Yielder, P., & Murphy, B. (2017). Exercise promotes neuroplasticity in both healthy and depressed brains: An fMRI pilot study. *Neural Plasticity, 2017*(1), 8305287. https://doi.org/10.1155/2017/8305287

Gregoire, M. (2003). Is it a challenge or a threat? A dual-process model of teachers' cognition and appraisal processes during conceptual change. *Educational Psychology Review, 15*, 147–180. https://doi.org/10.1023/A:1023477131081

Griesbauer, E. M., Manley, E., Wiener, J. M., & Spiers, H. J. (2022). London taxi drivers: A review of neurocognitive studies and an exploration of how they build their cognitive map of London. *Hippocampus, 32*(1), 3–20. https://doi.org/10.1002/hipo.23395

Haworth, J. (2019). 16-year-old fatally stabbed as dozens filmed him bleeding to death. *ABC News*. https://abcnews.go.com/US/teen-arrested-stabbing-boy-attacked-filmed-dozens-bled/story?id=65713494

Heimola, M., Paulanto, K., Alakuijala, A., Tuisku, K., Simola, P., Ämmälä, A. J., ... & Paunio, T. (2021). Chronotype as self-regulation: Morning preference is associated with better working memory strategy independent of sleep. *Sleep Advances, 2*(1), zpab016. https://doi.org/10.1093/sleepadvances/zpab016

Hoffman, B. (2015a). *Motivation for learning and performance.* Academic Press.

Hoffman, B. (2015b). *Which common educational myth limits student achievement?* PsychologyToday.com. https://www.psychologytoday.com/gb/blog/motivate/201509which-common-educational-myth-limits-student-achievement

Hoffman, B. (2017). *Hack your motivation: Over 50 science-based strategies to improve performance.* Attribution Press.

Hoffman. B. (2019). *Do you think more intelligently than the average person?* PsychologyToday.com. https://www.psychologytoday.com/intl/blog/motivate/201910/do-you-think-more-intelligently-than-the-average-person

Hoffman, B. (2025). Value and utility: What students learn and transfer from a graduate motivation course. *Scholarship of Teaching and Learning in Psychology*, Advance online publication. https://doi.org/10.1037/stl0000448

Horowitz, A., & Rubin, R. (1986). (You gotta) fight for your right (to party!). *Licensed to kill, III.* Def Jam.

Huberman, A. (2021, September 20). Toolkit for sleep. *Neural Network newsletter.* https://www.hubermanlab.com/newsletter/toolkit-for-sleep

Huberman. A. (2024, March 6). How to improve learning and performance by developing a growth mindset. *Neural Network newsletter.* https://www.hubermanlab.com/newsletter/how-to-improve-learning-performance-by-developing-a-growth-mindset

Huberman, A. (2024, May 15). Improve your sleep. *Neural Network newsletter.* https://www.hubermanlab.com/newsletter/improve-your-sleep

Immink, M. A. (2016). Post-training meditation promotes motor memory consolidation. *Frontiers in Psychology, 7*, 1698. https://doi.org/10.3389/fpsyg.2016.01698

Inzlicht, M., Werner, K. M., Briskin, J. L., & Roberts, B. W. (2021). Integrating models of self-regulation. *Annual Review of Psychology, 72*(1), 319–345. https://doi.org/10.1146/annurev-psych-061020-105721

James, W. (1890). *The principles of psychology.* Holt.

Jäncke, L., Koeneke, S., Hoppe, A., Rominger, C., & Hänggi, J. (2009). The architecture of the golfer's brain. *PloS One, 4*(3), e4785. https://doi.org/10.1371/journal.pone.0004785

Johnson, R. E., Taing, M. U., Chang, C. -H., & Kawamoto, C. K. (2013). A self-regulation approach to person-environment fit. In A. L. Kristof-

Brown & J. Billsberry (Eds.), *Organizational fit* (pp. 74–98). John Wiley & Sons, Ltd. https://doi.org/10.1002/9781118320853.ch4

Jones, K., Methley, A., Boyle, G., Garcia, R., & Vseteckova, J. (2022). A systematic review of the effectiveness of acceptance and commitment therapy for managing grief experienced by bereaved spouses or partners of adults who had received palliative care. *Illness, Crisis & Loss, 30*(4), 596–613. https://doi.org/10.1177/10541373211000175

Käfer, J., Kuger, S., Klieme, E. & Kunter, M. (2019). The significance of dealing with mistakes for student achievement and motivation: Results of doubly latent multilevel analyses. *European Journal of Psychology of Education, 34*, 731–753. https://doi.org/10.1007/s10212-018-0408-7

Kahneman, D. (2011) *Thinking, fast and slow*. Farrar, Straus, & Giroux.

Kalyuga, S. (2007). Expertise reversal effect and its implications for learner-tailored instruction. *Educational Psychology Review, 19*, 509–539. https://doi.org/10.1007/s10648-007-9054-3

Kamen, C., Heckler, C., Janelsins, M. C., Peppone, L. J., McMahon, J. M., Morrow, G. R., ... & Mustian, K. (2016). A dyadic exercise intervention to reduce psychological distress among lesbian, gay, and heterosexual cancer survivors. *LGBT health, 3*(1), 57–64. https://doi.org/10.1089/lgbt.2015.0101

Kansakar, U., Trimarco, V., Mone, P., Varzideh, F., Lombardi, A., & Santulli, G. (2023). Choline supplements: An update. *Frontiers in Endocrinology, 14*, 1148166. https://doi.org/10.3389/fendo.2023.1148166

Kawachi, I. (2017). It's all in the game—the uses of gamification to motivate behavior change. *JAMA Internal Medicine, 177*(11), 1593–1594. https://doi.org/10.1001/jamainternmed.2017.4798

Killingsworth, M. A., & Gilbert, D. T. (2010). A wandering mind is an unhappy mind. *Science, 330*(6006), 932–932. https://doi.org/10.1126/science.1192439

Kim, A., & Dennis, A. R. (2019). Says who? The effects of presentation format and source rating on fake news in social media. *Mis Quarterly, 43*(3), 1025–1039. https://doi.org/10.25300/misq/2019/15188

Kirschner, P. A., & Hendrick, C. (2020). *How learning happens: Seminal works in educational psychology and what they mean in practice*. Routledge.

Kivetz, R., Urminsky, O., & Zheng, Y. (2006). The goal-gradient hypothesis resurrected: Purchase acceleration, illusionary goal progress, and customer retention. *Journal of Marketing Research, 43*(1), 39–58. https://doi.org/10.1509/jmkr.43.1.39

Knoch, D., & Nash, K. (2015). Self-control in social decision making: A neurobiological perspective. In G. Gendolla, M. Tops, & S. Koole (Eds.),

Handbook of biobehavioral approaches to self-regulation (pp. 221–234). Springer. https://doi.org/10.1007/978-1-4939-1236-0_15

Kornell, N., & Son, L. K. (2009). Learners' choices and beliefs about self-testing. *Memory, 17*(5), 493–501. https://doi.org/10.1080/09658210902832915

Kouzes, T. K., & Posner, B. Z. (2019). Influence of managers' mindset on leadership behavior. *Leadership & Organization Development Journal, 40*(8), 829–844. https://doi.org/10.1108/lodj-03-2019-0142

Kühn, S., Düzel, S., Colzato, L., Norman, K., Gallinat, J., Brandmaier, A. M., ... & Widaman, K. F. (2019). Food for thought: Association between dietary tyrosine and cognitive performance in younger and older adults. *Psychological Research, 83*, 1097–1106. https://doi.org/10.1007/s00426-017-0957-4

Kuhn, T. S. (1997). *The structure of scientific revolutions* (Vol. 962). University of Chicago Press.

Lee-Kwan, S. H. (2017). Disparities in state-specific adult fruit and vegetable consumption—United States, 2015. *Morbidity and Mortality Weekly Report, 66*. https://doi.org/10.15585/mmwr.mm6645a1

Leopold, C., Sumfleth, E., & Leutner, D. (2013). Learning with summaries: Effects of representation mode and type of learning activity on comprehension and transfer. *Learning and Instruction, 27*, 40–49. https://doi.org/10.1016/j.learninstruc.2013.02.003

Li, P., Legault, J., & Litcofsky, K. A. (2014). Neuroplasticity as a function of second language learning: Anatomical changes in the human brain. *Cortex, 58*, 301–324. https://doi.org/10.1016/j.cortex.2014.05.001

Loewenstein, G., & Molnar, A. (2018). The renaissance of belief-based utility in economics. *Nature Human Behaviour, 2*(3), 166–167. https://doi.org/10.1038/s41562-018-0301-z

Loughrey, D. G., Lavecchia, S., Brennan, S., Lawlor, B. A., & Kelly, M. E. (2017). The impact of the Mediterranean diet on the cognitive functioning of healthy older adults: A systematic review and meta-analysis. *Advances in Nutrition, 8*(4), 571–586. https://doi.org/10.3945/an.117.015495

Maher, J. P., Gottschall, J. S., & Conroy, D. E. (2015). Perceptions of the activity, the social climate, and the self during group exercise classes regulate intrinsic satisfaction. *Frontiers in Psychology, 6*, 1236. https://doi.org/10.3389/fpsyg.2015.01236

Mark, G. (2023). *Attention span: A groundbreaking way to restore balance, happiness and productivity.* Harlequin.

Mayer, R. E. (2019). Computer games in education. *Annual Review of Psychology, 70*(1), 531–549. https://doi.org/10.1146/annurev-psych-010418-102744

Metcalfe, J. (2017). Learning from errors. *Annual Review of Psychology*, 68(1), 465–489. https://doi.org/10.1146/annurev-psych-010416-044022

Milani, R. V., & Lavie, C. J. (2009). Reducing psychosocial stress: A novel mechanism of improving survival from exercise training. *The American Journal of Medicine*, 122(10), 931–938. https://doi.org/10.1016/j.amjmed.2009.03.028

Moore, D. A., & Healy, P. J. (2008). The trouble with overconfidence. *Psychological Review*, 115(2), 502–517. https://doi.org/10.1037/0033-295x.115.2.502

Nelson, R. J., Bumgarner, J. R., Walker II, W. H., & DeVries, A. C. (2021). Time-of-day as a critical biological variable. *Neuroscience & Biobehavioral Reviews*, 127, 740–746. https://doi.org/10.1016/j.neubiorev.2021.05.017

Nikolić, J. (2018). Biases in the decision-making process and possibilities of overcoming them. https://scidar.kg.ac.rs/handle/123456789/13325

Noyes, J. A., Welch, P. M., Johnson, J. W., & Carbonneau, K. J. (2020). A systematic review of digital badges in health care education. *Medical Education*, 54(7), 600–615. https://doi.org/10.1111/medu.14060

Pennycook, G., & Rand, D. G. (2019). Fighting misinformation on social media using crowdsourced judgments of news source quality. *Proceedings of the National Academy of Sciences*, 116(7), 2521–2526. https://doi.org/10.1073/pnas.1806781116

Peters, U., Sherling, H. R., & Chin-Yee, B. (2024). Hasty generalizations and generics in medical research: A systematic review. *PLoS One*, 19(7), e0306749. https://doi.org/10.1371/journal.pone.0306749

Pignatiello, G. A., Martin, R. J., & Hickman, R. L. (2020). Decision fatigue: A conceptual analysis. *Journal of Health Psychology*, 25, 123–135. https://doi.org/10.1177/1359105318763510

Poly, C., Massaro, J. M., Seshadri, S., Wolf, P. A., Cho, E., Krall, E., ... & Au, R. (2011). The relation of dietary choline to cognitive performance and white-matter hyperintensity in the Framingham Offspring Cohort. *The American Journal of Clinical Nutrition*, 94(6), 1584–1591. https://doi.org/10.3945/ajcn.110.008938

Popova, M. (2023). 17 life-learnings from 17 years of the Marginalian. https://www.themarginalian.org/2023/10/22/17/

Raman, D. V., Rotondo, A. P., & O'Leary, T. (2019). Fundamental bounds on learning performance in neural circuits. *Proceedings of the National Academy of Sciences*, 116(21), 10537–10546. https://doi.org/10.1073/pnas.1813416116

Rankin, C. H., Abrams, T., Barry, R. J., Bhatnagar, S., Clayton, D. F., Colombo, J. et al. (2009). Habituation revisited: An updated and revised description of the behavioral characteristics of habituation. *Neurobiology*,

Learning, Memory, 92, 135–138. https://doi.org/10.1016/j.nlm.2008.09.012 https://doi.org/10.1016/j.nlm.2008.09.012

Reeve, J., & Cheon, S. H. (2021). Autonomy-supportive teaching: Its malleability, benefits, and potential to improve educational practice. *Educational Psychologist*, 56(1), 54–77. https://doi.org/10.1080/00461520.2020.1862657

Reeve, J., & Jang, H. (2006). What teachers say and do to support students' autonomy during a learning activity. *Journal of Educational Psychology*, 98(1), 209–218. https://doi.org/10.1037/0022-0663.98.1.209

Remskar, M., Western, M. J., & Ainsworth, B. (2024). Mindfulness improves psychological health and supports health behaviour cognitions: Evidence from a pragmatic RCT of a digital mindfulness-based intervention. *British Journal of Health Psychology*, 29(4), 1031–1048. https://doi.org/10.1111/bjhp.12745

Renninger, K. A., & Hidi, S. (2011). Revisiting the conceptualization, measurement, and generation of interest. *Educational Psychologist*, 46(3), 168–184. https://doi.org/10.1080/00461520.2011.587723

Roediger, H. L., & Butler, A. C. (2011). The critical role of retrieval practice in long-term retention. *Trends in Cognitive Sciences*, 15(1), 20–27. https://doi.org/10.1016/j.tics.2010.09.003

Rohrer, D., & Pashler, H. (2007). Increasing retention without increasing study time. *Current Directions in Psychological Science*, 16(4), 183–186. https://doi.org/10.1111/j.1467-8721.2007.00500.x

Sailer, M., Hense, J. U., Mayr, S. K., & Mandl, H. (2017). How gamification motivates: An experimental study of the effects of specific game design elements on psychological need satisfaction. *Computers in Human Behavior*, 69, 371–380. https://doi.org/10.1016/j.chb.2016.12.033

Sailer, M., & Homner, L. (2020). The gamification of learning: A meta-analysis. *Educational Psychology Review*, 32(1), 77–112. https://doi.org/10.1007/s10648-019-09498-w

Saner, H., & Burell, G. (2012). Exercise to reduce distress and improve cardiac function: Moving on and finding the pace. In P. Hjemdahl et al. (Eds.), *Stress and cardiovascular disease* (pp. 317–332). Springer. https://doi.org/10.1007/978-1-84882-419-5_18

Sardi, N. F., Tobaldini, G., Morais, R. N., & Fischer, L. (2018). Nucleus accumbens mediates the pronociceptive effect of sleep deprivation: The role of adenosine A2A and dopamine D2 receptors. *Pain*, 159(1), 75–84. https://doi.org/10.1097/j.pain.0000000000001066

Scheiermann, C., Kunisaki, Y., & Frenette, P. S. (2013). Circadian control of the immune system. *Nature Reviews Immunology*, 13(3), 190–198. https://doi.org/10.1038/nri3386

Schneiderman, N., Ironson, G., & Siegel, S. D. (2005). Stress and health: Psychological, behavioral, and biological determinants. *Annual Review of Clinical Psychology, 1*(1), 607–628. https://doi.org/10.1146/annurev.clinpsy.1.102803.144141

Seiler, A., Fagundes, C. P., & Christian, L. M. (2020). The impact of everyday stressors on the immune system and health. In A. Choukèr (Ed.), *Stress challenges and immunity in space* (2nd ed., pp. 71–94). Springer. https://doi.org/10.1007/978-3-030-16996-1_6

Seli, P., Risko, E. F., & Smilek, D. (2016). On the necessity of distinguishing between unintentional and intentional mind wandering. *Psychological Science, 27*(5), 685–691. https://doi.org/10.1177/0956797616634068

Sharot, T., & Garrett, N. (2016). Forming beliefs: Why valence matters. *Trends in Cognitive Sciences, 20*(1), 25–33. https://doi.org/10.1016/j.tics.2015.11.002

Sheffler, P., Kürüm, E., Sheen, A. M., Ditta, A. S., Ferguson, L., Bravo, D., ... & Wu, R. (2023). Growth mindset predicts cognitive gains in an older adult multi-skill learning intervention. *The International Journal of Aging and Human Development, 96*(4), 501–526. https://doi.org/10.1177/00914150221106095

Shen, X., Helion, C., Smith, D. V., & Murty, V. P. (2024). Motivation as a lens for understanding information-seeking behaviors. *Journal of Cognitive Neuroscience, 36*(2), 362–376. https://doi.org/10.1162/jocn_a_02083

Sio, U. N., & Ormerod, T. C. (2009). Does incubation enhance problem solving? A meta-analytic review. *Psychological Bulletin, 135*, 94–120. https://doi.org/10.1037/a0014212

Spears, R. (2021). Social influence and group identity. *Annual Review of Psychology, 72*(1), 367–390. https://doi.org/10.1146/annurev-psych-070620-111818

Stanovich, K. E., West, R. F., & Toplak, M. E. (2016). *The rationality quotient: Toward a test of rational thinking*. MIT Press.

Steffey, M. A., Risselada, M., Scharf, V. F., Buote, N. J., Zamprogno, H., Winter, A. L., & Griffon, D. (2023). A narrative review of the impact of work hours and insufficient rest on job performance. *Veterinary Surgery, 52*(4), 491–504. https://doi.org/10.1111/vsu.13943

Strain, T., Flaxman, S., Guthold, R., Semenova, E., Cowan, M., Riley, L. M., ... & Stevens, G. A. (2024). National, regional, and global trends in insufficient physical activity among adults from 2000 to 2022: A pooled analysis of 507 population-based surveys with 5·7 million participants. *The Lancet Global Health, 12*(8), e1232–e1243. https://doi.org/10.1016/s2214-109x(24)00150-5

Taber, K. S. (2018). Scaffolding learning: principles for effective teaching and the design of classroom resources. In M. Abend (Ed.), *Effective teaching and learning: Perspectives, strategies and implementation* (pp. 1–43). Nova Science Publishers.

Tan, L. H., Spinks, J. A., Gao, J. H., Liu, H. L., Perfetti, C. A., Xiong, J., ... & Fox, P. T. (2000). Brain activation in the processing of Chinese characters and words: A functional MRI study. *Human Brain Mapping, 10*(1), 16–27. https://doi.org/10.1002/(sici)1097-0193(200005)10:1%3C16::aid-hbm30%3E3.0.co;2-m

Tao, W., Zhao, D., Yue, H., Horton, I., Tian, X., Xu, Z., & Sun, H. J. (2022). The influence of growth mindset on the mental health and life events of college students. *Frontiers in Psychology, 13*, 821206. https://doi.org/10.3389/fpsyg.2022.821206

Theodoratou, M. (2023). Coping strategies in clinical psychology and neuropsychology. *Preprints 2023*, 2023101932. https://doi.org/10.20944/preprints202310.1932.v1

Tobler, P. N., Fiorillo, C. D., & Schultz, W. (2005). Adaptive coding of reward value by dopamine neurons. *Science, 307*, 1642–1645. https://doi.org/10.1126/science.1105370

Tomova, L., Wang, K. L., Thompson, T., Matthews, G. A., Takahashi, A., Tye, K. M., & Saxe, R. (2020). Acute social isolation evokes midbrain craving responses similar to hunger. *Nature Neuroscience, 23*(12), 1597–1605. https://doi.org/10.1038/s41593-020-00742-z

Tosini, G., Ferguson, I., & Tsubota, K. (2016). Effects of blue light on the circadian system and eye physiology. *Molecularision, 22*, 61. https://doi.org/10.63500/mv_v22_61

Touroutoglou, A., Andreano, J., Dickerson, B. C., & Barrett, L. F. (2020). The tenacious brain: How the anterior mid-cingulate contributes to achieving goals. *Cortex, 123*, 12–29. https://doi.org/10.1016/j.cortex.2019.09.011

Tsai, H. Y., Chen, K. C., Yang, Y. K., Chen, P. S., Yeh, T. L., Chiu, N. T., & Lee, I. H. (2011). Sunshine-exposure variation of human striatal dopamine D2/D3 receptor availability in healthy volunteers. *Progress in Neuro-Psychopharmacology and Biological Psychiatry, 35*(1), 107–110. https://doi.org/10.1016/j.pnpbp.2010.09.014

Turan, Z., Avinc, Z., Kara, K., & Göktas, Y. (2016). Gamification and education: Achievements, cognitive loads, and views of students. https://doi.org/10.3991/ijet.v11i07.5455*International Journal of Emergent Technology Learning, 11*(7), 64–69.

Unsworth, N., & Robison, M. K. (2018). Tracking arousal state and mind wandering with pupillometry. *Cognitive, Affective, & Behavioral Neuroscience, 18*, 638–664. https://doi.org/10.3758/s13415-018-0594-4

Valdez, P. (2019). Circadian rhythms in attention. *The Yale Journal of Biology and Medicine*, *92*(1), 81–92.

Vosniadou, S. (2013). Conceptual change in learning and instruction: The framework theory approach. In S. Vosniadou (Ed.), *International handbook of research on conceptual change* (2nd ed., pp. 11–30). Routledge. https://doi.org/10.4324/9780203154472.ch1

Warner, A. G. (2023). Arguing for the opposition: A position commitment shock to overcome confirmation bias. *Management Teaching Review*, 23792981231185713. https://doi.org/10.1177/23792981231185713

Weiner, B. (2021). An attributionally based theory of motivation and emotion: Focus, range, and issues. In N. T. Feather (Ed.), *Expectations and actions* (pp. 163–204). Routledge. https://doi.org/10.4324/9781003150879-8

West, R., Murphy, K. J., Armilio, M. L., Craik, F. I., & Stuss, D. T. (2002). Effects of time of day on age differences in working memory. *The Journals of Gerontology Series B: Psychological Sciences and Social Sciences*, *57*(1), P3–P10. https://doi.org/10.1093/geronb/57.1.p3

White, M. M., Olson, S. J., & Canning, E. A. (2024). Disentangling the impact of instructor mindset and demeanor on student experiences. *Motivation Science*, *10*(1), 83. https://doi.org/10.1037/mot0000322

Williams, P. T. (2001). Physical fitness and activity as separate heart disease risk factors: A meta-analysis. *Medicine and Science in Sports and Exercise*, *33*(5), 754. https://doi.org/10.1097/00005768-200105000-00012

Wilson, M. A., & McNaughton, B. L. (1994). Reactivation of hippocampal ensemble memories during sleep. *Science*, *265*(5172), 676–679. https://doi.org/10.1126/science.8036517

Winne, P. H., & Hadwin, A. F. (2008). The weave of motivation and self-regulated learning. In D. Schunk & B. J. Zimmerman (Eds.), *Motivation and self-regulated learning: Theory, research, and applications* (pp. 297–314). Erlbaum.

Wolters, C. (2003). Regulation of motivation: Evaluating an underemphasized aspect of self-regulated learning. *Educational Psychologist*, *38*(4), 189–205. http://dx.doi.org/10.1207/S15326985EP3804_1

Wolters, C. A., Benzon, M. B., & Arroyo-Giner, C. (2011). Assessing strategies for the self-regulation of motivation. In B. J. Zimmerman & D. H. Schunk (Eds.), *Handbook of self-regulation of learning and performance* (pp. 298–312). Routledge/Taylor & Francis.

Wulantari, N. P., Rachman, A., Sari, M. N., Uktolseja, L. J., & Rofi'i, A. (2023). The role of gamification in English language teaching: A literature review. *Journal on Education, 6*(1), 2847–2856. https://doi.org/10.31004/joe.v6i1.3328

Xu, J., Wu, A., Filip, C., Patel, Z., Bernstein, S. R., Tanveer, R., ... & Kotroczo, T. (2024). Active recall strategies associated with academic achievement in young adults: A systematic review. *Journal of Affective Disorders.* Update. https://doi.org/10.1016/j.jad.2024.03.010

Xu, S., Akioma, M., & Yuan, Z. (2021). Relationship between circadian rhythm and brain cognitive functions. *Frontiers of Optoelectronics, 14*(3), 278–287. https://doi.org/10.1007/s12200-021-1090-y

Yeager, D. S., & Dweck, C. S. (2020). What can be learned from growth mindset controversies? *American Psychologist, 75*(9), 1269–1284. https://doi.org/10.1037/amp0000794

Yorks, D. M., Frothingham, C. A., & Schuenke, M. D. (2017). Effects of group fitness classes on stress and quality of life of medical students. *Journal of Osteopathic Medicine, 117*(11), e17–e25. https://doi.org/10.7556/jaoa.2017.140

Zhan, Z., He, L., Tong, Y., Liang, X., Guo, S., & Lan, X. (2022). The effectiveness of gamification in programming education: Evidence from a meta-analysis. *Computers and Education: Artificial Intelligence, 3,* 100096. https://doi.org/10.1016/j.caeai.2022.100096

Zhou, J., Dai, Y., Zuo, Z., Liu, T., & Li, S. (2023). Famine exposure during early life and risk of cancer in adulthood: A systematic review and meta-analysis. *The Journal of Nutrition, Health and Aging, 27*(7), 550–558. https://doi.org/10.1007/s12603-023-1947-4

8

Epilogue

Chapter Outline

And So, It Goes   323

And So, It Goes

Hopefully by now you are convinced that passion is nothing more than a discretionary, internalized, biological reward and believe that neuropsychological evidence increases our understanding of motivated behavior. While successfully refuting the substance and application of the presented evidence is unlikely, you may still doubt that the recommended strategies work. In other words, deeply entrenched beliefs are resistant to persuasion. Any conclusions made are your choice, although some people will disagree! Science does not evolve when everyone believes in the same things and acts similarly, never questioning old practices or historical ways of thinking. Instead, scientific advancement minimally encourages debate and often breeds skepticism. Just be certain that any inferences advanced are based on sound replicable evidence like that presented throughout the book. Be certain that conclusions are not based on *"motivated reasoning,"* which is merely another way to assert the validity of one's personal choice.

Next, keep in mind that changing perspectives is not a sign of intellectual frailty, nor does change happen easily. Multiple persuasion attempts are often necessary to convince someone that one method is superior to another. Incremental change takes time, with radical shifts taking even longer. Nobel laureate and physicist Max Planck once decreed, "A new scientific truth does not triumph by convincing its opponents and making them see the light, but rather because its opponents eventually die, and a new generation grows up that is familiar with it" (Azoulay et al., 2019, p. 2889). You do not need to die to adopt different perspectives on passion and reward, but burying your old ideas is a prerequisite for personal growth.

Second, whether trying to persuade others or when embarking on a personal journey of critical thinking and intellectual awareness, we often act like junior scientists. Different approaches are tested using trial and error until we see what works best or until we receive feedback from trusted others showing us that one ideal perspective reliably produces better results than existing protocols. Only when the evidence is consistent and works in favor of our intentions are we willing to commit to a long-term change in behavior. Thus, patience is a worthy byproduct of acceptance, as is demonstrating the willingness to think differently.

Third, keep in mind the transitory nature of scientific research. While consideration of neuropsychological findings is important, as the months and years unfold, there will be variations in the availability and analysis of relevant evidence. Conclusions and assertions that appear truthful today may crumble into junk tomorrow. Information entropy does *not* devalue the veracity or impact of current findings; instead, it merely suggests that finer-grained analysis and new discoveries will induce different interpretations. Just as we no longer duel to settle disagreements, avoid publicly shaming misfits in the town square, and don't spank kids in school, how we apply neuropsychological evidence will continue to evolve. New interpretations and subsequent behaviors will replace those no longer useful, and much of the change may conflict with the prevailing scientific and cultural zeitgeist.

Fourth, beware the "experts." Do not listen to anyone proclaiming to be the preeminent guide to your decision-making and well-being. Carefully, scrutinize offers of free advice avoiding reliance on published sources that lack validation and only operate for the purpose of generating profit. While evidentiary interpretation can be assisted by those trained or experienced in a particular domain, strategy choice is a highly personal decision. Yes, when objectivity reveals knowledge or skill deficits, actively seek out advice. Ground your assessments in reality using accurate calibration not wishful thinking or resource convenience. Yes, when the goal is to learn more than you currently know, consider the perspectives of others as part of the learning process. Accept accountability for utility without deferring to anyone else besides yourself.

Finally, regarding all the evidence concerning neuromodulation and especially how DA is the catalyst for accomplishment, keep long-term objectives in the forefront of your consciousness. Celebrate accomplishments in moderation and minimize fixation on the inevitable obstacles that are part of the exploratory journey. Eventually you may realize that goal attainment, while gratifying, is not the brain's primary reward. The ultimate payoff is earning satisfaction through goal setting and by dedicating effort. Let progress be your passion.

Reference

Azoulay, P., Fons-Rosen, C., & Zivin, J. G. (2019). Does science advance one funeral at a time? *American Economic Review, 109* (8), 2889–2920. https://doi.org/10.3386/w21788

Glossary

Scientific Terminology	Simplified Description	What It Really Means/Example	Page
Affect(ive)	The resultant feeling from an emotional experience	The subjective psychological or physical perception of a wide variety of emotions	p. 131
Agency	Controlled and effortful action directed toward a task or goal	Planned and voluntary behaviors	p. 56
Attainment value	How much an individual believes that engaging in, completing, or mastering a skill has personal importance and is meaningful to the self	Will task completion really matter for my reputation and/or self-views or is the task merely an obligation?	p. 58
Autonomous motivation	Voluntarily engaging in an activity because of an inherent interest or personal endorsement of the activity's importance	Feeling like we can do what we want to do without worrying about contingencies or consequences	p. 73
Autonomy	Self-governance by freely pursuing wants, desires, and intentions without external coercion or pressure	Doing what you want, when you want to do it, while having discretion as to how to achieve the goal	p. 5
Autonomy supportive instructional behaviors	Teaching or learning strategies that emphasize the power of choice and individuality supporting student learning outcomes	Letting learners make decisions about what is learned, how the material is learned, and how mastery is determined	p. 290
Availability bias	Relying on more recent memories when contemplating a decision rather than considering a full corpus of experience or evidence	Using convenient or recent information as the basis of a decision because you are too lazy or busy to dig deeper	p. 282
Cognitive load	The degree of task complexity or mental effort needed to complete a task	How much challenge a person believes is associated with a particular task or learning objective	p. 129

(*Continued*)

Scientific Terminology	Simplified Description	What It Really Means/Example	Page
Cognitive miser	The proclivity for humans to avoid complex thinking whenever avoidable	Not wanting to invest time in things that require brain horsepower	p. 281
Competence	The need to feel effective and capable in one's interactions with the environment by exercising and expressing one's skills and abilities	The gratified feeling experienced when you are good at something, whether a skill or personal quality like honesty or friendliness	p. 5
Confirmation bias	Seeking evidence that supports one's beliefs while ignoring or rationalizing undesirable information	Justifying decisions by cherry-picking reasons that support your choice while ignoring contrary evidence	p. 223
Controlled motivation	Engaging in activities due to external pressures or internal demands, rather than by personal choice or interest	Obligations, requirements, duties, and responsibilities that are the requirements of civilized lifestyles/cultures	p. 74
Dispositions	Qualities, beliefs, and unique ways of viewing the world	General but subjective expectations concerning how the world works	p. 71
Drive	The attempt to satisfy a need through motivated effort	A psychological or biological investment of effort	p. 3, 107
Effect size	A quantitative measure indicting the strength of relationship among variables usually determined by controlled research and statistical significance	How much impact a variable, strategy, or context has on an experimental outcome or a measure of impact	p. 23
Engagement	Cognitive, emotional, or behavioral task focus	When attention is focused providing a memorable emotional or learning experience	p. 6
Entropy	When applied to human functioning, the gradual decline of psychological and physiological functioning that eventually results in death	A general state of disarray and chaos that diminishes capability	p. 256

Term	Definition	Description	Page
Essentialist	A philosophy or belief that contends concepts have a set of defined characteristics that are necessary to define the concept	Arguing about definitions and meanings instead of focusing on applying the concept	p. 8
Executive control	The command center of the mind that regulates higher-order cognition to regulate, control, and manage thinking and motivational processes	Where the brain focuses attention and effort	p. 114
Extrinsic motivation (EXMO)	Task engagement based on coercion or mandate and usually incentivized	Exerting effort toward a goal based on an external obligation or mandate, feeling coerced or manipulated	p. 5
Framing	Selecting certain aspects of a desired reality and making those attributes more prominent when communicating text, speech, or visuals relating to a message	A baseline point of view that presumes specific realities that support one's belief, a generalized framework to justify an opinion	p. 282
Gene expression	The interplay between genes and the environment that shapes an individual's behavior and overall functioning	When heredity results in certain behaviors emerging, while others stay dormant or repressed	p. 116
Goal orientation	The reason for task engagement, typically mastery or to achieve a desired outcome or appear competent	The approach taken toward academic or work pursuits, either looking good or striving for expertise and accomplishment	p. 59
Heuristics	Using learned assumptions and information to make decisions with a perceived high probability of success	Mental shortcuts or rules of thumb that the brain uses to make quick decisions or judgments	p. 281
Incentives/ reinforcers	A consequence of action designed to increase desired behavior or decrease undesired behavior	Usually, an externally derived reason to exhibit controlled behavior, pay for performance	p. 32, 88

(Continued)

Scientific Terminology	Simplified Description	What It Really Means/Example	Page
Internalization	Assimilation of beliefs, values, or dispositions as part of one's identity	When a person, team, social cause, belief, culture, ethnicity, or attribute defines your identity	p. 52
Intrinsic motivation (INMO)	Task engagement based on interest, curiosity, or personal desire. Engagement in a task for no apparent external payoff	Doing what we find to be personally rewarding and satisfying without feeling any obligation or mandate	p. 5
Intrinsic value	How much an individual subjectively enjoys doing and/or completing contemplated tasks	Something that is inherently interesting to the individual has intrinsic value	p. 58
Locus of control	A belief in the internal or external control over one's effort or destiny	Beliefs about how much control individuals have over their lives; internal locus assumes one can control what happens to them	p. 65
Motivated reasoning	The tendency of people to conform assessments of information to some external goal or end lacking consideration of accuracy	The tendency to find ways to believe what we want to believe, even when faced with contradictory evidence	p. 323
Neuropsychology	Science focused on applying the relationship among the brain, nervous system, and cognitive, behavioral, and emotional functioning to human behavior	Motivation research in neuropsychology examines which brain structures, neural circuits, factors influence attention, goal-directed behavior, beliefs, and decision-making	p. 6
Overjustification effect	The erroneous perception that in all circumstances offering rewards for something when a person already has interest reduces INMO	An experimental finding that led researchers to erroneously believe that rewards kill motivation under any circumstance	p. 199, 214

Term	Definition	Description	Page
P-hacking	Researchers searching for unplanned significant results from data collected for other purposes	A questionable practice designed to enhance the career of researchers in the quest for academic recognition	p. 41
Phasic release	Phasic release involves rapid, transient bursts of neuronal firing, resulting in brief but high potency increases in neural concentration.	The feeling of excitement generated by specific stimuli or events, like what happens when unexpected rewards are earned, or surprising information is discovered	p. 139, 156
Plasticity (neuronal)	The ability of the neuronal structure of the brain to change based on interaction with the environment	Whether we are aware or not, we learn from experience, and it changes the actual composition of our brain	p. 43
Pluralistic ignorance	Privately rejecting a personal belief by mistakenly believing that others (the majority) accept a different belief	Going along with what seems to be the consensus of opinion despite personal skepticism	p. 302
Practical significance	Deriving meaningful application of research findings to resolve real-world problems	Using statistically significant research results to solve practical problems that improve people's lives	p. 24
Relatedness	The desire to be connected to others, requited affiliation	Feeling like you are part of a relationship, group, organization, or culture	p. 5
Reward	A subjective outcome ancillary to task engagement valued by an individual	In a practical sense, rewards are earned when a person demonstrates a particular behavior or reaches a particular goal	p. 4
Self-beliefs	Subjective appraisal of personal motivations, emotions, dispositions, and task expectancies	How people think about themselves, their capabilities, and probabilities for achieving successful outcomes	p. 95

(Continued)

Scientific Terminology	Simplified Description	What It Really Means/Example	Page
Social desirability	Acting in ways consistent with the expectations of other people or the dominant culture	Behaving in ways that are believed to be appropriate and socially acceptable	p. 40
Tonic release	Tonic neuronal release is characterized by a slow, steady discharge maintaining a baseline level of a neurotransmitter	Typically, below consciousness, low-level firing of neurotransmitters influences long-term behavioral states and mood	p. 139, 156
Unjustified	Beliefs unsupported by evidence beyond personal experience	Opinions, intuitions, and wishful thinking, conspiracy theories	p. 25
Utility value	How much an individual believes that engaging in, completing, or mastering a skill is useful from an applied perspective	How can I use the experience or skill going forward; does task mastery have fringe benefits?	p. 58
Valence	The internal appeal (positive valence) or aversiveness (negative valence) of an event, object, or situation	An evaluation of the suitability or appeal of a particular situation, the evaluation of impact as positive or negative	p. 68, 225
Variance explained	Similar to effect size but a quantitative measure that indicates how much variation in an outcome is attributable to a specific cause	The magnitude and strength of an effect size in explaining an experimental outcome	p. 24
Volition(al)	The feeling of having free will to make choices	Causing things to happen in preferred ways based on personal preferences	p. 74

Appendix

Top 50 Cited Empirical Reward and INMO/EXMO Studies

Citations Counts Per Google Scholar as of June 13, 2025

Citation	Cite Total	5-year trend	Type (E/NE)	Sample size	% WEIRD sample	Constructs	Effect size	% Variance explained	Conclusions
[1]Pintrich, P. R., & De Groot, E.V. (1990). Motivational and self-regulated learning components of classroom academic performance. Journal of Educational Psychology, 82(1), 33-40. https://doi.org/10.1037/0022-0663.82.1.33	17,089	↑141%	NE	173	100	[6]Self-efficacy Intrinsic value Cognitive strategy use Self-regulation Performance	M	10-22	Self-efficacy and intrinsic value enhanced cognitive engagement and performance, with self-regulation the strongest predictor of academic success. Test anxiety negatively affected self-efficacy and exam performance.
[1]Davis, F. D., Bagozzi R. P., & Warshaw P. R. (1992). Extrinsic and intrinsic motivation to use computers in the workplace. Journal of Applied Social Psychology, 22 (14), 1111-1132. https://doi.org/10.1111/j.1559-1816.1992.tb00945.x	11,062	↑242%	NE	40	N/R	EXMO/INMO Perceived usefulness Enjoyment Usage intentions Usage behavior Task importance	S-M	15-75	Perceived usefulness primarily drove workplace computer usage, though enjoyment positively interacted with and amplified the impact of usefulness on intentions.

(Continued)

Top 50 Cited Empirical Reward and INMO/EXMO Studies

Citations Counts Per Google Scholar as of June 13, 2025

Citation	Cite Total	5-year trend	Type (E/NE)	Sample size	% WEIRD sample	Constructs	Effect size	% Variance explained	Conclusions
[3]Deci, E. L. (1971). Effects of externally mediated rewards on intrinsic motivation. Journal of Personality and Social Psychology, 18(1) 105-115. https://doi.org/10.1037/h0030644	8,910	↑228%	E	24	100	[6]EXMO/INMO Extrinsic rewards Verbal feedback	*	N/R	Monetary rewards reduced INMO, while verbal reinforcement and positive feedback increased INMO.
[1]Rich, B. L., Lepine, J. A., & Crawford, E. R. (2010). Job engagement: Antecedents and effects on job performance. Academy of Management Journal, 53(3), 617-635. https://doi.org/10.5465/amj.2010.51468988	6,987	↑135%	NE	245	88	[7]Job engagement Job involvement Job satisfaction Intrinsic motivation Task performance Organizational citizenship behavior	M	25-45	Engagement mediated the relationship between value congruence, perceived organizational support, core self-evaluations, and job performance more so than job involvement, job satisfaction, and INMO.
[1]Elliot, A. J., & McGregor, H. A. (2001). A 2x2 achievement goal framework. Journal of Personality and Social Psychology, 80(3), 501-519. https://doi.org/10.1037/0022-3514.80.3.501	6,893	↑60%	NE	148-180	100	Goals-mastery-approach, mastery-avoidance, performance-approach, performance-avoidance	S-M	15-40	Mastery-avoidance goals showed more negative results than mastery-approach, but more positive than performance-avoidance.

Reference	Citations	Growth	Type	N	Variables	Category	Range	Summary
[2]Skinner, E. A., & Belmont, M. J. (1993). Motivation in the classroom: Reciprocal effects of teacher behavior and student engagement across the school year. *Journal of Educational Psychology, 85*(4), 571-581. https://doi.org/10.1037/0022-0663.85.4.571	6,402	↑174%	NE	144	94	Autonomy support Engagement Intrinsic motivation Performance	S	13-23	Teacher behaviors, specifically involvement, structure, and autonomy support had reciprocal effects with student engagement. Positive interactions enhanced engagement, while disengagement may perpetuate negative teacher responses.
[1]Hackman, J. R., & Lawler, E. E. (1971). Employee reactions to job characteristics. *Journal of Applied Psychology, 55*, 259–286. https://doi.org/10.1037/h0031152	5,382	↑60%	NE	208	N/R	[6]Variety Autonomy Task identity Feedback Satisfaction Performance Work motivation Job involvement	M*	20-40	Jobs with high variety, autonomy, task identity, and feedback boosted motivation and satisfaction for employees with strong higher-order needs, with job design effectiveness relying on aligning job characteristics with individual needs.

(*Continued*)

Top 50 Cited Empirical Reward and INMO/EXMO Studies   Citations Counts Per Google Scholar as of June 13, 2025

Citation	Cite Total	5-year trend	Type (E/NE)	Sample size	% WEIRD sample	Constructs	Effect size	% Variance explained	Conclusions
[3]Lepper, M. R., Greene, D., & Nisbett, R. E. (1973). Undermining children's intrinsic interest with extrinsic reward: A test of the "overjustification" hypothesis. Journal of Personality and Social Psychology, 28(1), 129-137. https://doi.org/10.1037/h0035519	5,055	↑12%	NE	55	100	Intrinsic interest/ motivation Extrinsic rewards Self-perceptions Overjustification effect	S	N/R	When rewards were expected, children exhibited less future interest in drawing compared to those not rewarded. The effect was evident both in drawing quality during the experimental session and later during classroom observations.
[1]Ryan, R. M., Rigby, C. S., & Przybylski, A. (2006). The motivational pull of video games: A self-determination theory approach. Motivation and Emotion, 30, 344-360. https://doi.org/10.1007/s11031-006-9051-8	4,905	↑186%	NE	50-208	100	[6]Autonomy Competence Presence Enjoyment Intrinsic motivation	M-L	30-50	Needs for autonomy, competence, and relatedness predicted enjoyment and future gameplay, with autonomy and competence satisfaction tied to positive mood changes, applicable across single-player and multiplayer gaming contexts.

Reference	Citations	Growth	Type	N	Age	Code	Range	Findings
[1]Elliot, A. J., & Harackiewicz, J. M. (1996). Approach and avoidance achievement goals and intrinsic motivation: A mediational analysis. *Journal of Personality and Social Psychology, 70*(3), 461-475. https://doi.org/10.1037/0022-3514.70.3.461	4,526	↑32%	NE	84-92	N/R	[5]Achievement goals Intrinsic motivation Task involvement	M*	20-35	Performance goals aimed at avoiding failure undermined INMO, while goals focused on achieving success did not, with task involvement mediating the negative impact of performance-avoidance goals by reducing engagement.
[1]Grolnick, W. S., & Slowiaczek, M. L. (1994). Parents' involvement in children's schooling: A multidimensional conceptualization and motivational model. *Child Development, 65*, 237–252. https://doi.org/10.1111/j.1467-8624.1994.tb00747.x	3,192	↑159%	NE	456	98	Parent involvement Perceived competence Control understanding School performance	S	13-17	Children's perceptions of parental autonomy support and involvement positively influenced motivation, which predicted academic performance, motivation mediated the link between perceived parental context and school achievement.
[1]Grant, A. M. (2008). Does intrinsic motivation fuel the prosocial fire? Motivational synergy in predicting persistence, performance, and productivity. *Journal of Applied Psychology, 93*, 48–58. https://doi.org/10.1037/0021-9010.93.1.48	2,896	↑143%	NE	58	N/R	Prosocial motivation Intrinsic motivation Performance Persistence Productivity	S-M	20-35	INMO amplified the positive impact of prosocial motivation on persistence, performance, and productivity, enhancing persistence and boosting performance and productivity.

(*Continued*)

Top 50 Cited Empirical Reward and INMO/EXMO Studies

Citations Counts Per Google Scholar as of June 13, 2025

Citation	Cite Total	5-year trend	Type (E/NE)	Sample size	% WEIRD sample	Constructs	Effect size	% Variance explained	Conclusions
[2]Vansteenkiste, M., Simons, J., Lens, W., Sheldon, K. M., & Deci, E. L. (2004). Motivating learning, performance, and persistence: The synergistic effects of intrinsic goal contents and autonomy-supportive contexts. *Journal of Personality and Social Psychology, 87*(2), 246-260. https://doi.org/10.1037/0022-3514.872.246	2,792	↑79%	E	200-377	N/R	Intrinsic goals Extrinsic goals Autonomy-support Control Performance Persistence Autonomous motivation	M-L	10-26	Intrinsic goals and autonomy-supportive contexts independently enhanced deep processing, test performance, and persistence, while autonomous motivation mediated the effects of goal content and context on learning outcomes.
[1]Grolnick, W. S., Ryan, R. M., & Deci, E. L. (1991). Inner resources for school achievement: Motivational mediators of children's perceptions of their parents. *Journal of Educational Psychology, 83*(4), 508 –517. https://doi.org/10.1037/0022-0663.83.4.508	2,429	↑74%	NE	456	100	[5]Control understanding Perceived competence Relative autonomy Autonomy support Involvement Academic performance	S-M	13-17	Parent involvement indirectly affected children's school performance through motivational resources, with mothers' behavior and intellectual/cognitive involvement linked to performance, whereas for fathers, only behavior was connected via perceived competence.

Reference	Citations	Growth	Type	N	Measure	Constructs	Sample	Age	Findings
[3]Ryan, R. M., Mims, V., & Koestner, R. (1983). Relation of reward contingency and interpersonal context to intrinsic motivation: A review and test using cognitive evaluation theory. Journal of Personality and Social Psychology, 45(4), 736-750. https://doi.org/10.1037/0022-3514.45.4.736	1,955	↑158%	E	96	N/R	INMO Feedback (controlling, Informational), Rewards (performance-contingent, task-contingent)	*	N/R	The salience of controlling versus informational rewards mediated impact on INMO, with task-contingent rewards reducing motivation compared to no rewards when lacking performance feedback, while performance-contingent rewards either boosted or undermined motivation.
[3]Deci, E. L. (1972). The effects of contingent and noncontingent rewards and controls on intrinsic motivation. Organizational Behavior and Human Performance, 8(2), 217-229. https://doi.org/10.1016/0030-5073(72)90047-5	1,654	↑20%	E	40	N/R	[?]INMO Extrinsic rewards (contingent and noncontingent) Performance feedback Perceived locus of causality	*	N/R	Contingent monetary rewards decreased INMO, while noncontingent payments had no effect. Punishment threats and negative feedback decreased INMO, while positive verbal feedback enhanced INMO.
[1]Roberts, J. A., Hann, I. H., & Slaughter, S. A. (2006). Understanding the motivations, participation, and performance of open-source software developers: A longitudinal study of the Apache projects. Management Science, 52(7), 984-999. https://doi.org/10.1287/mnsc.1060.0554	1,532	↑1%	NE	288	N/R	INMO/EXMO Participation Performance	S-M	13-54	Developers' motivations were interrelated, as paid participation boosted status motivations but reduced use value motivations; both paid participation and status motivations increased contributions, while use value motivations decreased them.

(Continued)

Top 50 Cited Empirical Reward and INMO/EXMO Studies

Citations Counts Per Google Scholar as of June 13, 2025

Citation	Cite Total	5-year trend	Type (E/NE)	Sample size	% WEIRD sample	Constructs	Effect size	% Variance explained	Conclusions
[2]Ratelle, C. F., Guay, F., Vallerand, R. J., Larose, S., & Senécal, C. (2007). Autonomous, controlled, and amotivated types of academic motivation: A person-oriented analysis. Journal of Educational Psychology, 99(4), 734-736. https://doi.org/10.1037/0022-0663.99.4.734	1,305	↑73%	NE	4,498	4	Autonomous regulation Controlled regulation Amotivation Academic achievement Persistence	S	1-22	High school students with high autonomous/ high controlled motivation showed the best academic adjustment, while college students with an autonomous profile exhibited greater persistence, whereas an autonomous profile better supported college persistence.
[4]Vansteenkiste, M., Zhou, M., Lens, W., & Soenens, B. (2005). Experiences of autonomy and control among Chinese learners: Vitalizing or immobilizing? Journal of Educational Psychology, 97(3), 468-483. https://doi.org/10.1037/0022-0663.97.3.468	1,231	↑45%	NE	132	0	[6]Autonomous motivation Controlled motivation Autonomy support Psychological control Academic performance	S-M	5-25	Autonomous study motivation predicted adaptive learning attitudes, academic success, and well-being, while controlled motivation correlated with higher dropout rates, maladaptive attitudes, and ill-being, with parental autonomy support enhancing adaptive strategies and well-being by fostered student autonomy

Reference						
[3]Amabile, T. M., Hennessey, B. A., & Grossman, B. S. (1986). Social influences on creativity: The effects of contracted-for reward. *Journal of Personality and Social Psychology, 50*(1), 14-23. https://doi.org/10.1037/0022-3514.50.1.14	1,148	↑59%	E	115	100	[7]INMO/EXMO Creativity	N/R	N/R	Contracting to perform tasks for rewards diminished creativity, whereas non contracted rewards do not, demonstrating that working for rewards can decrease creativity.
[1]Fortier, M. S., Vallerand, R., & Guay, F. (1995). Academic motivation and school performance: Toward a structural model. *Contemporary Educational Psychology, 20*, 257-274. https://doi.org/10.1006/ceps.1995.1017	1,051	↑33%	NE	263	N/R	Perceived competence Perceived self-determination Autonomous motivation Performance INMO Amotivation External regulation	M	28	Perceived academic competence and self-determination enhanced autonomous academic motivation and positively affected school performance.

(Continued)

Top 50 Cited Empirical Reward and INMO/EXMO Studies

Citations Counts Per Google Scholar as of June 13, 2025

Citation	Cite Total	5-year trend	Type (E/NE)	Sample size	% WEIRD sample	Constructs	Effect size	% Variance explained	Conclusions
[1]Kuvaas, B. (2006). Performance appraisal satisfaction and employee outcomes: Mediating and moderating roles of work motivation. *The International Journal of Human Resource Management, 17*(3), 504-522. https://doi.org/10.1006/ceps.1995.1017	1,029	↑107%	NE	593	N/R	[7]Performance appraisal satisfaction INMO Work performance Affective organizational commitment Turnover intention	S	11	Performance appraisal satisfaction was related to affective commitment and turnover intention, INMO mediated the relationship between work performance and satisfaction, enhancing performance for highly motivated individuals and diminishing it for those with lower INMO.
[3]Eisenberger, R., Rhoades, L., & Cameron, J. (1999). Does pay for performance increase or decrease perceived self-determination and intrinsic motivation? *Journal of Personality and Social Psychology, 77*(5), 1026-1040. https://doi.org/10.1037/0022-3514.77.5.1026	982	↑47%	NE	435	N/R	[7]Self determination, autonomy INMO Performance-contingent rewards Desire for control Perceived organizational support	S	2-8	Rewards increased perceived autonomy and INMO. Performance-contingent rewards enhanced self-determination and mediated positive relationships between reward expectations and organizational support/mood/performance.

[1]Kusurkar, R. A., Ten Cate, T. J., Vos, C. M. P., Westers, P., & Croiset, G. (2013). How motivation affects academic performance: A structural equation modeling analysis. *Advances in Health Sciences Education, 18*, 57-69. https://doi.org/10.1007/s10459-012-9354-3	926	↑288%	NE	383	100	Autonomous motivation Controlled motivation Effort Academic performance	S	N/R	Relative autonomous motivation enhanced academic performance by fostering good study strategies and higher effort, and the influence was primarily indirect, mediated through study strategies rather than direct effects.
[3]Harackiewicz, J. M. (1979). The effects of reward contingency and performance feedback on intrinsic motivation. *Journal of Personality and Social Psychology, 37*, 1352-1363. https://doi.org/10.1037/0022-3514.37.8.1352	819	↑83%	E	93	N/R	[6]Intrinsic motivation Reward contingency Positive feedback Performance	M-L	33	Performance-contingent rewards undermined INMO more than task-contingent rewards, while positive feedback independently boosted INMO, and informational performance-contingent rewards decrease motivation more than non-informational ones.

(*Continued*)

Top 50 Cited Empirical Reward and INMO/EXMO Studies   Citations Counts Per Google Scholar as of June 13, 2025

Citation	Cite Total	5-year trend	Type (E/NE)	Sample size	% WEIRD sample	Constructs	Effect size	% Variance explained	Conclusions
[1]Vansteenkiste, M., Simons, J., Lens, W., Soenens, B., & Matos, L. (2005). Examining the motivational impact of intrinsic versus extrinsic goal framing and autonomy-supportive versus internally controlling communication style on early adolescents' academic achievement. *Child Development, 76*(2), 483-501. https://doi.org/10.1111/j.1467-8624.2005.00858.x	814	↑63%	E	130	100	Intrinsic goals Extrinsic goals Intrinsic motivation Extrinsic motivation Autonomy support Internal control	S-L	9-45	Intrinsic goal framing improved conceptual learning and long-term retention compared to extrinsic framing, with autonomy-supportive communication enhancing conceptual learning and internally controlling styles promoting rote learning.
[3]Eisenberger, R., & Rhoades, L. (2001). Incremental effects of reward on creativity. *Journal of Personality and Social Psychology, 81*(4), 728-741. https://doi.org/10.1037/0022-3514.81.4.728	787	↑27%	NE	435	N/R	[6]Creativity INMO Self-determination Performance-reward expectancy	M	N/R	Tying rewards to creativity increased creative performance. Expected rewards for good performance increased creativity by enhancing INMO and perceived self-determination.

[1]Jaussi, K. S., & Dionne, S. D. (2003). Leading for creativity: The role of unconventional leader behavior. *The Leadership Quarterly, 14*, 475– 498. https://doi.org/10.1016/S1048-9843(03)00048-1	732	↑17%	E	364	100	[5]Unconventional leadership behavior Transformational leadership Creativity Group creative performance INMO	L	0-14	Unconventional leader behavior boosted follower creativity, increased group cohesion beyond transformational leadership, and enhanced group creativity with high INMO, while transformational leadership strengthened cohesion.
[1]Tauer, J. M., & Harackiewicz, J. M. (2004). The effects of cooperation and competition on intrinsic motivation and performance. *Journal of Personality and Social Psychology, 86*(6), 849-861. https://doi.org/10.1037/0022-3514.86.6.849	663	↑111%	E, **	228	N/R	[5]Intrinsic motivation Performance Cooperation Competition Task enjoyment	M-L	40-172	Intergroup competition consistently boosted INMO and task enjoyment when compared to pure cooperation or competition, resulting in equal or superior performance.
[3]Fisher, C. D. (1978). The effects of personal control, competence, and extrinsic reward systems on intrinsic motivation. *Organizational Behavior and Human Performance, 21*, 273–288. https://doi.org/10.1016/0030-5073(78)90054-5	655	↑92%	E	82	N/R	[7]Intrinsic motivation Personal control Competence Pay system Performance	*	N/R	Personal control over performance strongly influenced INMO, surpassing the impact of reward system types, with motivation peaking when both control and competence are high.

(*Continued*)

Top 50 Cited Empirical Reward and INMO/EXMO Studies

Citations Counts Per Google Scholar as of June 13, 2025

Citation	Cite Total	5-year trend	Type (E/NE)	Sample size	% WEIRD sample	Constructs	Effect size	% Variance explained	Conclusions
[3]Anderson, R., Manoogian, S. T., & Reznick, J. S. (1976). The undermining and enhancing of intrinsic motivation in preschool children. *Journal of Personality and Social Psychology, 34*(5), 915-922. https://doi.org/10.1037/0022-3514.34.5.915	647	↑110%	E	72	0	External rewards INMO	L	N/R	Money and awards reduced INMO in preschool children, while positive verbal reinforcement increased INMO, and ignoring children caused a significant decline in motivation.
[1]Simons, J., Dewitte, S., & Lens, W. (2004). The role of different types of instrumentality in motivation, study strategies, and performance: Know why you learn, so you'll know what you learn!. *British Journal of Educational Psychology, 74*(3), 343-360. https://doi.org/10.1348/000709904 1552314	596	↓4%	NE	184	N/R	[6]Instrumentality Goal orientation Cognitive strategies Performance	M-L	N/R	Internal regulation and perceived course utility promoted adaptive goal orientation, INMO, effective cognitive strategies, and enhanced performance, whereas linking performance to extrinsic rewards without recognizing course utility yielded lower internal regulation and distal utility.

[1]Dysvik, A., & Kuvaas, B. (2008). The relationship between perceived training opportunities, work motivation and employee outcomes. *International Journal of Training and Development, 12*, 138–157. https://doi.org/10.1111/j.1468-2419.2008.00301.x	521	↑72%	NE	343	N/R	Perceived training opportunity Intrinsic motivation Task performance Organizational citizenship behavior (OCB) Turnover intention	S-M	13-24	INMO mediated perceived training opportunities and employee outcomes like task performance, OCB, and turnover intention, enhancing the effect on OCB for highly motivated employees, with no direct relationship between training opportunities and outcomes without this mediation.
[3]Ross, M. (1975). Salience of reward and intrinsic motivation. *Journal of Personality and Social Psychology, 32*(2), 245-254. https://doi.org/10.1037/0022-3514.32.2.245	507	↓42%	E	66	100	[6]Reward salience INMO Attribution theory Self-determination	S*	N/R	Children who received a highly salient reward showed less subsequent intrinsic interest in drum playing compared to those who received a non-salient reward or no reward. Children who were asked to think about the reward showed less intrinsic interest than those distracted from thinking about it.

(Continued)

Top 50 Cited Empirical Reward and INMO/EXMO Studies

Citations Counts Per Google Scholar as of June 13, 2025

Citation	Cite Total	5-year trend	Type (E/NE)	Sample size	% WEIRD sample	Constructs	Effect size	% Variance explained	Conclusions
[1]Corpus, J. H., McClintic-Gilbert, M. S., & Hayenga, A. O. (2009). Within-year changes in children's intrinsic and extrinsic motivational orientations: Contextual predictors and academic outcomes. *Contemporary Educational Psychology*, 34(2), 154-166. https://doi.org/10.1016/j.cedpsych.2009.01.001	493	↑21%	E	1,051	78	[6]Intrinsic motivation Extrinsic motivation Academic achievement	S	1-7	INMO/EXMO decreased from fall to spring, with adolescents showing a steeper decline in INMO and elementary students in EXMO; INMO and classroom achievement positively reinforced each other, whereas poor performance had a minimal link to increased EXMO.
[1]Vansteenkiste, M., Simons, J., Soenens, B., & Lens, W. (2004). How to become a persevering exerciser? Providing a clear, future intrinsic goal in an autonomy-supportive way. *Journal of Sport and Exercise Psychology*, 26(2), 232-249. https://doi.org/10.1123/jsep.26.2.232	441	↓5%	E	501	N/R	[5]Intrinsic motivation Extrinsic motivation Autonomous motivation Controlled motivation Persistence	M-L	N/R	Framing exercise activities with future intrinsic goals boosted effort, motivation, performance, and persistence, whereas future extrinsic goal framing undermined those outcomes, with an autonomy-supportive context yielding similar benefits to intrinsic goal framing.

⁷Zimmerman, B. J., & Kitsantas, A. (1996). Self-regulated learning of a motoric skill: The role of goal setting and self-monitoring. *Journal of Applied Sport Psychology*, 8(1), 60-75. https://doi.org/10.1080/10413209608406308	431	↑26%	E	50	50	⁵Goal setting Self-monitoring Task performance Self-efficacy Intrinsic interest	M	28-31	Process goals outperformed product goals in enhancing dart throwing skills and psychological processes, such as self-recording boosting skills, self-efficacy, and self-reactions. Goal setting had an enhanced impact on skill acquisition.
¹Van Yperen, N. W. (2006). A novel approach to assessing achievement goals in the context of the 2×2 framework: Identifying distinct profiles of individuals with different dominant achievement goals. *Personality and Social Psychology Bulletin*, 32(11), 1432-1445. https://doi.org/10.1177/0146167206292093	420	↓30%	E	333	N/R	Self-efficacy Perceived competence INMO/EXMO Interest Performance Amotivation	S	2-13	Preference for mastery-approach goals correlated with INMO and self-efficacy, performance-avoidance goals related to negative outcomes, while performance-approach goals exhibited a mix of positive and negative effects.

(Continued)

Top 50 Cited Empirical Reward and INMO/EXMO Studies

Citations Counts Per Google Scholar as of June 13, 2025

Citation	Cite Total	5-year trend	Type (E/NE)	Sample size	% WEIRD sample	Constructs	Effect size	% Variance explained	Conclusions
[1]Dodd, N. G., & Ganster, D. C. (1996). The interactive effects of variety, autonomy, and feedback on attitudes and performance. *Journal of Organizational Behavior, 17*(4), 329-347. https://doi.org/10.1002/(SICI)1099-1379(199607)17:4<329::AID-JOB754>3.0.CO;2-B	405	↑80%	E	197	N/R	Variety Autonomy Feedback Satisfaction Performance	S	3-7	Increased autonomy boosted satisfaction and performance in high-variety tasks but had minimal impact in low-variety tasks, while feedback enhanced performance only when paired with high autonomy.
[4]Hechanova, M., Alampay, R. B. A., & Franco, E. P. (2006). Psychological empowerment, job satisfaction and performance among Filipino service workers. *Asian Journal of Social Psychology, 9*, 72–78. https://doi.org/10.1111/j.1467-839X.2006.00177.x	404	↑10%	N/E	954	0	[?]Psychological empowerment Intrinsic motivation Job satisfaction Performance	M	21-23	Psychological empowerment correlated positively with job satisfaction and performance, although the effect on performance was weak; men reported greater empowerment than women even when controlling for job level and performance.
[1]Moran, C. M., Diefendorff, J. M., Kim, T.Y., & Liu, Z. Q. (2012). A profile approach to self-determination theory motivations at work. *Journal of Vocational Behavior, 81*(3), 354-363. https://doi.org/10.1016/j.jvb.2012.09.002	399	↑37%	NE	287	0	[5]INMO/EXMO Job performance Job autonomy Task identity Task significance Feedback	L	N/R	Five distinct motivation profiles were identified, each correlating with varying levels of need satisfaction, job performance, and work environment perceptions, with self-determined and motivated clusters yielding the most favorable outcomes.

Citation						Variables			Findings
Gagné, F., & St. Père, F. (2002). When IQ is controlled, does motivation still predict achievement? *Intelligence, 30,* 71–100. https://doi.org/10.1016/S0160-2896(01)00068-X	387	↓28%	NE	208	100	[6]INMO/EXMO Persistence Cognitive abilities Academic achievement	M	40	Cognitive abilities were the strongest predictor of school achievement, surpassing the predictive power of motivation, while motivation itself did not predict academic success.
Graves, L. M., Ruderman, M.N., Ohlott, P.J., & Weber, T.J. (2012). Driven to work and enjoyment of work: Effects on managers' outcomes. *Journal of Management, 38,* 1655–1680. https://doi.org/10.1177/0149206310363612	366	↑0%	NE	346	83	[6]Work Motivation Performance Career Satisfaction Psychological Strain	M-L	11-48	Work enjoyment boosts career satisfaction and performance, driven motivation does not. Driven motivation, however, increases performance under low enjoyment but also raises strain. High enjoyment minimizes the need for driven motivation.
Cameron, J., Pierce, W. D., Banko, K. M., & Gear, A. (2005). Achievement-based rewards and intrinsic motivation: A test of cognitive mediators. *Journal of Educational Psychology, 97*(4), 641–655. https://doi.org/10.1037/0022-0663.97.4.641	365	↑12%	E	119	N/R	[3]Creativity Intrinsic motivation Extrinsic motivation Interest	S-M	13-45	Achievement-based rewards during learning or testing boosted INMO, mediated by perceived competence and interest-internal attribution, fostering motivation for specific tasks and increasing general interest in related activities.

(Continued)

Top 50 Cited Empirical Reward and INMO/EXMO Studies

Citations Counts Per Google Scholar as of June 13, 2025

Citation	Cite Total	5-year trend	Type (E/NE)	Sample size	% WEIRD sample	Constructs	Effect size	% Variance explained	Conclusions
[1]Aunola, K., Leskinen, E., & Nurmi, J. E. (2006). Developmental dynamics between mathematical performance, task motivation, and teachers' goals during the transition to primary school. *British Journal of Educational Psychology, 76*(1), 21-40. https://doi.org/10.1348/000709905X51608	343	↑29%	NE	198	100	[6]Task motivation Performance	L*	34-75	Children's mathematical performance and task motivation created a cyclical relationship, where high performance boosted motivation; teachers' pedagogical goals centered on motivation or self-concept development relevant to students' task motivation in mathematics.
[1]Reeve, J. (1989). The interest-enjoyment distinction in intrinsic motivation. *Motivation and Emotion, 13*, 83-103. https://doi.org/10.1007/BF00992956	336	↑206%	E	57	N/R	[5]Interest Enjoyment Collative motivation Perceived performance	M-L	34-49	Collative motivation drove interest, while perceived performance predicted enjoyment, showing distinct determinants for INMO, with interest initiating attention and exploration and enjoyment sustaining engagement and persistence.

Citation						Variables			Findings
Tauer, J. M., & Harackiewicz, J. M. (1999). Winning isn't everything: Competition, achievement orientation, and intrinsic motivation. *Journal of Experimental Social Psychology, 35*(3), 209-238. https://doi.org/10.1006/jesp.1999.1383	330	↑27%	NE	260	N/R	[5]INMO Competence valuation Competition Achievement orientation Outcome feedback Task enjoyment Perceived competence	L	50	Competition's effect on INMO was moderated by achievement orientation, with high achievers enjoying competition more, while competitive context and outcome feedback independently influenced motivation, and competence valuation boosted enjoyment, particularly in the absence of negative feedback.
[1]Kuvaas, B. (2009). A test of hypotheses derived from self-determination theory among public sector employees. *Employee Relations, 31*(1), 39-56. https://doi.org/10.1108/01425450910916814	307	↑24%	NE	779	100	INMO Job autonomy Work performance	S-M	14-28	INMO mediated the relationship between job autonomy, task interdependence, and supervisor support with work performance, positively influencing INMO, which strongly predicted performance across tasks and functions.

(Continued)

Top 50 Cited Empirical Reward and INMO/EXMO Studies

Citations Counts Per Google Scholar as of June 13, 2025

Citation	Cite Total	5-year trend	Type (E/NE)	Sample size	% WEIRD sample	Constructs	Effect size	% Variance explained	Conclusions
[4]d'Ailly, H. (2003). Children's autonomy and perceived control in learning: A model of motivation and achievement in Taiwan. *Journal of Educational Psychology, 95*(1), 84–96. https://doi.org/10.1037/0022-0663.95.1.84	302	↓3%	NE	806	0	[7]Autonomy Perceived control Parental involvement Academic performance	L	51	Maternal and teacher autonomy support were key for children's autonomy and perceived control; without perceived control, autonomy negatively impacts performance, while external motivation boosted effort and performance when control is present.
[1]Fisher, C. D., & Noble, C. S. (2004). A within-person examination of correlates of performance and emotions while working. *Human Performance, 17*, 145–168. https://doi.org/10.1207/s15327043hup1702_2	299	↑115%	NE	114	N/R	[6]Task skill, difficulty, interest, and performance	L	43-56	Task difficulty, skill, interest, and effort significantly predicted momentary perceived performance, with task interest uniquely influencing performance beyond the effect on effort, and perceived performance explaining substantial variance in emotions beyond other predictors.

Coding: Citation Column: [1] = motivational influences; [2] = autonomy and control; [3] = rewards and motivation; [4] = cross-cultural applications

Construct column [5] = similar constructs given different names; [6] = terminology overlap; [7] = different names and overlap

*Implied significance of results at $p > .05$, **Meta analysis L=large, M=medium, S=small," E=experimental, NE = non-experimental

N/R = not reported, however 88% of the samples with this designation used psychology course students from Western universities.

For online source, see https://figshare.com/s/b5d640ad73c4dc452df3.

Name Index

Acevedo, B. P. 229
Agrawal, V. 283
Alcaro, A. 202
Alexander, R. 216
Altgassen, E. 28
Amabile, T. M. 31, 36, 39
Anderson, R. 31, 34
Andolina, D. 184
Angrist, J. 62
Arnett, J. J. 33
Aune, D. 273
Aunola, K. 28
Aupperle, R. L. 228
Avery, M. C. 154, 155, 175
Azoulay, P. 323

Bai, S. 301
Baik, J. H. 161, 218
Bak, S. 185
Bakermans-Kranenburg, M. J. 113
Balban, M. Y. 270, 271
Balsam, P. D. 128
Bandura, A. 90, 171, 263
Bar, K. J. 168
Bardach, L. 111
Barrett, L. F. 132
Baswani, S. 214
Batson, C. 59
Baumeister, R. F. 37, 61, 264
Bazzari, A. H. 220
Beach, S. R. 152
Beaulieu-Boire, I. 154
Bell, L. 31
Belmont, M. J. 39

Beltrao, A. 306
Benjafield, J. G. 109
Benjamin, A. S. 296
Benjamin, P. R. 178
Berke, J. D. 162
Berlyne, D. E. 211
Berridge, K. C. 93, 94, 124, 130, 134, 137, 213
Berscheid, E. 53
Bezzina, L. 208
Bhanji, J. P. 202
Bhardwaj, S. 134
Biddle, K. D. 181
Blain, B. 162, 200, 203
Boecker, L. 234
Boettiger, C. A. 265
Bolton, Ramsay 233
Born, J. 179
Borreca, A. 184
Bouarab, C. 177
Bouret, S. 123, 172
Bradler, C. 93
Brassey, J. 83, 266
Braver, T. S. 163
Brewer, M. 82
Bromberg-Martin, E. S. 201, 204, 222, 226
Browne, C. J. 176
Buch, E. R. 293, 299
Budygin, E. A. 161
Bureau, J. S. 290
Burnette, J. L. 287
Burns, E. C. 108
Burns, Emma 108

Name Index

Burton, A. 77
Büsel, C. 277
Bushman, B. J. 144
Butler, R. K. 174

Cacioppo, J. T. 235
Calnan, M. 89
Cameron, J. 31, 40, 62, 199
Carpenter, S. K. 297
Carron, A. V. 275
Centers for Disease Control 267, 281
Cepeda, N. J. 297
Cerasoli, C. P. 32, 52, 63, 70, 73, 76, 80, 215, 302
Chakroun, K. 309
Chan, D. 18
Chapkovski, P. 264
Charpentier, C. J. 223, 225, 226
Chatterjee, D. 292
Chelnokova, O. 231
Chen, B. 89
Chen, L. X. 309
Chew, B. 202
Chi, M. T. 300
Chinn, C. A. 224, 226
Chu, B. 183
Claus, E. D. 136
Clear, J. 154
Cloutier, J. 232
Coe, E. 266
Cohen, J. D. 120
Collingridge, G. L. 219
Collins, Francis 53
Colquitt, J. A. 89
Columbus, Christopher 139
Colwell, M. J. 175
Cools, R. 123
Corpus, J. H. 29, 33, 39
Correa, M. 123, 125, 161
Costanza, George 115
Covey, S. R. 3
Covington, M. V. 86

Cowan, N. 209
Cox, S. M. 226
Cozma, I. 51
Cragg, S. J. 180
Creswell, J. D. 275
Crum, A. J. 285
Csikszentmihalyi, M. 50
Curran, T. 5

Daniel, R. 205
Davey, C. G. 233
de Araujo, I. E. 169
De Bruyckere, P. 289, 294
Deci, E. L. 30, 32, 33, 35, 39, 50, 52, 63, 68, 72, 74, 77, 81, 83, 85, 86, 92, 93, 108–10, 180, 202, 213–15, 229
Decker, A. L. 238, 239
Dedovic, K. 184, 185
De Dreu, C. K. 182
Delgado, M. R. 203, 229, 230, 232
Dezza, I. C. 223, 226
Dhabhar, F. S. 184, 185
Dhamala, E. 118
Diamond, A. 165
Dickman, K. D. 181
Dodd, N. G. 39
Dogan, T. 91, 92
Dole, J. A. 221
Domes, G. 181
Duckworth, A. L. 3
Dunning, D. 284
Dweck, C. S. 3
Dysvik, A. 76

Eagly, A. H. 34
Ebbinghaus, H. 296
Eccles, J. S. 11, 33, 35, 36, 211, 263
Ecker, U. K. 307
Eisenberger, N. I. 170
Elliot, A. J. 54, 58
Erwin, M. 280
Esch, T. 140, 143, 275

Name Index

España, R. A.   173, 174
Esterman, M.   277

Falk, S.   8
Fareri, D. S.   229, 230, 232
Farrell, M. R.   177
Fay, D.   78
Feld, G. B.   179
Feng, C.   229
Ferrario, C. R.   163
Ferraro, P. J.   63
Ferreira-Vieira, T.   277
Ferster, C. B.   117
Finlayson-Short, L.   233
Finn, D. P.   174
Fischer, A. G.   175
Fisher, C. D.   28, 36
Flores, C.   161
Flowerday, T.   289
Franco, A.   18
Frank, M. J.   136
Fratiglioni, L.   229, 237, 256
Frey, B. S.   214
Fryling, M. J.   207
Fulmer, C. A.   89
Fulmer, I. S.   214

Gagné, F.   29
Galaj, E.   137
Galilei, G.   3
Galvão, D. A.   274
Ganster, D. C.   39
Garrett, N.   226
Gebauer, J. E.   91
Gegenfurtner, K. R.   67
Gerbier, E.   296
Gerhart, B.   78
Gillet, N.   73
Gilligan, C.   34
Gladstone, J. R.   58
Gladwell, M.   3

Gneezy, U.   63
Godoy, L. D.   183
Goldman, J. G.   292
González, J.   292
Gonzalez, O.   28, 29
Gonzalez-Lopez, E.   173
Gottman, J.   181
Gourgouvelis, J.   274
Grant, Adam   78
Greenberg, S.   82
Greenstein, A.   77
Gregoire, M.   221, 228, 309
Greiner, Laurie   1
Griesbauer, E. M.   292
Grill, F.   205
Gruber, M. J.   205
Guastella, A. J.   182
Gwenin, C.   236

Haam, J.   180
Haar, J. M.   93
Hallam, S.   63
Hamid, A. A.   138, 139, 160
Harackiewicz, J. M.   31, 40, 58
Harry, Deborah Ann   167
Harter, S.   77
Hartley, K.   220
Hasselmo, M. E.   179
Hattie, J.   54, 56, 57, 60
Hauser, T. U.   136, 220
Haworth, J.   280
Healy, P. J.   283
Heatherton, T. F.   264
Hebb, D. O.   218
Hegel, G. W. F.   4
Heimola, M.   267
Henderlong, J.   31
Henrich, J.   18, 33, 35
Hidi, S.   6, 30, 41, 108, 131, 209
Higgins, E. T.   93, 94
Hoffman, B.   7, 55, 71, 220, 263, 275, 280, 294, 297, 298, 303

Name Index

Horn, A. G. 19
Horowitz, A. 266
Hortop, E. G. 73
Howard, J. L. 76
Hsu, M. 222
Hu, Z. 118
Huang, C. 90
Huang, H. 6
Huberman, A. 69, 173, 268, 271, 273, 305
Hull, C. 107, 117
Hunter, J. E. 24
Hurst, C. 6

Immink, M. A. 293
Inagaki, T. K. 229
Inzlicht, M. 259
Izuma, K. 229, 233

James, W. 277
Jäncke, L. 292
Jegen, R. 214
Johnson, R. E. 303
Jones, C. 236
Jones, K. 273
Judge, T. A. 6

Kaanders, P. 224
Käfer, J. 296
Kahneman, D. 281
Kalyuga, S. 297, 307
Kamen, C. 274
Kandel, E. R. 218
Kansakar, U. 290
Kawachi, I. 301
Kellogg, K. C. 7
Kelly, M. E. 235
Kendi, I. X. 78
Kennedy, M. B. 218
Kidd, C. 211
Killingsworth, M. A. 275
Kim, A. 284

Kim, K. S. 85
Kim, S. I. 118, 200
Kimberlin, C. L. 22
King, R. B. 33, 88
Kirchler, M. 77
Kirschner, P. A. 278
Kivetz, R. 264
Kizilirmak, J. M. 205, 206
Klein, W. M. 227
Klug, H. J. 90
Knezevic, E. 184
Knoch, D. 265
Knutson, B. 216, 229
Kobayashi, K. 222
Kohn, A. 212
König, C. J. 18
Kornell, N. 295
Korpershoek, H. 34
Kouzes, T. K. 285
Kramer, R. M. 89
Kraus, J. 181
Kreek, M. J. 174
Krichmar, J. L. 154, 155, 175
Kringelbach, M. L. 128, 130
Kruglanski, A. W. 7, 70
Kühn, S. 305
Kuhn, T. S. 307
Kuvaas, B. 34, 75, 80
Kwon, M. 4, 78

Lang, A. E. 154
Lanza, R. 9
Lapper, M. R. 31
Latham, G. P. 54
Latif, S. 158
Lee, S. J. 205
Lee, W. 6, 108, 135, 199–201
Lee-Kwan, S. H. 267
Leigh, W. 1
Lembke, A. 154, 163, 167–71
Leonard, M. L. 19
Leopold, C. 300

Lepper, M. R.   33, 75, 215
Levison, Jessica   2, 4
Levy, A.   199
Li, P.   292
Lieberman, D. Z.   126
Likhtik, E.   220
Lin, A.   210
Lindsay, Couzens (friend)   218
Linke, J.   200
Liu, C.   158
Liu, Y.   92
Liu, Z. H.   166
Locke, E. A.   7, 70, 110
Loewenstein, G.   308
Lømo, T.   219
London, E. D.   161–3
Long, M. E.   126
Loughlin, L.   280
Loughrey, D. G.   274
Love, T. M.   182
Luria, E.   140, 198–200, 204
Luthans, F.   93

Ma, J.   298
McDougle, M.   170
Macoveanu, J.   175
Madoff, B.   280
Magee, J. C.   219
Mahalingam, G.   181
Maher, J. P.   275
Malenka, R. C.   219
Maloney, R. T.   152
Manohar, S. G.   31
Manolio, T. A.   53
Marder, E.   122, 153
Mark, G.   276, 278
Marsh, A. A.   182
Martin, A. J.   108
Martin, A. M.   174
Maslakci, A.   22
Maslow, A. H.   81
Mather, M.   173

Matsuzaki, M.   219
Matthews, G. A.   236
Mayer, R. E.   302
Medvedev, D.   32
Mertens, D. M.   23
Metcalfe, J.   296
Meyniel, F.   175
Michaelsen, M. M.   63, 140, 143
Miele, D. B.   54, 108
Milani, R. V.   274
Miller, E. K.   120
Miller, P. J.   35
Milyavskaya, M.   62
Mischel, W.   162, 163
Miyazaki, K. W.   175
Moeller, J.   51, 52
Mohebi, A.   201, 204
Moksnes, U. K.   92
Monti, D.   155
Monti, J. M.   155
Mook, D. G.   37
Moore, D. A.   283
Morelli, S. A.   233, 234
Morgan, J. P.   70
Morris, L. S.   200
Muis, K. R.   3, 4
Murayama, K.   84, 111, 204, 205, 213, 222
Murphy, P. K.   221
Mussweiler, T.   91

Nadelson, L. S.   221
Namboodiri, V. M. K.   118
Nelson, R. J.   278
Neumann, I. D.   182
Newman, James R.   256
Newton, Isaac   165
Ng, J. Y. Y.   63
Nguyen, D.   130
Niedenthal, P. M.   216
Nieh, E. H.   120, 213
Nikolić, J.   283, 284
Norbury, A.   127

Noyes, J. A.   264
Ntoumanis, N.   77
Nunes, E. J.   178
Nyugen, D.   130

Ogoshi, Y.   231
Oldham, S.   201, 206
Olguín, J. H.   166
Open Science Collaboration   18
Owens, D.   203
Ozcelik, H.   235
Özduran, A.   93

Palacios-Barrios, E. E.   238
Pariott, L.   37
Park, J.   30
Patall, E. A.   203
Patihis, L.   219
Peale, N. V.   3
Pelletier, L. G.   73, 77
Pennycook, G.   284
Pessiglione, M.   222
Peters, K. P.   199, 215
Peters, U.   282
Phelps, E. A.   121
Picciotto, M. R.   123
Pierce, W. D.   31, 62, 199
Pignatiello, G. A.   276
Pine, A.   162
Pink, D. H.   3, 6, 8
Planck, Max   323
Pollmann, S.   205
Poly, C.   290
Pope, Alexander   125
Popova, Maria   268
Posner, G. J.   221
Poulin, M. J.   89
Price, M. K.   63
Pugh, Z. H.   212

Raman, D. V.   256
Ramsey, D.   3

Ranaldi, R.   137
Rankin, C. H.   307
Ray, N. J.   179
Reeve, J.   4, 6, 28, 36, 108, 135, 203, 216, 290
Reeve, J. M.   72, 79, 82
Reiss, S.   7, 70, 110
Remskar, M.   275
Renninger, K. A.   30, 41, 131, 289
Reshotko, N.   69
Reynolds, L. M.   161
Richmond, B. J.   172
Ripollés, P.   205
Robble, M. A.   164
Robinson, M. D.   69
Robinson, T. E.   134
Roediger, H. L.   296
Rohrer, D.   297
Ross, M.   33
Rotgans, J. I.   132
Rousseau, D. M.   89
Ruff, C. C.   229
Russo, S. J.   217
Rutledge, R. B.   139
Ryan, R. M.   5–8, 32, 35, 36, 39, 50, 52, 54, 67, 68, 72, 74, 76, 85–7, 107–10, 180, 202, 229

Sailer, M.   264, 301
St. Père, F.   29
Salamone, J. D.   72, 123–5, 161
Samtani, S.   229
Sandel, M. J.   7
Sands, L. P.   122, 139
Saner, H.   274
Sapolsky, R. M.   5, 6, 116, 128, 152, 236
Sara, S. J.   123
Sardi, N. F.   305
Sarter, M.   179
Scales, A. N.   50
Schattke, K.   7, 110

Name Index 361

Scheele, D. 181
Scheiermann, C. 267
Schiffer, S. 2
Schippers, M. C. 90
Schmid, P. C. 135
Schmidt, F. L. 24
Schmidt, H. G. 132
Schneiderman, N. 182, 269
Schueller, S. M. 94
Schultz, W. 122, 125, 126, 137, 138, 155, 163, 165, 166, 200, 201, 204
Schunk, D. H. 31
Schutz, P. A. 3, 108
Sears, D. O. 36
Seiler, A. 270
Seli, P. 278
Senko, C. 76, 90
Sepah, C. 154
Sescousse, G. 206
Shadish, W. R. 37, 114
Shafiei, G. 226
Sharot, T. 162, 200, 203, 223, 224, 226, 308
Shaw, J. D. 214
Sheen, Charlie 233
Sheffler, P. 286
Sheldon, K. M. 90
Shen, X. 223, 228, 309
Shin, J. 78
Sicherman, N. 227
Silvia, P. J. 70
Simons, J. 34
Simpson, E. H. 128
Sinatra, G. M. 220
Sio, U. N. 298
Skinner, B. F. 117
Skinner, E. A. 39
Skitka, L. J. 78
Slattery, D. A. 182
Solinas, M. 169
Somerville, L. H. 232
Sowislo, J. F. 92

Spears, R. 308
Speer, M. E. 217
Spradley, J. P. 10
Spreng, R. N. 237, 238
Sridhar, S. 186
Stack, A. D. 144
Stanovich, K. 60
Stanovich, K. E. 276, 280, 281
Steel, P. 18
Stefano, G. B. 140
Steffey, M. A. 298
Strain, T. 267
Strasser, A. 177
Strathearn, L. 182
Stratton, S. J. 23
Stuber, G. D. 127
Stupnisky, R. H. 76
Sullivan, G. M. 24
Sunstein, C. R. 223, 224
Sürücü, L. 22

Taber, K. S. 298
Tan, L. H. 292
Tang, M. 73
Tani, Y. 235
Tao, W. 286
Tauer, J. M. 31
Taylor, G. 73
Taylor, W. D. 125
Teixeira, P. J. 77
Tellez, L. A. 169
Thalmayer, A. G. 24
Theodoratou, M. 270
Thorp, J. 219
Tobler, P. N. 202, 307
Tomova, L. 236, 275
Toplak, M. E. 129
Tosini, G. 305
Touroutoglou, A. 125, 132, 133, 168, 215, 216, 256, 305
Tsai, H. Y. 305
Tsow, F. 118

Turan, Z. 301
Turrigiano, G. G. 219
Twenge, J. M. 79, 199

Umberson, D. 181
Unsworth, N. 278
Urdan, T. 33, 35

Valdez, P. 276
Vallerand, R. J. 4, 49–53, 77
Van den Berg, I. 36
Van den Broeck, A. 76
Van Ijzendoorn, M. H. 113
Vansteenkiste, M. 76, 83, 85–7, 108, 109
Van Zessen, R. 177
Vassena, E. 208
Vitale, E. M. 238
Vosniadou, S. 307
Vrana, K. E. 173

Wagner, U. 229
Walker, G. J. 73
Walters, S. 3
Wang, K. S. 203
Warner, A. G. 282
Washington, George 115, 224
Waters, Roger 62
Weiner, B. 65, 269
Weinstein, H. 280
Weinstein, N. 83
Weinstein, N. D. 227
Werner, K. M. 60
West, R. 267
Westbrook, A. 163, 205
Westen, D. 223
Wheeler, J. 260

White, M. M. 287
Wieczorek, O. 112
Wigfield, A. 11, 33, 35, 36, 90, 211
Williams, J. 210
Williams, P. T. 273
Williams, S. E. 217
Wilson, M. A. 293
Winne, P. H. 10, 61, 260
Winterstein, A. G. 22
Wise, R. A. 164
Wolters, C. 263
Wolters, C. A. 62
Wood, P. B. 154, 155
Wood, W. 34
Wright, J. C. 78
Wrosch, C. 91
Wulantari, N. P. 264

Xu, J. 295
Xu, S. 267

Yakel, J. L. 180
Yamasue, H. 181
Yaple, Z. A. 238
Yeager, D. S. 285
Yeung, A. W. 112
Yoon, H. 207
Yorks, D. M. 275
Young, C. B. 217
Yu, R. 238
Yukhymenko-Lescroart, M. A. 50

Zhan, Z. 301
Zhang, J. 92
Zhang, Y. 173
Zhao, H. 50
Zhou, J. 273

Subject Index

abstinence 170–1
academic motivation 26, 42
accomplishment
   celebrating in moderation 324
   and dopamine 324
acetylcholine (ACh) 123, 178–80, 265, 277, 290
   attention and memory 178
   learning consolidation 179
   REM sleep 179–80
achievement goals 90–1
achievement-based rewards 40
active recall 295
addiction 164–71
   definition 164
   dopamine baseline 165
   food addiction 169–70
   tolerance development 166–7
adrenal glands 172
adrenaline. *See* epinephrine
advanced organizers 299–300
agency 56
alertness 267, 277
Alzheimer's disease 277, 290
amotivation 73
amygdala 114, 120–1, 136, 145, 159, 181, 183, 217, 223, 227, 233, 234, 265, 308
anterior cingulate cortex (ACC) 133, 136, 206, 227, 238, 239
anterior mid-cingulate cortex (aMCC) 168
anticipation phase 123–8
anticipation of rewards 201, 206, 216

anticipation *vs.* pleasure 154–5
assimilation need 82
associative learning 206–7
attainment value 58
attention 276–80
   contingent capture 277
   sustained attention 277
autonomic nervous system (ANS) 119
autonomous motivation 73–4
autonomy 5, 26, 30–2, 39–40, 84–5
   as basic psychological need 84–5
   and control 199, 203, 215, 237
   frustration of 85
   perception of 200, 203–4
   and reward effectiveness 202, 209, 216
autonomy-supportive behaviors 290–1
availability bias 282

backfire effect 258
basal ganglia 200, 205
Basic Psychology Needs Theory (BPNT) 84, 109
behavioral research limitations 113–15
belief change (BC) 221–8, 306–7, 322
   conditions for 221
   incremental nature of 322–3
   neural mechanisms of 222–4
   resistance to persuasion 322
   and reward perception 222, 226
belongingness. *See* relatedness

Subject Index

bias
  racial bias 33–4
  response bias 38
  sampling bias 25, 32–5
  self-selection bias 25, 35–6
  social desirability bias 40
binding factors of motivation 57–61
  costs and benefits assessment 60
  goals 58–9
  self-perceptions 57
  task evaluations 57–8
biology advantages over behavioral approaches 111–18
biology and motivation 9, 12
boomerang effect 143–4
boredom, rewards and 62
brain functioning 9, 12
brain localization 112, 115, 151
brain regions
  caudate 201, 217, 236, 239
  corpus callosum 292
  hippocampus 114, 121, 159, 183, 274, 292, 295, 299
  insula 201, 227
  locus coeruleus (LC) 172–3, 277
  nucleus accumbens (NAcc) 120, 139, 145, 159, 173, 176, 178, 181, 200, 201, 213, 216, 217, 222, 227, 232–4, 239
  orbitofrontal cortex (OFC) 118, 120, 133, 145, 206, 232, 236, 239
  prefrontal cortex (PFC) 114, 120–1, 133, 139, 145, 160, 175, 181, 183, 185, 200, 217, 222, 227, 230, 233, 238, 239, 264–5, 267, 272, 277, 308
  putamen 217, 239
  striatum 133, 136, 139, 144, 200, 201, 205, 222, 226, 233, 236
  substantia nigra 139, 145
  ventral striatum 144, 200, 204, 205, 217, 226, 227

  ventral tegmental area (VTA) 120, 125, 139, 144–5, 159–60, 173, 176, 181, 185, 200, 213, 222, 233, 236, 277
  ventromedial prefrontal cortex (vmPFC) 200, 201, 203, 224, 234
breathing techniques
  cyclic breathwork 270
  physiological sigh 271

caffeine 169
causality *vs.* correlation 18–19, 26
central nervous system (CNS) 119–20
change
  incremental *vs.* radical shifts 322–3
  as intellectual growth, not frailty 322
  time requirements for 322–3
chocolate consumption 168–9
choline 290
circadian rhythm (CR) 124, 155, 267–8
  strategies for optimization 268
citation analysis 20–2, 42
clearerthinking.org needs list 82
cobra effect 144
Cocaine effects 169
cognitive clarity 276–88
cognitive desires 132–3
cognitive enhancement strategies 279
cognitive evaluation theory 39
cognitive misers 281
cognitive utility 224
competence 5, 85–7
  as basic psychological need 85–7
  frustration of 86
  perception *vs.* actual skill 86
completion-contingent rewards 30–1
conceptual change (CC) 221

conceptual learning   209
confirmation bias   258, 282, 286, 294
construct clarity   27–30
construct validity   22, 28–9
controlled environments   26–7, 36–7
controlled motivation   74
control premium   203
correlational evidence   186–7
correlational studies   18, 26
cortisol   115, 124, 126, 183–4, 235–6, 270
   chronic effects   184
   short-term benefits   184
cost-benefit analysis   128–30
costs and benefits assessment   60
critical thinking   323
crowding out effect   214
cultural considerations   10
cultural influences   187–8
curiosity
   epistemic   211
   intellectual   205, 211
   perceptual   211

debiasing   282
decision-making, personal nature of   323–4
default brain network   237–8
delay discounting   162–3
detection error   281
differentiation need   82
distributed practice   296–7
dopamine (DA)   12, 120, 125–8, 131–2, 154–71, 201, 213, 217, 218, 226, 227, 259, 261, 263, 265, 270, 277, 290, 292, 301–2, 304–6, 324
   addiction mechanisms   164–71
   baseline fluctuations   165
   control pathway   160–1
   deficits and replacement behaviors   126–7
   "dopamine detox"   154, 170–1
   and extrinsic *vs.* intrinsic rewards   201–2
   and facial attractiveness   231
   and learning   205, 219–20
   and loneliness   236, 238
   misconceptions   154
   and mood   216–17
   neurons and pathways   120, 139, 144
   pathway interactions   160–1
   practical implications   162–4
   reward pathway   159–60
   and reward prediction error   202, 222
   role in wanting *vs.* liking   134
   synthesis and baseline   120, 125–8, 131–2
   synthesis modes   156–7
   synthesis strategies   305
   tolerance development   166–7
   tolerance plateau   305
dopamine pathways
   mesocortical   159–61
   mesolimbic   159–60
   Nigrostriatal (NSP)   158
   Tuberoinfundibular (TIDA)   158
dorsal raphe nucleus (DRN)   236–7
drive theory   107–8
dualistic model of passion (DMP)   49–50

effect sizes   23–6, 38–9
emotional regulation   272
emotion and mood   216–18
   negative emotions   217–18, 227
   positive emotions   216–17
endorphins   274
engagement   6
engagement-contingent rewards   30
entropy   256

Subject Index

environmental restructuring 264, 303
epinephrine 115, 172-4
    cost-benefit evaluation 173
    stress response 174
errorful learning 296
esteem needs 91-2
    downward comparisons 91-2
    upward comparisons 91
Eustress 184-5
evidence
    replicable, importance of 322
    transitory nature of 323
execution phase 128-34
executive functioning 161
exercise 273-6
    group *vs.* solo 275
    psychological benefits 274
expectancy-value calculation 138
expectancy-value theory 198, 211-12
experiential learning 208
experimental design 19, 26
expertise reversal effect 307
exploratory journey, obstacles in 324
external regulation 73
external validity 26
extrinsic motivation (EXMO) 5, 8, 9, 11, 19-20, 29, 30, 39, 69-80, 110-11
    advantages of 78-80
    dark side of 64-5
    definition 69-70
    effectiveness conditions 63-4
    vs. intrinsic motivation debate 198-204
    neural pathways 200-2
    prejudice against 78
    quantity-focused tasks 63-4
    and reward processing 201-2
    reward termination effects 64-5
    separable outcomes 80
    timing considerations 64-5

facial attractiveness 230-2
    and brain reward systems 230-1
    gender differences 232
feedback and learning 135-7
fight or flight response 119, 172, 183
fMRI studies 232, 236
food addiction 169-70
four binding factors of motivation 56
framing bias 282
functional magnetic resonance imaging (fMRI) 109

gamification 264, 301-2
gamma-aminobutyric acid (GABA) 176-8, 265
    inhibitory function 176
    reward regulation 176-7
gender representation 25, 34
gene expression 116-17, 151-3
    environmental influences 152
    methylation 152
    neural plasticity 152
generalizability concerns 18, 23, 27, 32-7
goal attainment *vs.* goal setting 324
goal gradient effect 264
goals 58-9
    instrumental *vs.* ultimate 59
    orientation 59
goal setting, satisfaction through 324
goal setting and achievement 90-1
"Go" and "NoGo" learning 136
growth mindset (GM) 284-8
    cultivation strategies 288
    definition 284-5
    interventions 287

habituation 202, 239
harmonious passion (HP) 50
    characteristics 50
    vs. obsessive passion 50-1
hazard ratios (longevity study) 230

Subject Index 367

hedonic hotspots 216
hedonic impact 130–1
hedonic set point 167–8
hedonic utility 223
heredity influences 187–8
heuristics 281
hippocampus. *See* brain regions
homeostasis 119, 126–7, 155, 166, 176, 184
homeostatic plasticity 219
Huberman protocols 268, 271, 305–6
hypothalamic-pituitary-adrenal (HPA) axis 183

identified regulation 73
immune system 267
implicit learning 143, 209–10
incentive salience 131–4
incentives *vs.* rewards 80
individual differences
    measurement 113–14
information entropy 323
information seeking
    cognitive utility 224
    hedonic utility 223
    instrumental utility 223
    subjective value of information (SVOI) 222, 226
instrumental goals 59
instrumental utility 223
integrated regulation 72–3
intellectual awareness 323
interest 12
internalization 52, 72–3
    degrees of 72–3
    spectrum figure 73
internal validity 26
intrinsic motivation (INMO) 5–9, 11, 19–20, 28–32, 34, 36, 39, 41–2, 69, 75–8, 131–2, 138–43
    advantages of 75–7
    cultural conflation with passion 53
    disadvantages of 77–8
    vs. extrinsic motivation debate 198–204
    the INMO mask 203–4
    learning benefits 76
    measurement challenges 70
    neural pathways 200–2
    neurological basis 131–2
    overconfidence risks 77
    relationship to reward 138–43
    and reward processing 201–2
    superiority claims 109–11
intrinsic value (SEVT) 58
introjected regulation 73
irrationality 280

Jessica Levison case study 1–2, 4
jingle-jangle fallacy 53
judgment 280–4

laboratory research limitations 10
laboratory studies 26–7, 36–7
learning
    active *vs.* passive 288, 295
    distributed practice 296–7
    and dopamine 205, 219–20
    efficiency strategies 294, 299–300
    from mistakes 295–6
    maximizing with reward 211–12
    neural encoding 218–20
    neuroplasticity and 292
    and performance 8, 12
    and reward connection 130, 135–7
    styles myth 294–5
    types of (associative, observational, experiential, rote, conceptual, implicit, social) 206–10
learning and memory
    acetylcholine role 178–80
    consolidation during sleep 179

Subject Index

"liking" vs. "wanting" distinction 130–4
limbic system 159
locus of control 65–6
   external locus 65–6
   vs. internalization 66
   internal locus 65
loneliness
   and brain networks 237–8
   consequences of 235–6
   demographics 235
   neural responses to 236–7
long-term depression 219
long-term objectives, maintaining focus on 324
long-term potentiation 219

magnetoencephalography (MEG) 109, 115
Maslow's Hierarchy of Needs 81
mastery goal orientation 59
measurement effectiveness 22–4
melatonin 124
memory
   consolidation 293, 297
   dual coding 295
   hippocampus role 274, 292, 295, 297
   rehearsal 295
mesocorticolimbic pathway 200, 203, 205
message valence 225–6
meta-analyses 28
methodological concerns 17–18, 22, 25–7
methylation 152
mindfulness 273–6
motivated reasoning 322
motivation
   definition (Latin "movere") 55
   evolution of 55–6
   four binding components 56

phases (anticipation, execution, reactivity) 123
   rainbow metaphor 68, 71
motivation science 2, 9, 10
multidisciplinary approach 8–10
multitasking myth 278

need frustration 83
need satisfaction 80–4
   as homeostasis 95
   as source of behavior 81
   variability between individuals 83–4
negative prediction error 126
neural circuits 158–61
neural distinctions (intrinsic vs. extrinsic) 201
neural encoding 218–20
neural pathways, shared vs. distinct 199–204
neural plasticity 152, 178
neural replay 299
neuroendocrinology 6
neuroimaging studies 205–6, 231
neurological evidence 62
neuromodulation 12, 121–3, 324
neuromodulators
   definition vs. neurotransmitters 153
   interactions 186–7
   team analogy 154, 171, 187
neuroplasticity 274, 287, 292
neuroprotective behaviors 256
neuroprotective strategies 229, 237
neuropsychological evidence
   application evolution 323
   importance of considering 323
neuropsychology 6, 10, 12, 13
   advantages over behavioral research 112–18
   definition and scope 112
   limitations 117–18

Subject Index   369

neurotransmitters. *See* specific types
neurotransmitters *vs.*
    neuromodulators   153
Nicotine effects   169
Nigrostriatal pathway (NSP)   158
norepinephrine (NE)   122–4, 172–4, 219–20, 227, 228, 259, 265, 270, 277, 290
nucleus accumbens (NAcc). *See* brain regions

observational learning   207
obsessive passion (OP)   50–1
    addiction-like qualities   50
    controlling nature   50
optimal performance   2, 8, 11
organismic integration theory (OIT)   72
outcome expectations   57–8
overconfidence   284
overjustification effect   199, 214–15, 301
overjustification hypothesis   34
Oxytocin   180–2, 216
    romantic relationships   181–2
    social bonding   180–4
    stress reduction   181

paradox of passion   2, 4, 5, 7, 51–2
parasympathetic nervous system   119–20
participant demographics   25, 32–5
passion
    as biological reward   236, 322
    correlation *vs.* causation issues   52
    cultural conflation with INMO   53
    definition and measurement   49–50
    definitions   4
    dualistic model   49–50
    identity infusion   52
    polarity determination   50
    progress as   324

quotes   3
research limitations   51–2
situational *vs.* personal factors   51
passion warriors   1, 7
patience, as byproduct of acceptance   323
performance-contingent rewards   30–2
performance goal orientation   59
performance optimization   13
peripheral nervous system (PNS)   119
personal factors *vs.* situational factors   51
personal growth, prerequisites for   323
persuasion   220–18, 306–9
    message characteristics   224–8
    multiple attempts often necessary   322
    neural mechanisms   222–4
    resistance to   322
phasic dopamine release   156–7, 169
phenomenal sources   67–8
physiological sigh   271
pleasure seeking/pain avoidance   93–4
Pomodoro method   279
positron emission tomography (PET)   109
practical significance   24, 38, 40–1
prefrontal cortex (PFC). *See* brain regions
publication bias   18
punishment predictive errors (PPEs)   139
purism, intrinsic   69
P-values   26, 37, 41

randomization   23
raphe nuclei   175
reactivity phase   134–7
reciprocal determinism   171
recognition need   92–3

rehearsal 295
relatedness 5, 87–8
　belongingness 87
　repression of 87–8
　unconditional relationships 87
reliability 22
REM sleep 179–80
reputation 229, 233–4
research bias 8
research methodology limitations 9, 12
"rest and digest" system 119
rest stops 298–9
reticular activating system 124
reward(s) 5, 8, 9, 12
　anticipation 154–5
　brain's primary reward 324
　contingencies 30–2
　effectiveness 63
　and learning 205–6
　personalization 302
　and persuasion 220–18
　and social relationships 228–9
　type and context 213–16
　valuation 213
reward pathway 159–60
reward prediction error (RPE) 127–8, 138–40, 156, 165–6, 176, 197, 202, 222, 228, 260, 262, 283, 297, 302, 306
　definition and function 127–8, 138–40
　relationship to learning 139–40
　positive *vs.* negative 126, 138–9
reward system 263–5
　components 144–5
rewards *vs.* incentives 80
rote learning 208–9

salient rewards 63
sample composition 25, 32–5
sample size concerns 34–5
scaffolding 297–8

scientific advancement
　and debate 322
　and skepticism 322
scientific research, transitory nature of 323
scientific truth, generational acceptance of 323
self-consequating strategies 263, 279
self-determination 73–4
self-determination theory (SDT) 5, 6, 32, 42, 72, 82, 108–11, 140
self-esteem needs 91–2
self-perceptions 57
self-regulation 57, 60–1, 259–66
　biological hijacking 61
　definition 260
　phases (planning, monitoring, reflection) 260
　self-regulatory lapses 61
　strategies 263–5
self-report limitations 8, 12
self-report measures 18, 26, 38, 40–1
self-talk 264, 286
serotonin 116, 122–3, 174–6, 227, 259, 263, 265, 274, 275, 290, 292, 301
　delay of gratification 175
　mood regulation 174–5
　risk assessment 175–6
situated expectancy-value theory (SEVT) 11, 58, 211–12
skill acquisition 208–9
sleep 267–8, 305
sleep and acetylcholine 179–80
SMART goals 279
social approach behavior 232–5
social connections 180–2
social isolation 235–8
　demographics 235
　neural responses 236–7
social learning 210
social rejection 235

social relationships and reward 228–9
social rewards
   and brain activity 229, 233–4
   and longevity 229–30
   neuroprotective effects 229
   types of 229
socioeconomic status (SES) 238–9
   and reward processing 238–9
   scarcity hypothesis 239
Socrates and motivation 69
somatic nervous system (SNS) 119
source *vs.* type confusion 67–8
spacing effect 296
statistical inference 37–41
statistical significance 24–6, 37–9
status quo bias 282–3
strategy choice, personal nature of 323
stress hormones 182–5
stress management 269–73
   cognitive appraisal 271
   emotional regulation 272
stress response
   distress *vs.* eustress 183–5
   sympathetic-adreno-medullar (SAM) axis 183
striatum. *See* brain regions
sympathetic nervous system 119
synaptic plasticity 178, 218–19

task-contingent rewards 31–2
task evaluation 57–8
team cohesiveness 186–8
teenage brain development 161
tolerance development 166–7

tonic dopamine release 156–7, 160, 162, 178
trial and error approach 323
trust as psychological need 89
Tuberoinfundibular pathway (TIDA) 158
tyrosine 305

ultimate goals 59
universal reinforcements 110
utility value 58

valence and motivation 68
validation, importance in sources 323
validity concerns 18, 22–3
value creation and assessment 128–34
variance explained 24–6, 38–9, 41
ventral pallidum 160, 177, 181
ventral tegmental area (VTA). *See* brain regions
vicarious reward processing 234–5
volunteer bias 25, 35–6

"wanting" *vs.* "liking" 130–4
Western, Educated, Industrialized, Rich, Democratic (WEIRD) samples 12, 25, 32–5
worked examples 299–300
working memory 156, 159, 173, 267, 274
workplace statistics 6

zeitgeist, scientific and cultural 323
zone of proximal development (ZPD) 297